Southern Cross

Southern Cross

*A New View
of Leonidas Polk and His Clashes
with Braxton Bragg*

AMANDA LOW WARREN

McFarland & Company, Inc., Publishers
Jefferson, North Carolina

LIBRARY OF CONGRESS CATALOGING-IN-PUBLICATION DATA

Names: Warren, Amanda Low, 1955– author.
Title: Southern cross : a new view of Leonidas Polk and his clashes with Braxton Bragg / Amanda Low Warren.
Other titles: New view of Leonidas Polk and his clashes with Braxton Bragg
Description: Jefferson, North Carolina : McFarland & Company, Inc., Publishers, 2024 | Includes bibliographical references and index.
Identifiers: LCCN 2024019380 | ISBN 9781476693828 (paperback : acid free paper) ∞
ISBN 9781476652382 (ebook)
Subjects: LCSH: Polk, Leonidas, 1806-1864. | Polk, Leonidas, 1806-1864—Adversaries. | Generals—Confederate States of America—Biography. | Confederate States of America. Army—Biography. | United States—History—Civil War, 1861-1865—Biography. | Episcopal Church—Clergy—Biography. | Plantation owners—Louisiana—Lafourche Parish—Biography. | Bragg, Braxton, 1817-1876. | BISAC: HISTORY / Military / United States | HISTORY / United States / Civil War Period (1850-1877)
Classification: LCC E467.1.P7 W37 2024 | DDC 973.7/3092 [B]—dc23/eng/20240503
LC record available at https://lccn.loc.gov/2024019380

BRITISH LIBRARY CATALOGUING DATA ARE AVAILABLE

ISBN (print) 978-1-4766-9382-8
ISBN (ebook) 978-1-4766-5238-2

© 2024 Amanda Low Warren. All rights reserved

No part of this book may be reproduced or transmitted in any form or by any means, electronic or mechanical, including photocopying or recording, or by any information storage and retrieval system, without permission in writing from the publisher.

Front cover images: Leonidas Polk digital painting based on a photograph from the Alabama Department of Archives and History (used with their permission); cover design and all elements by artist, Clyde Duensing III.

Printed in the United States of America

McFarland & Company, Inc., Publishers
Box 611, Jefferson, North Carolina 28640
www.mcfarlandpub.com

In memory of my father, Wilbur Moore Warren II,
who planted the seeds,
and
to John Evans, who shined the light that grew them to fruition.

Contents

Acknowledgments ix
Introduction 1

Chapter 1. From Cadet to Bishop to General 3
Chapter 2. "Gibraltar of the West" 15
Chapter 3. Shiloh 24
Chapter 4. Perryville 46
Chapter 5. Middle Tennessee 60
Chapter 6. Trouble in Army of Tennessee High Command 77
Chapter 7. Was Polk Insubordinate? 100
Chapter 8. Chickamauga 109
Chapter 9. Independent Command in Mississippi 140
Chapter 10. The Atlanta Campaign 160
Chapter 11. Historians' Negative Portrayal of Polk 173
Chapter 12. Polk's True Nature and Personality 199
Chapter 13. Bragg vs. Polk 204

Last Words 210
Chapter Notes 213
Bibliography 223
Index 227

Acknowledgments

Along this winding way, many have aided, blessed, encouraged, and debated me. I thank them all, and ask forgiveness in advance from those inadvertently omitted who deserve mention. First, I am most grateful to a man I met, fittingly, at the Atlanta History Center: John Evans, Polk expert extraordinaire and perennial "voice crying aloud in the wilderness" articulating and defending Polk's triune legacy.

I extend special and heartfelt thanks to the superlative artist John Paul Strain for generously granting permission to reproduce in my book his painting "Morgan's Wedding," a poignant, masterful depiction of the December 1863 nuptials at which Bishop-General Polk officiated.

I especially appreciate eminent Civil War authors Samuel W. Mitcham, Jr., and Philip Leigh for taking the time to review my manuscript and offer their endorsements. That they would do so for a new, unknown writer speaks to their gallantry.

Thanks go to Matthews Reynolds, associate director of archives and special collections at The University of the South, for kindly accommodating me during my exploration through Polk's correspondence and papers. I also thank Frank Clark who devotedly manned the Bell Historical Research Center of Cumming, Georgia, a treasure trove of valuable, obscure reference volumes and sad victim of historical (hysterical) cleansing. Melvin Dishong served as a special guide over the ground at Pine Mountain, taking time to locate for me the section of trench where my husband's great-great-grandfather, a 17-year-old private in the 37th Georgia, crouched under fire on the day of Polk's death. I am grateful to Ted Savas who offered much-needed advice and direction. Thanks also to Father Tim Watts who early on blessed this project, and to the many friends, fellow lifelong learners, excellent writers, speakers, and experts involved with the Civil War community of Atlanta who taught and encouraged me, with Dennis Elm the most enthusiastic encourager.

Most importantly, I am grateful beyond measure for my husband, Clyde Duensing III, who invariably urged me on, freely and lovingly offering forbearance—dare I say blessing?—upon my Civil War endeavors and excursions, and whenever asked contributed his own considerable talents, particularly the awesome cover design for this book.

Finally, reaching beyond the bounds of time (after all, the ultimate objective of history), I give thanks to my Lord and Savior Jesus Christ, bestower of life and author of truth, whom Leonidas Polk strove with every fiber of his being faithfully to serve. At a Moravian church where I worshipped in Winston-Salem, North Carolina, the pastor pronounced a profound truth: "God speaks to us through history." With that in mind, I apologize if my words contain any mistakes or cause any offense, and pray that this account approaches His higher standard of truth and aligns with His unknowable purposes.

Introduction

"Think of the scandal to our church. A minister's duty is to preach 'peace and good will to men.' He can bless [and] encourage them, but not fight with them."
—Elise Bragg to Gen. Braxton Bragg, July 5, 1861[1]

This was perhaps her first scathing criticism of newly minted Major General Leonidas Polk, initiating a string of exchanges between General Braxton Bragg and his wife Elise against the Episcopal bishop of Louisiana—*her* bishop rather than his. Although Bragg occasionally attended services and participated in parish affairs, he did not truly join the church until his 1863 baptism and confirmation—where Polk was present but notably did not officiate. Instead, Bishop Stephen Elliott of Georgia performed the sacrament during a visit to the Army of Tennessee.

Perhaps Elise's early objection to Leonidas Polk was motivated less by theology than a wife's ambitions for her husband. In her letter to Bragg as the western Confederates concentrated at Corinth in 1862, she offered brief, biting assessments of his fellow generals, especially Polk whom she pronounced "a wild enthusiast." Tellingly, Elise concluded by lamenting to her husband: "Could only you have had command … you are the only one capable of managing volunteers."[2]

Beginning with those Bragg letters, a tradition took hold of disparaging every aspect of Leonidas Polk's Confederate service: his generalship, personal integrity, relations with superiors, commitment to the Southern cause, even his vigor and manhood. The custom continues to this day. Rarely questioning whether he deserves such treatment, historians seemingly strive to outdo one another in casting aspersions upon his name. Polk is described as a disastrous blunderer and a conniving, sinister subordinate who never obeyed an order he didn't like. Strangely, the very historians who soundly condemn Polk in introductory pages often concede, albeit deep within their texts, that in a given situation he actually chose the correct course or achieved some measure of success.

Beneath all of the denigration, a truth emerges: in order to understand the antipathy directed at Leonidas Polk, one must examine the controversy that invariably swirled around Braxton Bragg. As an army commander, and indeed throughout his life, Bragg incited conflict with others, and none more than Polk. Those who censure Polk today in effect side squarely with Bragg by arguing *his* case against the bishop.

Introduction

The purpose of this book is not to make a corresponding mistake by taking Polk's side. Instead, by stepping back, clearing the slate and seeking to uncover simply what happened, some surprising attributes and accomplishments of Leonidas Polk come to light. Beginning with a sketch of Polk's antebellum years, this narrative journeys through the campaigns and battles of Polk's Confederate command: Columbus, Kentucky; Shiloh; Perryville; Murfreesboro and the ensuing controversies within the Army of Tennessee; Chickamauga and its resultant conflicts; independent command in Mississippi; and the Atlanta campaign until Polk's death in June 1864. Then follows a fresh examination of the treatment of Leonidas Polk in history, in which is seen throughout the imprint of Braxton Bragg and his issues with Polk—arising however innocuously from the whisperings of an influential wife.

Chapter 1

From Cadet to Bishop to General

The Cornerstone

On the mountain fastness a group gathered, encompassed by an explosion of fiery-hued leaves. Far below, a glassy lake gleamed and distant sounds from the valley drifted upward as a ceremony commenced beneath the piercing azure of a Southern autumnal sky.

It was October 10, 1860, and crowds ascended the mountaintop by foot, horse, beast-drawn conveyance, and even a loaned locomotive protesting the precipitous grade, all to affirm a dream conceived in the mind of Leonidas Polk. Four years of writing appeals, raising funds, consulting authorities, site seeking, speechmaking, and drawing plans culminated now upon a slight rise atop the mountain. There rested a solitary square rock: the cornerstone of The University of the South.

Bishop Polk stood before the immense marble monolith which had been wrested from the valley below and hauled up the mountain by the brute strength of 34 oxen. Resplendent white robes rippled and billowed round the monument as Dr. Quintard's arm waved a choir's voices upward to heaven and Dr. Otey, Episcopal bishop of Tennessee, uttered greeting words, followed by the bishops of Florida, North Carolina, Alabama, and Georgia offering Scripture, exhortation and prayer. Then Leonidas, bishop of Louisiana, stepped up to the stone wielding a maul in his mighty arm, resembling a fearsome Christian Thor. Thrice smiting the immense block he imparted words dedicating this University to "the cultivation of True Religion, learning and virtue" *(strike!)*, "that God may be glorified" *(strike!)*, "and the happiness of man may be advanced" *(strike!)*. Nonetheless, the sword spoke louder than well-meaning words, for a fractured nation would soon clash violently at this place. As to the lone, solemn stone, it was destined for destruction at the hands of Federal cavalrymen.[1]

The celebrants, knowing nothing of what was to come, feasted on speeches followed by food spread for them upon long tables that bright autumn afternoon.

West Point

Leonidas Polk had not always followed a religious path. Born into a worldly family and aspiring to a career in the military, he entered West Point in 1823. There

Leonidas thrived in academics (excelling in mathematics, struggling only with French) as well as the rigor and discipline of cadet life. An inherent personality trait which helped him endure adversity was his invariable cheerfulness. "[H]e rarely complained of his lot except when he felt himself the victim of injustice. He rarely gave evidence of despondency and often exhibited a buoyancy that was contagious. Good humor often sparkled with wit." Polk's roommate was future Confederate general Albert Sidney Johnston, and he befriended cadet Jefferson Davis, one class below. Other Civil War notables in his class included Philip St. George Cooke, future father-in-law of J.E.B. Stuart; Napoleon Buford, destined to serve as a general in the Union cavalry; and Gabriel Rains, powder-and-explosives mastermind of the Confederacy. Polk relished the academically challenging environment and visits to the Academy by great personages of the day.[2]

A controversy erupted during Polk's year as a second-classman (equivalent of a junior in civilian college). A course in drawing was required under the curriculum, and a common practice in completing some assignments was to trace at certain phases of preparation. Without warning, a long-disregarded rule forbidding this shortcut was arbitrarily enforced. While most cadets had engaged in the tracing, only a few, including Polk, came forward and admitted it, and these alone were subject to punishment. Polk's class standing plunged as a result. Not one to suffer unfairness in silence, he wrote letters of protest. It likely seemed to him that in this case the Honor Code punished the honest. His appeals gained him no relief, and following his father's advice he reluctantly accepted the outcome though staunchly believing an injustice had gone uncorrected.

Historical marker on the campus of the University of the South. The plaque marking the location of the cornerstone can be seen in the background (photograph by the author).

Some historians have exaggerated this incident, even referring to it as a "cheating scandal," to discredit Polk

Chapter 1. From Cadet to Bishop to General 5

and raise doubts as to his character. Those who do so lack an understanding of the artistic process of drawing. Even the greatest artists—*especially* the greatest artists—liberally use reference to create realistic images. Professional illustrators routinely trace, project, and incorporate finished components in composing an original work. Virtually no representational art springs unaided from the mind; the artist consults and utilizes forms and images in order to reproduce an accurate likeness. This reality is likely the reason for the rule going unenforced so long at West Point.

One historian even implies a causal connection between this controversy and Polk's subsequent conversion to Christianity. Such an untrue characterization wrongly belittles Polk's deep, lifelong faith walk. He came to the decision to commit his life to Christ

Section of stained-glass window in All Saints' Chapel, The University of the South, portraying Polk consecrating the cornerstone and Bishop Otey to his left placing a Bible in the inner chamber of the stone. Dr. Quintard is to Polk's right, with the choir behind him (photograph by the author).

not in an attempt to redeem himself from a passing disciplinary setback, but after reading probing essays juxtaposing spirituality and science and comparing world religions. Deeply moved (or as Christians say, "convicted"), Polk sought out the chaplain at West Point, Charles Pettit McIlvaine, future Episcopal bishop of Ohio. The cadet's overtures must have come as a surprise to McIlvaine, who had managed to cultivate little interest in religion at the Academy. After instruction by Chaplain McIlvaine, Polk made a public profession of faith, risking ostracism: "Henceforth he would be a marked man, … subjected to curious observations and ridicule, for there was no record of either a cadet or a professor at West Point ever professing religion."[3]

Some have further distorted the facts and sequence of Polk's conversion by falsely claiming that the young cadet fell passively under the influence of a domineering, persuasive chaplain. This was not at all the case; it was Polk who approached the unassertive cleric. Furthermore, had the West Point chaplain proselytized intensively, then Polk's conversion would likely not have been so rare.

His fellow cadets' response to Polk's profession of faith turned out differently than expected. Rather than ridicule him others followed his example, perhaps an indication of Polk's natural qualities as a leader and pioneer. During the next chapel service following his conversion,

> Cadet Polk, and only Cadet Polk, slipped from his seat onto his knees.... Within days half a dozen other cadets were calling on McIlvaine to profess themselves disciples of Christ, and subsequently students (and even some of the faculty) were coming in such numbers ... that the chaplain's largest room was filled to overflowing.[4]

Leonidas Polk graduated from West Point in 1827, ranking eighth in his class. This fact perhaps comes as a surprise to anyone who reads books on the Civil War. A common caricature of Polk promulgated by historians is that of a blundering, slow, indolent, clueless general named to high rank only by virtue of his close friendship with Jefferson Davis. (Although friends during their time at the Academy, he and Davis never corresponded for more than three decades before the Civil War.) Nonetheless, Polk's academic success at West Point as well as his subsequent writings, achievements, continued education, travel, and associates and correspondents serve as evidence that Leonidas Polk cannot by any stretch be considered intellectually deficient.

Immediately following graduation Polk entered seminary in order to devote himself to Christian ministry, the profession to which he now felt called. After considering a New York divinity school, he entered Virginia Theological Seminary in the fall of 1828. The sentiment he expressed regarding its arguably lesser reputation as compared to the New York institution demonstrates his self-motivation for learning, a key element of the intellectually gifted: "The real labour of an education in any branch devolves necessarily on the student himself."[5]

Antebellum Years

Leonidas Polk was ordained in the Episcopal Church on April 9, 1830, one day before his 24th birthday. He married Frances "Fanny" Devereux the following month and their first child, a son, was born on January 27, 1831. Polk accepted a position as assistant to the rector of Monumental Church in Richmond, Virginia, but stricken with serious illness he traveled to Europe later that year at the urging of doctors.

In 1833 he and Frances moved to Polk family land in Maury County, Tennessee, where he built a home, assumed the role of planter, and served as rector at St. Peter's in the nearby town of Columbia. Polk felt a special call to minister to African Americans in his parish, and was elected a delegate to the Episcopal General Convention.

Several years later Polk was notified that the General Convention had chosen

Chapter 1. From Cadet to Bishop to General 7

 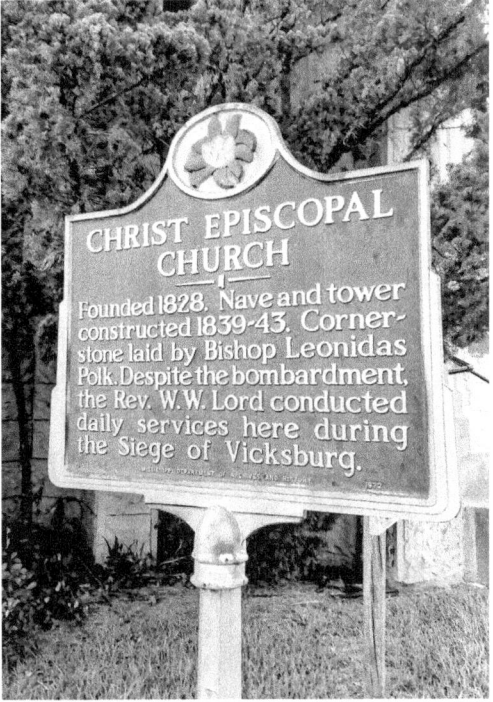

Christ Episcopal Church, Vicksburg, Mississippi, is one of numerous churches consecrated by Polk during his tenure as missionary bishop of the Southwest. Throughout the battles and siege of Vicksburg, from May through July 1863, the rector conducted daily services even as the church endured heavy bombardment by Federal field artillery to the north and east and Union gunboats on the Mississippi River (photograph by the author).

him as missionary bishop of the Southwest, for which he was ordained in December 1838. Thus began years of energetic, exhausting travel throughout the then-frontier regions of Louisiana, Mississippi, Arkansas, Texas, and the Indian Territory. In remote locations barely claimed from the wilderness, he tirelessly scouted opportunities for stirring up faith and founding new churches. These years dedicated to missionary work required extreme exertion and hardship (at times he slept in barns), disproving false portrayals of Leonidas Polk as a sluggard basking in luxury or an opportunist out for his own gain. Polk's religious vocation hardly entailed a life of comfort and ease. His efforts bore fruit in bringing the gospel to godless, hardscrabble settlements where vice and violence prevailed. The work took Leonidas away from home for months at a time; he often missed holidays with his growing family. Yet still Polk reflected, "I feel that I have done but too little in accomplishing the end of my creation."[6]

Polk and his brothers built a beautiful chapel on their land in Maury County, near Columbia, Tennessee. Consecrated St. John's Chapel in September 1842, it still stands today. During the Civil War, as General Hood's doomed Army of Tennessee passed through Columbia during their march toward the Battle of Franklin in November 1864, the army's finest division commander, General Patrick Cleburne,

St. John's Chapel, Columbia, Tennessee, built by Polk and his brothers in 1842 on their family land. After he was killed in the Battle of Franklin on November 30, 1864, the body of Major General Patrick Cleburne lay buried in the chapel's graveyard until 1870 when his remains were moved to Helena, Arkansas (photograph by Kraig McNutt, used with permission).

paused to admire St. John's. Gazing upon the picturesque churchyard which perhaps reminded him of similar scenes in his native Ireland, Cleburne mused to his aide, "It is almost worth dying to rest in so sweet a spot." A few days later Cleburne would be killed in battle, shot through the heart while charging formidable Federal works at Franklin, and buried in that very spot.[7]

In 1841 Polk took on the operation of a sugar plantation in Louisiana, and later that year he was named the first bishop of the new state diocese. As in Tennessee, he championed literacy and religious instruction for slaves, in accordance with his belief that

> the Gospel of Christ ... seeks to equalize the human condition; and to compensate ... for the disparities existing in the worldly circumstances of our race. It is eminently, therefore, the property of the poor.[8]

Though wealthy, the Polk family weathered tremendous hardship and setbacks during these years. In 1849 cholera struck in Louisiana; Polk fell gravely ill along with at least 300 plantation residents, black and white, and more than 70 died. Consequently crops failed for lack of labor, and severe financial difficulties followed. Then in 1850 a violent tornado struck the plantation home while the Polk family hosted dinner guests. The place was wrecked in a matter of moments. After struggling for years to recuperate, the Polks sold the property at considerable loss and moved to New Orleans.

Around this time, Polk conceived the idea of founding a superior Southern university. In 1856 he launched an ambitious drive toward that goal, pouring his considerable talents into the enterprise as described by Bishop John Henry Hopkins of Vermont:

> I was amazed and delighted at [Polk's] combination of original genius, lofty enterprise, and Christian hope, with the utmost degree of practical wisdom, cautious investigation, exquisite tact, and indefatigable energy.[9]

His mammoth effort culminated in the cornerstone ceremony of October 1860. The University of the South lives on as Leonidas Polk's supreme legacy. Of course, numerous souls contributed toward the founding of the university atop the mountain domain—but if there is one person whose vision and vigor brought it into being, that would be Leonidas Polk.

Stone marking location of Leighton, Polk's plantation in Lafourche Parish, Louisiana (photograph courtesy of the Sewanee Chapter, the Leonidas Polk Memorial Society, used with permission).

As an Episcopal bishop, Polk was widely beloved, largely because of the love and respect he demonstrated to all. He once refused to accept a decision submitted by a parish in Baton Rouge because women were excluded from voting. Never did Polk's high church position stultify him or fill him with pride or imperiousness. His was the heart of a servant, in compliance with Luke 22:26 ("he that is chief [shall be] as he that doth serve"). Even so, he was not so modest as to shrink away or turn the other cheek when controversy arose.

War Breaks Out

During the years leading up to the Civil War, Polk worried over the divisive forces at work in the South and the nation. He corresponded and met with church leaders in an attempt to foster unity and peace amid the growing political polarization.

By New Year's Day 1861 South Carolina had seceded from the Union, with Mississippi, Florida, Alabama, Georgia, Louisiana, and Texas following in rapid succession. In a letter to President Buchanan written on Christmas Day, Polk accurately prophesied the order of events as they came to pass. As a minister of the gospel, Bishop Polk had refrained from any public statement on the political turmoil, and

> [h]e was pleased to add that ... the Episcopal Church had ... confined herself to teaching and preaching the gospel of Christ. Pressure had often been exerted from both sides, yet neither her pulpit nor presses had contributed to "the radical and unscriptural propagandism which has so degraded Christianity."

Polk did incur some controversy when, following Louisiana's secession on January 26, 1861, he decreed by letter to the diocese that the creation of an independent nation rendered the Episcopal body within its boundaries *governmentally* distinct from the United States church. "Our affection for our brethren in the North has not been shaken," he explained. Separation was effected solely "to follow our nationality" as required by church doctrine, he believed. Much debate ensued among Episcopal bishops and scholars, while events took their rapid course.[10]

By May Polk's observations of the unfolding conflict expanded beyond purely ecclesiastical matters when he wrote a letter to President Jefferson Davis expressing concern over defense of the Mississippi River Valley. The river became a focus of great consternation early in the War, particularly for the northwestern states, in light of the waterway's importance as a commercial conduit. At the beginning the Confederacy adopted a policy of free and

Jefferson Davis, President of the Confederate States of America. Many historians inaccurately postulate that he commissioned Polk a major general because of their close, lifelong friendship. While the two had been friends at West Point, they went their separate ways after graduation, never corresponding until the outbreak of the Civil War (photograph by Mathew Brady, Library of Congress).

open trade on the river, but in the knowledge that gunboats were sure to follow, the Southern government began erecting forts and mounting cannon along its course.

The South-leaning governor of Tennessee, mindful of Polk's West Point education, from time to time consulted the bishop on military matters. In June Jefferson Davis invited Polk to the new capital in Richmond to confer on Mississippi River interests, and after a week of talks and meetings among various Confederate luminaries including Robert E. Lee, the president offered Polk a brigadier general's commission. At first he declined, but after visiting Louisiana troops amassing along future battle lines in Virginia and seeking the counsel of Bishop William Meade at Virginia Theological Seminary, he resolved to accept. By the time he returned to Richmond firm in his decision, Davis upgraded the proffered commission to major general and gave Polk command of a territory encompassing the Mississippi River Valley.

That Polk was made a general, even though he lacked any military credentials whatsoever beyond a West Point education, surely raised eyebrows. During a time when many clamored for command, what were Davis's reasons for choosing Polk for such a crucial position? Davis himself explained that he was impressed by Polk's confident leadership. Additionally, in those days of widespread trust in divine providence, it surely did not hurt that Polk was a man of the cloth.[11]

Some historians have pilloried Davis for commissioning Polk, and Polk for acquiescing. After inaccurately denigrating Polk as "not an especially learned man," Steven Woodworth portrays him as a smooth con artist for the manner in which he landed a military appointment:

> When war came, Polk quickly decided on a military role for himself in the conflict.... [His] chief talent ... was his tremendous persuasiveness and charisma. He had a way with people, and he could, it was said, be "extremely charming" in conversation.[12]

Woodworth's account has Polk burning with military ambition and plotting, conniving, and charming his way into a high rank in the Southern army. However, neither Polk's own words nor his actions suggest the intention or ulterior motive alleged by this historian. As previously noted, he declined the commission at first to engage in considerable soul-searching, even leaving Richmond to seek the counsel of his mentor Bishop Meade.

To support his contentions Woodworth quotes selectively from a letter that Polk wrote to his wife at this time, but conveniently omits the first sentence in which the bishop states his true motive: "I am quite well & have had good reason to know that my visit here has been of decided use to our cause in several important particulars." Polk's concern, clearly stated, was to be *of use to the cause*, not to obtain military rank or command for himself. His focus was on serving the greater whole over and above his individual interests. One cannot read anything more into the missive unless predisposed to take a derogatory view of the bishop.[13]

And that Steven Woodworth is so predisposed, there can be no doubt. Huston

Horn, recent biographer of Polk, refers to Woodworth as "a historian who enjoys needling Leonidas Polk's Civil War duty." Horn exposes Woodworth's error in asserting that Polk believed he was quoting the Bible upon accepting his commission, when he uttered the phrase "resistance to tyrants is duty to God." Polk knew the Scriptures thoroughly and would not have labored under such a mistake, nor was he averse to quoting other (even Presbyterian) authorities and thinkers. But this is the kind of liberty that Woodworth and others take in their ongoing "needling" campaign.[14]

In order to understand Polk's true state of mind with regard to the offer of a generalship, it is instructive to read from a second letter he wrote to his wife from Virginia, dated June 19, 1861. First, he relates his sobering impressions after a visit to the site of the Battle of Big Bethel, a small-scale Confederate victory:

> I went down to the battle ground at Bethel Church. I examined it in detail. The hand of God became revealed in that, truly. Never in the annals of war was there such a defeat with such a disparity of numbers.... I saw where the puddles of blood of the poor fellows on their side were spilled.

While divulging that friends are pressing him to "take part in this movement," he pours out to Frances his inner debate on whether to accept the generalship offered him:

> the president has twice brought it before me. He is desirous for me to accept the commission of Brigadier General in the Confederate Army & urged many considerations for my compliance. A number of New Orleans people seem to desire it also as well as many of my military friends. I have said I could give no answer to this now.... What my duty may be I have not yet determined.... I cannot ignore what I know. I cannot forget what I have learned. We cannot forget that I have been educated by the country for its service in certain contingencies. What may be the result I hope I may be guided from on high as determining & I trust in any event I may be permitted to see my way clear before me.[15]

These are the words of a man in the throes of decision, listening to voices around him but above all seeking divine guidance. He has gazed upon blood spilled on the field of strife and thus grasps the import of the choice before him. Polk goes on to tell his wife of visiting Louisiana troops and addressing soldiers there and in Norfolk, and his plan to seek advice from Bishop Meade the following day. Polk does not know yet whether he wants to accept, nor whether he *ought to* accept a commission. Nowhere in these writings is there a tone of crafty, underhanded finagling for rank as alleged by Dr. Woodworth.

Oddly, historian Albert Castel postulates the emergence of facial hair as some manner of pretense on the part of Polk upon assuming his new rank:

> Shortly after the war began in 1861, Davis appointed [Polk] a major general. It was a mistake. Although Polk grew a beard that made him look like a general rather than a priest, he proved at best mediocre, at worst, execrable, as a military leader.[16]

Aside from such innuendo and sarcasm, Davis's naming Polk to his new command in the West involved several key factors: most importantly, the pending arrival of Albert Sidney Johnston. Johnston was a larger-than-life figure in the U.S. Army known for sterling integrity and personal charisma, who had distinguished himself in the Mexican War, fought for Texas independence, patrolled the Western frontier in command of the storied 2nd Cavalry, led the 1857–58 Utah expedition, and most recently headed the Department of the Pacific in California. Jefferson Davis in particular harbored the highest regard for Johnston, but his esteemed reputation was universal. In the same letter that Woodworth cites as proof of Polk's shameless self-promotion, Polk wrote his wife: "We want and [Davis] wants Genl A.S. Johnston badly. He has not yet arrived." This suggests that Polk's position hinged on Johnston's eventually being given first priority. Indeed, at that very time Johnston was embarking on a grueling, overland trip across the desert Southwest, eventually reaching Richmond in September 1861. He then promptly replaced Polk as commander of Department Number 2 of the West, newly expanded upon Johnston's ascension. Thus, Polk's position was clearly temporary and awarded at a time when Jefferson Davis believed that he had a few months' leeway, as the Yankees surely would not attack the swampy lowlands during the summer months for fear of disease. Meanwhile someone was needed to get fortifications underway in defense of the Mississippi, and Polk filled that role.[17]

Davis had received numerous appeals from influential citizens for a suitable commander over the Mississippi Valley. Indeed, some of these called for Albert Sidney Johnston. But some lobbied for Polk as well. While mulling over Davis's offer of command, he learned "that there 'is a great wish on the part of my friends that I should take part in this movement'" whom Polk described as "persons of consideration" including "a delegation of planters and businessmen from Mississippi and Louisiana." Polk's appointment did not come out of the blue or through some whim of Davis, but had the express support of prominent men.[18]

Finally, in the earlier letter to his wife, Polk informed her that he "had several interviews with Lee" during his stay in Richmond. In spite of Woodworth's attributing Polk's promotion to his "extremely charming" conversation, the pragmatic Lee was not one to be easily charmed or persuaded. Rather than waste an entire week exchanging mere pleasantries, Lee and Polk would have engaged in the serious business of discussing riverine defenses, an area of expertise that Lee developed during his decades in the U.S. Army Corps of Engineers. Thus Lee had ample opportunity to judge the soundness of Polk's ideas and suggestions.

Given the support surrounding Polk's appointment, including his apparently passing muster with Robert E. Lee, and in light of the implied temporary status of his position pending A.S. Johnston's arrival, Davis's naming Polk to command takes on a more reasonable aspect than historians would have us believe.

Polk stepped up to the challenge of his new post as he always did: with determination, devotion to duty, and consciousness of his limitations. Polk entered the army simply "because it seemed the duty next me." During the following year, he attempted to resign on three separate occasions. Obviously this was not a man driven by personal ambition. He made it clear that he cared not for vainglory or power arising out of military command:

> As Bishop-General Polk descended the steps of the Virginia Capitol ... a friend stepped forward to congratulate him on his promotion. "Pardon me," said Polk gravely. "I do not consider it a promotion. The highest office on Earth is that of a bishop in the Church of God."[19]

Chapter 2

"Gibraltar of the West"

Polk was given temporary command of the upper Mississippi River Valley, with headquarters in Memphis, pending the arrival of Albert Sidney Johnston from his U.S. Army posting in California. On September 2 Polk's department was expanded to include Arkansas and Missouri. By September 15 Johnston arrived in Nashville to assume command in the West.[1]

In the meantime Polk had taken effective measures of his own, most notably his advance on Columbus, Kentucky, in order to employ its high bluffs and strategic position for defense of the Mississippi River. Polk's move involved him in a race of sorts against Ulysses S. Grant, whose department commander, General John Frémont, ordered him on August 28, 1861, to transport downriver from his post at Cairo, Illinois, and "occupy Columbus, Ky. as soon as possible." Polk beat Grant by one day.[2]

Among the most blatantly inaccurate and unfair charges brought against Leonidas Polk is that he singlehandedly violated Kentucky's neutrality on September 4, 1861, by advancing to Columbus, where he subsequently raised a strong, defensive Confederate bastion. Thomas Connelly goes so far as to pronounce Polk's taking Columbus "probably one of the greatest mistakes of the war." A close examination of the facts will demonstrate the fallacy and hyperbole of historians' railing against Polk over this issue.[3]

Kentucky's "Neutrality"

In May 1861 Kentucky officially declared its neutral status through resolutions passed by the state house and senate, and issued by Governor Magoffin. Kentucky was truly a divided state, and the legislature leaned strongly pro–Union while the governor sympathized with the South. Both presidents Lincoln and Davis made it known that they respected and intended to abide by Kentucky's neutral stance.

However, long before Polk advanced on Columbus, the Union had already contradicted its own policy of observing Kentucky's neutrality. As Connelly himself admits, "*In early August,* Harris [Tennessee's Confederate governor] learned that the Federals had established Camp Dick Robinson, south of Lexington, Kentucky, for the purpose of training and arming Kentucky Union recruits." This was of grave concern to Governor Harris, as a neutral Kentucky provided a buffer protecting Tennessee from Union incursions. However, in a brazenly neutrality-busting action, the U.S. Army had moved onto Kentucky soil for the purpose of running a military training installation—well before Polk crossed over into Kentucky! When Confederate-leaning Kentucky governor Magoffin objected, Federal authorities offered the disingenuous defense that troops at the camp had every right to drill under their national flag—but such a claim defies the very definition of neutrality. That same national flag was the standard of one of the belligerent parties to the conflict. The fact that recruitment and training for war were taking place beneath its billows signified that the state had chosen a side (or that said side was claiming the state), thereby nullifying its neutrality.[4]

One could not easily overlook Camp Dick Robinson. It was no small, out-of-the-way spot in the woods, nor was its operation discreet or under cover as some have said. Located on a leased farm, the camp occupied 425 acres with dimensions of one-half mile frontages at the intersection of two major roads. Not only did thousands of infantry drill on the grounds, but by the end of August when the 1st Kentucky Artillery with its six pieces trained there, the impact upon the region assumed a dramatic, audible dimension. By virtue of Camp Robinson alone, the Union had already resoundingly violated Kentucky's neutrality fully one month before General Polk supposedly did so.

Stanley F. Horn, in his classic 1941 history *The Army of Tennessee*, lists additional instances of the Union's ignoring the border state's neutrality, all of which predate Polk's move on Columbus. The Federals had named Major Robert Anderson, their hero of Fort Sumter, commander of the "Department of Kentucky" with headquarters initially in Cincinnati, Ohio. However,

> [o]n the first of September the Federal government threw off any pretense of recognizing neutrality and took active steps toward occupation. Major Anderson moved his headquarters from Cincinnati to Louisville. [General "Bull"] Nelson was commissioned a brigadier general and authorized to organize at Maysville, Kentucky, a force to operate in the eastern part of the state. The troops at Camp Dick Robinson were placed under the command of Brigadier General George H. Thomas. There were signs of an impending shift of troops from Cairo to Columbus.
> ....
> Major General Leonidas Polk moved up swiftly from his encampment at Union City in Tennessee and seized Columbus on September 4. He just barely got there ahead of Grant, for the latter was preparing to grab it on the following day.[5]

Connelly also discloses in a footnote Frémont's August 28 order to Grant "to occupy Columbus, Ky., as soon as possible." Clearly, numerous federal actions predated and provoked Polk's advance. But in spite of these facts, Connelly decries Polk's action: "in September 1861, when Leonidas Polk *broke the neutral barrier* and entered Kentucky," as though Polk was the first to violate the stated policy. Connelly further scolds: "A combination of ambition, lack of communication, and sheer dogmatism prompted [Polk's] move that officially broke Kentucky's neutrality." Why is Polk charged with breaking neutrality when the Union had already shattered it? And why do historians shrug their shoulders at the Federals' longstanding violations yet hurl the book at Polk for his eleventh hour, defensive move?[6]

Neutrality in fact ceased to exist under principles of law once the Union army initiated wartime operations in the state of Kentucky. Consider the legal doctrine of adverse possession: when an owner knowingly allows a party to trespass and fails to object or take action, the owner loses the right to claims down the line against the trespasser, and indeed to the land itself. The underlying principle is that one cannot rightfully complain about an action to which one has acquiesced for a designated period of time. The pro–Union legislature of Kentucky, by its silence regarding the operation of Camp Dick Robinson, General Nelson's organizing of forces, and Major Anderson's establishing Department of Kentucky headquarters in Louisville, had effectively rescinded its neutral status before General Polk ever set foot on Kentucky soil—and thus relinquished any right to charge him with violating a neutrality which had ceased to exist.

Kentucky Unionists howled at the specter of the Confederate flag waving over Columbus, even though it was initially raised not by Confederate troops but by the townspeople, *prior to* Polk's arrival. Colonel Gustave Waagner spotted the Stars and Bars when Grant sent him on September 2 to Belmont, across the river from Columbus, to reconnoiter. The theatrical uproar over Polk's crossing the border sent Southern-leaning politicians in Kentucky and Tennessee in hand-wringing mode, and Confederate government officials initially second-guessed themselves, even ordering Polk to withdraw his troops. However, Polk convincingly demonstrated to President Davis the military necessity of his move in light of Grant's imminent seizure of Columbus. Davis agreed, writing on September 16, "We cannot permit the indeterminate qualities, the political elements, to control our actions in cases of military necessity." Polk made a reasonable counter-offer to the state of Kentucky: "I am prepared to agree to withdraw the Confederate troops from Kentucky, provided she will agree that the troops of the Federal Government be withdrawn simultaneously." Unsurprisingly, this offer was ignored. The truth is that the United States government from the beginning disdained in word and disregarded by its actions Kentucky's neutral stance—and there was nothing that Kentucky could do about it.[7]

Nevertheless, internal inconsistency and illogic did not stop Kentucky's Unionists from making political hay out of Polk's foray. The chairman of the Kentucky Senate Committee professed his "profound astonishment." Denunciatory speeches reached a fever pitch, and in North-leaning newspapers ink poured into outraged headlines and editorials. Of course it was nothing more than theater, starring the politicians and press acting out the melodrama *du jour*.[8]

Historians' View of Polk and Columbus

Historians almost universally characterize Polk's move as a "blunder" and far worse—in the words of Steven Woodworth, "one of the most decisive catastrophes the Confederacy ever suffered. Kentucky's neutrality had been resoundingly flaunted." Yet no one pronounces judgment against the Federals who had already obliterated any pretense of neutrality. Was Kentucky's neutrality a principle binding only upon the Confederacy? Why the double standard—and more to the point, why do historians endorse it? How is it that the Union even today is deemed innocent in this matter, despite its training camps and occupation by an entire military department? Yet Polk incurs mountains of guilt for a single fort with a small contingent of troops, its guns pointed not at Kentucky nor even to the North, but westward toward the Mississippi River to protect Confederate positions downriver from "the Federals massing upward of forty thousand troops at Cairo for the obvious purpose of descending the river."[9]

Lincoln defended the Union's recruiting in Kentucky on the basis that it only took place "upon the urgent solicitation of many Kentuckians." Southern sympathizers in Kentucky had similarly urged the Confederate government to assume an active role in the state. However, while aware of the Union's violations, Richmond abstained out of respect for the state's neutrality policy. Given these facts, if the desire and consent of Kentuckians serves as an adequate defense for the U.S. Army's penetrating the state, should it not similarly absolve the Confederacy when it did finally enter Kentucky? Historian Earl Hess, who also impugns Polk for taking Columbus, nevertheless admits, "The citizens of Columbus itself also thanked Polk for his action." The ardent preference of the town's population, as evidenced by their choice of flags and their thanks to General Polk, was for the Southern Confederacy. Yet for some reason Lincoln's argument does not apply to the other side. Supposing Grant advanced one day earlier and took Columbus first, as was his intention, would he have been subjected to the same level of—or, indeed, *any*—condemnation? Or would it instead be hailed as another brilliant move by that bold, relentless fighter Grant?[10]

After being pre-empted by Polk, Grant occupied Paducah, Kentucky, the following day, September 5. Historians imply that the Federal general would never have ventured into the neutral zone on his own, but Polk's advance left him no choice. Paducah came under Union control only because Polk first seized Columbus, the story goes. This completely misconstrues the truth. Actually, it was Grant's aggression which forced Polk's hand:

> [A]s the Confederate forces approached this place, the Federal troops were found in formidable numbers in position upon the opposite bank, with their cannon turned upon Columbus. The citizens of the town had fled with terror.

In addition to these visual observations, Polk possessed intelligence of Federal troop movements in Missouri and Grant's impending advance. He knew that the Federals had no qualms over openly violating Kentucky's neutrality; they had already done so on numerous occasions and planned to do it again at Columbus. But such facts remain hidden, at best disclosed in endnotes, in the current storyline of Polk's unilateral foray into Kentucky.[11]

The sham does not end there. Historians magnify the narrative with some version of a claim that Polk destroyed any chance of Kentucky's aligning with the South, and that as a direct reaction to his impolitic invasion Kentucky was pushed irrevocably to the side of the Union. This is, of course, absurd. If believable, then the logical inverse would also be true: Polk beat Grant to Columbus by only one day. Supposing Grant entered Columbus first, would it have forced Kentucky into the Confederacy? The answer is a resounding no. Nor would Kentucky ever have sided with the South had Polk *not* taken Columbus. Unless we mistake political theater for reality, General Polk and Columbus in no way acted as the catalyst for Kentucky's going with the Union. The portrayal of this entire affair is draped with pretense and posturing, yet the underlying, undeniable fact is that Kentucky's lawmakers had already aligned with the Union and merely awaited a pretext by which to reveal it to the world.

All of this should be obvious. The unassailable truth is that Kentucky's neutrality was a farce; it was "cloaking a fiction" in the words of Polk's biographer Huston Horn. Author Glenn Tucker similarly calls Kentucky's stance "a sort of make-believe neutrality." Truly the uproar following Polk's move on Columbus was nothing more than Unionist political histrionics. Yet historians decry Polk as though he was the first party who breached neutrality, when in fact by then the policy had been abandoned in all but name only. And rather than take an objective view which one should expect from academic observers 160 years later, they align with the political bluster and journalistic hyperbole of the time by bringing their own egregious charges against Polk. The condemnation of Polk on this point has been taken up by others and repeated so often that it has morphed from opinion into presumed fact. The result is that Polk's name is rarely mentioned now without an ensuing string of increasingly imaginative insults. The Columbus incident early in the War, and in particular most historians' slanted depiction of it, is only the first illustration of a prevalent, inexplicable animus against General Polk.[12]

Some authorities, however, take a more measured approach by acknowledging that Kentucky's neutrality was a sham but holding that Polk still erred by upsetting the delicate political situation in the state. Even if the uproar over Columbus was all political theater, nevertheless it was Polk who caused it, they allege, which in turn caused his government to be assailed for his action. He certainly gifted Kentucky Unionists with considerable propaganda currency. This argument has some merit, and these potential ramifications surely gave Polk pause as he debated whether to advance into Kentucky. His second-in-command, Gideon Pillow, offered input on the weighty political question. From the first days of the war Pillow viewed Columbus as a prize to be won, and as early as May 1861 pushed the Confederate government for permission to take the position. Afterwards he turned his hyperactive attention in numerous other directions, but by September he urgently advised Polk in favor of moving on Columbus. By this time Polk well realized that Pillow was not one to offer dependable counsel as to military matters. As far back as the Mexican War he was well known to possess no martial talent; however, it is difficult to overstate Pillow's adeptness in the political arena. He was a major mover and shaker in local, state and national politics of the 19th century. Pillow had a hand in the selection of several Democratic presidential nominees, and his own name had even been considered in past contests. Polk likely felt he could rely on Pillow's judgment as to the political risks involving in moving on Columbus.[13]

Political ramifications are not the only issue surrounding Polk's advance into Kentucky; more importantly, there were military considerations. In addition to the widespread censure for his audacity in taking Columbus, some historians even go so far as to belittle the strategic worth of the town's location. Yet most are silent on this point, for few would deny the military desirability of Columbus. It was certainly appreciated by Federal general John Frémont, commander of the Department of the West. His August 28 order to Grant to take Columbus likely came at the recommendation of his Russian engineering officer, Charles Alfred de Arnand, who was educated at the Military School of Engineering in St. Petersburg. In early August Frémont sent him on a reconnaissance to scope out Polk's location and likely movements. Presumably Grant in turn perceived the military advantages of the position. Yet neither Grant nor Frémont has been criticized for their designs on Columbus.

Polk's advance into Kentucky was a military necessity. Grant was moving in to take Columbus, and Polk knew it. He had to act fast and decisively. Historians have heaped criticism upon Polk for not obtaining permission from the War Department in Richmond before occupying Columbus. But 19th-century communications were too slow in this situation. William Tecumseh Sherman said it well: "Occasions do arise when a prompt seizure of results is forced on military commanders not in immediate communication with the proper authority." The political controversy that Polk and Richmond weathered temporarily was preferable to the military disaster that would have ensued had Grant occupied the strategic position. Once the Confederacy lost Columbus, the Union would win immediate dominance over that crucial section of the Mississippi River.[14]

If Polk made any mistake militarily by taking Columbus, according to historian Glenn Robins, it was that he did not go far enough:

> [T]he bishop erred ... by overlooking the military importance of Paducah and by failing to include the city as one of his principal objectives. Together, Columbus and Paducah would have strengthened the Confederates' hold on the Mississippi River.[15]

Even without Paducah, the establishment of a Confederate bastion at Columbus, Kentucky, represents Polk's first major accomplishment during his service in the Civil War. The fort would fulfill its purpose during its effective life by serving as an impediment to Union incursions downriver.

He "pronounced them good"

Once Polk's force moved into and secured Columbus, he proceeded to erect strong fortifications and artillery emplacements on the high bluffs overlooking the river as well as farther down toward the waterfront. By this time General Sidney Johnston had visited Columbus, "examined the fortifications there, [and] pronounced them good." As readers of Civil War history can attest, Johnston's ready approval of Polk's earthworks was a rarity. Inevitably, fortifications erected by one general and inspected by another (or his engineering staff) were deemed faulty, wholly inadequate, deplorable, or worse. That the fort at Columbus won Johnston's endorsement demonstrates that Polk had not forgotten the principles of engineering and terrain learned during the West Point days of his youth.[16]

Johnston's long defensive line ran across the northern border of the western department of the Confederacy, from Columbus, through Bowling Green, Kentucky (where Johnston established his headquarters), to Cumberland Gap. Polk, now commander of Johnston's First Division, maintained his headquarters at Columbus and in addition oversaw other forts along the river as well as inland. He worked tirelessly to strengthen the defenses at

Brigadier General Gideon Pillow, second-in-command to Polk at Columbus. Never known for military ability in either the Mexican or Civil War, Pillow was a political powerhouse of the Democratic Party. As a Confederate officer he damaged what little reputation he had after disgracefully escaping Fort Donelson just before it fell, leaving others to face the enemy, only later to resurface briefly for minor combat roles at Murfreesboro and the Atlanta Campaign. Pillow rendered his best service to the Confederacy as a recruiter and administrator of the Conscription Bureau in Tennessee (photograph by Mathew Brady, National Archives at College Park).

Columbus. By January 1862 he had mounted 150 cannon, deployed in the river numerous submarine torpedoes (fashioned by his friend, the eminent Matthew Fontaine Maury), and extended a huge chain across the Mississippi River to obstruct the passage of Union gunboats. He had pushed for the construction of ironclad gunboats as roving defenders on the Mississippi. In addition, he obtained steamboats to be converted into gunboats, and arranged armaments purchases from Cuba. So strong was the Columbus bastion that General Henry Halleck, commander of the Union Department of Missouri, "termed it the 'Gibraltar of the West.' It was in fact so defensible that Halleck and his commanders began to think of alternatives to get around it." The Federal naval officer Andrew Foote wrote the secretary of the navy: "The works are of very great strength, consisting of formidable tiers of batteries."[17]

Retreat from Columbus

Major General Henry Halleck, a brilliant military engineer known as "Old Brains" who early in the war commanded the Department of Missouri, was not so dismissive of the value of Polk's defensive position at Columbus, Kentucky as are modern historians. He judged Polk's fort overlooking the Mississippi River as so formidable that he christened it "Gibraltar of the West" (photograph by J.A. Scholten, Library of Congress).

But even the invincible Gibraltar was eventually conquered by the English, and Polk's stronghold also fell, not by battle but in accordance with the same principle under which it was initially taken: military necessity. In January 1862 the eastern sector of Johnston's thin line commanded by General George Crittenden was overrun by a Union force under General George Thomas at Mill Springs, Kentucky. This loss along with the subsequent fall of Forts Henry and Donelson in February rendered Johnston's advance positions at Bowling Green and Columbus untenable, and Polk was ordered to evacuate although the defenses at Island No. 10 and Fort Pillow were to be retained. Polk, initially and perhaps quixotically, "with 'unbounded confidence in the strength of Columbus,' ... and with 'characteristic gallantry' insisted that he could hold the fort against any force as long as his supplies should last."

Nevertheless, with regret Polk obediently and expeditiously prepared to abandon the fort to which he had devoted so much effort and planning. Timely and successful evacuation was accomplished through diligent effort on the part of Polk, his staff, and the garrison:

> Polk's shutdown of the Columbus works was accomplished clandestinely and swiftly. "In five days we moved the accumulations of six months," Polk said, including 140 guns.... "we removed enough to supply my whole command for eight months."[18]

Chapter 3

Shiloh

Concentration in Corinth

Following the withdrawal of Confederate forces from their line stretching across Kentucky, including Polk's position at Columbus, it became apparent that the strategy long urged by generals Gustave Beauregard, Joseph Johnston and others for concentration of Confederate forces was advisable. Before this time, out of political expedience President Davis insisted on protecting the entire Confederacy, calling for defensive dispositions of Southern forces behind state boundaries and along the perimeter of the new nation. The problem was that dispersing limited military assets across non-strategic territory would inevitably result in defeat of the whole through incremental enemy attacks.

Beauregard had been dispatched by Davis to lend his considerable expertise to the vulnerable West, and there he and Sidney Johnston entered into an arrangement of co-command. Together the generals decided on Corinth, Mississippi, as a point to concentrate the scattered Western forces. General Polk brought his 17,000 from Columbus. From Pensacola and Mobile came General Braxton Bragg with 10,000 troops. General Mansfield Lovell in command at New Orleans reluctantly dispatched 5,000 of the city's defenders under General Daniel Ruggles. General Sidney Johnston led Hardee's 14,000 and Crittenden's 5,000 toward the railroad junction in northern Mississippi, and Beauregard called for General Earl Van Dorn to cross his force over the Mississippi River from Arkansas (although they did not arrive in time for the upcoming epic battle).

A formidable host was coming together, and on March 27 Beauregard, Johnston, Polk and Bragg met in Corinth to form the Army of the Mississippi. Beauregard organized the motley conglomeration into three corps under Polk, Bragg, and William Hardee. Johnston named former vice president John C. Breckinridge commander of the army's reserve corps. Braxton Bragg, an adept administrator, took on extra duty as chief of staff to aid Johnston in training the army and forging it into a cohesive force. "By early April Johnston had concentrated nearly 50,000 troops at and around Corinth, with more on the way."[1]

Braxton Bragg

The concentration of Confederate troops taking place in the region of Tennessee and northern Mississippi brought Leonidas Polk and Braxton Bragg together for the first time in their respective military roles. They had known each other in Louisiana, but the extent of their acquaintance is uncertain. Polk biographer Huston Horn has Braxton and Elise Bragg socializing with the Polks at their Louisiana plantation in the early 1840s. However, he is mistaken as Bragg did not meet Elise until 1849, and after they married that June they were off to distant army posts. Horn also refers to Bragg as "Polk's former sugar-plantation neighbor," but other than Bragg's visits to Elise's home in 1849, the two families did not reside at their Thibodaux homes during corresponding years. The Polks sold their property in 1853, while Bragg did not acquire his plantation until 1856. Nevertheless, from 1856 until the war broke out Bragg lived and planted sugar in Louisiana, occupying various civic positions, while Polk, dwelling in nearby New Orleans, served as Episcopal bishop of that state. According to Huston Horn, in October 1857 Bragg attended a church convention in Philadelphia as a delegate from St. John's Church in Thibodaux, at which Polk gave an address. And on January 1, 1861, Polk paid "a cordial holiday social call" upon Braxton Bragg in New Orleans. Clearly the two men had some association before the war, but the nature and extent of their relationship is unclear.[2]

General Pierre Gustave Toutant Beauregard, "Hero of Manassas," was transferred to the West after he ran afoul of President Davis. Assigned to Sidney Johnston's command, he arrived in time to implement a concentration of troops culminating in the Battle of Shiloh. When Johnston was killed on the battlefield, Beauregard assumed command of the Western army until the president replaced him with Braxton Bragg in June 1862 (photograph by Mathew Brady, National Archives at College Park).

Bragg and Polk provide a study of contrasting personalities. While the bishop, habitually cheerful, took a magnanimous view of his fellow man, tolerated human weakness, and employed the power of love to win over people, Bragg, universally known as "the best disciplinarian in the United States Army," suffered no fools, indulged no misbehavior (particularly if it involved alcohol), and drove himself and others relentlessly. General Edmund Kirby Smith succinctly summed him up: "a grim old fellow, but a true soldier."³

Before the transfer to Corinth, Bragg had spent almost one year in command of the Confederate training camp in Pensacola, Florida, where he whipped raw recruits into disciplined troops and defended against Fort Pickens, one of the few federally-occupied military installations holding out in the Confederacy. Bragg had previously served 18 years in the U.S. Army after graduating fifth in the West Point class of 1837. In 1849 he married Elise Ellis of Louisiana, who thereafter exercised profound influence upon Bragg's thinking and decisions. Ever the "true soldier," upon leaving the army he christened his new sugar plantation "Bivouac" and ran it like a disciplined military camp.

After resigning from the army Braxton Bragg maintained close friendships with fellow officers, including soon-to-be enemies, through personal visits and prolific correspondence. He helped William Tecumseh Sherman obtain his position as president of the Louisiana Seminary of Learning and Military Academy (precursor of LSU), and retain the post as sectional tensions increased, by "defending his old friend against charges of abolitionism and introducing him to a number of important politicians." Even after South Carolina seceded in December 1860, Bragg wrote Sherman, "should the worst come, we shall still be personal friends." Bragg called on George Thomas earlier that year when the latter came to New Orleans, and another army friend, Henry J. Hunt, who later masterminded the savage artillery attacks against Confederates at Malvern Hill and Gettysburg,

General Braxton Bragg commanded the Army of Tennessee from June 1862 until he resigned in December 1863 following a disastrous defeat at Chattanooga. While fully dedicated to the Southern cause, controversy and conflict were his constant companions, for which he blamed everyone but himself. A Texan serving under him observed that Bragg "seems to vent his evil spleen by arresting his generals." Lieutenant General Kirby Smith described him best: "a grim old fellow, but a true soldier" (Library of Congress).

visited Bragg and Elise at Bivouac. Even after the firing on Fort Sumter, Bragg wrote a warm letter to Hunt, who replied, "We still have a personal regard for each other, whatever course our sense of duty may dictate."[4]

In the case of Bragg, his sense of duty elevated him first to the rank of major general in the Louisiana state army, then brigadier general in the Confederate States Army and commander of the post at Pensacola. On December 27, 1861, orders came for Bragg to assume command in the Trans-Mississippi, but Bragg was given discretion whether to accept, and he did not. When the call came in early 1862 to concentrate Western forces in the vicinity of Corinth, Mississippi, Bragg fully supported the strategy. He had written President Davis earlier to "abandon his attempt to defend every Confederate state and concentrate all 'means and resources' in the most vital regions of the country.... [T]he 'whole of Texas and Florida should be abandoned.'" He must have been gratified, then, to find his advice coming to fruition, even though it meant abandoning Pensacola to the Yankees.

Bragg traveled to Jackson, Tennessee, by mid–March and began fault-finding no sooner than he arrived, with Polk as one of his first targets. Beauregard was in command at Jackson, but ill and overly worried, Bragg thought, over the military situation. He wrote to Elise that Polk was fretful as well and actually hindered Beauregard's recovery by burdening him with problems. This criticism was mild, though, compared to the vitriol with which he painted Polk to his wife over the following weeks.[5]

Bragg was appalled at what he perceived as a wholesale lack of discipline among the troops arriving in Tennessee and later Corinth. Elise egged him on by railing against his fellow commanders. Her husband was the only man who could manage volunteer recruits, she insisted; the others commanded mere mobs. Bragg castigated the assembling forces as "poorly supplied and badly organized, instructed and disciplined." He found Corinth in a state of "disorder and confusion." Some arriving troops, finding no provisions, were accused of plundering, and Bragg ordered one of his units to "drive 'the swine' back to their camps with bayonets. 'No plundering has taken place since,'" he wrote Elise.[6]

Bragg chafed with frustration at men he saw as incompetents who ranked him, with Polk as his primary focus. Although Elise volunteered plenty of vituperation toward Sidney Johnston in her letters, she and Bragg reserved their most hostile assessments for Polk. The truth is that Braxton Bragg seethed with contempt for Leonidas Polk from the very beginning of their association in the army. Bragg harangued his wife constantly with his criticisms against Polk and his command. Although "[p]lundering was widespread throughout the army" (and no doubt even Bragg's well-disciplined men were not innocent), Bragg complained, "Polk and Johnston do nothing to correct this. Indeed the good Bishop sets the example, by taking whatever he wishes." His accusing Polk personally of stealing seems extreme and surely Bragg did not literally believe it, but the disgust emanating from his words cannot be missed. Pouring out his contempt for Polk's men, he "described them as 'a mob that we have miscalled soldiers'" not only in private venting to his wife but as part of a long, disgruntled diatribe to General Beauregard, superior officer over both Bragg and Polk. Indeed, Bragg no doubt harbored an ulterior motive, kindled by his wife: he made no secret of his conviction that he should be in overall charge.

Perhaps Elise's objections to Polk centered primarily upon his religious vocation, as expressed in her strongly worded quote heading the introduction to this book. Elise pressed her opinions liberally upon her husband and appears to have had great impact upon his outlook. Perhaps their mutual disapproval of their bishop's serving as a general was the underlying reason for historian Thomas Connelly's opinion that "Bragg had never considered Polk a soldier."[7]

The Union Army at Shiloh

While Bragg fretted and tried his best to impose order upon Polk and Johnston's unruly soldiers, the Confederates were not the only combatants assembling in the vicinity of Corinth, Mississippi. By now the Union army had overrun Forts Henry and Donelson and gained free access to the Tennessee and Cumberland rivers. For his next step General Halleck focused on the important railroad junction at Corinth where the Mobile & Ohio crossed the Memphis & Charleston line, and sent General Charles F. Smith's command to the nearest point on the Tennessee River. He also ordered Don Carlos Buell to march overland from Nashville to join Smith. "[A]s unified commander, he was concentrating his forces by the book." Upon arriving in the area, General Smith suffered an injury that laid him up at headquarters and shortly thereafter caused his death from infection of the wound. Henry Halleck appointed Grant to take command; he arrived in Savannah on March 17.[8]

For weeks steamboats plied the Tennessee bringing large contingents of Grant's force in and around Savannah downriver from Pittsburg Landing, future site of the Battle of Shiloh. After a miserable foray through flooded swampland south of Eastport, Mississippi, in an unsuccessful attempt to cut the Memphis & Charleston Railroad, Sherman's division made its way back to Pittsburg Landing. "Once on firm soil, Sherman took a detailed look around the high ground at Pittsburg Landing and liked what he saw; it 'admits of easy defense by a small command, and yet affords admirable camping ground for a hundred thousand men.'" Union units steadily arrived and spread out across the "admirable camping ground," mobilizing for a battle they believed theirs to initiate. Five divisions commanded by Sherman, John McClernand, W.H.L. Wallace, Benjamin Prentiss, and Stephen Hurlbut bivouacked in the vicinity of Shiloh Church. Lew Wallace's division was posted several miles north.[9]

With Grant's army camped 22 miles away unsuspecting of any attack, and knowing that Buell's Army of the Ohio would soon arrive, General Albert Sidney Johnston in Corinth decided to take the offensive before the Yankees united to outnumber him.

March to Shiloh

The spark that ignited the Battle of Shiloh originated within Polk's command. His Second Division commanded by General Benjamin Franklin Cheatham had been detached to Bethel Station in the vicinity of Purdy, twelves miles north of Corinth, to guard the Mobile & Ohio Railroad. On March 28 Cheatham telegraphed Polk that he was threatened by Union general Lew Wallace's division advancing in his direction from Crump's Landing on the Tennessee River, where they had disembarked from transports. Upon receipt Polk dispatched the urgent message to Beauregard, who wrote across it a dramatic endorsement: "Now is the moment to advance and strike the enemy at Pittsburg Landing." He forwarded the fateful telegram to Sidney Johnston.[10]

On the night of April 2 Johnston, message in hand,

Major General Ulysses S. Grant (later elevated to lieutenant general over all Union armies) assumed command of Federal forces at Shiloh after Major General Charles F. Smith died from a fluke injury. Grant never admitted to being surprised by Sidney Johnston's attack in April 1862, but the first day of battle ended with a grim situation for the Federals. In a drenching storm Sherman approached him standing beneath a tree, sheltered from the rain only by the brim of his hat, and commiserated that it had been "the devil of a day." Grant laconically replied, "Whip 'em tomorrow, though," and that is what he did. Such single-minded perseverance was the bedrock of his success (Library of Congress).

conferred with his chief of staff Bragg and verbal orders were issued for the army to advance early the following morning. Beauregard and Johnston then met to craft written marching orders and battle plans. Johnston envisioned the overall operational goal—to turn the Union army toward the left (west) away from the Tennessee River—and delegated to Beauregard the responsibility for formulating a tactical plan that would achieve the objective. Thomas Jordan, Beauregard's chief of staff, actually wrote the battle plan using Napoleon's Waterloo orders as a rather questionable model. Thus, the Confederate attack formation would assume a Napoleonic configuration, with the three corps extended in long, parallel lines: Hardee's in front, Bragg's 1,000 yards behind, and Polk's corps the same distance back, third in line. This model would prove problematic on the ground, as it is difficult for a corps commander to maintain control of a battle line well over one mile long. It is as though the idea was simply to wash over the Federal army like a wave, rather than actually fight them.[11]

The first order of business was to accomplish a surprise assault upon the Federals' camp. Beauregard choreographed complicated marching orders to move his army over the elaborate road network connecting Corinth to Pittsburg Landing. His directions would have proven difficult under ideal circumstances with seasoned soldiers, but confusion, miscommunication, weather, and mud injected inevitable reality into the process. Although early on April 3 the troops were "awakened by the long roll that was sounded throughout the camp [and] [e]verybody was in motion ... [d]rums were beating, trumpets sounded, fifes blowing, brass bands playing, and men hurrying," by noon any forward motion was brought to a halt as a massive jam of officers, soldiers, animals, wagons, artillery, couriers and commissary officers, all bent on doing their duty, crammed the streets of Corinth.[12]

General Beauregard later blamed Polk for the back-up in Corinth and the Southerners' subsequent failure to open the Battle of Shiloh on schedule. Beauregard charged that on the morning of April 3 Polk's First Corps blocked the Third Corps of General William Hardee from launching their march at the head of the column. However, it is difficult to see how Polk's troops could have impeded anyone in Corinth since his First Division, commanded by General Charles Clark, was "not even in the town" (they bivouacked two miles from Corinth), and Cheatham's Second Division lay some twelves miles away at Purdy.[13]

Larry Daniel, in his book *Shiloh: The Battle That Changed the Civil War*, elaborates that Beauregard's perception of Polk's culpability came from an aide dispatched to investigate the cause of the Corinth traffic jam. The staffer reported Clark's division standing at arms with its wagons blocking Ridge Road. He claimed that Polk held them up insisting on a written order. The story continues that upon receiving this intelligence, Beauregard sent the aide to clear the road which was done promptly. However, the aide's report on its face seems contradictory. If Polk had Clark's division standing in readiness, then he was already several steps into following prior verbal orders. In compliance with the orders and aware of his assigned position, Clark's division remained stationary, not for want of written orders but to allow Hardee's corps to pass. That Polk would supposedly hold up the works demanding a written order while already strictly complying with the oral direction seems unlikely and illogical.

The second problem with the aide's report is the contention that Polk's men and wagons blocked the road. Larry Daniel joins with Timothy Smith and Parks in arguing that Beauregard was mistaken:

> William Polk, the bishop's son, convincingly rebutted the charge. Charles Clark's 4,500 men were encamped two miles outside of town, in fields and woods. William Polk, who happened to be present, attested that neither troops nor wagons came onto the road until after Hardee's corps had passed.

Connelly concurs that General Clark's division stood ready to march, "*clear of the road* and was waiting for Hardee to move."[14]

The illogic compounds further, taking into account both factors: if Polk's men were standing in readiness yet not moving, clearly there was a reason for their not advancing. The reason was that Hardee's corps was to precede them. If they were waiting for the purpose of allowing Hardee's corps to pass by, then it makes no sense that they would block the road thus preventing Hardee from passing.

Finally, the aide's report implies Hardee's corps stood ready to march but for Polk's impeding the road. Clearly Beauregard's aide did not simply check to see whether Hardee was in fact bottlenecked down the road, for if he had he would have found it was not the case. In fact, if anyone was waiting for a written order, it was General William Hardee. "Hardee waited for a written order to move, which he did not receive until after 3 p.m.," explains Connelly. Specifically, what General Hardee wanted was a second, more specific written order than the vague one received earlier from Bragg acting as Johnston's chief of staff.[15]

It is interesting that Beauregard's attribution of blame upon Polk, repeated years after the war, rests entirely upon an aide's report. As shall be seen in a notorious episode during the Battle of Chickamauga, aides' reports were not always reliable in accurately assigning responsibility for delays.

Problems abounded in Bragg's corps as well. When written orders to move "tomorrow" were delivered to First Division commander General Daniel Ruggles at 3:30 a.m. on April 3, he interpreted "tomorrow" to mean that he was to march early on April 4! This misunderstanding naturally had delayed his division's departure by the time Ruggles realized the mistake.[16]

In spite of all the confusion, the Army of the Mississippi finally moved out of Corinth by 3:00 on the afternoon of April 3, and as flags fluttered and bands blared, the soldiers' "long-restrained ardor burst into a blaze of enthusiasm." However, the marching madness had only just begun. The route from Corinth involved several winding roads known by multiple names and linked by intersections. Polk's and Hardee's corps marched primarily along the western road, while Bragg on worse roads to the east was scheduled to link with Polk's corps by two intersecting routes. Thence arose the trouble on April 4, as Polk's column waited three hours for Bragg at one of the crossings after Bragg had changed his route but failed to notify Polk. Connelly details Bragg's woes:

> Bragg found only bad roads, poor guides, and raw troops in his move on Monterey. Due to these conditions, he was forced to route both of his divisions onto the Ridge Road via the Monterey-Savannah road. This move threw the Rebel column into more turmoil. Hardee was slowed, for Bragg asked him to wait until his corps moved up in support before Hardee deployed.[17]

And, of course, there waited Polk's single division as well. Once a messenger finally brought word of the altered plan, Polk proceeded onward and bivouacked for the night at a crossroads.

And what a night it was. Torrential rains and even hail pelted soldiers lacking shelter, delaying the formation of battle lines which had been originally scheduled for 3 a.m., April 5. Polk's men waited as Withers' division of Bragg's corps moved ahead, then marched in their rightful place behind Bragg in accordance with their assigned position in Beauregard's battle plan. However, unbeknownst to Polk and even Bragg, the latter's First Division, that of Daniel Ruggles, went missing. Under the watchful eye of Sidney Johnston, Hardee's men formed their battle line in front, then Bragg's corps began filing in behind Hardee. Once Jones Withers' division assumed its position, Bragg's next division commanded by Daniel Ruggles became suddenly conspicuous by its absence. After waiting on Ruggles for what seemed an interminable period of time, General Johnston lost his patience, unleashing his frustration: "This is perfectly puerile! This is not war!" he growled. "Let us have our horses!" and he set off with his staff to locate the disappearing division. Upon reaching an intersection on the Corinth Road, Johnston found Ruggles's column to the rear of Polk's, which had timely moved out after Bragg passed, unaware that another Second Corps division lagged behind. The army's senior commander then set to work directing traffic so that the tardy Ruggles could take his proper place in line of battle.[18]

Sidney Johnston was not the only general overwrought with tension that day. Blame began flying among corps commanders trying to absolve themselves from responsibility for the delays. It was fittingly prophetic that Polk's and Bragg's corps became entangled during the march to Shiloh, as it represented the beginning of what would become an enduring struggle of personalities between the two generals. During the dreadful march, Bragg's previously private hostility toward Polk spilled out into the open. The problem had begun, of course, before the army even left the city limits of Corinth, when Polk was wrongly blamed for the jam in town. Then Bragg blamed Polk for allegedly blocking him along the way. As Timothy Smith describes it, "April 5 was nearly gone, and the only fighting that took place that day was among the Confederate corps commanders blaming each other for the delay." Bragg, cursed with deplorable roads, had rerouted his columns and in spite of an intricately timed plan requiring coordination among the corps, failed to notify Polk of the change. Bragg must have been persuasive in his complaints, however, for "[m]ost blamed Polk, and Beauregard wrote of 'quite a controversy about that march, between Gen'ls Bragg & Polk....' William Preston Johnston later declared that Polk held his own: 'The plucky old bishop unhorsed his accusers right on the spot.'" Here Polk exhibited a lifelong trait of arguing forcefully when he was certain of his rectitude, rather than abide an untrue accusation.[19]

Clearly the bishop was not at fault for the delays. Larry Daniel has Beauregard "[u]nfairly blaming Polk (as he would after the war) for all the mounting problems." Most modern historians, however, withhold blame for the difficulties and pitfalls of the march. The truth is that bad weather, adverse conditions, terrible roads, overly elaborate plans requiring precisely timed junctures, changes of route, and human fallibility all contributed to the army's predicament. Nevertheless, at the time Bragg *appeared* at fault on two occasions: when Colonel Randall Gibson, in front of Sidney Johnston, questioned Bragg over communication breakdowns concerning the march and battle plan (for which Bragg never forgave Gibson), and when Ruggles's division turned up missing as Bragg's corps formed its battle line (for which Bragg blamed Polk).[20]

By early evening of April 5, after more torrential showers described as "[o]ne of the hardest rains fell I ever saw in life and wound up in considerable hail," Bragg's now-united corps completed its formation 1,000 yards behind Hardee's, with Gladden's brigade moved up to extend the right of Hardee's front line for protection of its flank on Lick Creek. As Polk's corps, now reunited with Cheatham's division, formed the third line, "Polk himself ranged ahead to keep the correct interval from Bragg's troops…. Thus situated, the Confederate army was within a mile of the Union camps." Even the weather cleared, portending a better day on the morrow.[21]

In addition to holding him in the highest personal esteem, President Davis regarded General Albert Sidney Johnston as the Confederacy's best martial hope, and trusted him above any other to win Confederate independence on the field of battle. During the calamitous march to Shiloh when others advised turning back, Johnston expressed his gratitude for Polk's backing his decision to go on. Polk, he told a staff officer, "is a true soldier and friend." Tragically, Johnston was killed while leading troops at Shiloh. His body was first buried in New Orleans, then removed in 1867 to Texas where he had fought for independence in 1836–37 and served as secretary of war for the Republic (National Portrait Gallery, Smithsonian Institution).

Still, all was not well among the high command. That night a council of war considered the question of whether to proceed with the attack. Because of the Confederates' noisy, chaotic advance; skirmishing on April 4 between Alabama cavalry and the 72nd Ohio training in a field near the Rebels' staging area; Southern bands playing and troops cheering and firing their weapons to test whether the powder had remained dry throughout the rainy march; and woodland animals and even a few Rebel dogs rushing into federal camps, Beauregard felt certain that the Federals had detected their presence and believed that the foe by then would be "entrenched to the eyes." The Creole also voiced concern that the delayed march had resulted in an acute shortage of rations among the troops. Polk agreed with the latter point only, affirming that

> his soldiers had already exhausted their rations and he had none in reserve. Bragg indicated that his men had enough food and that they would share it with Polk's troops. It seems doubtful that Bragg enjoyed such a surplus, and it should be noted that he did not follow through with his offer.[22]

The food shortage was a minor point of agreement between Polk and Bragg. As to the larger question, whether the attack should proceed, they fell on opposite sides of the issue. First Breckinridge, who rode up just after completing the disposition of his reserve corps behind the main line, spoke out insisting "that a retreat 'will never do.' Polk, asked for his opinion, concurred: 'We ought to attack.'" At this juncture Bragg agreed with Beauregard that the attack should be cancelled; however, Connelly lists Bragg on the pro-attack side. Daniel posits a second gathering around 8:00 p.m. when "Bragg had by now changed his opinion, leaving Beauregard unsupported." Whatever Bragg's position, Johnston decisively broke off all debate, proclaiming, "Gentlemen, we shall attack at daylight tomorrow." Shortly afterwards Johnston declared to a staff officer his deep appreciation for Polk's support: "*Polk is a true soldier and friend.*"[23]

During the surprisingly cold April night, soldiers lay on their arms unaware of the wrangling in high ranks. Some no doubt reflected on Johnston's stirring proclamation read earlier which "'made a deep impression on all the men,' and a Mississippian declared it to be the 'best written and most thrilling address I have ever seen.'" Other men pondered what might await them on the morrow. "The Great Battle of the Mississippi Valley has come to issue at last I reckon," wrote one soldier to his wife.[24]

Battle of Shiloh, Day One

The Battle of Shiloh proper opened at first light on Sunday, April 6, 1862. With Polk's corps deployed behind both Hardee's and Bragg's lines, he was not involved in the first stages of the engagement. By the time his men advanced, Federal forces under Sherman and McClernand were offering stubborn resistance from a strong position on a ridge overlooking Shiloh Branch, a steep-banked creek lined with swampy, miry, briery ground. Polk's reinforcements provided welcome assistance to Patrick Cleburne's battered brigade of Hardee's corps. The left side of Polk's advance came under heavy artillery fire as his men moved across Fraley Field. At that point, Polk's force aligned such that two brigades went in on Cleburne's right and two to his front heading for Shiloh Church. From Union lines Col. Jesse Hildebrand of Ohio, who ran his headquarters out of the church, expressed amazement that "so many Confederates kept pouring out of the woods to his front."[25]

Polk's Corps at Shiloh

FIRST DIVISION Brig. Gen. Charles Clark (w) Brig. Gen. A.P. Stewart	SECOND DIVISION Maj. Gen. B.F. Cheatham (w)	CAVALRY
First Brigade **Col. Robert Russell** 11th Louisiana 12th Tennessee 13th Tennessee 22nd Tennessee Bankhead's Tennessee Battery	**First Brigade** **BG Bushrod Johnson** (w) **Col. Preston Smith** (w) Blythe's Mississippi 2nd Tennessee 154th Tennessee Polk's Tennessee Battery	1st Mississippi
Second Brigade **BG Alexander P. Stewart** 13th Arkansas 4th Tennessee 5th Tennessee 33rd Tennessee Stanford's Mississippi Battery	**Second Brigade** **Col. Wm. Stephens** **Col. George Maney** 7th Kentucky 1st Tennessee Batt. 6th Tennessee 9th Tennessee Smith's Mississippi Battery	Mississippi and Alabama Battalion

SOURCE: From O. Edward Cunningham, *Shiloh and the Western Campaign of 1862* (El Dorado Hills, CA: Savas Beatie, 2007).

General Bushrod Johnson's brigade of Cheatham's division, Polk's corps, proved of great help to Cleburne as well as to General Patton Anderson's brigade of Bragg's corps, supporting both on their right. The Tennessee battery of Captain Marshall T. Polk, a cousin of Leonidas, unlimbered in a well-chosen position at Rhea Field and at first fired effectively upon the artillerists of Allen Waterhouse's Illinois battery, which had wrought considerable damage on the Confederates all morning. During this exchange Marshall Polk was severely wounded in the leg and in quick time his battery suffered extensive damage as well. As he formed his lines for successive advances, Bushrod Johnson was shot in the stomach and taken to the rear. While awaiting treatment at a field hospital, he coolly read a Northern newspaper found earlier on the field.[26]

Meanwhile, Robert Russell's brigade of Polk's First Division was positioned at Rhea Field in support of Cleburne. There the Tennesseeans and Louisianans of the brigade found themselves enmeshed in "the same old attack-and-repulse sequence that had played out all morning." The first problem was the rough terrain: they were forced to advance "through woods, through thickets, through briars, through sloughs, through mud and water." But Sherman and McClernand's determined stand posed the major problem faced by the Rebels in this sector of the fight. Polk wrote, "The resistance at this point was as stubborn as at any other on the field." In the course of several brave attempts to overrun Waterhouse's battery, General Clark was shot in the shoulder, and command of his division went to Russell. With the wounding of General Clark, Polk stepped forward and "compensated for his loss by 'frequent exposure of himself to the hottest of the enemy's fire.'"27

During the battle Albert Sidney Johnston ranged over all of the sectors of the battlefield giving orders, inspiring the troops, leading them into position and even charging to the front when he felt a situation called for a special display of bravery. Up until this time Polk's corps had spearheaded its effort toward the central part of the field. At one point as Johnston galloped eastward to shore up the effort there, he saw Polk and ordered him to send Alexander Stewart's brigade to the right. Johnston personally led Stewart's men part of the way toward the desired position. Beauregard funneled Polk's last brigade, that of William Stephens, to fill in a gap at center field which opened up as Johnston ordered other units to the right.28

With all of this shifting and redirecting of troops, overall command fragmented somewhat as divisions, and even brigades, were broken up. It was not possible for a general to lead his own units once they were spread out over an approximately four-mile front. This situation gave rise to an impromptu arrangement among the corps commanders. Bragg, as Johnston's chief of staff, directed Polk to oversee the center, anchored on the main Corinth road, while he tended to the right. Hardee meanwhile was already providing overall command on the left.

This improvisation is of particular interest in the context of Polk's relations with Bragg. Historians would later hold Polk accountable for a state of extreme acrimony that plagued the Western Army during Bragg's future tenure

Captain Marshall T. Polk, Jr., a young cousin of Leonidas, commanded a battery at Shiloh where he was wounded and his leg amputated. In spite of his impairment, years after the war he challenged Pollock Lee, a former Bragg aide, to a duel because of a false story Lee allegedly reported during the Battle of Chickamauga in an attempt to incriminate Polk (*treasury.tn.gov/ Explore-Your-TN-Treasury/Meet-Treasurer-Lillard/ History-of-TN-Treasurers/ProfileMarshall-T-Polk*).

as commanding general. Polk would be accused of insubordination, disrespect, disobedience of orders, plotting and intriguing behind the commander's back, even mutiny—all attributable to his alleged personality flaws including obstinacy and imperiousness. However, during the time leading up to Shiloh Polk hinted of no acrimony toward Bragg, while Bragg on the other hand wrote and thought disparagingly of Polk as well as Johnston. In this transaction during the heat of battle General Polk, even though he outranked Bragg, deferred to him on the basis of the latter's ancillary position as chief of staff, asked him for orders, and willingly obeyed the direction to assume responsibility for a section of field as assigned by Bragg, not Johnston. It is difficult to reconcile this incident with the heinous picture to be painted of Polk

Brigadier General Charles Clark commanded a division in Polk's Corps at Shiloh where he was wounded. He returned to the army under General Breckinridge, and during the attack on Baton Rouge in August 1862 was again wounded, this time severely. No longer able to fight, he was elected governor of Mississippi in 1863 ("Clark, Charles," House Divided: The Civil War Research Engine at Dickinson College).

in the future—so difficult that it brings into question the accuracy of such portrayals. At Shiloh we see a cooperative Polk sacrificing even his personal safety in order to inspire his men and putting aside questions of rank in favor of the army's heroic effort on the field of battle on a sunny spring Sunday morning in Tennessee.

However, this spirit of cooperation did not go both ways. Bragg's pent-up resentment toward Polk was at the forefront of his mind during the battle that morning, as evidenced by his condemnation of the 11th Louisiana. The regiment was forced to retreat after Bragg ordered it to attempt a near-impossible task: the capture of Waterhouse's battery situated in a dominant position on the field. Historian Larry Daniel assesses the 11th Louisiana effort: "They made a pretty good showing, considering their numbers, but were staggered by infantry and artillery fire.... Although the flag-bearer held firm, Marks's men scurried back to the creek." When the 11th made another attempt in conjunction with the 22nd Tennessee, resulting in the Louisianans' "fleeing in wild disorder.... [Bragg] was dismayed to see the 11th Louisiana scrambling back in full retreat. *'They belonged to Polk's mob,'* he disgustedly wrote Elise." But Bragg was wrong; the 11th Louisiana had only recently been assigned to Polk's corps. They came to Corinth as part of the New Orleans units sent by General Lovell, under General Ruggles, *one of Bragg's division commanders.*[29]

During the afternoon of April 6, once Sherman and McClernand had gradually fallen back and sheltered their forces behind the Tilghman Branch ravine, Polk's command turned to the fight against the Union position known as the Hornets' Nest. Bragg was in the midst of the action here, ordering repeated frontal attacks on the stronghold. Col. Randall Gibson pleaded for artillery support on behalf of his 13th Louisiana who were being slaughtered, but Bragg refused and ordered the Louisianans in again. After numerous Confederate assaults were repulsed, Daniel Ruggles finally massed artillery from various commands and a coordinated effort caused the Federal line to contract and become nearly surrounded. General W.H.L. Wallace, commander of the Federal Second Division, determined to cut a way out for his command but was shot while standing in his stirrups to plot their course. General Polk saw Wallace fall and inquired as to the identity of the brave officer.[30]

As many as 2,200 Federals surrendered when the Hornets' Nest was finally given up. They lost the position, but accomplished their tactical purpose of occupying large numbers of Confederates while Grant and his artillerist chief of staff, Colonel Joseph Webster, prepared a strong position in the rear for the Federals' final stand of the day. Sixth Division commander General Benjamin Prentiss is the Union officer most associated in history with the heroic, doomed stand at the Hornets' Nest, but the mortally wounded W.H.L. Wallace deserves as much credit. Prentiss surrendered his sword to Polk's acting First Division commander, Colonel Robert Russell, who in turn passed it to Polk. Shiloh historian Edward Cunningham relates another instance in which General Polk was the would-be recipient of a surrendered sword:

> General Polk arrived in the Third Iowa camp just as [senior company commander (in charge after the regiment's colonel had been wounded) Captain Samuel] Edgington ordered his men to drop their weapons, and the captain surrendered his sword to the "Fighting Bishop." Always courteous, General Polk saluted Captain Edgington and returned the blade, although the captain and future colonel of the regiment had the sword taken away from him by his guards later.[31]

Polk did not rest on his laurels, but quickly sent his cavalry to pursue those who managed to escape capture at the Hornets' Nest. Lieutenant Colonel John Miller of the 1st Mississippi Cavalry rounded up all of the guns but one, plus the cannoneers, of the 2nd Michigan Battery as they fled down a ravine attempting to elude their pursuers.

Meanwhile Polk and his infantry advanced in search of Sherman and McClernand, no doubt believing victory at hand—until they viewed Grant's final, formidable position facing them. According to Shiloh historian Timothy Smith: "[T]here was no body of men on earth that could break that line with all that artillery. Polk remarked, 'Here the impression arose that our forces were waging an unequal contest.' And at that point, they were."[32]

Around this time Beauregard, now overall commander after Albert Sidney Johnston's death on the field earlier that afternoon, ordered the attack halted, believing the Confederates could finish the fight successfully the following morning. One source of Beauregard's complacency was a seemingly reliable but false report that Buell's army was not reinforcing Grant at Pittsburg Landing after all, but had been spotted marching southward toward Alabama. In fact, under orders to take the Memphis & Charleston Railroad, Buell had detached only his Third Division, and that was the "army" that Beauregard's source saw marching toward northern Alabama—a sizable force, to be sure, numbering around 10,000, but hardly Buell's entire army. Commanding the Third Division was General Ormsby Mitchel, and from his headquarters during the move south was launched the famous Andrews's Raid upon the Western & Atlantic Railroad in north Georgia, in turn giving rise to the storied "Great Locomotive Chase" of April 12, 1862. (The railroad raiders used the cover story, as they raced their stolen train northward from Atlanta, that they were rushing powder to General Beauregard at Shiloh!)[33]

Regardless of the questions surrounding Buell's movements, by nightfall Beauregard's exhausted army required food and rest. After fighting all that long Sunday they were incapable of mounting an attack against a fortified foe, down a deep ravine and up its far, steep bank bristling with artillery. Later, Beauregard's order halting the Confederates' advance became the subject of much controversy and condemnation. Bragg in particular attempted to rewrite history by recounting his supposed shock and vehement opposition upon receipt of the order to withdraw. However, no one around him at the time remembered it that way. The reality was that the Confederate army as a whole had no more fight left in them by early evening of April 6.[34]

Historian Steven Woodworth stands with Bragg in condemning Beauregard for calling off any further attack on April 6. First, Woodworth's entire account is open to question based on inaccuracies he employs to cast subtle doubt on Beauregard's competency:

> He had been at the rear of the battle all day and stayed there even after taking command. He was also "greatly prostrated" from the nervous ailment with which he had been suffering for two months and was not physically equal to the requirements of army command.[35]

Beauregard was not "at the rear of the battle all day." This allegation comes from a false story later put forth by detractors who maliciously portrayed Beauregard as confined to an ambulance during the entire battle. The story has long been debunked. It is true that Beauregard took on the command role of overall direction of troops from headquarters, while Johnston ranged forward in the field (the reverse of respective roles played by Beauregard and another Johnston at the Battle of First Manassas). But field headquarters moved forward as the Confederates pushed the enemy back; by mid-day Beauregard set up his center of operation in Shiloh Church where Prentiss had headquartered that morning. Beauregard was not "prostrated" during the battle but remained actively engaged every moment. It is true that Beauregard suffered from serious debilitation at this time, but by no stretch could it be accurately termed a "nervous ailment." The general had undergone throat surgery while commanding in Virginia, after which his army duties prevented his taking sufficient leave to recover properly. His health issues were entirely physical, over which by sheer will power he prevailed, and to characterize him as suffering from a "nervous" condition is a sly attempt at questioning Beauregard's mental or emotional competency. In fact, despite his compromised health, Beauregard exhibited abundant energy and perspicacity in issuing orders, directing troops, and exercising control over the battle.

Woodworth buys into Bragg's supposed reaction to Beauregard's final order of the day, related in a *postwar* account of Bragg's aide Colonel Lockett: "Upon receiving Beauregard's message, which contained the words, 'the victory is sufficiently complete,' Bragg burst out, 'My God, was a victory ever sufficiently complete?'" Bragg's biographer Grady McWhiney adds to this another dramatic exclamation: "Bragg, looking to his left, saw Polk's force withdrawing. 'My God, my God, it is too late!' he sobbed." As moving as the scene may be, its accuracy is questioned by Thomas Connelly:

> Bragg some ten years after the war ... managed to assume the post of a thwarted warrior who had violently protested Beauregard's order. He charged that another assault would have captured Grant's force.... Yet Bragg had two versions of the story. When he wrote his wife on April 8, 1862, he stated that as the Army approached the river landing, it came under a heavy fire from the gunboats. Bragg described the Confederates as "disorganized, demoralized, and exhausted." Bragg also admitted to his wife that on the night of April 6 he was confident that Grant would be beaten the following morning.... There is even some contradictory evidence on Bragg's alleged shock at the news of Beauregard's order. Captain Clifton Smith, a Beauregard aide who bore the order to Bragg, later stated that Bragg took the news without a comment. Bragg's medical director, Dr. J.C. Nott, stated that he also heard Bragg raise no protests after he received the order.[36]

Exactly what was Polk's position on the order to pull back in the early evening of April 6 has been a matter of disagreement among historians. Woodworth numbers Polk among those allegedly opposed to Beauregard's decision: "Bragg, Hardee and Polk were unanimous afterward in stating that the withdrawal order had cost them their last chance for victory." He and McWhiney cite excerpts from official reports in support, but at least as far as Polk's report is concerned, his meaning was not so clear cut. For example, Timothy Smith agrees with a straightforward reading of Polk's statement, previously quoted, that the Confederate forces upon coming up against Grant's strong line "were waging an uneven contest," thus justifying the order to withdraw. McWhiney cites the same quote but views its prefatory words ("Here the impression arose") as a qualifier, i.e., he assumes Polk meant that the impression belied the reality, thereby bolstering the opposite conclusion that Polk felt the withdrawal was not justified.

Another statement of Polk's on this matter can be construed either for or against Beauregard's withdrawal. Connelly explains:

> Polk's report was also quoted to the effect that an hour of daylight remained, and nothing prevented a victory save Beauregard's order. Yet on April 10, 1862, Polk wrote his wife that the victory would have been complete if only they had had another hour of daylight.

Polk's ambiguous lament was typical of his occasional unclear communications that could cause problems, particularly later in the Kentucky Campaign. This example at Shiloh has been used to support each side of the debate over Beauregard's order, which is perhaps emblematic of the overall misuse of Polk in history: too many scholars have repeatedly contorted and twisted his motives and actions and words. Timothy Smith's straightforward, direct interpretation more accurately reflects the true man, as Polk was not coy in voicing his opinions. In a letter to his daughter one year after the battle, he did imply, however, that "the friends of Genl Beauregard," in particular his chief aide Thomas Jordan, might not be pleased with some of the statements he (Polk) made in his official report written five months after the battle. But as for his comments during the days following Shiloh, his biographer Joseph Parks writes simply, "He offered no criticism of Beauregard's decision."[37]

As to whether Bragg truly raged against Beauregard at sunset on April 6, 1862, fearing that the withdrawal order deprived the army and perhaps the Confederacy of ultimate victory, a simple detail related by Edward Cunningham effectively casts doubt upon Bragg's later version. Cunningham describes Bragg's visiting Beauregard's headquarters, which had been confiscated from Sherman earlier in the day:

> Generals Hardee and Breckinridge went in to see Beauregard to find out the plans for the next morning. Bragg also came in. Beauregard instructed the officers to assemble their commands for action at the earliest possible moment the next morning. There would be no effort to round up the scattered Confederate commands that night. The other officers soon drifted off, leaving Beauregard and Bragg, who climbed into Sherman's bed for some much needed sleep.

Thus Bragg ended the day, not remonstrating against his commander for the despised order nor protesting nor arguing nor even silently agonizing, but seeking sleep. It is difficult to imagine his crawling into bed and slumbering alongside a man who he truly believed had dashed the hopes of Confederate nationhood that day. There is no doubt, however, that Bragg *later* blamed Beauregard for the failure at Shiloh.

General Polk did not join the gathering at Beauregard's headquarters on Sunday night; instead, he bivouacked with Second Division commander Frank Cheatham and his troops at Cheatham's campsite of the prior night. Other portions of Polk's command from Russell's division remained nearer the front in captured Yankee tents around Shiloh Church.[38]

Battle of Shiloh, Day Two

Early the next morning Beauregard was awakened by firing from the left. Pond's brigade of Bragg's corps somehow had not received the withdrawal order of the night before. Finding themselves alone far to the left front, they desperately contested a strong Federal advance first thing Monday morning. Beauregard immediately began dispatching his corps commanders to assemble their forces at assigned points along the front lines. Because he had spent the night farther to the rear, Polk was not at hand for this initial advance shortly after dawn. However, Russell's brigade played a key role:

> Robert Russell noted, "At the discharge of the first guns I formed my brigade in line of battle." Russell had the most intact brigade on the Confederate left early in the fight. Thus fell to him the initial duty of holding that critical flank.[39]

Timothy B. Smith, in his masterful work *Shiloh: Conquer or Perish*, provides an altogether new and thorough treatment of the second day of battle at Shiloh. While most authors brush by April 7 with the simple summation that the reinforced Yankees ran the Rebels off the field, Smith shows that the day's progress was in fact not altogether one-sided. He takes time to detail the considerable, strong Confederate effort, and his readers also learn with some surprise (given his failures of April 6) that the most effective Union contribution of the second day should rightfully be credited to General Lew Wallace. Here we uncover another unfortunate lesson in the manipulation and distortion of history, and this time the culprit is none other than Ulysses Grant. It was Grant's practice not only to discredit but destroy those subordinates and peers who for some reason (or no valid reason) fell into his disfavor. Lew Wallace found himself unfortunately and unjustifiably among that group.

Monday morning Polk took position in his lines by 10:00, quite dramatically according to the account in Volume I of Beauregard's ghost-written memoir:

> Dashing forward, with drawn sword, at the head of Cheatham's fine division, [Polk] soon formed his line of battle at the point where his presence was so much needed, and, with unsurpassed vigor, moved on, against a force at least double his own, making one of the most brilliant charges of infantry made on either day of the battle.

If this image is somewhat exaggerated, Polk nevertheless led his troops energetically, actively giving orders—again, as on the previous day, sometimes to units not a part of his corps. Like Sunday's arrangement, the three corps commanders informally assumed control over general sectors of the battlefield, although this day Hardee led the right and Bragg the left, with Polk again overseeing the center/left. Smith shows that "the entire Confederate line was not as cobbled together as commonly thought." Polk's corps is described by Smith as less organized than the others but he attributes this to attrition from the previous day's fight, particularly in Stewart's "shattered" brigade, "the most devastated in the army."[40]

Contrary to Woodworth's image of a debilitated Beauregard hiding out in the rear, the general ranged over the field, particularly the left. "He went himself to rally the men and prevail on them to hold and perhaps even counterattack to continue the previous day's victory." Beauregard performed admirably, as a proactive general in touch with his army both by personal appearance and constant reporting by staff.

Beauregard retained much more organization and control than often thought, and he thus fought better than often realized. One Union artilleryman declared on this second day, illustrating the power of the Confederate legions, "It was worse than the day before."

As the day progressed the Confederates successively formed three strong lines and held their own at each position. During a particularly fierce and close fight, at times involving hand-to-hand combat, a "patchwork line" worked by General Polk and General Ruggles was able to stop an advance of General Stephen Hurlbut's Division.[41]

Union numbers began to tell, however. During the week prior to battle Major General Don Carlos Buell's Army of the Ohio (less the Third Division as previously noted) had made their way slowly through central Tennessee to link with Grant at Pittsburg Landing. As they passed through Maury County some of Buell's soldiers entered St. John's Chapel, the church built by Polk and his brothers, and destroyed the pipe organ. Finally, by the late afternoon of April 6 and all through that night Buell's army arrived on the Shiloh battlefield, with McCook's division still taking its place in line during mid-morning of April 7.

Beauregard had no such reinforcements, and by 2:00 it became clear that the Confederates could not regain the ground lost during this second day of battle. An orderly, fighting retreat commenced and Beauregard's army—exhausted, hungry, pelted by rain and hail, and many wounded—made its way back to Corinth over the next two days. Several days later, in a letter to his wife, "for his own deliverance 'from the thickest of the storm,' Polk gave credit to God. 'It was He who covered my head in the day of battle.'" Timothy Smith adds that "Polk had much to be thankful for in addition to his own safety; two of his sons were safe as well, one on his staff and one in Bankhead's Battery."[42]

On both days of Shiloh Polk had functioned effectively as corps commander and his men fought well. In a spirit of hope and optimism typical of Polk, he believed that the army could have won a total victory on the first day if only they had one more hour of daylight. "The second day he judged a draw. 'We left them, and they did not follow us.... The army is now refreshing itself for another attack.'"[43]

True to his nature, after Shiloh Polk commended his army for their valiant effort, and trusted in the future for a better outcome. In contrast, no sooner was the battle over than Bragg began writing bitterly to Elise against his compatriots. First among his victims was Col. Randall Gibson, temporary commander of the Louisiana Brigade during the battle. In both his official report of the battle, and especially his private letters to Elise, Gibson came under fire from Bragg. Elise knew Gibson personally as he attended Yale with her brother Towson, and Gibson's property abutted Bivouac. The conflict between him and the Braggs predated the war, but the specifics are unclear. Gibson alluded to their relationship during that time as having turned "disagreeable." According to historian Earl Hess, Bragg disliked Gibson's father and brother Claude. More recently, there was the incident during the march to Shiloh when Gibson embarrassed Bragg to the commanding general's face. In Bragg's official battle report of Shiloh, he got revenge by implying that he was forced to step in and rally Gibson's command which began the action "in rear of its true position" and was "driven back" in "considerable disorder due entirely to want of proper handling." When newspapers published the report, Gibson was furious. He and the regimental commanders of his Louisiana Brigade engaged in vigorous correspondence denying Bragg's account. Gibson would have been more livid had he known what Bragg wrote to Elise immediately after the battle. To her he expanded his claim of having rallied Gibson's brigade, to include a dramatic scene of taking up the Louisianans' colors. "I gave them a talk, took their flag, and led them in, but it was no use—they were demoralized and nothing could induce them to go—A want of confidence in their leader Gibson—destroyed theirs. *Entre nous*, he is an arrant coward."

Brigadier General Randall Gibson came from a patrician family and was educated at Yale. He owned land adjacent to Bragg's plantation in Lafourche Parish where the two had apparently become enmeshed in an unspecified conflict. Gibson was a colonel commanding the 13th Louisiana Infantry and led the Louisiana Brigade during the Battle of Shiloh. In his battle report Bragg defamed Gibson's performance at Shiloh, and thereafter Gibson believed that Bragg unjustly hindered his promotion (Andrew D. Lytle Collection, Mss. 893, 1254, Louisiana and Lower Mississippi Valley Collections, LSU Libraries, Baton Rouge, Louisiana).

It is interesting that Bragg claimed to Elise that he personally bore the regiment's flag. What actually happened is that he sent a staff officer, Major Samuel Lockett, to rally the brigade, and it was Lockett who seized the 4th Louisiana flag. Col. Henry Allen, future Louisiana governor, demanded his colors back and instructed Lockett to go tell Bragg they must attack the flank rather than attempt more frontal assaults. This was not the only time Bragg would write his wife that he, rather than a staff officer, performed an act at a crucial point during battle.[44]

It is important to shine a light on the conflict with Gibson, as it demonstrates Bragg's proclivity to stir up controversy by bringing unjust and untrue charges against fellow officers. Historians repeatedly accuse Leonidas Polk of instigating the acrimony surrounding Bragg that later gripped the

Army of Tennessee, but Bragg's attack on Gibson shows his capacity for picking fights with those against whom he harbored preconceived prejudice. This tendency had already become a pattern with Bragg.

Nevertheless, it is fair to bring out some points regarding Bragg's correspondence with Elise. In general, letters to wives should not be viewed in the same manner as other writings, as they constitute private musings and supportive ego boosting within the unique spousal relationship. In much the same way that people assume the role of heroes in their own dreams, wives and husbands typically share delusions of grandeur and private prejudices which should not be interpreted as their objectively held viewpoints. Examples abound of historians' deliberately discrediting the self-image and motives of historical men based on letters to their wives; George McClellan and Edmund Kirby Smith are two examples. On the other hand, we should keep in mind Elise's experience which perhaps differed from other Civil War generals' spouses. While obviously and understandably an ardent supporter of Bragg's interests and desirous of his advancement, she was an experienced army wife who had accompanied him at postings, even to the far Western frontier, and interacted extensively in military society and culture. She was also present with the army during key points of Bragg's Civil War service; for example, she was at Murfreesboro during the great battle there. Thus she was inured to army men's competitive sizing up and squabbling for position. Bragg did not need to impress Elise, nor could he easily misconstrue to her the workings of command, for she was sufficiently knowledgeable to form her own valid opinions. Finally, his correspondence with her should not be written off as mere venting. For these reasons, Bragg's letters to his wife repeatedly berating his comrades can be seen as a straightforward expression of his negative attitudes and outlook.[45]

But even accounting for Elise's special understanding of military matters, nowhere is the contrast between Bragg and Polk more evident than in their respective letters to their wives following Shiloh. Bragg's captious finger-pointing contrasts sharply with the simple, humble sentiment of Polk's self-assessment written to Frances after Shiloh: "I believe from what I know and hear, you will have no reason to be ashamed of your husband or your sons."[46]

Chapter 4

Perryville

Movement of Armies into Kentucky

The next full-scale battle for the Confederate army of the West did not come until many months later, and under a new army commander. Just days after Shiloh, President Davis on April 12 appointed Braxton Bragg a full general. Continuing their private railing against Polk, three days later Elise gloated to her husband over his new status: "Your usefulness is thereby increased, & you are relieved from obeying the commands of our vain glorious Bishop [Polk]."[1]

A mammoth Federal army, now personally commanded by Henry Halleck, slowly advanced toward the Confederate army ensconced in Corinth, Mississippi. Beauregard quickly realized that Corinth was no place to weather a siege. Its water supply, both as to quantity and quality, could not support an army, and men languished sick and ill-nourished. Beauregard orchestrated a masterful retreat from the town, deceiving Halleck's Federals right up until they marched into the abandoned works. After his army escaped safely, Beauregard took leave at last to recuperate from his own health problems. Jefferson Davis, grievously saddened over the loss of Sidney Johnston and never a fan of Beauregard, relieved the latter and named Braxton Bragg overall commander in June 1862.

Bragg resolved to take offensive action. Strategizing with General Edmund Kirby Smith of the Department of East Tennessee, the two generals planned a joint campaign into Middle Tennessee with the objective of retaking Nashville, now occupied by General Buell's command, and possibly advancing into Kentucky. The idea behind this movement did not originate with Bragg or Kirby Smith, but instead emanated from the mind of Robert E. Lee as expressed in a letter to Jefferson Davis. Nevertheless, Bragg deserves rightful credit for acting on it and executing the first major wartime transfer of troops by rail when he transported his army (excluding the artillery which traveled more slowly overland) in a matter of days from Tupelo, Mississippi, to Chattanooga, Tennessee, on a roundabout route over rickety Confederate rails. By the end of August 1862 Bragg's forces assembled and set out on a grand march northward. They trailed Kirby Smith who had left Chattanooga over a week earlier with his command and a portion of Bragg's.[2]

Before departing Chattanooga, Bragg "did everything in his power to be rid of Polk, but the president sustained his friend." Having failed to dispense with his nemesis, Bragg reorganized the Army of the Mississippi. He assigned Polk as commander over the Right Wing, composed of the First Division under General Cheatham and the Second under General Jones Withers. The left wing, comprising General Simon Bolivar Buckner's and General S.A.M. Wood's divisions, was commanded by Hardee.[3]

Polk's march began on August 28 over the rough, barren Walden Ridge. He reached Sparta, Tennessee, by September 5 where the cavalry command of Colonel Nathan Bedford Forrest, following a successful raiding expedition in Middle Tennessee, joined Bragg's juggernaut to "scout the advance of his army, screen his movements, and harass Buell's attempt to pursue." Forrest was placed under the temporary command of Polk and as always performed his tasks well; however, by the end of September Bragg detached Forrest from the army with orders to recruit a new cavalry regiment in Middle Tennessee.[4]

It was in Sparta during that first week of September where new, improved flags were distributed to Polk's corps. The original Polk flag, designed by Leonidas, featured a red St. George cross emblazoned upon a blue background containing white stars without standard number or placement. The new issue retained the St. George cross now edged in white, with eleven stars aligned in a regulated pattern. Moving forward, "banners to the breeze," Polk's men must have felt like a holy, conquering host with their scarlet crosses aloft, marching in the vanguard of the army's bold advance northward into Union territory.[5]

Meanwhile Kirby Smith, racing far ahead, won a dramatic victory in Richmond, Kentucky, on August 30, thanks largely to Cleburne's brigade loaned to him from Bragg's army. By September 1 Kirby Smith established himself in Lexington and spread his forces around its vicinity, sending Union authorities at Louisville and Cincinnati into a panic.

Don Carlos Buell's Army of the Ohio, initially posted in and around Nashville, was by now marching northward to intercept Bragg and Kirby Smith's advance into Kentucky. The movements and maneuvering of the respective armies produced considerable confusion and conflict as Bragg attempted to negotiate some kind of cooperative arrangement with Kirby Smith and unite both forces into battle against Buell. The repercussions from the resultant controversies reverberated long after the army's incursion into Kentucky, and historians continue vehemently to disagree upon and debate them to this day. Three major issues arose at this time, pitting Bragg against Polk:

    1. the questions and misperceptions surrounding the location of the bulk of Buell's force and where its main thrust would be brought against Bragg's army;

    2. Bragg's October 2 order for Polk to advance the army northward from Bardstown, Kentucky, in a flank attack against a portion of Buell's force advancing upon Frankfort; and

    3. Bragg's October 7 order for Polk to take Cheatham's division to Perryville

Leonidas Polk designed his corps flag based on the Episcopal Church shield. This artifact is a small-sized personal flag owned by a trooper in the 12th Battalion, Tennessee Cavalry. The Polk flag remained the standard of his corps until early 1864 when Joseph Johnston, upon assuming command of the Army of Tennessee, ordered the army's sundry flags to be standardized. Polk's troops, by then commanded by General Hardee, would thereafter carry the better-known Confederate battle flag, although Cleburne's division was allowed to retain their distinctive Hardee flag with its blue background emblazoned by a white circle in the center (Case Auctions, used with permission).

and join with Hardee to "give the enemy battle immediately, rout him," then return to Harrodsburg where Bragg planned the climactic battle of Kentucky.

Issues (2) and (3) deal with specific orders from the commanding general. For purposes of this chapter they will be cited during the sequence of events of the Battle of Perryville. But it was not until months after the Kentucky Campaign that the (then named) Army of Tennessee erupted in conflict and Bragg revisited these matters, touting both as evidence to support his accusations against Polk for alleged insubordination. The problems and ramifications surrounding those orders will be more thoroughly analyzed in Chapter 7. Issue (1) relates to Polk's role in ascertaining and communicating his understanding of Buell's dispositions, and since this sheds light on Polk's performance during the Battle of Perryville that point will be primarily taken up in this chapter.

Polk's forces, at the head of Bragg's army, arrived in Glasgow, Kentucky, on September 13 where General Bragg issued a stirring proclamation to the people of the state. Then the following day word arrived at headquarters of a setback on the Green River several miles north of the main army. General Chalmers, hoping for easy glory and underestimating the strength of Fort Craig near Munfordville based on erroneous reporting by a cavalry officer, attacked the garrison only to meet a bloody defeat. Bragg, who "did not wish to 'allow the impression of a disaster to rest on the minds of my men,' ... decided to reverse the debacle." On September 15 he marched the entire army to Munfordville. Once "Polk's wing got into position on the Green River's north bank," the fort was surrounded and vastly outnumbered.[6]

An odd and rather amusing exchange ensued before the Yankees finally agreed to surrender. Colonel John Wilder, the fort's commander, politely requested information as to the strength of Bragg's force before he would agree to capitulate. He even sent a message to General Simon Bolivar Buckner based on the latter's reputation as a gentleman, asking his advice and requesting an opportunity to inventory in person the Rebel artillery arrayed against him! Buckner, taken aback, complied with the unorthodox request by transporting a blindfolded Wilder across the lines to assess the Confederate cannon, whereupon the colonel concluded that his best course indeed would be surrender.

Once that side drama was resolved Bragg again turned his attention toward uniting with Kirby Smith and, turning away from the Federal force, advanced his army to Bardstown. With Bragg no longer opposing him on his front, Buell was free to proceed across the Green River northward to Louisville. There he would consolidate and launch his counter-attack to save Kentucky. Bragg has been criticized for his decision to clear the way for Buell, but Bragg alone could not have blocked the Army of the Ohio. Before Bragg could successfully fight Buell, it was necessary for him to combine forces with Kirby Smith.[7]

By the end of September 1862 Bragg placed Polk in temporary command of the Army of the Mississippi posted in and around Bardstown, Kentucky, while the commander set off on a political mission. Now that Confederate forces occupied much of eastern Kentucky including the capital city, Bragg traveled to Frankfort to install Richard Hawes as Confederate governor of the state in order to gain some political traction, as well as recruits for his army. The inauguration and associated festivities were scheduled for October 4, and Bragg along with his staff had many arrangements to make and details to complete. Kirby Smith and two of his divisions under Henry Heth and Carter Stevenson joined Bragg in Frankfort.

While Bragg was away Polk kept the commanding general informed of intelligence he received from Louisville regarding Buell's army. In particular, he noted: "all around agree in the great demoralization of Buell's army arising from Lincoln's proclamation." By this time the Battle of Antietam had provided the Union a victory of sufficient significance that Lincoln deemed it politically safe to issue his Emancipation Proclamation, albeit not to take effect until January 1, 1863. Polk went on to warn Bragg that Buell might put his army "in motion as a measure of safety to him," i.e., to counteract the plunge in morale following the Proclamation, and prevent desertion. In addition, Polk wrote of logistical matters and his concerns over the security of the army's supply depot at Bryantsville.[8]

Meanwhile, just as Polk predicted, on October 1 General Buell moved, launching a four-pronged advance from Louisville. General Joshua Sill led fewer than 20,000 toward Frankfort while the bulk of the Army of the Ohio, some 55,000, moved in parallel columns toward Bragg's army, then under Polk's watch at Bardstown. Buell's larger force quickly pushed back Confederate cavalry and advance infantry posts including Cleburne's at Shelbyville; Polk reported the massive movement to Bragg on October 2 and followed up with updates received from Col. John Wharton's cavalry. Mistaking the smaller column marching toward Frankfort for Buell's main force, Bragg nevertheless decided that he had time to proceed with the inauguration as scheduled. He also saw the opportunity for an artful attack, and "immediately ordered Polk to 'put your whole available force in motion by Bloomfield and strike [Buell] in flank and rear.' Bragg wished to use Kirby Smith's command as a blocking force from the east while Polk came up from the southwest and smashed into the Federals from the flank." This order is the one referenced in issue number (2) above, and the body reads in full:

> GENERAL: The enemy is certainly advancing on Frankfort. Put your whole available force in motion by Bloomfield and strike him in flank and rear. If we can combine our movements he is certainly lost. Your information of the 30th was correct, but your courier was two days and nights getting here. Dispatch me frequently to Frankfort.[9]

Unfortunately, Bragg's order was based on a gross misperception on his part, and could have grave consequences. Bragg thought that Buell's principal thrust was headed toward him and Kirby Smith, and thus desired Polk to advance to the support of the small force at Frankfort. Marching swiftly, Polk could overwhelm Buell from the rear, or so Bragg believed. But the order quickly proved problematic for Polk at Bardstown.

> Buell's intentions had since become clearer; the Federal main effort was clearly aimed at Bardstown, not Frankfort.... [B]y the morning of October 3, the Federals stood about a day's march from Bardstown. Moving as ordered would cause the Confederates to collide with McCook's thirteen-thousand-strong I Corps near Bloomfield, east of Bardstown. Fighting McCook would delay the Confederate movement to Frankfort and would enable the rest of Buell's army to concentrate and smash Polk's force.[10]

What Polk decided to do about it is taken up in Chapter 7. What follows here is an examination of issue (1) above: *when and to what extent* Polk knew with certainty that he, not Bragg and Kirby Smith in Frankfort, faced the majority of Buell's army.

Christopher Kolakowski's explanation quoted above, supported by other authorities, clearly recites that Polk realized on October 2 that he was dangerously outnumbered by Buell. However, that opinion is not unanimous among historians because of two factors: Bragg's later claims regarding what Polk knew and when, and Polk's vague, ambiguous communications—a chronic problem between him and Bragg.

Over the next few days Bragg repeatedly changed his perceptions and his plans. *Within 24 hours he countermanded the order* for Polk to move toward Frankfort for a flank attack:

> DEAR GENERAL: ... I have sent you several dispatches since yesterday morning desiring you to move your force on the enemy, who was making a descent on this point. That move has proved to be only a feint and has ceased. You will act accordingly....[11]

On October 4 as Sill's detachment menaced the capital, Bragg and other Confederate military dignitaries in attendance, hearing the roar of approaching artillery, fled a post-inauguration luncheon. Bragg arrived in Harrodsburg on October 5, whereupon he ordered all Confederate forces, including Kirby Smith's, to move in his direction to concentrate for a great battle against Buell.

Kirby Smith, however, loath to give up his quasi-independent command in the Lexington vicinity, reported that he was threatened by the columns of McCook and Rousseau. This was inaccurate but, as Kenneth Noe states in his fine battle study of Perryville, Bragg believed Kirby Smith over Polk. On the basis of his irrational prejudice against Polk, Bragg abandoned his plans for concentration at Harrodsburg.

> [B]oth Kirby Smith and Polk indicated they were facing the larger Union force. One of them had to be wrong, and Bragg long had felt contempt for the bishop, whereas Kirby Smith seemed to possess a gift for mesmerizing Bragg.... Accordingly, on the morning of October 7, Bragg issued new orders putting into motion his previous decision to take the army north.... Boldly pointing to a map, Bragg told his staff that the great battle of Kentucky was about to occur at Versailles. He could not have been more wrong, for the bulk of the Union army was in his rear, approaching the village of Perryville even as he spoke.[12]

Polk compounded Bragg's erroneous perception by employing message phraseology that, based on other concurrent writings and warnings, he clearly did not mean literally. In Harrodsburg on October 6 pursuant to Bragg's order to concentrate there, around midnight Polk forwarded to Bragg a note from Hardee asking for reinforcements ten miles away in Perryville. There Hardee had halted his march so that his men could obtain water (scarce during the severe drought of that summer and autumn) from standing pools in the bed of Doctor's Creek. Hardee had been closely pursued by a Federal column all day but was uncertain as to its strength. In forwarding Hardee's note to Bragg, Polk added a comment that he did not know what numbers they were facing, but "I cannot think it large." Yet according to Noe, Polk did not really mean this. He explains and expostulates on the ramifications of the vague communication:

> Much has been made since the event of Polk's ambiguous "I cannot think it large" comment. What did "large" mean to the bishop? And did he refer to an entire force or only an advance column, as his biographer-son later claimed? Certainly he thought it was more than a mere feint. On the night of the sixth he essentially ordered half of the gray-clad army, Hardee's entire wing supported by additional cavalry, to hold Perryville.... That he suspected most of Buell's army lay somewhere nearby as well, an assertion often dismissed, also is clear in a letter written to his wife the next day.[13]

Admittedly careless wording, "I cannot think it large" should not be construed as a definite assessment. Polk should be held responsible for poor communication skills, both in his failure to provide Bragg with sufficient updates at this time ("Bragg ... still had received no definite news from Polk") and his poor choice of wording in the October 6 message. Yet Bragg later seized upon and magnified the sloppy message in order ultimately to blame Polk to a degree that goes way beyond this single communication:

> Bragg's reports of his conversations with Polk in regard to the matter differ entirely from his chief lieutenant's. According to Bragg, Polk indicated to him that the Union force behind them was truly small and nonthreatening, convincing him to continue with his plans of withdrawing to the north.

Noe concludes,

> *"The weight of the evidence rests with Polk's account.* The letter to his wife is clear, and, like Hardee, he continued to maintain after the campaign that he had informed Bragg that a sizable Federal force was approaching. Bragg, in contrast, displayed selective memory on several occasions after the campaign."[14]

Regardless of the fine points of who-said-what-when-to-whom, Polk's one vague, short sentence does not cancel out all of his other communications and, more importantly, his actions which indicate an awareness that he faced a significant Federal force. In earlier letters to Bragg, he gave fair warning that Buell was moving toward his position. Clearly, *Polk was right*; three Federal corps threatened his army, in spite of some historians' attempts to obscure that simple fact. Similarly, Bragg had his own reasons for later overemphasizing Polk's single, poorly-worded phrase: to cover the truth that he (Bragg) was wrong in his understanding of the whereabouts and strengths of Buell's columns.

Battle of Perryville

The full realization of *how* large a force loomed before him did not completely dawn on Polk until after initial shots were fired on Peters Hill west of Perryville in the early morning hours of October 8, 1862. General St. John Liddell's brigade, sent forward to feel out the enemy, tangled with men of General Sheridan's division who were just as thirsty as the Confederates and advanced toward Doctor's Creek to fill their canteens. Sheridan ended the short but intense fight by pushing back Liddell's Arkansans, securing not only Peters Hill but Bottom Hill beyond. Although eager to press on, Sheridan's advance was halted by his corps commander, General Charles Gilbert.

Leonidas Polk, Confederate commanding general on the field, after considering the ferocity of Sheridan's fight and observing substantial Union columns amassing on the hills across from his position, wisely judged that the "immediate" attack ordered by Bragg (the order referenced as [3] above, more thoroughly discussed in Chapter 7) should be postponed. The text of Bragg's October 7 order reads as follows:

> In view of the news from Hardee you had better move with Cheathams Division to his support, and give the enemy battle immediately. Rout him and then move to our support at Versailles.
> No time should be lost in these movements.

Clearly Bragg's order was issued under the belief that Polk faced a small detachment that could be routed quickly and easily. But seeing the formidable host on yonder hills, Polk adopted a defensive-offensive stance to gain a better idea of the strength of the force before him. He observed McCook's corps moving up to the left of Gilbert's, and in order to bolster his right accordingly and if possible overlap the Federals' left, Polk preemptively ordered his sole division on the field, that of General Frank Cheatham, to shift to the far right. Once in place, Cheatham proceeded to stack the brigades of Donelson, Stewart, and Maney, respectively, in parallel lines with 200 yards between them.[15]

Polk's Corps at Perryville
(Withers' Division not present, marched on to Versailles, Kentucky.)

CHEATHAM'S DIVISION Maj. Gen. Benjamin Franklin Cheatham	CAVALRY
Donelson's Brigade **Brig. Gen. Daniel S. Donelson** 8th Tennessee 15th Tennessee 16th Tennessee 38th Tennessee 51st Tennessee Carnes's Tennessee Battery	**Wharton's Cavalry Brigade** **Col. John A. Wharton** 2nd Georgia Cavalry 1st Kentucky Cavalry 4th Tennessee Cavalry Davis's Tennessee Cavalry Battalion 8th Texas Cavalry
Stewart's Brigade **Brig. Gen. Alexander P. Stewart** 4th Tennessee 5th Tennessee 24th Tennessee 31st Tennessee 33rd Tennessee Stanford's Mississippi Battery	
Maney's Brigade **Brig. Gen. George Maney** 41st Georgia 1st Tennessee 6th Tennessee 9th Tennessee 27th Tennessee Melancthon Smith's Mississippi Battery	
Smith's Brigade **Brig. Gen. Preston Smith** 12th Tennessee 13th Tennessee 47th Tennessee 154th Tennessee 9th Texas Scott's Tennessee Battery	

SOURCE: From Kenneth W. Noe, *Perryville: This Grand Havoc of Battle* (Lexington: University Press of Kentucky, 2001).

Meanwhile, hearing no guns, Bragg galloped to Perryville that morning overcome with anger at Polk for not following his order to attack "immediately," Bragg's irritation also extended to what he believed was a small Yankee force trifling with him, delaying *his* plan to fight a major battle to the north. Bragg "refused to believe that Buell's entire army was present or approaching the field." From the moment he arrived in Perryville Bragg assumed overall command, and "[o]verruling any objections from Polk and Hardee, Bragg ordered an immediate offensive." He placed Polk in command on the right, consistent with the shift in that direction already accomplished by Polk's sole division, and assigned Hardee the left and center, with the attack to begin on the right.[16]

As he scanned the field, Bragg noted a ridge which he ordered seized by General S.A.M. Wood (of Hardee's corps) "immediately, or else that the enemy would be firing down upon you in five minutes." Wood quickly pushed back Yankee skirmishers and gained the height, from which he viewed a sobering sight: "two of Rousseau's three brigades in all of their martial glory." Wood sent to Polk for help, and in response the battery of Captain William Carnes was dispatched to the hill, although briefly delayed from one of its guns becoming snagged, and then extricated from a gate post. Donelson's 8th and 51st Tennessee infantry regiments went in support of the battery. Carnes opened fire on Loomis's Union guns, and a one-and-one-half-hour artillery duel ensued. Carnes found himself at a disadvantage with his smooth-bore guns, but once General Cheatham substituted Stanford's Mississippi battery with its rifled pieces the Federal battery was silenced.[17]

Cheatham's infantry attack began at 2:00, his men "moving out as if on dress parade." Disappearing into the ravine of Doctor's Creek, they "rose up out of nowhere onto the steep bluffs across the creek" and quickly began suffering heavy casualties largely inflicted by the Federal battery of Lieutenant Charles Parsons from a prominence known as Open Knob. Cheatham sent in Maney's brigade to the right of Donelson (whose brigade was temporarily reduced after two of his regiments were detached to support Carnes's battery) in an attempt to overlap the Federal flank and attack Parsons's battery. Under galling fire, Maney's Tennesseeans along with a lone, green Georgia regiment took refuge behind a fence which provided no real shelter from the storm. Maney exhorted his men to charge; together they rose up and emitting a chilling Rebel yell, killed Yankee division commander General James Jackson and overran the battery. Union brigade commander "General William Terrill and Lieutenant Parsons had to be physically dragged from the guns to avoid capture," the Yankees managing to save only one of the pieces. (General Terrill had a brother who fought for the Confederacy, and was a cousin of J.E.B. Stuart.)[18]

As Maney advanced, Cheatham calmly smoked a pipe and rode along beside his men 100 yards to their right as he "looked down the lines between the contending forces," later referring to the experience as "the most exciting few moments of my life." Cheatham placed Turner's two cannon 200 yards from the Federals' left flank, and they proceeded to decimate Parsons's supporting infantry, greatly aiding in the capture of that battery. During the height of their fire,

[o]ne of Turner's crewmen was interrupted by a voice behind him saying, "Let me try my hand at them." The soldier wheeled and found Cheatham at his shoulder. As the young artillerist stepped aside, Cheatham took over, directed the aiming and firing of the cannon, and enjoying himself immensely.[19]

After his adventure with the artillery, Cheatham ordered Maney to bring the 1st Tennessee up from reserve to take a second battery that had unlimbered 500 yards away on the position now known as Starkweather Hill. The 1st Tennessee managed to kill most of the Yankee artillerists but could not hold their position without support and, although briefly taking the guns, had no way to carry them off. Donelson came back in with his two regiments previously diverted for artillery support; the enhanced advance pushed back the second Union line and captured four guns from an Indiana battery.

Cheatham's incremental victories added up. By the end of the day his men shattered McCook's corps, beating them back over 1,200 yards. (Con-

Born into a prominent founding family of Tennessee, Major General Benjamin Franklin Cheatham led a division in Polk's Corps. Polk and Cheatham shared a close bond, described by a staff officer as the fondness of a father and son—or perhaps more accurately, a *prodigal son* given Cheatham's proclivities. In contrast, Bragg despised Cheatham for his alleged lack of discipline over himself and his command. During their foray into Kentucky, the Shakers of that state kindly shared abundant provisions with Cheatham's men, but one described those Rebels as "more like the bipeds of pandemonium than beings of this earth" (Losson, *Tennessee's Forgotten Warriors*, 64) ("Cheatham, Benjamin Franklin," House Divided: The Civil War Research Engine at Dickinson College).

nelly gives the distance as "almost two miles.") As he had at Shiloh, Polk granted Cheatham a great deal of latitude to direct his division independently. The division commander "had ample reason to be proud of his men. He had been well served by both his artillery and infantry throughout the day." Cheatham's men bore much of the brunt of the fight at Perryville, with Maney's brigade suffering the greatest casualties. "Cheatham praised his men for their achievements, ... and noted that 'never did men fall on any field fighting more gallantly.'"[20]

Meanwhile the fight on the left began when Hardee attacked up the Old Mackville Road around 3:00 with Bushrod Johnson, then Cleburne assailing and scattering the Union line behind the Russell farmhouse. S.A.M. Wood's brigade rushed beyond the farmhouse to take the Dixville crossroad, but the Yankee line there held thanks to the timely reinforcement of Prussian veteran Colonel Michael Gooding's brigade. His men were hit so hard that Gooding felt certain he faced Cleburne's entire division rather than one brigade.[21]

Just as the ubiquitous General Liddell had charge over the first attack of the day, he would also command the last. He advanced in a gap between Polk's and Hardee's wings and drove back the last remnant of the Union lines in the vicinity of the Dixville crossroad, capturing General McCook's artillery chief and McCook's headquarters ambulance containing a cache of papers, as well as a canteen of bad whiskey! "Its wretched, sickening taste led me to doubt that the property was [McCook's]," Liddell complained, "but someone present who knew him well said, 'He drinks no other kind.'" Also among the spoils were General McCook's clothing. Later, the corpulent McCook wrote to Hardee asking for the return of his uniforms, pointing out that "they must be too large for any Confederate General except [equally corpulent] Humphrey Marshall. But Bragg had disposed of the effects."

As Liddell prepared his final advance, in the dim light of day's end he was uncertain whether the men before him were friend or foe. Expressing his quandary to Polk, the latter performed a remarkable deed:

> I was just about to give the order to forward with bayonets fixed when General Leonidas Polk rode up. I don't know whence he came…. I inform[ed] him of my men having fired by mistake into Cheatham's Division. General Polk seemed shocked at the accident and said, "What a pity, I hope not. I don't think so. Let me go and see. Open your ranks." It was done. The brave old man spurred his horse through the opening. My suspense was but for a few seconds when he hastily returned, explaining, "General, every mother's son of them are Yankees!" The news was circulated loudly, "Yankees!" The trumpet sounded to "fire." A tremendous flash of musketry for the whole extent of the line for nearly one quarter of a mile in length followed.

During the time that Liddell spent in "suspense" awaiting his superior's return, Polk engaged in a harrowing adventure with the mystery soldiers obscured by smoke:

> Polk rode through Liddell's soldiers to the next battle line and inquired, "What troops are these?" The reply chilled him, "The 22nd Indiana, Lt. Col. Squire Keith commanding." Polk, the second highest-ranking Confederate on the battlefield, was now among Union troops. As Polk ordered him to cease firing, Keith asked, "Who are you that gives this order?" General Polk again commanded him to cease firing or be court-martialed, which caused Keith to order his men to lower their weapons. The general rode along the 22nd's battle line, all the while feeling what he later described as "a thousand centipedes … traveling up and down my backbone." At the end, he spurred his horse back to Liddell's men and cried, "General, every mother's son of them are Yankees! Open fire!"

After Polk's close call with the enemy (and probably the closest he ever came to uttering profanity), Liddell's brigade fired *en masse* and so many Indianans fell, including Lieutenant Colonel Keith, that their regiment sustained the highest casualties of any engaged at Perryville. Liddell hankered to advance further, but Polk, perhaps shaken by his close call behind enemy lines, refused. "I want no more night fighting," he pronounced.[22]

Another novel occurrence of the fight on the left was "the first street combat of the Civil War." Carlin's brigade, including a regiment of fleet Norwegians, pursued the small brigade of Tennessee Colonel Samuel Powell right into the town limits of Perryville, whereupon musketry and artillery fire crisscrossed amidst the mostly deserted residences and businesses. General Gilbert, "[f]earing a trap," and "not in an aggressive mood," called off the fight on account of the darkness.[23]

Retreat from Perryville

Once the fighting of October 8 finally subsided, many were the descriptions of the horrible battlefield scenes beneath the eerie light of a full moon. A Wisconsin soldier recounted, "I tell you it was a ghastly sight, dead men so close that one could walk on them for rods and not touch the ground." An Indianan "remembered his great sadness as he surveyed the dead of Powell's [Confederate] brigade: 'Their faces were very pale, and the light of the moon glittered in their eyes. It was fearful to behold.'" On Peters Hill "Sheridan's exhausted men lay down and slept among the dead and wounded 'whose cries of anguish ascended from every part of the blood-stained battle ground.'" A major from Donelson's brigade

> found "a scene revolting to humanity—the house, yard, and every available space upon an acre of ground were covered with the wounded—The night was quiet, and the moon shone as calmly and as placidly as if nature looked with approving smile upon the terrible drama which had just been enacted." As he walked stunned among the wounded, [he] could not help but wonder "why Christian men could approve and encourage such a wholesale butchery."[24]

Indeed, perhaps these same thoughts were on General Polk's mind as he sought refuge the following morning within the nave of St. Philip's Episcopal Church in Harrodsburg. With him was the Rev. Charles Todd Quintard, chaplain of the 1st Tennessee of Maney's brigade. During the battle Quintard had taken on another role, for in addition to Episcopal priest he was a highly trained medical doctor. He performed surgery, neither pausing nor eating, from early afternoon on October 8 until collapsing with exhaustion at dawn the following day. In later reminiscences recalling that morning in the church sanctuary,

> Quintard wrote, "General Polk threw his arms about my neck and said: 'Oh, for the blessed days when we walked in the house of God as friends! Let us have prayer!'" Polk knelt at the altar railing as Quintard "vested myself with surplice and stole" and began praying.... As Quintard blessed the general, Polk remained kneeling at the altar and wept, his tears the culmination of fatigue, sadness, and bitterness. During the Battle of Perryville the bishop-general had sent one of his divisions into what was perhaps the most desperate charge to occur in Kentucky during the Civil War. In fact, many of the veterans who survived the fight recalled that Perryville was one of the most intense battles of the entire conflict.[25]

In the immediate aftermath of the battle while conferring with Polk and Hardee, Bragg "at last learned that their fifteen thousand men were facing Buell's entire army" and "early on the ninth, the victorious but battered Rebel army fell back to Harrodsburg." Bragg ordered Kirby Smith's army to meet him there, and many officers and soldiers eagerly anticipated that once the two armies united, they would again battle Buell and win a resounding victory. Indeed, this seemed to be Bragg's intention as well, but overcome with second thoughts he ordered Polk to move away toward the main supply depot at Bryantsville "before Buell's horsemen could seize it."

Meanwhile, Kirby Smith fought a small action at Dry Ridge against Buell's diversionary force under Joshua Sill which had so effectively deceived Bragg. Sill evaded the Rebels' thrust and Kirby Smith arrived in Harrodsburg on October 10 to find most of Bragg's army already departed, bound for Bryantsville.[26]

On the night of October 12 Bragg made the final decision to abandon Kentucky altogether. The retreating army endured a miserable, demoralizing march through barren, mountainous terrain in horrible weather, half-starved and -clad. The Kentuckians in his ranks particularly felt discouraged and downhearted over leaving their state. A universal viewpoint in the army, in addition to the civilian populace, was that after the losses at Forts Henry and Donelson, Shiloh, New Orleans, and now this ignominious retreat, the Confederacy could hardly endure another setback.

Recriminations soon began to fly in all quarters. It is important to note in light of later controversy, that on October 12, only four days after the fight, General Bragg wrote to Adjutant General Samuel Cooper his report of the battle at Perryville. He stated that prior to the battle, "General Polk was at the same time heavily pressed at Bardstown, and he, *in accordance with previous orders*, fell back toward Harrodsburg." Contrary to the commander's later arguments, Bragg explicitly acknowledged in this report made just days after the battle that Polk's withdrawing was in obedience to his order. Bragg continued:

> Hearing on the night of the 7th that the force in front of Smith had rapidly retreated, I moved early next morning to be present at the operations of Polk's forces. After consulting with the General, reconnoitering the ground, and examining his dispositions, I declined to assume command, but suggested some plans and modifications of his arrangements which he promptly adopted.

Bragg here indicates satisfaction with Polk's handling of the situation, and again confirms the latter's prompt obedience. Bragg went on to extol his army and his subordinates:

> From the time engaged it was the severest and most desperately contested engagement within my knowledge. Fearfully out-numbered, our troops did not hesitate to engage at any odds ... [and] drove the enemy about two miles. But, for the intervention of night we would have completed the work.... The ground was literally covered with his dead and wounded.
>
> To Major General Polk, commanding the forces, Major General Hardee commanding left wing, two divisions, and Major Generals Cheatham, Buckner and Anderson, commanding divisions, is mainly due the brilliant achievements on this memorable field. Nobler troops were never more gallantly led—The country owes them a debt of gratitude....

> Ascertaining that the enemy was heavily reinforced during the night, I withdrew my force early the next morning to Harrodsburg and thence to this point.[27]

The report gives every indication that immediately following the battle Bragg held a supremely positive opinion of Polk's efforts at Perryville.

In the October 12 communication to Cooper, Bragg went on to complain about the unwillingness of the people of Kentucky to "rise *en masse* to assert their independence." This had proven a vexing problem for Bragg throughout the campaign, and was a primary reason for his decision to retreat from the state. In a letter he had written Polk from the capital city, Bragg sarcastically voiced his disgust over Kentucky's reaction to the Confederates' entry into their state: "Enthusiasm is unbounded but recruiting at a discount. Even the women are giving reasons why individuals should not go [with the army]."[28]

A number of high-ranking officers, not only those from Kentucky, groused over the retreat. Among them was General St. John Richardson Liddell, who led the first and last attacks of the Battle of Perryville. Expressing his disagreement with the decision to withdraw from Kentucky, Liddell "spoke outright" to General Bragg, for which he claimed Bragg never forgave him. During the southward march Liddell also complained bitterly to General Hardee about giving up Kentucky and consequently in his opinion, Tennessee. In response Hardee assured Liddell "that when all the facts were known, General Polk would be credited for saving Bragg's army in causing its timely retreat from Kentucky." The record bears out Hardee's point, although historians fail to give Polk credit. Bragg, by orders dated October 16, assigned to Polk numerous duties with the object of holding back the enemy from pursuing of the Army of Tennessee as it marched out of Kentucky, including rendering assistance to Kirby Smith in bringing out the army's cumbersome trains and destroying specifically named bridges.

The vanguard of the army finally reached Morristown, Tennessee, on October 20. From there they rode the railroad cars to their next fateful destination: Murfreesboro.[29]

Chapter 5

Middle Tennessee

Rest and Reorganization

During the weeks following Perryville both the Union and Confederate armies in the West took on new names, and the Federals gained a new commander as well. Beginning on November 12 Bragg posted his force, thereafter known as the Army of Tennessee, in the region encompassing Tullahoma and Murfreesboro. Bragg also reorganized the army at this time, but it soon needed further reconfiguration with additional shifting of commanders and the transfer in December of an entire division (Carter Stevenson's) to Vicksburg, Mississippi. Polk's corps remained unchanged, with its two divisions still under Jones Withers and Frank Cheatham. In Hardee's corps the deserving Patrick Cleburne rose to division command when Buckner was moved to head the Department of East Tennessee in place of Edmund Kirby Smith, who in December ascended to his dynasty in the Trans-Mississippi. Only McCown's division of Kirby Smith's former corps remained with Bragg. The army's cavalry was placed under the overall leadership of Joe Wheeler.

Following the demoralizing retreat from Kentucky, a loss of confidence in Bragg pervaded the army, from privates to top infantry commanders. Polk, Hardee and Kirby Smith were summoned separately to Richmond, resulting not only in the shuffling described above, but the creation on November 24 of a new, overall theater command under Joseph Johnston. Johnston's territory was as broad (extending from the Mississippi River to the Appalachian Mountains) as his duties were nebulous, in spite of his constant queries to Richmond to clarify the parameters of his authority. Johnston established his headquarters in Chattanooga. After accusations and complaints flooded Richmond over Bragg's erratic leadership, indecision, and dispersal of forces during the Kentucky expedition, the departmental figurehead General Johnston visited the army in December, accompanied by commander-in-chief Jefferson Davis.

The only military action of note in the vicinity that month was John Hunt Morgan's successful raid on December 7 against the Federal garrison at Hartsville, Tennessee. His object comported with the Confederate strategic goal of disrupting the enemy's supply and communications to and from Nashville. Morgan's bold, daring raid led to the wounding and capture of over 2,000 while he incurred only 139 casualties: an embarrassing loss which mortified Washington.[1]

This masterful painting by eminent artist John Paul Strain, *Morgan's Wedding*, depicts the December 1862 nuptials of the dashing cavalryman Brigadier General John Hunt Morgan and socialite Mattie Ready of Murfreesboro, Tennessee. Bishop-General Polk, after donning his clerical garb over his uniform, performed the ceremony in the Ready parlor. From left: Major General Benjamin Cheatham, Alice Ready (the bride's sister), Martha Ready (the bride's mother), Charles Ready (the father of the bride), Mattie Ready, Brigadier General John Hunt Morgan, Colonel Basil Duke, Lieutenant General Leonidas Polk, Lieutenant General William J. Hardee, Mary Breckinridge (wife of General Breckinridge), Major General John C. Breckinridge, and Brigadier General Roger W. Hanson. The gala wedding brought a whirl of parties and dinners and balls to the Army of Tennessee (The Historical Art of John Paul Strain, used with permission).

His reputation soaring, John Hunt Morgan returned to Confederate camps enlivened not only with martial, but marital celebration surrounding his wedding to Murfreesboro belle Mattie Ready on December 14. This social event of the season glittered in brass with generals Bragg, Breckinridge, Hardee and Cheatham serving as groomsmen. As Bishop-General Polk performed the ceremony, he made quite an impression upon Colonel Basil Duke, brother-in-law of the groom: "Clad in his uniform of Lieut. Genl., I thought him one of the noblest looking men I had ever seen, and I was impressed with his grand and benignant manner. He was one of the finest specimens of the ante-bellum gentleman I ever saw."[2]

No objective observer would imagine that a terrible battle loomed just beyond the festivities at Murfreesboro that month; most assumed active campaigning concluded for the winter. Although Polk's corps and Breckinridge's division bivouacked in and around Murfreesboro, Bragg's forces were otherwise spread out along a broad expanse for subsistence purposes, as the country had been stripped by government commissary officers supplying Lee's army in Virginia.

On the Federal side no such complacency existed. Two weeks after Perryville the commander of the Army of the Ohio, General Don Carlos Buell, was replaced by General William Rosecrans, recent victor at the Battle of Corinth on October 3–4. Rosecrans promptly renamed his host the Army of the Cumberland (although the name would not be officially recognized by the U.S. government until January 8, 1863) and during November 7–18 marched most of his army to Nashville.[3]

There Rosecrans set about rehabilitating the army, directing special attention to supply and other departments neglected by Buell, particularly the medical corps. He fortified the city to an extent previously unknown, transforming Nashville into an impregnable Union stronghold. Meanwhile, Lincoln and Secretary of War Stanton exhorted their generals to attack the enemy before winter froze momentum as well as the roads. Lincoln personally pushed them to take on "hard, tough fighting that will hurt somebody." Rosecrans, not one to overreact to prodding, rebuffed threats to replace him if he would not soon act. Finally, on Christmas Day, deeming his army ready, he held a council of war to map out an attack on Bragg's army at Murfreesboro. Rosecrans crowned his battle orders with a zealous admonition: "Press them hard! Drive them out of their nests! Make them fight or run! Fight them! Fight them! Fight I say!"[4]

Battle of Murfreesboro, Day One (December 31, 1862)

The Federal advance began on December 26 with 46,000 men split into three columns snaking toward the Confederates, at that time contemplating constructing cozy winter quarters throughout the countryside. Wheeler's cavalry skirmished with the Federals, managing to impede their progress sufficiently to give Bragg time to bring his scattered forces together at Murfreesboro. By December 30 Bragg had his army in its initial positions with Hardee's corps to the right on the east bank of Stones River, Polk across the river on the left, and McCown's division, temporarily attached to Hardee's corps, to the far left. It was at this point that Polk made a major contribution to the fortunes of Bragg's army, which has gone virtually uncredited by historians:

> The night of December 30, Bragg held a council of war. He planned to attack the next day up the Nashville Pike; such an assault would likely have failed. Polk countered with a plan to "turn the enemy's right where we outflanked him"; Bragg agreed. The Confederate left would attack in a grand right wheel, pushing the Federals northeast *toward* the Nashville Pike.[5]

To prepare for attack, Polk aligned the four brigades of Withers' division in front and Cheatham's four brigades to the rear in support. Once his corps had taken position Polk and Cheatham inspected the lines, after which Polk delivered a short speech to his men, "then turned to Cheatham and said: 'General, talk to them in your way.' The Tennesseean straightened his legs in his stirrups and shouted: 'Men, give them hell!'" This exchange typified the fond relationship between devout, cultured Polk and Cheatham, the profane horse racer.[6]

The Yankees lined up with McCook's corps on the right, Thomas in the center, and Crittenden on the left crossing the Nashville Pike and railroad running beside it. Coincidentally, Rosecrans crafted almost identical battle orders to Bragg's (the latter derived from Polk's idea), with each commander's respective attack to begin from his left on the morning of December 31. Here, perhaps, is where Rosecrans's personal predilections put him at a disadvantage. Known for his late-night social gatherings where his officers and staff were invited to partake in philosophizing, religious discussions, and cultural performances—frequently enjoying, for example, the fine tenor voice of General Alexander McCook—Rosecrans was not an early riser. Thus, he scheduled his December 31 attack for 8:00 a.m., whereas Bragg ordered his advance to begin two hours earlier at 6:00. During the night Cleburne's division forded the cold river to line up behind McCown in support; General Hardee also crossed to direct the complex advance which involved the whole left wing's wheeling to the right in order to press Rosecrans to the river.[7]

McCown's attack that morning came as a complete surprise to McCook's men who believed they would be doing light duty this day: merely holding the Rebel force in place at their front while their own left executed the hard attack. Consequently many Yankees were cooking breakfast when the Southerners smashed into them, and General

Major General William S. Rosecrans commanded the Army of the Cumberland at the Battle of Murfreesboro after replacing Don Carlos Buell for the latter's perceived slowness and unsatisfactory performance at Perryville. Rosecrans was a brilliant eccentric; before the war he suffered severe burns while inventing a process for refining oil. A devout Catholic, he kept a priest always nearby on his staff. Early in the war he prevailed over Lee in western Virginia for which McClellan took credit, and he later fell into a similar dynamic with Grant who discredited his victories at Iuka and Corinth, ignored his masterful maneuvers in the Tullahoma Campaign, and after Chickamauga exiled him to isolated command in Missouri (photograph by Mathew Brady, National Portrait Gallery).

McCook came galloping out to his lines with shaving lather still on his face! By 7:00 McCook's right flank had completely collapsed.[8]

Bragg's plan went awry when McCown's men, rather than wheel to the right as directed, headed northwest in pursuit of the fleeing Federals in their front. As a result, Cleburne's division advanced believing themselves behind McCown's line, when in fact they were moving into a gap created by the latter's deviation. Cleburne's men found themselves confronting the division of Union general Jefferson Davis, now alerted by the disaster unfolding to his right and prepared for attack. Colonel Michael Gooding, 22nd Indiana, who had reinforced the Yankees at a dramatic moment in the Battle of Perryville, stood observing as "[t]he enemy made their appearance in great numbers, advancing in solid column." Others described the scene more colorfully: "The Rebels came 'firing upon us and yelling like Indians.'"[9]

General Polk made a spur-of-the-moment decision while his corps, positioned for battle, waited in line to advance. Perhaps remembering how the difficult terrain at Shiloh compelled the senior generals on the field to adjust by assuming responsibility for adjacent sectors of the battleground, he similarly re-assigned his division commanders. As things stood, Withers' division occupied the front with Cheatham lined up behind. Just before they went in, Polk decreed that Cheatham would command the two left brigades, front and rear, while Withers would control the corresponding brigades on the right. This order instantly placed half of his command under unfamiliar leadership without sufficient time to adjust.[10]

Colonel Loomis's brigade (of Withers' division) was the first of Polk's corps to advance, at 7:00 a.m. They marched over a cotton field toward Colonel William Woodruff's brigade of Davis's division awaiting them behind a fence within the protection of woods. The first volley "staggered" Loomis's line, wounding Loomis seriously enough that he left the field and after the battle resigned from the army. Colonel John Coltart assumed his command. By 7:15 three regiments on Coltart's right advanced, "executed a left half-wheel and then came straight forward" as described by a lieutenant in the 24th Wisconsin: "Their banners flying, and uttering a horrid yell, they advanced heeding neither shot, shell, or bullet." The 24th retreated, exposing the flank of a neighboring Illinois regiment which nevertheless held determinedly, then counter-charged pushing the Confederates back. During the Yankees' charge their esteemed and beloved General Joshua Sill was instantly killed.[11]

It was past time for Cheatham to advance his units in support. His first brigade to go in was Colonel Alfred Vaughan's (Vaughan standing in for the absent General Preston Smith). Vaughan advanced into the same hot fire that had driven back Loomis, with the same effect on his men. Cheatham personally rallied and led Vaughan's troops in a second charge. Manigault's brigade went in next at Cheatham's direction but fled when they too experienced excessive exposure in a cotton field. Finally, Cheatham sent in his and another brigade together, whereupon one regiment, the 9th Texas, was able to break Woodruff's line, causing other Yankee units to withdraw. A combatant in the 21st Michigan described the chaos:

Polk's Corps at Murfreesboro

CHEATHAM'S DIVISION Maj. Gen. Benjamin Franklin Cheatham	WITHERS'S DIVISION Maj. Gen. Jones M. Withers
Donelson's Brigade **Brig. Gen. Daniel S. Donelson** 8th Tennessee 16th Tennessee 38th Tennessee 51st Tennessee 84th Tennessee 39th North Carolina Carnes's Tennessee Battery	**Loomis's Brigade** **Col. John Q. Loomis** (w) **Col. John Q. Coltart** 19th Alabama 22nd Alabama 25th Alabama 26th Alabama 39th Alabama 17th Alabama Battalion Sharpshooters 1st Louisiana Regulars Robertson's Alabama Battery
Stewart's Brigade **Brig. Gen. Alexander P. Stewart** 4th & 5th Tennessee 19th Tennessee 24th Tennessee 31st & 33rd Tennessee Stanford's Mississippi Battery	**Chalmers's Brigade** **Brig. Gen. James R. Chalmers** **Col. Thomas W. White** 7th Mississippi 9th Mississippi 41st Mississippi Blythe's Mississippi Regiment 9th Mississippi Battalion Sharpshooters Garrity's Alabama Battery
Maney's Brigade **Brig. Gen. George Maney** 1st & 27th Tennessee 4th Tennessee Provisional Army 6th & 9th Tennessee Maney's Company Tennessee Sharpshooters Turner's Mississippi Battery	**Anderson's Brigade** **Brig. Gen. James Patton Anderson** 24th Mississippi 27th Mississippi 29th Mississippi 30th Mississippi 37th Mississippi 45th Alabama 39th North Carolina Barret's Missouri Battery
Smith's Brigade **Col. Alfred J. Vaughan, Jr.** 12th Tennessee 13th Tennessee 29th Tennessee 47th Tennessee 154th Tennessee Allin's Company Tennessee Sharpshooters 9th Texas Scott's Tennessee Battery	**Manigault's Brigade** **Col. Arthur M. Manigault** 24th Alabama 34th Alabama 10th South Carolina 19th South Carolina Waters' Alabama Battery

SOURCE: From Larry J. Daniel, *Battle of Stones River* (Baton Rouge: Louisiana State University Press, 2012).

[T]hey drove us into a swamp. Our unit was nearly surrounded and cut to pieces. They fired into us from front and rear and piled our men in heaps. The balls were thick as hail. Shot and shell cut down trees like scythes cutting grain. It was awful to see trees falling and riderless horses running around. I hope never to see such a desperate time again.[12]

At around 8:00 Manigault made a third attack with Maney's Tennessee brigade by which time Davis's position had completely collapsed, but Confederate advances came up against a more formidable line under General Sheridan near the Wilkinson

Pike. Bloody and savage fighting took place in the vicinity of the Harding house and brick kiln, where Colonel George Washington Roberts led four Illinois regiments in a bold bayonet attack against the flank of the South Carolina regiments of Manigault's brigade. Fighting raged back and forth until the Yankees were pushed back north of the Wilkinson Pike where, according to Sheridan, "when Cheatham advanced, 'the contest then became terrible'"—so terrible that the site later became known as the "Slaughter Pen."[13]

Rumors had Cheatham intoxicated from the time of his division's advance early in the morning. His attack was undeniably tardy and some second-hand accounts describe him falling from his horse while addressing the troops. Whether true or not, Cheatham clearly did not begin the day well with his late, piecemeal, and uncoordinated attacks, but by the time his men advanced to the Wilkinson Pike against the fierce resistance of Sheridan's division, Cheatham had risen to the occasion. "Both Maney and Vaughan reported that Cheatham accompanied his units as they assailed the Wilkinson Pike line, with Cheatham at the head of Maney's regiments." If Cheatham had earlier been drunk as rumored, then the exigencies of battle sobered him up.[14]

Polk's other division under Jones Withers also contributed significantly to the Confederate effort in the Slaughter Pen. Manigault's, Anderson's and Chalmers's brigades made a concerted advance against Sheridan's final position along McFadden Lane. As the Mississippians of Anderson's brigade absorbed savage punishment, Stewart's brigade of Cheatham's division moved up in support; "they marched 'in

Major General Jones Withers served as mayor of Mobile, Alabama, before the war. A division commander in Polk's Corps during the Kentucky Campaign he missed the Perryville fight, having marched his men on to guard the Confederate supply depot. At Murfreesboro he earned commendations from Polk and Bragg. Because he suffered frequent health problems, he turned his division over to Thomas Hindman and was assigned command of reserve forces in Alabama for the remainder of the war. He was numbered among Bragg's strongest supporters in the controversies that rocked the army (photograph by Mathew Brady, U.S. National Archives).

Chapter 5. Middle Tennessee

splendid order and with a cheer.'" General Polk personally ordered Stanford's Mississippi battery in position, and "[t]he Confederates began to close the vise on the Slaughter Pen—Manigault's brigade fighting east of Harding Lane, Maney's brigade left of the lane, and Vaughan's Tennesseeans on Maney's left"—a coordinated effort on the part of Polk's corps, followed by an encore performance against Negley's division to Sheridan's left.

> The Federal resistance finally crumbled in the face of Cheatham's furious assault. Cheatham was aided by Withers, who plowed into the Union flank with Patton Anderson and A.P. Stewart's brigades. Just as Withers struck, Cheatham's legions overran several gun crews on the other side of Wilkinson Pike. While Cheatham slashed with his sword, his troops broke the Union line and slaughtered the Yankees who desperately tried to hurl them back. The cost was staggering, and Sheridan wrote that there were three assaults along the Wilkinson Pike before his troops were battered back.[15]

Sheridan's stubborn stand north of the Wilkinson Pike cost him immensely, eventually killing all three of his brigade commanders (General Joshua Sill and Colonel George W. Roberts; the third, Colonel Frederick Schaefer, fell after he led two of his regiments to assist in the continuing fight to their left). Sheridan's division performed admirably by holding for as long as they did according to orders "no matter what the outcome," giving Rosecrans time to align a new defensive position at the juncture of the Nashville Pike and the railroad: the Round Forest.[16]

General Polk has been roundly criticized for his subsequent handling of the Confederate assault against the Round Forest salient. Some historians, including Larry Daniel in his study of Stone's River, hold Bragg primarily to task for the slaughter there: "Bragg's ultimate decision to continue hammering the Round Forest would prove disastrous." Daniel's opinion as to Bragg's culpability remained unchanged in his recent book, *Conquered: Why the Army of Tennessee Failed*. He not only blames Bragg for "launch[ing] a series of near-suicidal piecemeal attacks, all of which were repulsed," he goes further by refuting Earl Hess's arguments that Polk was responsible. Connelly also points the finger at Bragg: "Not only did Bragg choose to attack the strongest position on the line, but he also did not mass enough troops to promise any hope of victory." The English military analyst Field Marshal Viscount Wolseley takes this point further:

> At the Battle of Stone's River [Bragg] successfully planned and carried out an attack upon the right flank of Rosecrans's army. But when everything was going in his favor, he abandoned his advantage and, instead of crushing in the defeated wing upon the other wing, made a gratuitous attack upon the strongest intact position left to the enemy, and at a point where his previous success gave him no advantage.

In fact, Hardee called in vain for reinforcements to the left in order to "crush the defeated wing" as Wolseley suggests.[17]

Bragg's decisions concerning Breckinridge's division played a major role in the debacle at the Round Forest. The latter's 6,000 men had remained largely idle on the east side of the river throughout the morning's fight. "Bragg's key task was to monitor the situation and decide the best use of Breckinridge's division.... *The mismanagement of this division ultimately cost Bragg the battle.*"[18]

Around mid-morning Polk began the attack on the Round Forest by sending in Chalmers's brigade of Withers' division. General Chalmers was wounded in the attempt and his advance repulsed. Next in support of Chalmers came Donelson's brigade, "no finer troops in the Confederate army," according to a Federal observer. Nevertheless, they were mowed down by Union artillery and musketry, many "sliced down, 'left dead upon the spot where they halted dressed in perfect line of battle.'" Part of the problem was that Confederate lines moving into the position were forced to divide in order to move around a burned farmhouse, breaking up their cohesion. The intensity of fire was unprecedented even to these veterans of Shiloh and Perryville. "[F]or a while it seemed all the artillery shells, canister, & solid [shot] in the universe had turned loose," wrote a Tennessean.[19]

By 1:00, after Chalmers and Donelson had been repulsed (although Donelson's 8th Tennessee met with some success, capturing hundreds of prisoners south of the Round Forest), a lull gave the Federals time to reinforce their position. Meanwhile, the first of Breckinridge's brigades from across the river reported to Polk. Breckinridge and Bragg had remained distracted all morning by illusory cavalry reports of Federal forces advancing from the east. Finally determining there to be no threat, Bragg ordered Breckinridge to begin crossing his three remaining brigades over Stone's River to support the Round Forest effort. (According to Larry Daniel, Jackson's brigade had already crossed and participated in the last attack on Negley's position before noon, but Kolakowski has Jackson reporting to Polk with Adams at 1:30 and his brigade advancing on the Round Forest before Adams was repulsed. Cozzens reports Jackson's advance "[a]s quickly as Adams cleared the field," i.e., after Adams was repulsed.)[20]

Breckinridge's next brigade to cross, commanded by General Daniel Adams, was composed mainly of Louisianans. Upon reporting to General Polk, Adams was given optimistic orders: "Look at yonder battery. Take it and the day is ours." Contradicting his earlier stated position, Larry Daniel then places all responsibility for the subsequent failure upon Polk: "Rather than wait for Preston and Palmer to arrive, the Bishop foolishly committed the brigades piecemeal; it would prove disastrous." Adams's attack began at 2:00, and like those before, their march was divided by the Cowan farmhouse, whereupon "Gibson's front line entered a virtual killing zone." "The savage fire sent the graycoats reeling back in confusion." Adams was wounded in the arm, and while recuperating in hospital laid the blame for his and his brigade's misfortune upon both Polk and Bragg: "How or why Genl. Polk who gave the order or Gen. Bragg *who was standing by when it was given* expected me to take it [Round Forest], I cannot imagine.... I cannot help but regard the order as a very imprudent and unwise one." However, Peter Cozzens, definitely no fan of Polk, absolves the bishop somewhat for ordering in Adams: "The bishop was reluctant to commit [Adams's] brigade, but orders were orders."[21]

Breckinridge crossed the river with his last two brigades, those of General Joseph Palmer, former mayor of Murfreesboro, and General William Preston, brother-in-law of the late Albert Sidney Johnston. As Breckinridge reported to Polk, he "was horrified to see his Louisianans [Adams's brigade] retreating in 'considerable disorder.'" Cozzens speculates, "We can only imagine his wrath, directed at Polk, who had committed the brigades before their supporting lines had forded Stones River." In spite of allowing for Polk's reluctance (quoted above), Cozzens here condemns him soundly: "Although Bragg had ordained the attack, he had left its timing and execution to the bishop; certainly Polk could have waited the hour necessary to muster all four brigades, rather than commit them individually to almost certain defeat."[22]

It is not entirely true that Polk sent in all of Breckinridge's brigades individually, for at 4:00 Palmer's and Preston's advanced together, the former on the left and latter to its right, although Hess credits Breckinridge with sending in the two brigades in tandem. General William Hazen, lauded for holding the Union position at the Round Forest, later recalled the spectacle: "At about 4 p.m. the enemy again advanced upon my front in two lines. The battle had hushed, and the dreadful splendor of this advance can only be conceived, as all description must fall vastly short." Colonel Thomas B. Smith of the 20th Tennessee, Preston's brigade, swung his regiment to the right in an attempt to circumvent the Round Forest, but encountered Federals in the outlying position hidden by woods along the river bluff. The Tennesseeans managed to capture some prisoners, but then with no other units in support were forced to pull back, prisoners in tow. Meanwhile Palmer's and the rest of Preston's brigades met with no more success than any of the prior attacks. Daniel describes their effort as "feeble," while Cozzens describes each commander halting his march short:

> [C]ertainly the sight of nearly one thousand dead or wounded strewn over just four acres was enough to give [General Preston] and his men pause as they neared the Cowan farm. Any notion Preston may have had of continuing forward he abandoned as his lines became snagged in the farmyard.... [W]ith Preston stopped so far short of his objective, Palmer saw no reason to sacrifice his command. So, after a loss of just two men killed and twenty wounded, Palmer instructed his men to bivouac for the night alongside what remained of Stewart and Coltart's brigades.

And with that, "[d]ue to the lateness of the hour, and the fact that Polk had by now lost stomach for more blood letting, the attacks ceased, although the firing continued until dark."[23]

Civil War generals, North and South, typically shared a personality trait: denial of ever committing any error. Accordingly, Sherman and Grant insisted they were not surprised at Shiloh; Hood blamed the loss of Atlanta on subordinate commanders and private soldiers' cowardice—the list goes on. Leonidas Polk stands out by offering frank self-criticism following Murfreesboro. Interestingly, he attributes his failure at the Round Forest to a cause opposite that set forth by later critics. Peter

Cozzens, for example, admonishes Polk for sending Adams in too early, and not waiting for Breckinridge's final two brigades to arrive (even though they required three hours to cross the river and align), so that all three could attack together. Polk believed, however, not that he attacked too soon with separate units, but rather that the entire effort came too late: "The bishop decided to use [Adams and Jackson], as he later explained, 'to drive in the enemy's left and ... dislodge him from his position in the Round Forest. Unfortunately, the opportune moment for putting in these detachments had passed.'" Christopher Kolakowski concludes: "Nevertheless, Polk decided to proceed with the plan. General Bragg was observing from the rear and could have countermanded these attack orders, but he took no action."[24]

Polk's biographer Joseph Parks focuses on the issue of timing, specifically the delayed river crossing of Breckinridge's command:

> Bragg ordered [Breckinridge's] brigades to cross over to Polk's assistance. They came but not in time. It was two hours after Donelson's bloody repulse before the two brigades under J.K. Jackson and D.W. Adams arrived. Another hour passed before the brigades of William Preston and J.B. Palmer ... were on the scene. Piecemeal attacks merely added to the slaughter of the attackers.

Parks then quotes Polk's optimistic, "what-if" appraisal:

> "Could they have been thrown upon the enemy's left immediately following Chalmers' and Donelson's assault in quick succession," Polk later contended, "the extraordinary strength of his [the enemy's] position would have availed him nothing. That point would have been carried."[25]

Contemporary commentators and historians alike consistently condemn Polk for the piecemeal assaults, and his own self-analysis acknowledges this failing. Polk accepted responsibility.

Even though the slaughter at the Round Forest was largely incurred by Confederates, the Yankees suffered, too:

> Cobb's Kentucky battery, reinforced by a section of the Washington Artillery, had torn large gaps in the Federal lines with well-directed fire from atop Wayne's Hill. In fact, one of Cobb's rounds almost robbed the Army of the Cumberland of its commander. While riding by Sheridan's reserve column on the way to the Round Forest, a solid shot flew past Rosecrans, sparing the general but decapitating his closest friend in the army, [his aide] Julius Garesché.

The fighting around the Round Forest mercifully came to an end as darkness fell, leaving the Federals "masters of the original ground on our left," in the words of Rosecrans.[26]

Battle of Murfreesboro, Day Two (January 2)

New Year's Day of 1863 found the armies eyeing one another across the lines, neither attacking nor retreating. A retreat was exactly what Bragg expected of Rosecrans, and perhaps the Union general would have done just that but for words spoken during a council of war the previous evening. As Rosecrans polled his senior commanders, General George Thomas uttered the famous line: "*This Army does not retreat.*" This declaration galvanized Rosecrans's resolve to fight on, and he then pronounced a benediction upon the meeting: "Go to your commands and prepare to fight and die here." During the night the Federals dug fortifications to the north, abandoning their Round Forest position which Polk's men promptly occupied.[27]

The day's only movement of note seemed minor, but had tremendous repercussions upon the following day's action as well as the ultimate outcome of the battle. Union Colonel Sam Beatty, commanding Van Cleve's division, crossed the river to occupy a high ridge running along the east bank. This ground should have stood out to Bragg as an essential height to be taken from the first, but the Southern commander had neglected to secure it. Now the Federals' possession of the limestone eminence by the end of day, January 1, threatened Polk's entire position on the west side of the river. Without consulting his two corps commanders, Bragg quickly concocted a plan utilizing Breckinridge's division to drive the Yankees from the height.[28]

When Bragg outlined his plan to Breckinridge the following morning, the division commander vehemently protested. For one thing, directly issuing orders to Breckinridge without going through corps commander Hardee represented a breach of military protocol on Bragg's part, but Bragg would entertain no argument. That morning Polk and Hardee conducted a reconnaissance and discovered the problematic Federal position. But Polk knew nothing of Bragg's plan to attack it until 3:00 that afternoon when Bragg rode over to his headquarters and ordered Polk to support Breckinridge's imminent advance with an artillery barrage.[29]

Polk had already opened his artillery early that morning upon the Union line on the west bank which "caught them by surprise." The Federals' response compounded their own problems when one battery, brought forward to counter-fire on Polk's, mistakenly directed its fire at Bradley's Union battery which was simultaneously under attack from Polk! When Captain Bradley galloped toward the offending gunners to stop the friendly fire, his horse was shot and he was forced to run the rest of the way.[30]

As orders for the afternoon attack were passed down to Breckinridge's brigade commanders, all adamantly protested. In fact, "the volatile" General Roger Hanson "denounced the order as 'murderous' and threatened to go to army headquarters and 'kill Bragg.'" (Cozzens adds that "Breckinridge and Preston had to restrain him from shooting Bragg.") Hanson's assessment turned out to be a self-fulfilling prophecy, with himself as one of the victims of Bragg's "murder." He even had a premonition of his impending death in the assault.[31]

To add to the havoc of the Confederates' preparations for their ill-fated assault, General Gideon Pillow appeared unexpectedly on the scene begging Bragg for a command. Pillow, after incompetent decision-making and erratic leadership since the beginning of the war, had disgraced himself in February by fleeing his command at Fort Donelson, leaving General Buckner holding the bag to surrender to Grant. Pillow had been a thorn in the side of Leonidas Polk during the early days at Columbus, stirring up conflict, grousing and sulking over imagined slights, all the while championing only one cause: his personal glory. In spite of his checkered history, Bragg inexplicably awarded him command of Palmer's brigade on the spot, just before the attack began.

The Confederates advanced precisely at 4:00 "in beautiful order." As was often the case with the Southern army on so many battlefields, at first they met with success by overrunning Beatty's position and driving his men across the river. However, Captain John Mendenhall, General Thomas Crittenden's artillery chief, had amassed 58 cannon atop McFadden's Hill. (Kolakowski states 57 guns.) The Confederates, zealously pursuing the fleeing Yankees, came into range and were torn to pieces by Mendenhall's bombardment as well as the musketry of Stanley's and Miller's brigades awaiting them. A Yankee counterattack followed consisting of Negley's division, Hazen's brigade, even Grose's and Grider's brigades which had been overrun in the initial attack. The Confederate advance ended in a complete disaster.[32]

The battered Rebel brigades fell back and formed a defensive position in anticipation of Rosecrans's attacking the following morning. During the rainy night Bragg brought Cleburne's and McCown's divisions back across the river to shore up this line, leaving Polk's corps alone on the west bank. As the rains washed over the bloody battlefield strewn with wounded men and corpses, the rising river threatened to isolate Polk's two divisions, Cheatham's and Withers', with two Union corps at their front. Given their perilous position, that night both division commanders sent a dispatch to Bragg advising that the army retreat, which Polk endorsed.[33]

Bragg, awakened upon the arrival of this message, retorted in effect that *his* army does not retreat, either: "We shall maintain our position at every hazard." The following morning, however, Bragg changed his mind. Once again, as at Perryville, General McCook's papers landed in Confederate hands, and the information they contained led Bragg's staff erroneously to calculate Rosecrans's numbers at a higher total than they actually were. Furthermore, Federal reinforcements were reported on the way to Murfreesboro. For these reasons, Bragg reversed himself and decided to withdraw. And again, as at Perryville General Liddell admonished that the fight continue and the field not be abandoned, but Bragg and his lieutenants agreed retreat was necessary.[34]

Thousands of wounded were successfully evacuated by wagon, but over 1,400 had to be left behind, along with volunteer surgeons and assistants to care for them, all facing certain capture by the enemy. Unfailingly concerned over the medical care of his men, their plight moved Bragg to tears. Nonetheless, during the night of January 3–4 the Southern army quietly left Murfreesboro, leaving their dead and the unfortunate portion of wounded behind. Polk's column nearly reached Shelbyville, having marched 20 miles mostly in the rain. Bragg set up his headquarters at Tullahoma, and his army finally began constructing their long-awaited winter quarters.[35]

Tullahoma Campaign

All during the spring and early summer of 1863, the two Western armies of the North and South camped only 30 miles apart (Polk's corps at Shelbyville lay a mere 20 miles from the enemy). Each contended with problems of supply and two types of mud: the usual variety caused by wet weather, and the other kind associated with intrigue and politics (as to the Southern army, mostly internal wrangling, but for the Yankees, primarily outside pressure). Cavalry skirmishes were frequent and, at the urging of staff officer and future president General James Garfield, Rosecrans reluctantly approved a mule-mounted raid commanded by Colonel Abel Streight against Bragg's supply line. A small but determined column under General Nathan Bedford Forrest pursued Streight's 1,700 horse- and mule-men across northern Alabama, and trapped them into surrendering outside of Rome, Georgia, on May 3.[36]

Monument atop the height at Stones River (Murfreesboro) National Battlefield Park from which Federal artillery bombarded and broke Breckinridge's attack (photograph by the author).

Washington continually prodded Rosecrans to attack the Rebel army in force, but he desisted for weeks while amassing supplies at depots and building immense fortifications in Murfreesboro and other locations to protect them. Finally, on June 24, 1863, Rosecrans conceived an ingenious advance through the gaps of the Highland Rim of Middle Tennessee. Bragg's army was posted along the main roads through the gaps and cavalry patrols ranged ahead, but his lines were thin and Rosecrans's well-planned approach caught the Southerners off-guard. Rosecrans's meticulous outfitting of his cavalry—for example, his procuring of repeating rifles—finally paid off in this operation, providing them distinct advantages.

As at other key points in the war, Bragg's fatal flaw of faulty intelligence-gathering once again came back to haunt him. Another familiar pattern, which would recur in the future, was Bragg's failure to plan against a certain eventuality.

Bragg continued to await developments. Underlying this apparent lack of concern ... was a fundamental uncertainty among the army's senior commanders concerning Bragg's strategy, never resolved in spite of the Army of Tennessee's six months of relative inactivity in Middle Tennessee. Everyone—from Johnston and Bragg on down to the privates in the ranks—expected Rosecrans to move eventually. What the Confederate response should be when that day came, however, never crystallized into a plan of action.[37]

By June 26 the Federals had pushed Hardee's corps and the Southern cavalry through two of the three gaps. On that date Bragg met with Polk in Shelbyville to propose a counterattack by Polk's corps at Liberty Gap for the following day. Polk was "appalled" at the plan, "believed [it] deeply flawed, and 'objected, considering the position he was about to be thrown in nothing short of a man-trap.'" Not surprisingly, Steven Woodworth criticizes Polk for his objections. As it turned out, however, the plan was rendered moot when Stewart's division failed that afternoon to hold Hoover's Gap and the Manchester Pike. David Powell and Eric Wittenberg, in their excellent study of the Tullahoma Campaign, expound upon the aborted plan and expose the fallacy behind Steven Woodworth's criticism of Polk's generalship. In the fight at the Highland Rim gaps, as at other Civil War junctures, Woodworth attempts to cast Polk as saboteur of Bragg's would-be brilliant brush with victory:

> In a 1998 essay, historian Steven Woodworth postulated that Polk served Bragg poorly here and that Bragg's offensive could have worked—likely forcing, if not the destruction of Rosecrans's army, a hasty retreat to Murfreesboro and an abrupt, ignominious end to the Union offensive. It is hard to see how such a victory could have played out.... Shifting Polk's force north of the Highland Rim would have exposed it to complete disaster, much as Polk feared.[38]

In the face of Rosecrans's relentless, multi-pronged advance through and beyond the Highland Rim gaps, the entire Army of Tennessee retreated to Tullahoma on the night of June 26. The next afternoon Wheeler's cavalry fought a rearguard action north of Shelbyville against Union cavalry brigades under Robert Minty. The Yankees trapped 300 troopers in a field, taking them prisoner and pushing the remainder of Wheeler's men in a disordered retreat through the town, whereupon even more were captured in pursuit toward the Duck River.[39]

By June 28 Rosecrans's army had consolidated in Manchester, threatening Bragg's railroad supply line in his rear. If the Federals cut that line, Bragg's army would be isolated. On June 28 Buckner's reinforcements moving from East Tennessee to aid Bragg saved a key railroad bridge from a crack brigade of mounted infantry under General John Wilder (the same Wilder who surrendered Munfordville to General Buckner, gentleman to gentleman, 10 months earlier). Nevertheless, the Yankee horsemen managed to reach the railroad junction of Decherd in Bragg's rear, where they cut telegraph wires and destroyed railroad track before returning to their lines.

On June 29 Bragg hunkered down at his position around Tullahoma and resolved to fight there, until Polk and Hardee confronted him with the reality of the army's dangerous situation. By the following day Bragg conceded the obvious and ordered his army to retreat to Decherd; they moved farther back to Cowan on July

2. Now he was backed up to mountains—the Cumberland Plateau—and once again Bragg considered making a stand. Hardee and Polk both supported his stance, voting to "fight at the mountain," and Bragg deployed a line of battle. But the commander, although no pressure was being exerted by Rosecrans at that particular time, inexplicably opted "without consulting his corps commanders" to retreat over the mountain all the way to the safety of Chattanooga. Bragg during this time was ill and stress-ridden; indeed, throughout the entire crisis Bragg seemed shaky. "[S]ince abandoning Tullahoma, Bragg appeared indecisive and unsure of his next course," so much so that Hardee expressed concern over his fitness for command. "Bragg's defeatist attitude and unpredictable conduct exacerbated the ongoing command crisis within his army. His senior subordinates no longer trusted his decision-making. Bragg's vacillations at both Tullahoma and Cowan proved hugely damaging. In each case he seemed to show every intention of fighting, … and then abruptly changed his mind." On July 3 in Cowan he confided to Charles Quintard, medical doctor, chaplain of the 1st Tennessee and Bragg's spiritual adviser, that he felt "utterly broken down." He further admitted, "This [the army's retreat] is a great disaster." As to Polk's view of the recent unfortunate turn:

> Polk shared the disappointment resulting from retreat but made no effort to saddle Bragg with sole responsibility. "Of our falling back to this place I have to say I thought it judicious, and advised it," he [later] wrote President Davis.[40]

On July 3 during the retreat, General Polk's corps marched up Sewanee Mountain and halted to rest at University Place. There Bishop Leonidas Polk beheld for the last time the sacred site of his yet-unrealized, greatest life mission: The University of the South, represented only by the marble cornerstone dedicated to God that beautiful October afternoon in 1860. Around 2:00 a.m. Polk arrived on the mountaintop and tarried for much of the day. As the flesh is weak, he surely first sought sleep, but perhaps awakened early—before breakfast was prepared, horses tended, orders issued, and other mundane tasks of the world intruded—in order to pray.

Neither church nor chapel yet in existence, he might have taken a short walk to the consecrated ground around the cornerstone. He would have launched into his devotions using the eloquent language of the Episcopal Book of Common Prayer, and then perhaps found himself praying extemporaneously as he did the day after battle at Perryville when he ventured into church with Chaplain Quintard and beseeched God for blessed days when believers North and South could be reunited as friends. His thoughts then likely turned to the solitary stone beside him, earthly emblem of his ardent aspiration tragically suspended by war. Perhaps he importuned God for a time soon to come when young men's brains, no longer pierced by Minié ball or spilled by canister shot, would instead gain education and enlightenment at this place. Leonidas Polk surely prayed to see in his lifetime the fulfillment of his mission, yet in the same breath he just as certainly uttered, "Not my will but thine be done." Knowing that the University Domain would soon lie behind enemy lines, he undoubtedly dreaded the wanton vandalism that the Yankees would wreak upon this cherished space, and felt some small relief that no university buildings had yet been erected. The stone and its contents hidden within were all that presented themselves. Even if the Yankees obliterated it, neither their destruction nor explosives nor any other force could ever reverse the holy consecration of this place.

Signal Corps officer Mercer Otey recorded his observations of Polk's activities later that morning. Mercer was the son of James Hervey Otey, late bishop of Tennessee who officiated with Polk during the consecration of the university cornerstone and had died recently, in April 1863. The young Otey recounted that

> Gen. Polk ... called his body servant, Altamont, to fetch his cane chair ... and had it placed at a point that had been cleared of surrounding trees, called "inspiration point," I think, commanding a full view of the great valley stretched at our feet ... here we rested for an hour or more on historic ground, and together talked of the hopes and plans that he and my father entertained for the building of the great university.[41]

His devotions and reminiscences completed, many duties and cares awaited the general's attention. Most of the soldiers had already marched on; only Wheeler's cavalry remained. That afternoon—as Pickett's and Pettigrew's and Trimble's divisions receded from their high tide at Cemetery Ridge, and Pemberton negotiated with Grant surrender terms for Vicksburg—Leonidas Polk and his staff retreated from his sacred mountain to catch up with Cheatham's division marching ahead. By the next day, July 4, his corps completed its crossing of the Tennessee River.[42]

Chapter 6

Trouble in Army of Tennessee High Command

General Braxton Bragg as Army Commander

Bitter disappointment pervaded the Army of Tennessee after withdrawing from the greater portion of its namesake state. At least the Confederates still possessed Chattanooga, a vital center of transportation, supply and raw materials for their new nation. They also barely held East Tennessee—little consolation with its largely hostile, Unionist population. With bad news from Pennsylvania and the Mississippi River only magnifying despondency in the ranks, blame and recrimination eroded what little morale the men maintained.

A pattern of advance/initial success/defeat/withdrawal had now become an old, bad habit of the Army of Tennessee. After Perryville, Murfreesboro, and now Rosecrans's nearly bloodless victory in Middle Tennessee, the Western Confederate army, and indeed the nation, sought a scapegoat. Responsibility naturally fell upon Bragg as commander, but Bragg himself was the quickest to point fingers. Polk's position as senior subordinate conveniently placed him at the receiving end of Bragg's torrent of blame. This chapter and the next explore the increasingly harmful high-command intrigues following each setback of the Army of Tennessee.

In his seminal study of the Western Confederate campaigns, Thomas Connelly points out that a commander's personality played a more crucial role in Southern armies than in those of the Union.[1] We see evidence of this in the naming conventions of units; in contrast to the elaborate, numbered system of the U.S. Army, Confederate brigades, divisions and corps were designated by the *name* of their original commander: for example, the famous Stonewall Brigade, Pickett's Division, Polk's Corps, and lesser-knowns such as Clingman's Brigade. Thus, for better or for worse, the Southern fighting unit was stamped with the identity and personality of its commander. This emphasis perhaps arose from the unique culture of the South which valued personal honor and family identity.

General Bragg himself conflated family and army relationships, as seen in a message to his men transmitted through General Liddell: "I have no children. Hence, I look upon the soldiers of my army as my own—as *my* children." Perhaps in no other fighting force, not even Lee's, did a leader's personality influence his command's atmosphere and outcome as did Bragg; even long after he had resigned, Bragg "considered the Army of Tennessee as his own." Like a family, the army was subject to the strengths and gifts, as well as the faults and quirks, of its "parent."[2]

Thus, it is instructive to explore the personality of Braxton Bragg in order to understand how he shaped his army, and why conflicts with Polk and other subordinates inevitably arose and in turn undermined the army's effectiveness. Before launching into Bragg's faults, however, it should be pointed out that he was a complex and contradictory man. Although his public persona was perceived as harsh, he hid a softer side. "A soldier claimed Bragg 'sedulously avoided giving public evidence of the tender feeling which he entertained for the suffering and unfortunate.'" Having seen this side of the general during his hospital visits to the wounded, army surgeons invariably held him in the kindest regard. Dr. T.G. Richardson, Bragg's staff surgeon, noted in a letter to Army of Tennessee medical director Samuel Stout that Bragg "had the interests of the hospitals very much at heart." From many accounts, it appears that Bragg cultivated a warm and familial atmosphere with his staff officers. But most of the rank and file knew only their "chieftain of rough and somewhat forbidding exterior."[3]

Thomas Connelly elaborates on some of Bragg's troublesome traits which inevitably colored his leadership style:

> [Bragg] was irritable and impatient, even with his friends.... If Bragg could irritate a friend, he could infuriate an enemy. He never left his enemies any escape mechanism, but instead relished complete victory in any dispute.
>
> On and off the field, Bragg was indecisive. In ... campaigns, he had shown ability in preparing plans, only to waver at the final moment.
>
> ....
>
> Paradoxically, Bragg was as rigid as he was indecisive. Once he had made a decision in his field tactics, he seemed unable to adjust to a changing confrontation.
>
> Bragg became easily upset when obstacles seemed to jeopardize his plans, and he tended to magnify problems out of proportion.

Perhaps one of the most perspicacious analyses of Bragg was offered by a visiting English military observer, Lieutenant Colonel Garnet Joseph Wolseley, later Field Marshal Viscount:

> General Bragg was a commander who seems to have been very uncertain in his action. At times he was both skillful in his arrangements and enterprising in his movements. Suddenly his skill deserted him at the most critical moments.

Wolseley puzzled over Bragg's "strange mixture of qualities."[4]

Bragg's own brother John suggested that the bitter disappointments which followed Bragg's pattern of initial-success-turned-failure could be attributed to his overexcitable, anticipatory nature:

> He has a way of announcing his successes which is very unfortunate and always reacts against him. The public are led to believe a great deal more has been effected than really has been. The whole trouble of B[raxton] in this respect arises from his impulsive and sanguine temper. He ought to try to subdue this tendency. Even under the flush and excitement of victory calmness and moderation are always more becoming as well as most politic.[5]

Chapter 6. Trouble in Army of Tennessee High Command

Braxton Bragg inevitably accomplished more at the beginning of an enterprise than upon its conclusion: for example, his bold, innovative railroad troop transfer which got the Kentucky Campaign off to an auspicious start; the army's spectacular performance at Perryville as well as their surprise attack the first morning at Murfreesboro; and later, in the last days of 1864, the initial success at Fort Fisher when the Union fleet aborted its first attempt against the North Carolina bastion. As his brother observed, Bragg gleefully but prematurely declared victory at these junctures, only to see it washed away by a disappointing outcome. It was not that he lacked energy nor was he reticent in applying himself. The Confederacy did not lose the war through any want of exertion on the part of Braxton Bragg! But he seemed somehow unable to sustain his initial successes and see them through to solid wins in the end.

Modern observers have tried to impose on Bragg modern psychological diagnoses, such as Noe's hypothesizing narcissistic personality disorder. Whether or not the general can be so neatly labeled, it is clear that his inherent nature and internal contradictions generated problems throughout the Army of Tennessee, leading to damaging rifts with key subordinates including Leonidas Polk.[6]

Many historians blame Polk entirely for the falling-out with Bragg. In his book *This Terrible Sound: The Battle of Chickamauga*, Peter Cozzens starts right from the beginning portraying Polk as hateful toward Bragg. Upon first introducing the reader to Polk as soon as page 3, he writes: "Polk had little Christian charity where Braxton Bragg is concerned. In his eyes, Bragg was 'a poor, feeble-minded, irresolute man of violent passions ... uncertain of the soundness of his conclusions and therefore timid in their execution.'" This passage casts Polk as a mean-spirited, hypocritical fault-finder who unilaterally poisoned the generals' relationship. By quoting these words so atypical of Polk in the opening pages of his book, Cozzens subtly suggests it to be the foundation of the disharmony between the two men. However, Polk did not write these words until the end of 1863 after Bragg unjustly dismissed him from the army without charges. Cozzens altogether omits the context. In reality, Polk had long exercised forbearance of Bragg's personal hostility toward him as the command structure slowly deteriorated under Bragg's leadership. Furthermore, the passage quoted was lifted from a personal letter to Polk's daughter who was upset over Bragg's unfair, very public censure of her father. Under these circumstances Polk should be granted some leeway for private venting.[7]

When Braxton Bragg was named overall commander of the army he brought considerable baggage with him to his new position: the same prejudices and conflicts and alienation that had come between him and fellow generals during his tenure as corps commander at Shiloh and earlier. He constantly complained that virtually no one under him was good enough in his eyes. It was not long before his harshness began to have a pronounced effect on the vast organization which he oversaw:

> Within the army, he drove his enemies to the wall, humiliated them, and forced them into the anti–Bragg element. He often spoke of his officers' not meeting his expectations, of their shortcomings.... Always the same theme persisted—Bragg was right and his generals wrong.[8]

Bragg's intimidating management style produced three unfortunate results in the Army of Tennessee. First, it stymied initiative. Where an atmosphere of blame abounds, subordinates are unlikely to risk responding creatively or even adequately to situations. Second, it fostered the unhealthy formation of "pro-Bragg" or "anti-Bragg" factions. Even the young clerks working on Bragg's staff took sides. This gradually ate away at the camaraderie necessary to a successful army. Third, because negativity and fear are contagious, men otherwise not prone by nature to such attitudes found themselves echoing them, or at least became inured to constant contentiousness among those fighting supposedly on the same side.[9]

General Richard Taylor, who had formerly served on Bragg's staff, visited him in Chattanooga shortly after Bragg transferred his army there by rail in 1862. Taylor at that time was departing the Army of Northern Virginia, where he had fought under Stonewall Jackson, bound for a new assignment in his home state of Louisiana. During conversation over dinner with Bragg, with staff officers and others present, Taylor was appalled at Bragg's public debasement of his own subordinates. In his book *Destruction and Reconstruction*, Taylor adhered to the Victorian, gentlemanly practice of not naming the slandered party, but historians unanimously (with the exception of one, discussed at length in Chapter 11) agree that Bragg spoke of Polk on this occasion:

> Bragg openly expressed his caustic feelings toward this general. "_____ [Polk] is an old woman," he declared in front of Taylor and other officers, who had joined the two at a dinner. "[He is] utterly worthless."
> Taylor was shocked by Bragg's outburst. When the two were alone, he asked, "By whom [do you] intend to relieve General _____ [Polk]?"
> "By no one. I have but one or two fitted for high command...."
> "You can hardly expect hearty cooperation of officers of whom [you] speak contemptuously."
> "I speak the truth," Bragg snorted, refusing to alter his position.... "From that hour," Taylor wrote, "I had misgivings as to Bragg's success."[10]

It is important to note that this conversation took place *before* the Kentucky Campaign when Polk's alleged malfeasance, of which Bragg accused him months later, supposedly took place. This exchange demonstrates that Bragg's hostility toward Polk was primarily personal, not based on any behavior of Polk, nor upon objective professional assessment, because it predated the wrongdoing with which Bragg later charged the bishop.

General Liddell observed similarly that Bragg castigated some subordinates unjustly, while showing undeserved favoritism to others:

> [Bragg] had such poor judgment of character.... I have known him to overlook men whose actions and zeal entitled them to wiser consideration, and it became the general belief that not service or enterprise entitled men to credit and promotion, but favoritism only.

This unfortunate trait led to alienation in the officers' corps that tore at the fabric of the army's cohesiveness.[11]

The commander's mistrust and bashing of his own colleagues spilled over onto his staff and spread down the chain of command, as antagonism unchecked is wont to do. Many historians quote army staff surgeon Dr. David Yandell's charges against General Polk of November 1862, which sound as though they could have come from the pen of General Bragg:

> "I saw enough of [Polk] at Shiloh & Perryville to cause me to place no great confidence in him. He will *prevaricate*." "He did say he was going to do this and going to do that, but the old man forgets." Unless "he is transferred to house *duties* [some unimportant post]," concluded Yandell, "we will all go to the Devil out here."

It is interesting, however, to note how historians edit this damning quote so that it seemingly applies only to Polk. The full text, rather than the above expurgated version, reveals that the good doctor in the same passage actually disparages Bragg even more severely, calling him "either stark mad or utterly incompetent ... ignorant of both the fundamental principles and the details of his noble profession." And just before the call for Polk to be "transferred to house duties," appears the clause "*if Bragg isn't removed* & Polk transferred ... we will all go to the devil out here." Bragg apologists invariably omit those comments![12]

Lieutenant General Richard Taylor, son of President Zachary Taylor and brother-in-law of Jefferson Davis, began the war as a volunteer aide to Bragg in Pensacola, until he gained command of a Louisiana brigade under Stonewall Jackson. In July 1862 he was transferred to his home state of Louisiana where he defeated General Nathaniel Banks in the Red River Campaign, and toward the end of the war commanded the Department of Alabama, Mississippi, and East Louisiana, Polk's former command ("Taylor, Richard," House Divided: The Civil War Research Engine at Dickinson College).

Ironically, Dr. Yandell himself unknowingly became a victim of Bragg's predilection to scorn officers in his own army. "Bragg, according to his brother John, considered Yandell 'a *miserable dog*.'" One sees how hostility malignantly magnifies as it ricochets throughout an organization. In the end, Dr. Yandell evinced his own penchant for controversy. In 1863 he overstepped his position by publishing a defense of Joseph Johnston after the latter came under government condemnation for failing to save Vicksburg. As his writings undeniably revealed that he had gained improper access to command communications, President Davis banished the doctor to the Trans-Mississippi. The following year he ran afoul of a colleague there and Richmond directed that Kirby Smith dismiss him.[13]

Bragg habitually berated not only individuals, but entire classes of people as well. He made no secret of his caustic prejudice against Tennessee troops which, like many of his attitudes, was planted, or at least nurtured, by his wife:

Dr. David Yandell was born into a renowned medical family in Kentucky: his father founded and taught at the University of Louisville medical school, and two brothers were also physicians. He was Albert Sidney Johnston's personal physician at Shiloh, but the commanding general ordered him to tend to wounded soldiers. Had he been close by when Johnston was mortally wounded, he could have saved the general's life. Dr. Yandell's opinionated personality caused some troubling run-ins during his military service. After meddling in a controversy involving Joseph Johnston, he was banished to the Trans-Mississippi, and was ultimately dismissed from that position as well. Yandell was known for entertaining fellow officers with uncanny imitations, and on one occasion was highly embarrassed when Bragg walked in as the doctor was mimicking him ("Yandell, David Wendel," House Divided: The Civil War Research Engine at Dickinson College).

> Bragg's patrician wife, Elise, who in many ways dominated her soldier husband, felt an almost pathological hatred of Tennesseeans that invariably rubbed off. She wrote him constantly that men from the Volunteer State were cowards who could not be trusted.
>
> "Dear husband," [Elise] wrote in a letter to Bragg, "please do not trust the Tennessee troops." She thought that they would prefer to plunder civilians rather than assail an adversary. "Put [them] where your batteries can fire on them if they attempt to run," she said. "Shame them into fighting."

Bragg agreed in a later reply: "I never realized the full correctness of your appreciation of them until now."[14]

Of course, such stereotypes promulgated by the army's leader passed down to the men, ironically even among the 11th Louisiana castigated by Bragg as part of "Polk's mob."

Charles Johnson of the 11th Louisiana claimed that petitions were circulated within his outfit asking that it not be brigaded with Tennesseeans. When subsequently assigned to Robert Russell's brigade with three Tennessee regiments, Johnson concluded that the men would have to "be content with being lashed to the tail of a Tennessee rabble."[15]

It is difficult to tell against whom Bragg's animus clashed more: Polk or men of Tennessee. Perhaps the bishop, because his clan had settled in the vicinity of Columbia, Tennessee, received the double portion of General Bragg's prejudice.

Even though Bragg may have been conspicuous for his disgust against this individual or that group, nevertheless this trait does not entirely characterize the man. One misunderstood aspect of Bragg's nature is the extent to which his irascible image belied his inner self. In addition to the surprising soft spot in his heart for wounded soldiers, few suspected that beneath his grim visage and brusque, contentious manner dwelt an optimist—one might even say, idealist. Indeed, this might explain the underlying motive for much of his anger toward subordinates: they never measured up to *his vision of perfection.* Of all the Confederate generals, Bragg probably burned most fervently with the purest zeal for the cause. He gave his utmost to his nascent nation, even to the sacrifice of his health and disposition, not to mention his home and land where he had mightily toiled and sweated alongside slaves wresting pure sugar from the unyielding cellulose and slicing leaves of cane stalks laboriously cultivated in the swampy, sweltering Louisiana lowlands. That Bragg was a secret idealist is evident in his abhorrence of pre-war Louisiana political corruption, which overwrought him then to such an extent that he broke out in boils. It could only have been idealism that moved Bragg to pledge eternal friendship to Tecumseh Sherman on the eve of war (about which Bragg incidentally had no illusions, but foretold "would rage from one end of the country to the other"). Bragg's idealism would spring up unpredictably and anomalously on the field. For example, while in the throes of retreating from Kentucky, he sent a message to Polk on October 16, 1862, with detailed instructions to facilitate the army's retreat. Bragg added a surprisingly cheerful P.S.: "I have no doubt we can whip the force behind us. B.B."[16]

However one chooses to characterize Braxton Bragg, whether pathologically narcissistic, incongruously idealistic, or downright toxic, his personality issues undeniably caused significant problems in the Army of Tennessee. A pattern soon emerged following his army's major battles: he initiated inquisitions and condemned and purged scapegoats. During what should have been times of rest and refitting, the high-command circle of the Army of Tennessee went into crisis mode almost as stressful as battle. And typically, these episodes worsened with each successive occurrence.

Witch Hunts and Purges

When Braxton Bragg involved himself in an endeavor, he gave it his all—and true soldier that he was, it seemed that every effort morphed into a battle. But he ever believed in the final outcome and his ability to achieve it. Perhaps it was this ultra-confidence that drove him to inflict sweeping purges upon his army after the disappointing retreats and defeats following Perryville and Murfreesboro. *Someone* had not done his duty; somewhere a weak link had compromised the outcome—and it must be exposed and eliminated.

Unbeknownst to Polk, his relationship with Bragg began to unravel in the spring of 1862 when Bragg focused his hypercritical eye on Polk's command before and during the battle of Shiloh. Similarly, the Kentucky Campaign that autumn generated contention, although the backlash in the army following Perryville and the demoralizing retreat back to Tennessee was rather muted and mild compared to later imbroglios in the wake of Murfreesboro and Chickamauga. At least on the surface, post–Perryville intrigues within the army command maintained a gentlemanly decorum limited to letter writing, recriminations in official reports (some in the form of omissions), and the airing of criticism and grievances behind closed doors in Richmond. The public sphere was another matter; newspapers and politicians, especially those from Kentucky with Southern sympathies, bluntly and loudly decried the army's failure to unite the border state under the Stars and Bars.

Toward the end of October Richmond summoned Bragg to confer on the outcome of his Kentucky expedition. Accusations preceded him in the person of an aide who had traveled there on behalf of Kirby Smith, armed with a list of criticisms over Bragg's handling of the campaign. "The dogs of detraction were let loose upon me," he wrote Elise after arriving in Richmond. President Davis, however, had by this time built up a defensive obliviousness to journalistic and political clamor, and gave Bragg the benefit of the doubt as the general defended his decisions.[17]

The president then sent for Polk, followed by Kirby Smith, to sound them out on their views of the campaign and the army's continued confidence in Bragg as commander. Both "told the President they considered Bragg responsible for the failure of the Kentucky campaign … [and] that Bragg had lost the confidence of his men." Never one to dwell solely on the negative, in addition "Polk acknowledged Bragg's great ability as an organizer and disciplinarian." Furthermore, Polk went to Bragg's defense by expounding on the command confusion that arose from the combining of separate departments: "Polk also presented Bragg's case for unifying [Kirby] Smith's army with his own.... How differently the Kentucky campaign might have ended if it had been effected in time."[18]

After arbitrating everyone's point of view, Davis retained Bragg; promoted Polk, Kirby Smith and Hardee to lieutenant general; and named Joseph Johnston overall commander of the West, shouldering him with the (impossible) task of overseeing, coordinating, and reinforcing, as needed, Bragg's forces in Middle Tennessee and General John Pemberton's at Vicksburg. Shortly thereafter Kirby Smith, who had announced to Davis that he preferred not to be associated with Bragg in any future campaigns, was named commander of the Trans-Mississippi.[19]

Early in December Bragg reorganized his army, now officially known as the Army of Tennessee. The conflicts seething over the past two months became subsumed into the social whirl of the Christmas season and the balls, horse races, and other festivities culminating in the gala wedding of dashing newly promoted

Brigadier General John Hunt Morgan and Miss Mattie Ready of Murfreesboro, officiated by Bishop Polk. However, holiday celebrations soon came to an abrupt halt with Rosecrans's advance toward Murfreesboro. The still-unresolved controversy arising out of the Kentucky Campaign would have to wait; in the future it would rear its ugly head over the Army of Tennessee.

Bragg's January 11 Circular Letter

Trouble came mere days after the Battle of Murfreesboro. A newspaper writer accused Bragg of retreating from the battlefield against his subordinate generals' counsel, and predicted that he would be removed from command. Bragg brooded over the article. Despite the advice of his closest supporters, including former staff surgeon Dr. Josiah Nott who urged him to ignore controversies generated in the press, Bragg took action. On January 11 he chose the astonishing course of drafting a circular letter to his corps and division commanders asking them to correct the falsehood which had been published in the Chattanooga *Rebel*. He wished his lieutenants to confirm in writing that they had, in fact, advised the retreat from Murfreesboro. But the controversy compounded when some of the recipients (as well as most subsequent historians) read more in Bragg's letter than was intended: in addition to requesting the specific statement that they supported the retreat, they interpreted the letter to solicit a vote of confidence in Bragg as army commander.[20]

Connelly explains that Bragg actually created two drafts of the letter. The first version directly asked for an opinion of whether the army had lost confidence in him. Bragg's staff emphatically (and wisely) advised against opening this can of worms, and redrafted the letter omitting the confidence question. Nevertheless, the revised letter still included a *statement* that if Bragg had lost the confidence of his lieutenants, he would resign from command, thus leaving intact the *implied* question.[21]

The letter caused quite a stir among Bragg's subordinates. Word of it spread through the army and even reached Jefferson Davis in Richmond. Like most of the intended recipients, an aghast Davis also interpreted the letter to request input as to Bragg's fitness for continued command. Unfortunately for Bragg, the floodgates opened, and a torrent of no-confidence votes began streaming into headquarters. Hardee replied that he, Cleburne and Breckinridge agreed that Bragg should resign. Breckinridge sent the additional message that he had polled his brigade commanders and they too no longer supported Bragg's remaining in command. An identical missive came from Cleburne. Tallying up the replies to the circular letter, Bragg's assistant adjutant general, George Brent, concluded that dissatisfaction with Bragg was greater in Hardee's Corps than in Polk's. And apparently there was a widespread notion that an impressionable Hardee could not think for himself. While many historians deem him as having been influenced by Polk to turn against Bragg, Brent postulated instead that Hardee had been "seduced by Breckinridge."[22]

Polk's reply to Bragg's January 11 letter was delayed as he was away from the army on leave, visiting his family in Asheville, North Carolina. Either the first version was inadvertently sent to Polk, or he read the second version more carefully than the others and perceived the ambiguity. Polk first responded "that he had seen two questions in the original circular, but understood that his division commanders had seen only one—the question regarding a retreat." (Thus Polk openly disclosed that he had engaged in exchanges with the other generals over the questions raised by Bragg's letter.) Polk asked Bragg for clarification before submitting his response. Bragg answered by letter dated January 30, 1863:

> I hasten to reply to your note.... To my mind that circular contained but one point of inquiry and it certainly was intended to contain but one—and that was to ask of any Corps + Division commanders to commit to writing what had transpired between us in regard to the retreat from Murfreesboro.
>
> I believed it to have been grossly + intentionally misrepresented ... for my injury. It was never intended by me that this should go further than the parties to whom it was addressed....
>
> The paragraph relating to my supercedence was only an expression of the feeling with which I should receive your replies should they prove I had been misled in my construction of your opinions + advice.

From that explanation artfully crafted by Bragg, Polk confined his reply to the single query, verifying that he had indeed advised retreating from Murfreesboro.[23]

Meanwhile, Bragg had a self-created crisis on his hands. Other than Polk's careful reply, the majority of Bragg's subordinates were now on record as lacking confidence in his leadership, under his declaration that he would resign if that were the case. This odd move by Braxton Bragg—broaching the question of his army's confidence in him, and conditioning upon their responses nothing less than his retirement—demonstrates the hidden trait previously discussed: his underlying optimism. Even though he did not intentionally ask his generals' opinions of his fitness for command (in the amended version), his letter touched around the edges of the question and brought negative feedback that Bragg obviously never expected. Now he was forced to scramble out of a hole that he had dug for himself.

The matter unleashed a storm of controversy into already troubled relations. In fairness to Bragg, as clarified to Polk he meant for the matter to remain confidential within the closest circle of his immediate subordinates. Nevertheless, the damage had been done and President Davis, anguished upon hearing of the uproar, ordered General Joseph Johnston to go to the army personally and investigate. Johnston arrived in Tullahoma around the end of January, and within days received a message from the secretary of war offering him the option of replacing Bragg as commander of the Army of Tennessee. Johnston demurred, instead stating his strong support of Bragg and his opinion that the controversy would pass, thus ignoring the testimony of numerous generals including Polk that serious problems with Bragg threatened to fracture the army's cohesion. Johnston insisted to Richmond that complaints against Bragg had little merit and the army was in fine morale and condition. Bragg gloated that Johnston's support "'completely knocked the pegs' from the 'scoundrels who

Chapter 6. Trouble in Army of Tennessee High Command

were abusing me.'" If Bragg did not get the validation he sought from subordinates, he did win vindication from Johnston.²⁴

Around the time Johnston issued his glowing report, Polk wrote to Jefferson Davis on March 30, 1863, a letter marked "Private." He felt it his duty to inform the president that he would have responded to Bragg's inquiry in the same manner as the others, i.e., he too had lost confidence in Bragg *in his current position*. Polk's detractors trumpet this letter as conclusive evidence of the latter's scheming behind the back of his superior. It is important to cite this correspondence at length so that the reader can judge whether it truly contains any note of treachery:

General Joseph E. Johnston originally commanded in Virginia until he was wounded at Seven Pines and Lee permanently inherited his army. Tensions had arisen between Johnston and Jefferson Davis over rank, protocol, and disregard for the president's authority. Once he recovered, Johnston found himself appointed to an ill-defined post in the West: an advisory role with no troops under his command. In January 1863 he was ordered to investigate a conflict that had erupted between Bragg and his subordinates, and took the gentlemanly course of backing his brother officer—only to be treacherously repaid by Bragg a year and a half later (photograph by Mathew Brady, National Archives).

> My idea is—my conviction rather—that if the presence, and offices of Genl B. were entirely acceptable to this army, the highest interests—military interests—of the Confederacy would be consulted by transferring him to another field—where his peculiar talent—that of organization and discipline—could find a more ample scope.... The application of that talent is not always easy & agreeable where it exists. Yet there are few armies which would not be benefitted by it, even if the benefit came from without. My opinion is that the Genl could be of service to all the armies of the Confederacy if placed in the proper position.... Assign him the duties of Inspector General. And from my observation while in Richmond, it would be a great relief to Genl Cooper, whose energy + business capacity, great as they are, seemed well nigh overtaxed.
>
> The Genl could not object to the position on the score of rank as the ranking Officer of the army now holds that position ... as his specialty is that which the Office of Inspector General covered, his resources + capacity would be felt throughout the army.²⁵

Polk was not attempting to depose his superior from the army. On the contrary, what Polk suggested was in effect a *promotion* of Bragg to the upper echelons of army administration. Even if Davis did not take his advice at this time, Polk offered a positive and insightful recommendation which eventually came to pass quite satisfactorily when Davis named Bragg his military adviser two years later.

Nevertheless, for now Bragg stayed on as commander of the Army of Tennessee. He won this first round, and gloried in it. Earl Hess points out that "Bragg began to relish the fight with his generals for it released his naturally combative spirit." In his glee he crowed to William Whann Mackall, soon to assume the position of Bragg's chief of staff: "My prowess for accomplishing this has been most distasteful to many of my senior generals, and they wince under the blows. Breckinridge, Polk & Hardee especially."[26]

Hess frames the entire affair surrounding Bragg's January 11 letter as the definitive point when Bragg lost credibility as a leader. Bragg himself raised the issue of whether his officers had confidence in him. He named his own penalty if he had lost their confidence. The replies verified that he no longer had their confidence. But Bragg did not keep his word; he did not retire as promised.

> Bragg wrote of his willingness to step aside if the good of the service demanded. The response to the round-robin letter obviously demanded it, but Bragg refused. This is the most damning criticism of Bragg in the entire war. Faced with open expressions of distrust in his ability coming from his most important subordinates, he dug in his heels and fought back instead of gracefully leaving the Army of Tennessee.... From now on the general fought increasingly for himself and not solely for the common good; it would ruin his war career.[27]

The whole matter was created and carried out by Bragg, against the advice of his staff, and he could blame no one but himself.

Murfreesboro Battle Report

Bragg set about to punish his intra-army enemies, now identified openly, in the form of his official report on the Battle of Murfreesboro. The primary target of Bragg's report was General John Breckinridge, who would indeed "wince under the blow." Bragg assumed that Breckinridge was behind the hostile newspaper articles, as some of the information and accusations contained in them could have come from Theodore O'Hara, a former newspaperman now serving on Breckinridge's staff. Not only had O'Hara held a grudge against Bragg ever since Pensacola where the latter dismissed him from his post as colonel of the 12th Alabama, but he was the sort of man generally that Bragg despised. First and foremost, O'Hara was overly fond of whiskey, a trait for which Bragg had no tolerance. Further, he was a self-indulgent *bon vivant*, a musician and poet (most notably author of the famous poem "Bivouac of the Dead"), a dandy in dress and manner, a staunch Democrat and ally of Gideon Pillow in his political intrigues of the Mexican War (incurring the disapproval of Regular Army adherents), a foreign adventurer given to Latin American revolutions and filibustering, and of course a journalist, one profession for which Bragg harbored deep mistrust.

Chapter 6. Trouble in Army of Tennessee High Command   89

Despite Breckinridge's denial that any members of his staff had taken part in the criticisms of Bragg's retreat, it was easy for Bragg to assume that O'Hara was really operating with his master's tacit approval.... [I]t was assumed at army headquarters that [Breckinridge] was behind the disaffection in Hardee's corps.... Bragg had convinced himself that Breckinridge was the chief malcontent in the army.[28]

Bragg's report spared Breckinridge nothing, blaming the bloody draw at the Round Forest position on the latter's delay in crossing his brigades over the river on December 31, and censuring him entirely for the failure of January 2. Bragg cooked up evidence against Breckinridge by calling on artillerist Capt. Felix Robertson, who took part in the January 2 attack, to submit a revised report directly to him. Robertson's first report had been generally innocuous, but for the second version Bragg solicited wording that would impugn Breckinridge. Robertson complied. "The report was a 'tissue of lies' from beginning to end.... Robertson himself eventually admitted that he knowingly wrote an incorrect report at Bragg's suggestion."[29]

Robertson's role during the January 2 attack was rather extraordinary on a number of points. An artillery officer in Withers' division whom Peter Cozzens describes as "obsequious," Bragg singled out Robertson on January 1 to conduct a reconnaissance in preparation for the attack, then authorized him to form his battery into an impromptu, independent command. Robertson thus saw himself as a kind of detached freelancer not subject to Breckinridge as commanding officer of the January 2 attack, but rather answerable only to Bragg—he even refused to obey Breckinridge's directions for placing his battery on the day of battle. It is possible that Bragg first learned of Felix Robertson's sycophantic nature during the early days of the war when Bragg commanded at Pensacola and Robertson served there as staff officer to General Gladden. At any rate, the young artillerist certainly proved himself a willing accomplice, going so far as to supply the amended (some would say falsified) battle report at Bragg's behest. The situation was additionally controversial by virtue of Bragg's flouting normal chain-of-command considerations in his interactions with Robertson, who notably served in Polk's corps.[30]

At the same time Bragg used his Murfreesboro report to embarrass and infuriate his enemies, he gave excessive credit to subordinates such as Patton Anderson whom he viewed as loyal to him. Meanwhile, the sensational attack against Breckinridge, disguised as a battle report, was not lost on anyone. When the paperwork arrived in Richmond, Robert Kean of the Confederate War Department commented, "Bragg's report of the battle of Murfreesboro has been received.... It bears hardly on Breckinridge attributing the failure on the right to his blundering. There are deep quarrels in that army, and Bragg is cordially hated by a large number of his officers." Breckinridge was, of course, outraged, particularly after Bragg's Richmond lobbyists had the report published. Ever the statesman, Breckinridge refused to entertain his supporters' calls for him to resign and challenge Bragg to a duel, but he did defend himself in writing to Confederate adjutant general Samuel Cooper and request a court of inquiry. The matter was never addressed, and in May Breckinridge and his Kentucky regiments were transferred out of Bragg's army to Mississippi.[31]

To grasp the import of Bragg's attack on Breckinridge, it is necessary to understand the degree of popularity that Breckinridge enjoyed not only throughout the Confederacy, but even among many in the North from his days as vice president and senator. Perhaps no incident illustrates Breckinridge's esteem more than the reaction of his own beloved Kentucky brigade upon their commander's transfer from the Army of Tennessee:

> Gen'l Breckinridge sent around an order for all the brigade to assemble at brigade Hd. Qrs. at a given signal—that he wished to speak to the "boys." He got up on a stump, and commenced by telling them that he had received orders from Gen'l Bragg ... to hold himself in readiness to move on the cars.... [K]nowing that they would object to making a campaign in a climate so deleterious to health [in Mississippi], especially in the summer season, he had ... request[ed] that the Kentucky troops of his division be permitted to remain with the army of Tennessee, and Mississippi troops be given him instead.... Gen'l Bragg left it to his option whether the Ky. troops would go or stay.... Bragg and Breckinridge had been at "loggerheads" since the battle of Murfreesboro; and the boys felt that if they did not vote to follow their Maj. Gen'l, outsiders would think they also condemned him as well as Bragg, so when the vote was put, they not only held up their right hands, to a man, but cheered loudly.

That his men would risk the deadly summer climate of Mississippi rather than be separated from their commander, speaks volumes of the affection Breckinridge held among his "Orphan Brigade."[32]

Major General John Breckinridge, congressman from Kentucky, vice president of the United States under President John Buchanan and presidential candidate in the fractured 1860 election, incurred Bragg's wrath by failing to wrap up his attack on Baton Rouge, Louisiana, in time to accompany Bragg's army into Kentucky. Imagining that Breckinridge could have brought in thousands of recruits in his native state, Bragg blamed him for the army's failure at Perryville, and again for its defeat at Murfreesboro. Breckinridge went on to serve under Lee in Virginia and ascended to the post of Confederate secretary of war in February 1865, too late for his effective measures to make a difference (Library of Congress).

Breckinridge was not the only victim of the Murfreesboro report. Bragg's censure of General Frank Cheatham also drew a backlash throughout the army. Bragg the teetotaler had been scandalized by rumors of Cheatham's drinking the morning of the battle, and was disgruntled that Polk had not punished Cheatham with any severity. Like Breckinridge, Cheatham enjoyed ample popularity among the troops, especially the soldiers of Tennessee who viewed him as an emblem of pride and manliness. He also had powerful political connections in Richmond. In addition, Randall Gibson, of no small influence himself, took issue with Bragg's unfair portrayal of his performance at Murfreesboro, as he similarly had after Shiloh.

The clamor and controversy over the battle report finally induced Davis to act. In March he dispatched Joseph Johnston back to Tullahoma—no longer suggesting, but *ordering* that he relieve Bragg and take command of the army. However, once Johnston arrived he found Bragg at the bedside of Elise who was desperately ill with typhoid fever. Johnston, like Bragg a devoted husband in a childless marriage, did not have the heart to depose Bragg at such a time. Then when Elise finally recovered, Johnston in turn fell ill and was incapacitated for duty, his condition exacerbated by lingering effects from the wounds he had suffered at the Battle of Seven Pines on the last day of May 1862. In the meantime, Davis sent his trusted aide, a son of the late General Sidney Johnston, to investigate the condition of the Army of Tennessee. When his report came back to Richmond mildly favorable to Bragg, and in the absence of an obvious successor, Davis decided that Bragg would remain in command.

Public Perception and Rumors

During this time controversy swirled around Bragg not only within the army and Richmond political circles. The public also weighed in on the worsening predicament in the West after yet another retreat by the Army of Tennessee, subsequent squabbles troubling the army's high command, and Bragg's Murfreesboro battle report which condemned and insulted popular leaders of men. Particularly with regard to Breckinridge, Bragg won no sympathy in the Southern Confederacy by attacking the former vice president, who

> enjoyed enormous popularity with the public. Almost every faction in the military and government circles respected and admired him. Lee thought very highly of the man.... Beauregard and Johnston thought highly of him, as had Sidney Johnston ... his only bitter enemy in the whole Confederacy seemed to be Bragg.[33]

All of these setbacks and conflicts in Bragg's army generated widespread consternation which compounded after each blow. Two letters written to Polk during that anxious time epitomize a change in public sentiment during the first half of 1863 as Bragg's troubles became known.

The first, dated February 15, 1863 (before the Murfreesboro report), came to Polk's headquarters from Colonel John M. Huger. Huger had served as an aide to General Bragg, but it is difficult to pin down the precise timeframe. He was one of the prominent South Carolina Hugers, and according to his obituary fought in the Second Seminole War in 1835 with the rank of major. At some point he moved

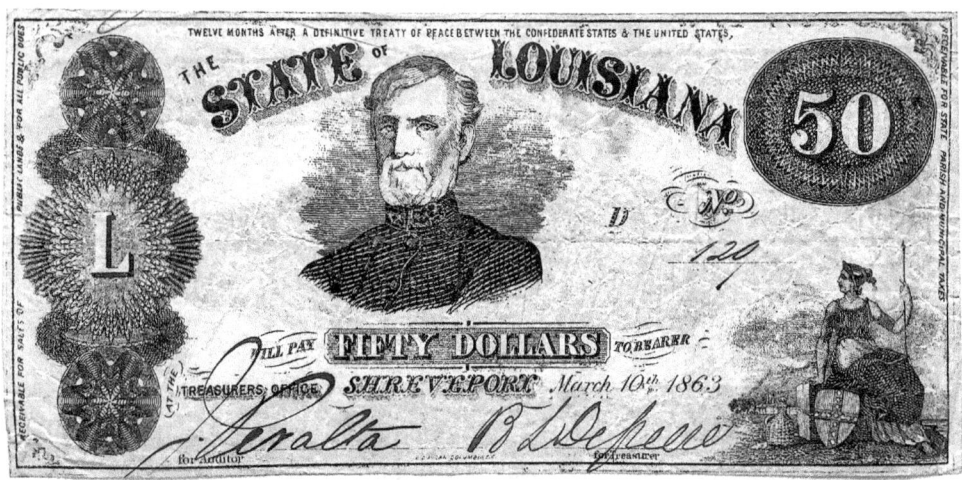

A $50 State of Louisiana note bearing Polk's image is evidence of the high regard in which the general was held in his adoptive state (photograph by the author).

to Louisiana where he operated two sugar plantations and formed a close friendship with the Polks. After the fall of Nashville early in 1862, two of Polk's daughters resided in the Huger family home in New Orleans as refugees, and a few weeks before Polk's death in 1864, Huger's son William would marry Polk's daughter Elizabeth. Huger waged frequent personal campaigns by correspondence. For example, on July 30, 1862, he wrote President Davis from Mobile urging the easy recapture of New Orleans. This letter was likely not well received in that it recommended General Beauregard, Davis's enemy whom he had recently relieved, as the potential hero of the operation.[34]

At the time of the February 1863 letter to Polk, Colonel Huger was traveling with his wounded son William, a first lieutenant with the 1st Louisiana Infantry, to place him "in his mother's safe keeping in Mobile," then planned to return to Richmond "on private business." Presumably, then, at the time of the letter he was not serving in a military capacity, and indeed seemed to be estranged from Bragg whom he "frankly admit[s]" having "wronged" in some manner. Whatever might have occurred between the two, he staunchly maintained loyalty toward Bragg, and later returned to his position as aide-de-camp to Bragg when the latter served as advisor to Jefferson Davis in Richmond. (A roster of "President Davis' military family" compiled by a Confederate artillery officer includes Huger listed alongside Bragg aides colonels Chesnut and William Preston.) Biographer McWhiney, however, describes Huger simply as a civilian. He likely rotated on and off duty at will, as was often the case with volunteer aides.[35]

In his letter Huger first touches on his disillusionment brought about by Bragg's foray into Kentucky and the subsequent Battle of Murfreesboro:

> It grieves me beyond expression, to hear from all quarters the unqualified disapproval of my chief's conduct on the occasion. I thought him wrong when he crossed the Cumberland and

Chapter 6. Trouble in Army of Tennessee High Command

left Buell in Nashville, … but I love justice and would gladly know the truth. From commanders of divisions to privates, I heard of his want of soldierly qualifications in the battle of Murfreesboro until I turned away heart sick from disappointment that he had crushed my hope that he might be <u>the Man of the Occasion</u> as I had once thought him.

In spite of these sentiments, however, Huger does not give up on Bragg. Upon reflection he concludes that he and others have judged Bragg too harshly, and he implores Polk on Bragg's behalf to set the record straight. The language he employs, appealing to a sense of justice and truth, demonstrates that he knows Polk well:

> The mist of prejudice is now somewhat dispelled, and my hope revived, and I look to you to assist in raising the vail [sic] and letting the public see the truth—you will not—you <u>cannot</u> refuse your aid to dispel an error and ward off a wrong from a meritorious public servant—it is a necessity of your nature to seek the truth, and as a corollary, the necessity to do justice must be imperative to an equal degree. Now, as I frankly admit that I have wronged a noble warrior who has risked every thing in the cause of his country, property—life—honor, I call upon you to lend me assistance in wiping out an impression from the public mind unjust as it is injurious to Genl Bragg, and not less harmful to the noble cause which has made us all willing victims at the altar of patriotism.

Still perhaps slightly in doubt as to the truth himself, Huger next begs Polk to write him and provide his "opinion in reference to the recent battle" which he trusts will "roll back the wave of popular error … which now dims the bright shield of your brother warrior." The armor had begun to crack ever so slightly, but this Bragg supporter cannot bring himself to believe it, and calls on Polk to shore up his and the public's shaky hope. The letter having come when the furor over Bragg's first circular letter had died down, and before the appearance of his objectionable Murfreesboro report, Huger may have found at this point a receptive audience in Polk.[36]

The second letter was written by another in-law to Polk. William D. Gale had married Polk's daughter Katherine in 1858 and served on his father-in-law's staff. Also like Huger, this letter written by a mobile correspondent similarly conveyed the pulse of the public picked up along his journey.

By late March 1863 Bragg's official report on Murfreesboro had hit Richmond with a storm which newspapers quickly spread throughout the Confederacy. On the 27th of the same month Gale found himself laid over in Atlanta "on account of a smash up" on the railroad. In his letter he reflects on the repercussions of Bragg's battle report:

> I heard in Chattanooga that Genl Breckinridge had certainly sent in his resignation, as soon as he heard of the manner in which he had been censured in the report of the comdg. Genl, but that Genl Johnston had induced him to withdraw it.

He continues to relate Richmond rumors riding the rails:

> I have just seen an officer who left Richmond four days since. He says he heard thro' Genl Henry + Senator Foote + others that Genl Bragg had been telegraphed to go to the capital and was expected last Sunday.… Genl Bragg's report was much talked off [of] and had created quite a commotion in army + political circles. This officer says Genl Henry informed him that Genl Bragg censured Genls Breckinridge, Cheatham + McCown, the first he charges

with having disobeyed positive orders on three different occasions, the 2nd he says did not do his duty and the last was also charged with some act of insubordination. This has raised a storm in congress.... General Henry says, however, that Genl Bragg will not be removed. Others speak with equal confidence of his being retired at an early day and say that is the object of his being ordered to Richmond at this time.... I venture to predict his certain removal. His Report has done the work, which is the <u>2nd most unfortunate document that has emanated from his pen</u>. The Ky and Tenn interests combined will do that which neither could separately.... There is great talk of sending Genl Hood + his division to Tenn—He is willing to come but Genl Lee says no....

(One wonders what Gale considered Bragg's *first* most unfortunate document—the January circular letter?)[37]

This letter, in comparison with the first, clearly sets forth how much the situation had deteriorated in a mere six weeks. Gale describes a commander who has declared war on his own generals, a pattern which continued unabated until Bragg would be relieved of his command eight months later. By now the truth of Bragg's vendetta mindset had come out in the open for all to see. No longer does the writer appeal to Polk to smooth things over and avoid harm "to the noble cause" as Huger had begged. He simply reports the disaster that he believes will surely end Bragg's career, and one imagines the bishop shaking his head sadly at the spectacle. (Gale's mention of Hood is ironically prophetic since Bragg would be instrumental in placing him in command of the Army of Tennessee the following year.)

Both letters provide an objective and revealing picture of how the prevailing public perception of Bragg rapidly disintegrated during the spring of 1863. Additionally, they demonstrate that the uproar over General Bragg did not involve any alleged scheming on the part of Leonidas Polk. The first writer saw Polk in quite the opposite role: Bragg had been misjudged and Polk could rehabilitate his image. But by the time the Murfreesboro report was released Bragg's habitual disputes with his subordinates had spilled out way beyond the close circle of army command, and were reverberating throughout the Confederacy. The second letter evinces the truth that the general commanding was doing a highly effective job of stirring up conflict all by himself, with Polk and his staff in the role of incredulous spectators.

Braxton Bragg's private war against his generals germinated in his own mind. But what started it? Clearly a false newspaper report was the catalyst that led to the January 11 round-robin letter. When that attempt to absolve himself backfired, Bragg's efforts at damage control brought him to a kind of turning point, as set forth in a letter he wrote to Jefferson Davis in late February. To the president he resolved: "Assailed myself, for the blunders of others, and by them and their friends, my mind is made up *to bear no sins in the future* but my own."[38] His mind "made up," he would no longer assume blame for others' wrongs, only his own. But because he virtually never acknowledged any wrongdoing on his part, the net effect was that Bragg would let himself off the hook from then on. He willfully and consciously adopted this skewed viewpoint as policy. From that date forward his program would be to argue his case by assailing fellow officers, as he quickly demonstrated in the Murfreesboro battle report. Bragg's own "report has done the work," observed Gale. This attack and those that followed can hardly be pinned on Polk, nor did they target only him, but instead vectored out in many directions. Bragg was like a man out of control, punching and hitting with abandon.

April 13 Circular Letter

After Bragg survived in command of the Army of Tennessee, he would not content himself with this narrow victory over his enemies, but pursued them anew. Not one to quit while he was ahead, incredibly he issued another circular letter, this time targeting Polk's "disobedience of orders" leading up to the battle of Perryville in October. Bragg sent this April 13 letter to the brigade, division and corps commanders who had participated in Polk's councils of war in Kentucky. While Bragg was absent from the army on a political mission in the state capital, Polk had convened two or three such conferences to seek input as he attempted to reconcile the disparity between the situation developing on their front and Bragg's ever-changing orders. (The specific orders, as listed in Chapter 4, and Polk's decisions regarding them, will be analyzed in Chapter 7.) Bragg's new circular accused Polk's subordinates of "advising a disobedience to my orders" and demanded that they "inform me to what extent you sustained [Polk] in his acknowledged disobedience." The edict amounted to nothing more than a trap crafted to indict not only Polk, but eventually the letter's recipients, of insubordination—i.e., they were expected to testify against themselves! Most refused to respond.[39]

It is hard to imagine how Bragg justified to himself the convoluted mess he was creating. Rather than simply bring charges against Polk for disobeying his orders, if that is what he believed occurred, he took the approach of corralling eight generals and threatening *them* to lodge charges! This scheme of Bragg's reveals a man in manic mode propelling his army into escalating crisis. The only results Bragg achieved were destructive, forcing his subordinates onto the defensive and uniting them firmly against him. Both sides, now entrenched, then took the fight outside the army by aligning with allies in the Confederate Congress, further putrefying relations within the army's command structure.

Why did Bragg make this incredible choice: to issue a highly irregular communiqué to subordinates, *again,* after a similar measure in January almost cost him his command? Historians continue to puzzle over this question, but perhaps an answer has emerged through a little-known historic document that has come to light.

It was not in Polk's nature to stand by passively when faced with an injustice committed against a fellow, honorable officer. When Bragg used his Murfreesboro battle report to slander Breckinridge, Polk evidently did some investigating on his own. A note from Polk (in his atrocious handwriting) to Breckinridge, dated April 2, 1863, not housed in any institutional collection but published online and sold to a private collector, seems to explain what drove Bragg to his April 13 inquisition. Although it is unlikely that either the purveyor or buyer grasped the significance of this correspondence, it solves a longstanding historical mystery. In the note Polk transmits a copy of Felix Robertson's first Murfreesboro report to Breckinridge and indignantly declares that "[i]t is not the paper I asked Capt Robertson to send me. And I thought myself very explicit in asking him for the report you wished—his report to General Bragg. I have promptly asked him for a copy of *that* report." Polk was apparently onto the fact that there were *two* reports made out by Felix Robertson: the routine post-battle report, and a later one elicited by Bragg which was sent directly and covertly to him, and differed from the first report by casting Breckinridge unfavorably.[40]

Some might argue that Polk stepped out of line by poking into the compilation of his commanding general's battle report. But Polk had every right to probe into this discrepancy. Robertson was Polk's subordinate: an artillery captain in his corps assigned to Withers' division, Loomis's brigade (commanded by Col. Coltart upon Loomis's wounding). Therefore, Polk's "request" to Robertson rightfully should have been taken as an order. Polk's irritation over Robertson's evasive bait-and-switch, in which he furnished another copy of the report that his corps commander already had while withholding the one clearly requested, as well as Polk's determination to get to the bottom of the matter, come across clearly in the note to Breckinridge. Just as Col. Huger

Polk's April 2, 1863, note to Breckinridge concerning his investigation into artillerist Felix Robertson's second report on the Battle of Murfreesboro. Historians have puzzled over why Bragg again resorted to a bombshell circular letter after the first one almost got him fired. This little note reveals Bragg's motive: he undoubtedly learned of Polk's probing into the matter, and went on the attack to distract from his own duplicity and breach of military protocol (photograph by Heritage Auctions: HA.com).

had urged, Polk was working to uncover the truth—but the truth was not exonerating Bragg as Huger hoped.

Robertson surely reported to Bragg, probably in a panic, that Polk was hounding him for a copy of his second report which had gone only to Bragg rather than through the normal chain of command ("that report"; "his report to General Bragg"). The irregularity of the secret, revised report and the possibility of their scheme being uncovered had to make both Robertson and Bragg nervous. It would seem that Polk's short, quickly scribbled note provides the key to what happened next: the puzzle piece that explains why Bragg took the extraordinary, desperate action of sending out another controversial circular to his subordinates. Contrary to historians' rumination on the subject, the April 13 letter did not come out of the blue, and Bragg's motive for issuing it is no longer inexplicable. Exactly as he had resolved in his letter to President Davis, Bragg would never again accept blame, but instead chose to go into attack mode. Threatened by Polk's scrutiny (evidenced by the April 2 note), Bragg turned away from his Breckinridge vendetta and focused his full fury upon Polk.

Historians routinely accuse Polk of instigating the feud with Bragg. But this sequence of events suggests that Polk was merely responding to Bragg's incriminating action. Nevertheless, rather than hold him accountable for violations of military protocol in compiling his Murfreesboro battle report, as well as his bizarre April 13 letter, some of these same historians sympathize with Bragg. Admittedly, most mildly concede Bragg's poor judgment in vindictively attacking subordinates within battle reports and issuing provocative circular letters. Yet they resoundingly attribute Bragg's mounting troubles to his lieutenants, first for their alleged failure to support him adequately, then by charging that Polk and others *drove* Bragg to extreme measures. These historians accuse Polk of diabolically conniving against Bragg, yet during this time the latter showed a marked predilection of his own for plotting and manipulating against men of his own camp whom he perceived as enemies.

What was Bragg's object in issuing the second circular letter? First, it was a simple case of overreaction. Constitutionally unable to let issues drop, Bragg obsessed over media criticism following Murfreesboro to such a degree that he circulated the January 11 letter. Now, the public uproar over Bragg's published Murfreesboro battle report, plus the news that Polk was sniffing around and inquiring into Felix Robertson's questionable role in that report, generated another cycle of obsession and overreaction, culminating with Bragg's April 13 letter.

Secondly, the objective of the April circular was to gather incriminating material for a second report on the Battle of Perryville. Bragg was on a roll. The brief report he had filed immediately following Perryville paled in comparison to his Murfreesboro epic. Creating a full-blown narrative of the Kentucky battle provided an opportunity for him to rehash the unresolved issues from the campaign that had brought to bear against him, and would hopefully rehabilitate his image.

Finally, in his February 27 letter to Jefferson Davis, Bragg himself stated his motive for lashing out: "Assailed myself, for the blunders of others, … my mind is made up to bear no sins in the future but my own." Bragg believed he had shouldered blame that should have fallen on others. In his mind, he had quietly borne their "sins"—but would do so no longer. Now he would hit before he got hit. Bragg determined to pin all accusations and wrongdoing upon his subordinates. And his next target would be Polk.

Elise was present with her husband during this time, thus there are no letters to reveal what influence she might have wielded by steering her husband to set his sights on the bishop. Since the beginning of the war she and Bragg had nursed a protracted resentment and disdain for Polk. Now that Bragg's excoriation of Breckinridge had run its course, perhaps it was she who redirected his ire toward Polk by pinpointing him as Bragg's true enemy within the ranks.

As occurred in the wake of the first circular letter, voices of reason attempted to persuade Bragg to back off from his new vendetta. One of the recipients of the April 13 circular, General Simon Bolivar Buckner, refused to reply directly to the interrogation contained in the letter, but instead answered with a plea that Bragg make allowances for errors that inevitably occur in war. Buckner appealed to Bragg that

> whatever opinion about the Kentucky campaign might prevail among the general officers "you were sustained in your authority by the whole weight of your character." He begged for an effort on Bragg's part to remove the accumulated asperities by frank personal explanation. Having been upheld by the Government, General Buckner thought that Bragg ought to be satisfied and take a course which without any sacrifice of his own dignity would "redound so much to the advantage of the Republic."[41]

This appeal went nowhere because "advantage to the Republic" was no longer Bragg's priority. Now his supreme focus was on vindicating himself and punishing those who questioned his fitness to command. Ironically, his very actions brought his fitness into question.

General Bragg, albeit lacking the supportive evidence he sought from subordinates, submitted his lengthy, revised Perryville report under date of May 20, 1863. His initial report, written within days after the battle, had praised Polk, Hardee and others; to them was "mainly due the brilliant achievements of this memorable field. Nobler troops were never more gallantly led. The country owes them a debt of gratitude." The revised report contained no such encomium for any generals but torturously detailed Bragg's self-serving account of Polk's alleged failures to obey his orders and accomplish his designs.[42]

During the time that these ugly conflicts roiled the army's senior command and rippled through the ranks, a miracle happened which must have gladdened Polk's heart: Bragg found religion.

> Bragg was so busy that he ordered his staff not to disturb him. But on June 1, a caller arrived at his doorstep, and insisted on seeing the general. "It is a matter of life and death," he claimed. The sentry guarding the headquarters tent went inside, delivered this message to Bragg, and

Chapter 6. Trouble in Army of Tennessee High Command

was told to bring the visitor to him. Bragg immediately recognized Episcopal chaplain Charles Quintard.

"What can I do for you?" Bragg said coldly, "I am quite busy, as you can see."

Quintard, well aware that Bragg had a reputation of "being so stern and so sharp in his sarcasm that many men were afraid to go near him," stammered while explaining his purpose for coming to Bragg. He had come to save his soul. Quintard was so scared, he could not bring himself to look directly at the general. "I fixed my eyes upon a knothole in the pine board floor," he admitted later, "and talked about our Blessed Lord, about the responsibilities of a man in [his] position." When Quintard glanced up, he saw "tears in the General's eyes, and [I] took courage to ask him to be confirmed."

Bragg rushed up to Quintard and took hold of both his hands. "I have been waiting twenty years to have someone say this to me," he cried. "Certainly I shall be confirmed if you will give me the necessary instruction."[43]

Dr. Charles Todd Quintard was a medical doctor and Episcopal priest who served as chaplain to the 1st Tennessee Infantry Regiment, and stepped in as a surgeon when needed. During the Atlanta campaign he helped found St. Luke's Episcopal Church, fittingly named for the disciple who was also a physician. After the war Quintard became bishop of Tennessee and fulfilled Polk's vision for the University of the South by bringing to pass its opening in 1868 (photograph by Mathew Brady, Library of Congress).

In June 1863 Bragg was baptized in the Episcopal rite at the Shelbyville First Presbyterian Church. Lieutenant Colonel Arthur Fremantle, an observer from the British army, witnessed the ceremony performed by Bishop Stephen Elliott of Georgia who happened to be visiting the army at the time. "Immediately afterwards he confirmed General Bragg, who then shook hands with General Polk, the officers of their respective staffs, and myself [Fremantle], who were the only spectators." In spite of everything to that point, the cleansing and renewal of holy water did seem, for a time thereafter, to quell the strife dividing Bragg and Polk.[44]

CHAPTER 7

Was Polk Insubordinate?

One of the main charges brought against General Polk by Bragg, echoed by numerous historians, is his alleged failure to follow the orders of his superior officer. Authors such as Steven Woodworth, James McDonough and others excoriate Polk for disobedience and intransigence. Bragg's biographer Grady McWhiney even supplies an explanation for Polk's supposed defiance, postulating that "Polk probably had been a bishop too long to be a successful subordinate."[1] This theory not only expresses a dim view of the clerical vocation (not surprising in a 20th-century academic), but a misunderstanding of it as well. A church leader of the 19th century, although accorded reverent respect, was also perceived as, and expected to act with the heart of, a servant. Contrary to McWhiney's notion, a bishop should ideally make the finest subordinate, for he is in the habit of yielding his personal will to God and devoting his time and effort to the service of his church. Submission is a way of life for him.

More importantly, Polk's critics avoid examining whether Polk's so-called disobedience turned out to be the correct course in any instance. Perhaps they assume such an outcome as irrelevant ("orders are orders") or impossible with regard to Polk, by definition an "incompetent" and therefore never correct. The general, in their view, was rigidly bound to follow orders, right or wrong, without question.

While such is indeed the case for enlisted men and noncommissioned, company, and field-grade officers, on the other hand a corps or division (and in certain situations brigade) commander, while certainly beholden to the orders of a superior, is equally encumbered with a duty to assess the situation on the ground in front of him. Particularly when the commander is not on the scene (as Bragg was not in each case) and written orders no longer comport with a fluid situation, a general must not blindly obey the inapplicable order but should adjust it to fit the conditions at hand. Otherwise a disaster, which might have been easily avoided, can result. For example, consider how upset was General Lee at John Magruder for advancing on Malvern Hill with tragic results. Afterwards Lee implored him, "General Magruder, why did you attack?" Magruder replied, "In obedience to your orders, twice repeated." But Lee's orders were based on faulty intelligence, as were Bragg's at Perryville.

General Thomas Wood serves as another notorious example of a general obeying an order which contradicted the reality confronting him at Chickamauga on

September 20, 1863. The result was a complete rout, but in this case his superiors, General Rosecrans and General Thomas Crittenden, bore the consequences.

There is a caveat in situations when a high-ranking subordinate on the field perceives an imperative to deviate from orders. The field commander is then duty-bound to inform his superior promptly with a thorough explanation. If there is any phase in the process where Polk can be faulted, this is it. His inadequate and vague messages forwarded to Bragg at times contributed to confusion rather than allay it. Communications were chronically dysfunctional throughout Bragg's command structure.

Some historians seemingly begin with the premise that Polk was in the wrong, then radiate outward from that preconception to interpret the facts. On occasion Polk did not adhere to the letter of orders given him, but this does not mean he was in the wrong. Four such instances occurred: two will be examined in this chapter and the remaining two, which occurred before and during the Battle of Chickamauga, in Chapter 8. The first incident took place during the lead-up to the Battle of Perryville, Kentucky, in October 1862.

Bardstown

The situation was this: At the end of September and first days of October 1862, General Buell, commanding approximately 80,000, advanced his army from Louisville, Kentucky, toward Bragg's dispersed force. A diversionary column of 20,000 under General Joshua Sill moved toward Frankfort, where Bragg had traveled with Kirby Smith and a coterie of generals and VIPs to install the Confederate governor, Richard Hawes. While away, Bragg left Polk in command of the army at Bardstown. Bragg mistakenly believed that Buell's entire army, rather than Sill's smaller force, approached him at Frankfort, and with Kirby Smith's army on hand he thought he saw an opportunity. On October 2 Bragg ordered Polk's force at Bardstown to move northward quickly and destroy Buell's columns in flank while Kirby Smith would attack from the front. Unfortunately, Bragg failed to understand that the bulk of the Union advance was in fact not directed at his and Kirby Smith's front. Instead, marching on parallel roads, three Union corps—Gilbert's, Crittenden's and McCook's—threatened Polk in *his* front at Bardstown, as Polk informed Bragg by dispatch dated October 2. Therefore, if Polk were to march northward per Bragg's order, it would have been *his* flank that would be destroyed—by the three Federal corps advancing on him. Polk replied that he would strike one of Buell's isolated columns, if presented with an opportunity, but if attack was "inexpedient" he would fall back. This was a reference to a previous order ("suggestion") given when Bragg departed for Frankfort, which *directed Polk to fall back eastward in the event he was faced with an overwhelming force*, in order to protect the main Confederate supply depot near Bryantsville. (The supply depot was located at the former Federal Camp

Dick Robinson, which the Confederates renamed Camp Breckinridge.) Bragg's initial report on the battle endorses Polk's decision: in his October 12 dispatch to General Samuel Cooper, adjutant general of the Confederate States Army, Bragg stated, "General Polk was at the same time heavily pressed at Bardstown, and he, *in accordance with previous orders*, fell back toward Harrodsburg."[2]

Faced with the majority of Buell's army moving rapidly toward him, Polk consulted with Hardee and his division commanders, and determined that they must disregard Bragg's October 2 order to march northward. Instead they would comply with the earlier directive to fall back. This decision to disobey Bragg's October 2 order, point (2) as enumerated in Chapter 4, grew into a contentious issue between the two generals during spring of the following year as their relationship, and Bragg's grip on his command, began to deteriorate. In addition, the controversy has fueled anti–Polk diatribes in the writings of many historians since that time.

As it turns out, the entire question is in fact moot, for Bragg countermanded the October 2 order even before he received word from Polk advising of his retreat.[3] But that fact has not extinguished the flames surrounding the issue and Polk continues to be branded an insubordinate. Therefore, the question should be examined thoroughly.

Inauguration ceremonies at the Kentucky capital took place on October 4, 1862. While bands played, the Confederate flag flew atop the Capitol and Governor Hawes delivered his speech in a pouring rain until ominous artillery fire erupted on the horizon, bringing the festivities to a premature end. Bragg quickly departed the truncated ceremonies to return to his army, during which time he remained confused about the true positions and strengths of Buell's columns. He ordered Polk to Harrodsburg and traveled there himself, arriving on October 5.

Although it was Bragg's intention to combine his force with Kirby Smith's Army of Kentucky and bring battle against Buell, Kirby Smith insisted on remaining north of the Kentucky River, away from Polk's position. Smith added to Bragg's confusion by sending contradictory reports throughout October 6 that Buell was then concentrating at *his* front, and pleading for help. He was mistaken; Buell's force was moving rapidly to the rear of Polk and Hardee's eastward march, so closely that when the Confederates halted at Perryville the armies collided in the massive, vicious battle of October 8.

Much has been made of Polk's refraining from making the flank attack ordered in Bragg's (remanded) October 2 dispatch. McDonough theorizes that "it is entirely possible that Polk's failure to move on October 3, as Bragg had instructed, cost the Confederates a victory." Steven Woodworth, in his caustic manner, scolds: "Bragg had sent Polk an order to attack, and that should have been straightforward enough. Apparently, it was not. Besides being a basically incompetent general, Polk had the added fault of hating to take orders…. Polk's disobedience probably cost the army a victory." He goes on to lambaste "the culprit" Polk for "obstinacy" and a mysterious, bewitching mesmerism which put his subordinates "thoroughly under his spell," "the plodding Hardee" "completely in the thrall of Polk." How convenient to postulate an imaginary, would-be victory, then condemn that troublemaker Polk for sabotaging it![4]

One might surmise that Woodworth's and McDonough's opinions are predicated upon the theory of Civil War authority Herman Hattaway and co-author Archer Jones:

> On October 2 Bragg ordered Leonidas Polk to move his corps north to Frankfort to attack the enemy there in flank while Kirby Smith attacked the front. Bragg's plan for a bold Napoleonic concentration unfortunately was based upon faulty intelligence, but nevertheless could have achieved a brilliant partial success had Polk moved rapidly as ordered, [but he] decided on his own to retreat to Danville.[5]

There are fundamental problems with this analysis. First is the dubious idea that any plan "based upon faulty intelligence" has much of a chance for success. Then, there is the oxymoron "a brilliant partial success." Is any partial success brilliant? Is any brilliant success partial? Should a general march his army to its likely doom in blind obedience to an order?

Presumably the authors qualify Bragg's would-be success as partial because the hypothetical victory would have been won only over Sill's column, a mere fraction of Buell's army. In fact, Sill's force was sent as a diversion in the *hope* of distracting and engaging the enemy away from Buell's main advance and his primary purpose of gaining Bragg's rear, isolating him and cutting him off from his supply base and retreat route. Had Polk moved Bragg's army northward as ordered, not only would the left flank of his columns, vulnerable in transit, have invited certain attack by McCook's advancing corps, but Polk's move would have left the Confederate supply depot at Camp Breckinridge wide open to Buell's advancing hordes even with a guard detachment posted there. The latter factor is of major importance, as the difficulty in procuring rations proved an Achilles' heel during Bragg's entire foray into Kentucky. At decisive junctures during the campaign, such as Bragg's decision of September 19 not to take a stand against Buell at Munfordville, the army's supply shortage played a major role.[6]

Finally, Hattaway and Jones assert inaccurately that Polk "decided *on his own* to retreat to Danville." As noted earlier, Bragg's orders to Polk upon leaving him in temporary command at Bardstown included a provision that Polk should fall back eastward toward Bryantsville if confronted with an overwhelming force. The greater portion of Buell's command menacing Polk, numbering at least 55,000, could certainly be considered an overwhelming force. Therefore, Polk was not "acting on his own" as Hattaway and Jones contend; instead, he was proceeding in accordance with the orders of his commanding officer under the very conditions specified by said orders. When he left his army under Polk's temporary command Bragg correctly anticipated the possibility of just such a contingency, and Polk correctly complied with the order when the contingency materialized.[7]

Woodworth and McDonough neglect to address these underlying issues; they expand on Hattaway and Jones's "brilliant partial success" by hypothesizing a squandered "victory"—nothing partial about it in their minds, but a sure and glorious win forever forfeited by the incompetent Polk.

Other authorities defend Polk's judgment call, relying on reality rather than speculation. Of Bragg's October 2 order, Stanley F. Horn writes:

> Now he [Bragg] ordered him [Polk] to move on Frankfort by way of Bloomfield to strike Buell's flank and rear while Kirby Smith attacked in front. The theory was entirely erroneous. *Polk, fortunately for the safety of the army,* took the liberty of disobeying orders. He felt himself pressed so closely on his own front that it was out of the question for him to do anything except fall back slowly before the superior force, in line with the original instructions.

Connelly agrees, explaining that Polk was threatened by "the Yankee advance on the Mount Washington Road within twelve miles of Bardstown, and a heavy force in line of battle pushing up the Shepherdsville road." At this same time "Polk received Bragg's order to make the flank attack. It was obvious that Bragg did not understand the situation.... *Polk's decision was a necessary one.* His position at Bardstown was collapsing, and he certainly could not move north as requested."[8]

Horn and Connelly state the situation as it was, not as it might have been. General Hardee said it most succinctly: "Had Polk followed Bragg's order at Bardstown, the army would have been destroyed." There will always be different opinions but, in particular, Woodworth's emphatic, exaggerated personal denunciations bring into question his point of view. He subjects his readers to such a continuous stream of derogatory descriptions and digs that one concludes that he rarely if ever has anything positive to say about any leader on the Southern side. For example, as to the appearance of General Joseph Johnston, universally described as impeccably groomed and having an impressive bearing, Woodworth offers only this snide remark: "In appearance Johnston was short and bald," and then continues with a correspondingly dour assessment of his personal qualities. Everyone has his faults, but to Dr. Woodworth it seems that Southern generals, especially Leonidas Polk, were riddled with them. Rather than bolster his position, excessive, serial sarcasm brings into question an author's objectivity.[9]

Perryville

Polk opted to override another order when the Battle of Perryville opened. While he pulled Bragg's army back toward Harrodsburg as Buell advanced, Hardee's corps, nipped at the heels by the III Corps of newly minted General Gilbert, halted in Perryville for two reasons. First and foremost was a dire need of water. Kentucky suffered that season under a severe drought that dried up streams and wells, and armies marching amidst clouds of dust thrown up by thousands of feet, hooves and wheels could not go far without hydration. Doctor's Creek near Perryville promised a flow of the vital liquid. The Federals, close behind and equally desperate for water, skirmished unsuccessfully against General Wheeler's rear guard in an attempt to reach the few watery pools under the full moon of October 7.

The question that arises at Perryville on October 7 is set forth as issue (3) in Chapter 4: whether Polk was at fault for allegedly disobeying Bragg's October 7 order that Polk "give the enemy battle immediately, rout him," then move on Versailles where Bragg believed the climactic battle of Kentucky would be fought. He still believed that the force advancing on Frankfort comprised the bulk of Buell's army, which he and Kirby Smith would draw back to Versailles. Whatever columns Polk faced in the meantime, Bragg thought, were negligible and could be easily and quickly brushed aside. In a follow-up communiqué, Bragg ordered Polk and Hardee to march to Versailles, unite with Kirby Smith, "strike a blow," and defeat the Federals.[10] The only problem with this scenario was that the enemy was nowhere near Versailles!

Meanwhile, Hardee, always with an eye for favorable terrain, saw some advantages to the ground surrounding Perryville. Aware of a large force amassing across the riverbed, he "appealed to Bragg for reinforcements. In response, Bragg late in the afternoon of the seventh directed Polk to divide his corps and move with Cheatham's division to Hardee's relief, while Withers's division should continue on its way to Versailles. As noted, Bragg instructed Polk to 'give the enemy battle immediately' at Perryville." Clearly, Bragg gave little thought to Perryville, a minor inconvenience in the scheme of his grand plan. In his mind Polk could quickly rout the small Federal force believed to be there. By the following morning of October 8, "Polk, now in command of the Confederate force at Perryville, had taken a good position on a ridge along the east side of Chaplin Fork, slightly in advance of the town, with his three divisions arrayed from right to left under Buckner, Patton Anderson, and Cheatham, respectively."[11]

Admittedly neither Polk nor Hardee, and certainly not Bragg, had any sure idea of the magnitude of the Union force before Perryville, at least not initially. Bragg, partly relying on intelligence from Kirby Smith, still believed that the lion's share of the Yankee force marched in the latter's direction far north of Perryville, and on October 7 announced to his staff that "at Versailles [where Kirby Smith had ostensibly agreed to concentrate with Bragg] would occur the great battle for Kentucky." Bragg was certain that Hardee and Polk could easily defeat the small force on their front in the meantime, then rapidly join him in Versailles for the real action.[12]

On October 8 some fighting occurred west of Perryville in the early morning hours as several Union regiments took Peter's Hill, previously occupied by the 7th Arkansas. Believing themselves outnumbered, the Yankees held back from pressing forward any farther, giving the Southerners time to form a new line. Nevertheless, vastly outnumbered, the Arkansans had to give up their position. The fight served to enlighten Polk as to the extent of the force that he faced, giving him pause concerning Bragg's order to "attack immediately." But just that morning he had dispatched a message to his commander, assuring him, "Understanding it to be your wish to give them battle we shall do so vigorously." Kenneth Noe explains Polk's dilemma:

Not long after dispatching the report, Polk rode out to examine the rough line of battle his subordinates had laid down in the darkness of the night before. What he saw shook him. For the first time, Polk dimly perceived the reality of his army's task. A large Federal force, at least a corps, lay beyond his lines west of the river. To cross the dry riverbed and attack such a host with three outnumbered and below strength divisions seemed inadvisable to say the least. Yet Bragg, unaware that most of Buell's army lay in wait at Perryville, had ordered just such an assault. Such orders, Polk concluded, should not—could not—be obeyed.... Polk resolved "to adopt the defensive-offensive, to await the movements of the enemy, and to be guided by events as they developed."[13]

Polk did decide to move his force across Chaplin River to secure a better position from which to move them into battle at such time that it became advisable or necessary. But the execution was slow, and the Federals filed into their lines at a leisurely pace as well. Other than the early morning engagement at Peter's Hill, by noon still no fighting had taken place.

Bragg, hearing no sounds of battle from his headquarters at Harrodsburg, in spite of his attack order and Polk's enthusiastic response, galloped to Perryville. Disgusted with Polk's reticence, he took command and set about preparing for the immediate attack he had ordered.

And how Polk's command did fight! A hardened veteran from Tennessee later described the charge of Polk's corps as "the most desperate charge in Kentucky during the Civil War," and Perryville "one of the most intense battles of the entire conflict."[14]

Nevertheless, once again an order had gone disregarded and disobeyed by that stubborn Polk! Was Polk in fact an irresponsible, defiant subordinate as some say, indifferent to the will of his commander? One historian who would answer in the affirmative is Steven Woodworth, never one to miss an opportunity for lame sarcasm:

> Bragg's orders called for Polk to use Hardee's troops to destroy whatever enemy force they confronted early the next morning, but as usual Polk was slow to obey. Though Bragg's order had used the word "immediately," Polk would later excuse his disobedience on the ground that it was not really clear what was meant by the term.[15]

James McDonough cites another explanation also hinging on the interpretation of a different, single word: "Polk claimed that he never disobeyed Bragg's order. His reasoning was that Bragg had told him to move with his whole 'available' force, and that, 'since the largest part of Buell's army' was in 'my immediate front,' there were simply 'no troops available.'" McWhiney uses the controversy to take a shot at Polk's religious vocation: Polk's "available force" rationalization, he writes, was "the argument of a bishop, not a general." Obviously neither Woodworth, McDonough nor McWhiney conceded any validity to Polk's decisions.[16]

In the midst of scolding Polk for his alleged disobedience, these analysts overlook the potentially disastrous outcome had Polk obeyed Bragg's order to attack "immediately." Dangerously outnumbered, the Confederates had already obtained a taste of what lay ahead when Liddell's Arkansans were pushed back by the aggressive

Sheridan. Fortunately, General Gilbert called off Sheridan from advancing further. The success that the Confederate army achieved on October 8 occurred only because the Federals, in spite of their superior numbers, remained oddly hesitant. One reason for Buell's reticence lay in his own misunderstanding of the size of the Confederate force before him: he believed he faced Bragg's entire army. Thus, had Polk attacked first thing in the morning, the Federals would likely have exhibited great fierceness, for believing themselves outnumbered, like a cornered animal they would have been fighting for their very survival! As it turned out, the Confederates' attack later in the day lulled Buell into dismissing it as a minor action, and Buell advanced little more than one of his three corps. The Federals' all-out attack came much later, not until 4:00. Before that time Buell, neither expecting nor even hearing the battle due to an acoustic shadow, failed to direct his forces effectively.

Another factor would have been in operation had Polk followed the letter of Bragg's order and attacked on time, i.e., at dawn. It is unknown whether the acoustic shadow that prevented Buell from hearing the battle would have been in place that morning, as wind direction or other factors that cause this phenomenon might have differed hours earlier. But assuming that a morning acoustic shadow hindered his awareness of the battle in the same way that it did later in the day, once sufficient reports reached him and convinced him of its magnitude Buell would have come alive to the fight much earlier, still in the late morning. Therefore, he would have had many more hours of daylight to throw his entire host against Bragg. The Confederates fought like tigers, it is true—but they got out of this battle primarily because of Buell's atmospheric deafness. Had they faced Buell's entire three corps for most of the day, it is difficult to imagine an outcome other than Bragg's army being overrun. These factors support the finding that *Polk's judgment and timing were correct*, even if somewhat unwittingly.

Connelly never faults Polk for refraining from the attack: "After the campaign Polk claimed the order to attack was disobeyed because he considered a 'great disparity' of numbers to exist." He goes on, however, to hold Polk accountable for his failure to communicate effectively with Bragg: "Nothing Polk wrote Bragg indicated he thought he was outnumbered. Yet if he felt, as he later wrote, such a disparity of numbers existed, why did he not tell Bragg? Bragg had ordered an attack, yet Polk did not even tell him the troops had gone on the defensive." Once again, the Army of Tennessee found itself plagued with communication breakdown, and Polk was a party to it.[17]

Based on Polk's early message to Bragg, it was his intention to follow the attack order; he assured his commander that he would give battle "vigorously." Then reality intruded. Although unaware of just *how* right he was—not realizing the precise number of Buell's army that he faced (54,000 men before another division began arriving that morning, as opposed to around 20,000 Confederates), Polk was, in fact, right to refrain from attacking such a host. Kenneth Noe, author of the definitive study of the Battle of Perryville, agrees:

In the years to come, many participants and scholars would excoriate Polk and Hardee for not doing what Bragg wanted that morning.

....

[O]ne cannot fault Polk for assuming a defensive posture that morning any more than one can criticize Robert E. Lee for doing the same thing a few weeks earlier in the face of a numerically superior enemy along Maryland's Antietam Creek. Polk's force was outnumbered, and it lay miles from both its commander and desperately needed reinforcements. In that light, insubordinately and furtively to be sure, *Polk in fact made the best decision possible*.[18]

Another historian who faults Bragg for failing to grasp his perilous plight at Perryville is David A. Powell:

Perryville was a confused affair. Bragg was heavily outnumbered and confronted the entire Federal army with just a portion of his own, but he badly misread the situation and contemptuously overrode the objections of his principal subordinates to order an attack against desperate odds. Only Federal blunders saved Bragg from a serious disaster.[19]

It was not until the night after the battle that Bragg finally understood that most of Buell's force was arrayed against him at Perryville. Once he grasped the number opposing him, the commanding general opted to retreat overnight even though his army had largely prevailed that day. Bragg knew he could not take on Buell's entire army himself; first he must have Kirby Smith's army close at hand. Yet he persisted in railing against Polk for wisely hesitating to attack those same numbers. This is not a rational stance, but a vendetta.

Clearly it is an erroneous simplification to charge Polk with disobeying Bragg's October 2 and October 7 orders without considering the circumstances and conditions which caused him to decide on a different course. Larry Daniel agrees: "Both instances proved justified." Blindly following either order could have resulted in disaster; in the case of the first, disaster would have been a likely outcome.[20]

Chapter 8

Chickamauga

As previously noted, Bragg made a habit of scapegoating his subordinates. This tendency hardened after his February 1863 epiphany when he officially resolved to accept no blame for setbacks or defeats; others would thereafter be held responsible. The practice magnified as time went on and culminated, in Polk's case, at Chickamauga. As shown above, Polk was correct in his decisions and actions taken at Perryville, contrary to the commanding general's (and some historians') charges against him. But Bragg's antipathy toward the bishop only continued to grow stronger and colored his perception of events before and during the Battle of Chickamauga, which finally led to Bragg's angry dismissal of General Polk, incongruously in the wake of the only glorious victory enjoyed by the Army of Tennessee.

The Coming Crisis

By August 1863 General William Rosecrans's Army of the Cumberland had penetrated the gaps of the Highland Rim in Middle Tennessee, forcing Bragg's army to cross the Tennessee River and retreat all the way back to Chattanooga. Once the Southern army took refuge in the city, a sense of crisis engulfed Leonidas Polk as he contemplated the situation facing the country at that crucial time. This came one month after Lee's army met defeat at Gettysburg and the fall of Vicksburg and Port Hudson split the Confederacy in two. But Polk's disquiet was not so much a matter of military setbacks. From the beginning he had realistically anticipated those and steeled himself against losing faith in the face of hardship and loss. But now his grave concerns centered on the changing public opinion of the war as well as a deficit of effective, inspirational leadership to guide the Southern people through their time of trial.

In early August Polk received a brooding letter from his friend General William Hardee expressing his own discouragement. Hardee had just been transferred to Mississippi and found the army in his department to be in poor condition. Hardee's duties at his new position were as yet undetermined and he felt himself useless and in a state of limbo. "I know I wish I were back at Chattanooga with my corps," he declared. He added ominously, "The present is a dark hour for the Confederacy."[1]

Apparently Polk empathized with his friend's sense of gloom, for he wrote two back-to-back letters in which he took up a similar theme. The first went to his brother-in-law, Kenneth Rayner, husband of Polk's sister Susan. "To my mind nothing is clearer than that we are approaching a crisis in the history of our affairs," the bishop pronounced gravely. He worried that the army was not strong enough and the administration not sufficiently energetic or "decided," and questioned "whether it will prove equal to emergencies still more stringent, yet to come."

But the alarming development, in Polk's opinion, was "the tendency now manifesting itself in different States among the people, to let down." He was scandalized by reports that the Raleigh *Standard* advocated a return to the Union and a former North Carolina governor supported that stance. Similar feelings, he heard, were cropping up in Alabama and Georgia. Polk called for "immediate attention on the part of those who do not mean to allow our efforts to rid ourselves of Yankee rule to fail." Polk proposed a forceful counter-measure to the malaise infecting the government and populace: to "take them by the forelock and open communications with France, the only power from whom we might expect aid."[2] One can sense his desperation and determination in the underlinings and exclamation points throughout his writing.

The following day Polk sent a heartfelt letter to Bishop Stephen Elliott of Georgia, marked *private & confidential*. In this epistle he poured out his soul and gave voice to his fears concerning Jefferson Davis and the spiritual state of the beleaguered Confederacy. Polk seemed almost surprised at his own feelings while confessing that he found himself unwilling to trust Davis's judgment.

> [Davis] is proud, self reliant, and I fear stubborn. I do not think such a mind should be allowed independent, untrammeled, & final action in such a case. We are deeply intrenched—too deeply not to have a hand in shaping measures which are to fix our destiny. Davis is not quick to perceive coming events & … believe[s] that things are possible, which history has shown were not possible nor even probable … strong men should see to it, that things are not allowed to drift to a point where they may be beyond control out of a too great confidence in the man at the helm.

Nonetheless, even in his anxiety Polk's innate optimism shines through: "I am confident we have had, abundantly, the means to defy the Yankees and this possibly forever—had they been judiciously used. I believe … we could recover what has been lost." He goes on to attribute the setbacks of the country to the sinfulness of its people and the necessity to "amend our lives."[3]

During this time, Polk's wife and two daughters were visiting him, but they soon departed when the Yankees appeared outside the city and began shelling it. One battery even targeted Polk's headquarters after a deserter pointed out its location. Everyone knew a major battle was looming. Perhaps Polk's uncharacteristic distress during this time was a contributing factor to his less-than-stellar showing at Chickamauga the following month.[4]

Once Rosecrans's columns approached Chattanooga in force, the Army of Tennessee abandoned the city on September 8 to avoid entrapment. By mid–September

Rosecrans divided his army to facilitate passage through and over the gaps and mountainous ridges of northwest Georgia. The Union general aimed for Confederate industrial centers, railroads and, of course, Bragg's army.

Pea Vine Road/ Rock Spring Church

Topology and poor cavalry service kept Bragg in constant confusion over the whereabouts of the various strands of Rosecran's advance. Bragg colorfully described to General D.H. Hill the challenges involved with maneuvering in North Georgia's rough terrain. (Hill appeared on the scene to take command of Hardee's corps after Hardee's transfer to Mississippi.) Bragg expounded to Hill:

> It is said to be easy to defend a mountainous country, but mountains hide your foe from you, while they are full of gaps through which he can pounce upon you at any time. A mountain is like the wall of a house full of rat-holes. The rat lies hidden at his hole, ready to pop out when no one is watching. Who can tell what lies hidden behind that wall?[5]

Lieutenant General William J. Hardee served with Polk at Shiloh, Perryville, Murfreesboro, and the Tullahoma Campaign, and the two enjoyed a friendly, trusting relationship. He was a solid officer of the Old Army, known for authoring a tactics manual used by both sides, and for his amiable, tactful disposition. Soldiers called him "Old Reliable." He tired of Bragg's intrigues and *un*reliability, and late in the summer of 1863 transferred to serve under Joseph Johnston in Mississippi. Thus, he did not take part in the battle of Chickamauga; instead, D.H. Hill was brought in to command his corps. When Bragg dismissed Polk after that battle, he and Hardee changed places and Jefferson Davis implored Hardee as he took command of Polk's corps to bring his natural tact and courtesy to bear upon the troubled relations in the Army of Tennessee ("Hardee, William Joseph," *House Divided: The Civil War Research Engine at Dickinson College*).

Nevertheless, Bragg perceived opportunities of his own to pounce on isolated segments of the Union army. One such opportunity came and went at McLemore's Cove on September 10. To Bragg's intense frustration, the reluctant General Hindman (whose division was under Polk's corps but detached at that time, thus Bragg's order went directly to Hindman) and General Buckner dragged their feet in attacking a Union force that was nearly trapped within the cove. No doubt his disgust at that failure contributed to Bragg's belief three days later that Polk caused a similar opportunity to slip by.

General Polk had been camped with Cheatham's division at Rock Spring Church until Bragg summoned them to his headquarters at La Fayette, Georgia, on September 11. Then on the morning of September 12 he ordered the division to return to Rock Spring Church for a possible attack on Crittenden's corps known to be moving in that general vicinity. When cavalry reports placed one of Crittenden's isolated divisions (Palmer's) on Pea Vine Road two miles north of Polk's headquarters, Bragg dispatched orders for Polk to attack at daylight on the 13th. Bragg ordered Hindman's division and W.H.T. Walker's reserve force to reinforce Polk, but Hindman did not arrive until one hour before the projected time of attack.

The night before Polk had conducted a reconnaissance and found not an isolated division in his front, but three Federal divisions within two miles of the point of attack. He notified Bragg of the situation and his opinion that he did not have sufficient numbers on hand and would go on the defensive unless attacked first. In fact, he expected to be attacked. In his reply Bragg seemed to assent to a defensive posture yet clung to the hope that the enemy would precipitate a fight. He also promised to send General Buckner's corps the following morning for additional support.[6]

Bragg rode with Buckner on September 13 and arrived at Polk's location around 9:00 a.m. (He "stormed into Polk's headquarters" in Cozzens's melodramatic account.) There he found Polk's force not positioned for assault but in a defensive line. At that time a cavalry advance reported Crittenden moving toward Lee and Gordon's Mill, and Polk sent Cheatham's corps in that direction, yielding nothing but some minor skirmishing. In fact, the prey had already escaped. ("*Crittenden had completed his concentration at Lee and Gordon's by the night of the twelfth.*") Thus, before Polk was even ordered to attack, Crittenden was actually no longer in place.[7]

Walker's corps advanced up Pea Vine Road by early afternoon, but no enemy was found. Bragg was angry with Polk, believing that his hesitation allowed the enemy to escape, but in fact, as explained by Connelly, "Bragg had been badly served by his intelligence.... Crittenden was never where Bragg believed him to be." Connelly further states, "Bragg believed that only Polk's slowness had prevented victory." Bragg complained later that Polk had more than ample force on hand, but included in his count Buckner's numbers which had not arrived by the time Polk was originally ordered to attack.[8]

This incident has been revised by later historians to serve as yet another example of Polk's disobedience. Woodworth tells it this way: "Polk thought the enemy in front of him was too strong and informed Bragg that he was taking up a good defensive position." His words "Polk thought" imply unfounded imagination on Polk's part; the author fails to reveal that the opinion was based on Polk's own ground reconnaissance. He goes on: "Bragg was certain that if Polk had access to all the information that he (Bragg) did, he too would see the need to strike at once." Bragg's information was, of course, based on a report more than 24 hours old by cavalry whose reconnoitering throughout the month had been consistently contradictory, confusing and unreliable. Nevertheless, Woodworth continues to blame Polk:

> [Bragg] cautioned Polk against waiting for the arrival of troops before attacking lest "another golden opportunity … be lost by the withdrawal of our game." It was no use. Polk was not in the habit of obeying Bragg, and thought he knew more than his commander anyway. Once again Polk disobeyed…. The Federals discovered the danger they were in, withdrew, and another "golden opportunity" was lost.[9]

Woodworth misconstrues the sequence to make it appear that it was Crittenden who "discovered the danger they were in" and withdrew before Polk could get around to attacking. In fact, the entire Federal army was in rapid movement, for it was Rosecrans, not Crittenden, who had discovered *his* dangerous position. Earlier he had believed reports of faux deserters sent by Bragg to plant the notion that the Southern army was demoralized and retreating to Atlanta. Once Rosecrans realized the ruse and concluded that Bragg was in fact not retreating but rather stalking his isolated segments, he drew them together rapidly. Crittenden's westward march was part of this urgent concentration ordered by Rosecrans.

Woodworth presents the incident as completely the fault of Polk, with the patient Bragg wronged once again by his dense, stubborn, self-important subordinate. Horn, however, explains it differently: "Bragg wrote Polk on the evening of the twelfth ordering him to attack at Peavine Church on the Graysville Road. He thought Crittenden's divisions still separated. Of course he was all wrong."[10]

Peter Cozzens, author of a trilogy on the battles at Murfreesboro, Chickamauga, and Chattanooga, aligns with the Woodworth school of sarcasm and vituperation. In relating this incident, Cozzens's every sentence involving Polk spits with invective against the general. As to his reconnaissance on the evening of the 12th, "the bishop completely misread the situation…. Polk had no idea that Crittenden's corps was actually concentrated in defensive positions near the mill." Cozzens in effect contradicts himself here; in advancing one argument he cancels out another. While berating Polk for poor reconnaissance, in so doing he acknowledges that Crittenden's force, no longer divided and now miles away at Lee and Gordon's Mill, had vacated the Pea Vine Road position—both conditions for attack specified by Bragg in his September 12 order. Therefore, Polk cannot rightfully be faulted for not attacking a force no longer there. Nevertheless, Cozzens castigates Polk for "tossing aside Bragg's order," in spite of having already established that the order no longer even applied to the situation![11]

Thankfully, recent accounts correct Woodworth's and Cozzens's distortions. David Powell, Chickamauga authority and author of a masterful three-volume study of the battle, offers the following in a separate essay on Forrest's role in the campaign:

> Bragg determined to strike at the XXI [Crittenden's] Corps, which he believed was equally scattered between Ringgold, Rossville, and Lee and Gordon's Mill. Bragg ordered…. Lieutenant General Leonidas Polk to waste no time in striking the enemy.

In fact, by the twelfth, this opportunity was also gone. Pegram's and Forrest's reports were out of date by at least twenty-four hours. By then, the XXI Corps was already concentrated at Lee and Gordon's Mill, holding a strong position on the west bank of West Chickamauga Creek. Polk was, in fact, outnumbered. Despite Bragg's repeated prodding, *Polk, who had a better grasp of the situation, wisely eschewed blundering into a foolish assault.* Bragg belatedly came to realize this fact when he arrived on the thirteenth, though he still felt Polk's slowness had cost the rebels yet another spectacular chance to damage a Federal column. *In fact, Crittenden's men were reunited and strongly posted even before Bragg issued his first attack order.*

In the first volume of his exhaustive study of Chickamauga, Powell provides much more detail on the factors that prevented success at Rock Springs Church. (Connelly and Cozzens give the location as Rock Spring; in Powell's version it is Rock Springs.) First, he clarifies that Buckner's reinforcements were not the only number wrongly included by Bragg as part of Polk's available force, but in effect Hindman's division could not rightfully be added, either:

> Bragg's error was his assumption that Polk would have his entire corps in place for the attack. Hindman spent most of the night extracting his division from McLemore's Cove and marching 13 difficult miles to La Fayette.... Hindman would not be able to resume his march to join Polk until 10:30 p.m., and getting there would require another all-night march.... Bragg assumed Polk would have 25,000 troops to fall on Palmer's Yankees; Polk understood that when he received the attack order he had only Cheatham's 7,000 men plus Walker's roughly 6,500 ... Hindman was sick, so Patton Anderson once again assumed command of that division. The troops were tired, having made a second night march in a row.

Powell goes on to describe the skirmishing and even an artillery duel that took place the morning of the 13th as portions of Polk's force probed the Federals' positions. "By midday Bragg concluded there was no chance of catching the XXI Corps divided, and reluctantly called off Polk's previously ordered assault."[12]

One of the accusations consistently brought against Polk is that he defiantly and resolutely avoided attacking in all situations and at all costs. Cozzens makes the sweeping statement that by issuing an attack order at Rock Spring Church, "Bragg was wasting his breath. Polk was no more inclined to attack than Hindman had been [at McLemore's Cove]." In fact, there is no basis for linking these two separate incidents. Unlike McLemore's Cove, there was no opportunity to be lost at Rock Spring Church. As far as the assertion that Polk never showed an inclination to attack, Powell discloses the whole truth. Shortly after midday when Bragg called off his attack order, all of Polk's reinforcements were up and he was fully apprised of Crittenden's position.

> Ironically, it was now Polk who wanted to attack. Buckner's column had arrived and taken up position behind Cheatham's division. With more than 30,000 men on hand, Polk argued that Crittenden "was only five miles away, and the creek was easily fordable."

It was not true that Polk would not attack; he simply looked before leaping. Once ready he was willing, even eager, to attack. However, Bragg's attention was suddenly redirected by an alarming report from D.H. Hill warning of McCook's corps approaching La Fayette. The threat was already dispelled by the time this message reached Bragg, but it ended any further action on Polk's front.[13]

Polk's Corps at Chickamauga

CHEATHAM'S DIVISION Maj. Gen. Benjamin Franklin Cheatham	HINDMAN'S DIVISION Maj. Gen. Thomas C. Hindman
Jackson's Brigade **Gen. John K. Jackson** 2nd Battalion, 1st Confederate 2nd Georgia Sharpshooters 5th Georgia 8th Mississippi	**Anderson's Brigade** **Brig. Gen. James Patton Anderson** 7th Mississippi 9th Mississippi 10th Mississippi 41st Mississippi 44th Mississippi 9th Mississippi Sharpshooters
Maney's Brigade **Brig. Gen. George Maney** 1st & 27th Tennessee 4th Tennessee 6th & 9th Tennessee 24th Tennessee Sharpshooters	**Deas's Brigade** **Brig. Gen. Zachariah C. Deas** 19th Alabama 22nd Alabama 25th Alabama 39th Alabama 50th Alabama 17th Alabama Sharpshooters
Smith's Brigade **Brig. Gen. Preston Smith** 11th Tennessee 12th & 47th Tennessee 13th & 154th Tennessee 29th Tennessee Dawson's Sharpshooter Battalion	**Manigault's Brigade** **Brig. Gen. Arthur M. Manigault** 24th Alabama 28th Alabama 34th Alabama 10th & 19th South Carolina
Strahl's Brigade **Brig. Gen. Otho F. Strahl** 4th & 5th Tennessee 19th Tennessee 24th Tennessee 31st Tennessee 33rd Tennessee	Artillery Dent's Alabama Battery Garrity's Alabama Battery Water's Alabama Battery
Wright's Brigade **Brig. Gen. Marcus J. Wright** 8th Tennessee 16th Tennessee 28th Tennessee 38th Tennessee 51st & 52nd Tennessee	
Artillery Carnes's Tennessee Battery Scogin's Georgia Battery Scott's Tennessee Battery Melancthon Smith's Mississippi Battery Sanford's Mississippi Battery	

SOURCE: From David A. Powell, *The Chickamauga Campaign: A Mad Irregular Battle* (El Dorado Hills, CA: Savas Beatie, 2014).

Dr. William Mecklenberg Polk, investigating this incident while working on a biography of his father, wrote to Archibald Gracie, Jr. (author of a Chickamauga study also focused on *his* father), a scathing account of Bragg's role and Polk's desire to attack once Crittenden's true location was ascertained. Notably, he takes issue with Bragg for his recurring habit of wrongly attacking his own generals in his battle reports:

General Bragg explicitly states in his official report that the force marching toward Rock Spring from the east had been allowed to escape by Polk, and that therefore Polk was responsible for the failure to cripple Crittenden. General Bragg having made up his mind that Crittenden's command was here the afternoon and night before, he could see no reason next morning why it should not have been here then. The fact that Forrest and Polk could not find it here at daylight the next morning was no proof to him … and he could not comprehend how it had gotten away. He was confused as he always was under such circumstances.… Information from General Forrest showed Polk that it had left there before dark on the afternoon before. Further investigation by Forrest located the whole of it at Lee & Gordon's Mill.… Bragg would have none of it.… General Bragg with Polk, Buckner, Cheatham and Walker … could then and there have moved straight to Lee & Gordon's mill and made a successful attack upon Crittenden.… Polk urged Bragg to move against Crittenden.… [who] would have been first eliminated and then the remaining portion of Rosencrans' [sic] army could have been dealt with as they moved north.

General Bragg was a conspicuous example of a General who falsified records by telling only a part of the truth, halting when the truth condemns himself.[14]

Once again, as also occurred twice at Perryville, Bragg from a distance away ordered Polk to attack based on a misunderstanding of the circumstances in Polk's front. Perryville differed from Pea Vine Road as to the reasons why Bragg was in the dark. In Kentucky Bragg reached an erroneous conclusion within his own mind that Buell's force was headed toward him rather than Polk's position at Bardstown. On the other hand, the misinformation that reached Bragg regarding Pea Vine Road came from cavalry reports, and Bragg cannot be faulted for relying upon them as he was already overburdened with monitoring his "rat holes" at that time. Considering all of the facts, Pea Vine Road cannot be deemed a "lost opportunity" akin to McLemore's Cove, in spite of Cozzens's equating the two.

Chickamauga "Breakfast Myth," September 20

An incident supposedly occurred at the Battle of Chickamauga which epitomizes the systemic falsehoods alleged against General Polk. It is instructive to examine this story in some depth, for over time its implications have been used in an attempt to paint Polk inaccurately as a man of flawed, slothful character.

First, the story: During the evening of September 19, 1863, after the first full day of battle at Chickamauga, General Bragg made plans and issued orders for the following morning, involving a wholesale reorganization of the Confederate high command due to the arrival of General Longstreet that night at 11:00. Polk was to oversee the right wing with D.H. Hill, who would no longer independently command his own (formerly Hardee's) corps, but function instead as second-in-command under Polk. Longstreet was assigned the left wing. The battle plan consisted of an attack to open at daylight beginning on the Confederate right and moving *en echelon* toward the left. Longstreet was to hold his forces in position awaiting the sound of Polk's guns on the right.

A number of problems doomed the plan, even if everything went according to program—which, of course, it did not. The first breakdown occurred in the area chronically infecting the Army of Tennessee: communications. First, Bragg provided only oral orders to Polk. Then, due to circuitous travels through the dark, foggy, forested wilderness during the night, neither Bragg's nor Polk's couriers were able to locate D.H. Hill, who in turn got lost seeking Polk's headquarters. As a result, Hill never received the order for a morning attack; it reached only Cheatham and Cleburne, Hill's subordinates in the newly improvised command framework.

Meanwhile Breckinridge's division of Hill's corps, miles away to the south, had been ordered to move to the far right and open the attack in the morning. After a grueling march they arrived tired and hungry at Polk's headquarters by 10:00 p.m. Polk indulgently granted them permission to bivouac near his headquarters rather than continue on to their launching-off position of the morrow; this compassionate but unwise decision, of course, jeopardized the timeliness of the next day's attack. Polk also failed to clarify to Breckinridge the orders to attack at daylight. When Breckinridge's men rose two hours before dawn to resume their march, Breckinridge stated that even then Polk did not specify the daylight directive, but said only that he should attack "as soon as possible."

Needless to say, by the time Breckinridge reached the battleground, affairs were not in order for a timely attack. Hill, still unaware of the order to attack at first light, was busy adjusting lines and also allowed his men, many of whom had not eaten for 24 hours, to prepare breakfast.

Polk arose before daylight and learned around 5:00 a.m. that his courier had never found Hill during the night, whereupon he dispatched another horseman with the attack order addressed directly to Cleburne and Breckinridge. He then gathered his aides, saddled up, and prepared to gallop to the front to assist in preparations for attack. At this time Major Pollock Lee arrived from Bragg's headquarters to learn why the attack had not opened. The report he brought back to Bragg, a disputed account which we shall call "the breakfast myth," is as follows:

> [Major Lee] found Polk about an hour after sunrise, sitting on the porch of a farmhouse three miles behind the lines, reading a newspaper, and waiting for his breakfast. Polk then told Lee that he did not know why the attack had been delayed, as he had not yet ridden to the front.[15]

This story, if true, evinces a shocking indifference, neglect of duty, and concern solely for his own creature comforts on the part of Polk. Connelly, however, immediately casts doubt on the credibility of the story:

> There seems no doubt that Lee gave Bragg this story. It was quoted to Hill by Bragg about 8 a.m. after the commanding general himself rode to find out the cause of the delay on the right wing. Also, in two letters written to his wife within a week after the battle, Bragg repeated the story. The story, however, does not coincide with the version of several witnesses, and two weeks after the battle, Lee himself allegedly denied telling Bragg such a tale.[16]

Connelly goes on to refute the story point by point, demonstrating conclusively that *the story can be considered nothing more than a complete fabrication.* Keeping in mind that Thomas Connelly's two-volume study of the Army of Tennessee is considered a definitive source on the Civil War in the West, and the second volume containing the story and his analysis discrediting it was published in 1971, below is a sequential examination of the various ways that historians have nevertheless chosen to repeat this account and present it as fact.

The first source, Don Carlos Seitz's biography of Braxton Bragg published in 1923, of course cannot be held accountable to Connelly's analysis because it predates it. Still, the credibility of the story had been refuted by numerous witnesses beginning immediately after the incident allegedly occurred; therefore, any historian should at least question its veracity. Seitz prints Bragg's entire September 22 letter to his wife Elise in which, interestingly, Bragg casts *himself*, not his aide Major Lee, as the party who caught Polk luxuriating over his morning routine! This was not the first time in a letter to Elise that Bragg claimed to do an act actually performed by an aide; he had made a similar distortion in his written narrative to Elise of the battle of Shiloh. In the current instance, two days after Chickamauga he complained to his wife:

> On Saturday night I brought up all my forces from every point and ordered a vigorous assault at daylight on Sunday morning. General Polk was to commence. Not hearing him, I sent at 7 o'clock and found him two miles from his troops sitting in a rocking chair at a house, waiting his breakfast, and did not know why the action was not commenced.[17]

This is just the sort of yarn that Bragg and his wife Elise enjoyed involving Polk. It is instructive to have Bragg's account even with its first-person variation. However, Seitz then goes on to contradict Bragg by naming Major Lee as the discoverer of Polk's dereliction:

> Bragg, on tenterhooks, strained his ears for sounds of conflict and hearing none sent his aide, Major Lee, to find out the trouble. He discovered Polk sitting comfortably in a rocking chair at his headquarters awaiting breakfast, "supposing" an attack had been made, as he had ordered it.

Seitz does not stop there. He then blames Polk for Longstreet's delayed advance:

> Polk was responsible for the delay. He had not attacked at daylight as instructed and Longstreet had not moved because his orders were to act on hearing the sound of Polk's guns.... Lee rode away to stir the generals, but it was eleven o'clock before the battle became general. The delay in Polk's progress on the right had, of course, been reflected on the left, where his movement had been awaited until the advantage of early effort was lost.[18]

The problem with this expanded blame is twofold. First, Polk's attack, admittedly delayed, actually got underway at 9:30 a.m., well before "the battle became general." It was Longstreet who did not attack until after 11:00, for reasons of his own not connected with the problems on the right. Longstreet's force was not, as implied here, ready and waiting at dawn, cooling their heels in line of battle waiting for Polk! (Anyone familiar with General Longstreet knows that his habit was to advance only when he was good and ready, not a moment before.)

Steven Woodworth, never one to miss an opportunity to slam Leonidas Polk,

Chapter 8. Chickamauga

not only reports the bogus "breakfast myth" as though fact in his 1990 book *Jefferson Davis and His Generals*, but adds considerable embellishment:

> Daybreak came and went. Bragg, listening at his headquarters for the roar of cannon on the right that would indicate the attack was under way, was perplexed by the silence. As more time passed and nothing happened, he dispatched a staff officer to Polk's headquarters to see what was causing his delay. The staff officer found Polk an hour after sunrise, sitting on the porch of the farmhouse he was using as his headquarters three miles from the fighting front, placidly reading a newspaper, and waiting for his breakfast. Did he know why there was no firing on the right? He did not. When the staff officer reported this to Bragg, the normally temperate commander responded with what his aide euphemistically called "a terrible exclamation," jumped on his horse, and galloped off to find Polk himself. Arriving at the farmhouse, he found that Polk, having foreseen some such visitation, had just left to look into the matter. "Do tell General Bragg," he had said as he went out the door, "that my heart is overflowing with anxiety for the attack. Overflowing with anxiety, Sir."

Steven Woodworth was certainly well familiar with Connelly's study on the Army of Tennessee; in fact, it was an important enough source that he describes it in his introduction as "heavily researched, highly critical, and much acclaimed." Nevertheless, he apparently disregards the highly acclaimed authority's debunking of this myth, preferring instead the colorful account related by Shelby Foote in Volume II of *The Civil War*, the sole source listed in Woodworth's footnote to this passage. In fact, the above quote contains each and every element from Foote's account. The problem is that Shelby Foote's work fails to name sources, and although his masterpiece stands undeniably as a magnificent, sweeping treatment of the Civil War, its author was known for using anecdotal accounts of doubtful veracity for literary purposes (and admitted as much—for example, his memorable scene of William Sherman bathing in the Chattahoochee River just before crossing toward Atlanta).[19]

Given the doubts surrounding this story, it is surprising that Steven Woodworth relates it with no conditional language but instead presents the tale as though established fact. One should expect an academic historian to exercise more prudence than would a prominent writer of fiction such as Foote; however, from its presentation a reader would never guess that Woodworth's account was anything other than factual reporting.

Another author who related the story was Judith Hallock in her 1991 Volume II to McWhiney's biography of Bragg, which also lists Connelly's work in the bibliography. She quotes from a memorandum Bragg wrote on the Battle of Chickamauga:

> "Before the dawn of day," he reported, "myself and staff were ready for the saddle.... With increasing anxiety and disappointment I waited until after sunrise without hearing a gun, and at length dispatched a staff officer to … Polk to ascertain the cause of the delay and urge him to a prompt and speedy movement." The staff officer, Major Pollock B. Lee, informed Bragg that he found Polk at his headquarters two miles from his line of troops at 7:00 a.m., sitting in a rocking chair reading a newspaper. Lee contended that Polk "was much surprised" that the attack had not been made, and "he proposed to go soon and ascertain the trouble."[20]

Now on to Peter Cozzens's 1994 account. He at least expresses some doubt as to Major Lee's story, and even offers an explanation for the fabrication:

> The bishop then sat down to a hasty breakfast. As he was eating, Major Pollock Lee of Bragg's staff rode up, sent by the commanding general to find out why the attack had not begun. He did not know the reason, Polk told Lee between bites, since he had not had a chance to ride to the front.
>
> The bishop's demeanor, breakfasting when he should have been attacking the Yankees, made quite an impression on Lee. Like most of Bragg's staff, Lee was a sycophant intent on giving the commanding general whatever he wanted. Knowing Bragg's need for scapegoats, Lee decided to distort the truth to help create one. He reported to Bragg that he had found Polk three miles behind the lines, sitting placidly on the front porch of a farmhouse reading a newspaper while awaiting his breakfast. Understandably, Bragg was enraged. Calling his staff to attention, he mounted up and galloped off to find Polk himself.[21]

Although Cozzens has Polk eating breakfast, albeit a hasty one, and casts him as oblivious and indifferent to his duty regarding the impending battle, he does concede Major Lee's story to be a distortion. But notice the subtle implication: "Lee decided to distort the truth *to help create one*" (emphasis added). How can a lie create a truth—perhaps when one feels it should, or might as well, be true? Cozzens seemingly believes that Lee's mendacity, his factually inaccurate account, nonetheless conveyed a truth about Polk. Perhaps the "truth" that Cozzens so artfully implies is found in his scolding Polk for "breakfasting when he should have been attacking the Yankees," a point which closely resembles the wrongdoing essential to Major Lee's story. It appears that Cozzens's questioning the veracity of Lee's story represents nothing more than lip service, for he manages to reinsert into the narrative an underlying, unfounded indictment against Polk while covering himself for repeating a known falsehood.

Cozzens abandons all subtlety several pages later while summing up Polk's role on the morning of September 20: "We are left to conclude that Polk, having no faith in Bragg's plan of battle, was doing his best to subvert it through malignant neglect." Such a charge, based as it is on false evidence, amounts to nothing more than malicious slander, with its author arrogantly presuming to know a man's mind and heart.[22]

Samuel J. Martin, in his 2011 biography of Bragg, offers a slightly altered version of the breakfast myth although it contains most of the elements included in other accounts. He too lists *Autumn of Glory* in his bibliography yet disregards Connelly's rebuttal. At least Martin employs a mild qualifier before his tale ("he claimed"):

> Pollock Lee arrived at Polk's camp. He claimed that he found the Bishop seated in a rocking chair, perusing a newspaper, awaiting his breakfast. When asked why he had not yet assaulted the enemy, Polk apparently could not bring himself to admit the truth. "Oh," he said lamely. "I ordered it." Bragg was hurrying toward the Bishop's headquarters. Upon receiving Lee's report of Polk's nonchalant behavior, he had responded by cursing, "a terrible exclamation," Lee recalled, and called for his horse. Bragg meant to confront Polk. When he reached the Bishop's command post, Bragg found only Wheless, just returned from the front. "His manner betrayed considerable impatience," Polk's aide recalled. He informed Bragg that his superior had just gone to the front to confer with Hill but had left behind a note. "My heart is overflowing with anxiety for the attack," the Bishop had written. "Overflowing with anxiety."[23]

Like Woodworth, Martin cites Shelby Foote as his only source, but distorts that account by claiming Polk's alleged sarcastic message was written in an absurdly worded note. One can be sure that is one document that never made it into the Official Records!

Finally, Earl Hess in his 2016 Bragg biography follows Cozzens's example by conceding it to be "unfortunate" that the story was made up, "but the truth was bad enough."[24] This kind of coloration enables an author to present an admitted falsehood with impunity, while nevertheless subtly influencing the reader.

In contrast to the bandwagon of authors who pass off Major Lee's fabricated story as though it were history or otherwise use it in an underhanded way, those who respect truth by omitting it altogether should be recognized. Stanley Horn's *The Army of Tennessee*, published in 1941 and therefore without benefit of Connelly's refutation, includes a detailed account of the morning's snafus on the Confederate right, but with no breakfast nonsense. Respected Chickamauga expert and park ranger Lee White, in his *Bushwhacking on a Grand Scale*, similarly leaves out the invented story and instead relates only facts: "Polk mounted his horse just as a member of Bragg's staff arrived to inquire why the attack had not begun. Quickly briefing the staffer about the miscarriage of orders, Polk then rode forward to join Cheatham." David Powell, in his Chickamauga masterpiece, also demonstrates his integrity by unequivocally refuting the breakfast concoction. Larry Daniel similarly dispenses with the story, simply stating: "It was a lie, but Bragg believed it." Finally, historian William Glenn Robertson, in his essay "A Tale of Two Orders: Chickamauga, September 20, 1863," published in the excellent collection *Gateway to the Confederacy*, thoroughly demonstrates the story's fallacy.[25]

But it was Thomas Connelly who decisively exposed the falsehood of Major Lee's account. (Arguably, one could just as well attribute authorship of the story to Bragg since Lee reportedly denied having concocted it.) First, the tale takes place at Polk's headquarters allegedly located in a farmhouse, where the general is seated in a rocking chair on the porch (the original account uses the quaint word "gallery") awaiting his breakfast. Some of the versions place this farmhouse three miles behind the front, while others have it two miles away. Overlooking the mileage discrepancy, Connelly points out two fundamental problems with the supposed setting. First, Polk's headquarters was "in a forest clearing, only 1200 feet behind Walker's reserve corps." In describing the confusion of the prior evening when neither Polk nor Hill could locate one another, Connelly concedes that there was some uncertainty over the exact location of Polk's headquarters, but it is a known fact that Polk, like Bragg, slept not in a bed or a house but in an ambulance wagon. Not only was Polk's headquarters *not* a house, but the final blow to the story's reliability is that *"there was no farmhouse nearby."* Therefore, this fundamental detail of Lee's account, including the related props such as the rocking chair and likely the newspaper as well, are simply not true—but were concocted out of thin air.

Second, Connelly shows the story's fallacy in connection with the "time element" which "does not seem consistent with available facts." "None of the times given by Bragg appears to have been possible." Without belaboring the fine points here, Connelly meticulously and convincingly demonstrates the impossible time factor, another strike against the story.[26]

Third, Pollock Lee's claim of finding Polk seated, some accounts add "placidly," in a rocking chair waiting for breakfast as though he had all the time in the world, are refuted by testimony of several witnesses who saw Polk mounted and moving to the front when Bragg's staffer arrived. William Glenn Robertson states definitively: "*Contrary to the story that would later be repeated in numerous accounts of the battle, Polk had been busy since first light.*" Robertson addresses the breakfast myth in this manner:

> Major Pollock Lee of Bragg's staff appeared. Lee had been sent to learn the cause of the delay in starting the "day-dawn" attack. Polk explained that Hill had not received the attack order during the night and that he was in the process of rectifying the matter.... Lee would later report to Bragg that he had found Polk sitting on the porch of a house, reading a newspaper, waiting for his breakfast. Bragg believed the story to be factual rather than the hyperbole it obviously must have been, and repeated it in two private letters to his wife.[27]

Here we have it confirmed that Polk was in fact active and busy, neither placidly lounging nor passively waiting.

The other major element to the story, the conversational exchange between Polk and Lee, is handled inconsistently across the various versions. However, a common theme threads through them all: Polk is portrayed as clueless, apathetic, and not in control of the situation. This perhaps represents the crux and purpose of the fable, a twisted anti-moral that the reader takes away, even if unconsciously.

Martin and Woodworth, following Foote's lead, go further by adding the sarcastic, mocking line supposedly uttered by Polk: "My heart is overflowing with anxiety for the attack. Overflowing with anxiety, Sir." This language is so obviously contrived and out of character that it scarcely needs addressing. The purpose behind it comports with the implications contained in the story proper: that Polk is haughty, insubordinate, lazy, indifferent, neglectful, and self-indulgent. But one must keep in mind that *if the story is not true, then neither is its implied moral.* The entire matter amounts to nothing more than a patently false portrayal.

Although conclusively debunked, successive authors nevertheless continue to repeat the Polk breakfast myth. At the mercy of their scholarship, unsuspecting readers believe the ugly slander. The authors covered above are not writers of fiction, but professional historians representing themselves as purveyors of truth and accuracy. Yet we find Woodworth and Hallock repeating the false story verbatim as though undisputed fact; Martin prefacing his version with "He claimed" as a lame disclaimer; and Cozzens and Hess admitting the story to be fabricated but nonetheless using it to cast aspersions on General Polk. Is it too much to complain that these authors, in passing on a story they know (or should know) to be untrue and originally conceived as malicious gossip, have betrayed the trust of their readership? At the very least one can conclude from the mere act of reporting this nonsensical story, that they deem certain subjects undeserving of fair treatment.

Interestingly, long before modern historians wrongly recounted Pollock Lee's fable, a relative of General Polk dealt with it in a characteristic 19th-century fashion: by challenging the tale spinner to a duel! An August 1913 letter of James H. Polk (1842–1926, son of Leonidas's brother George Washington Polk), to Polk's son, William Mecklenburg Polk, recalls the incident. James had been present when his cousin "Marsh" encountered Pollock Lee and issued a challenge to him. Marshall T. Polk (1831–1884), a first cousin of Leonidas but closer in age to his children, graduated from West Point in 1852 and commanded a Confederate battery at Shiloh. There he was severely wounded and his leg amputated. By the end of the war he had risen to the rank of Lieutenant Colonel.

When Marsh Polk's path crossed that of Pollock Lee in the post-war years, he loudly called him "a liar and a coward" over the false report at Chickamauga, and issued his challenge. Lee refused to duel on the basis that the one-legged Marsh was "a cripple." Marsh retorted that he still had his "trigger finger," whereupon Pollock Lee "slunk away like a cur"!

Cousin James, writing the letter three decades after the feisty Marsh's death, laments that "this lying detraction of Lee has been revived." He assumed that it had surely been buried with finality by "history bearing the stamp of truth." Over a century later, his lament still applies.[28]

Order to Attack, September 20

There were two fundamental problems with Bragg's order to attack Rosecrans's line on the morning of September 20. First, Union troops under General Thomas, opposing Polk's wing on the Confederate right, had been building strong fortifications all night long. Numerous sources contain accounts of Southern soldiers unable to sleep for the sound of Yankees' axes felling trees. By morning D.H. Hill's divisions confronted formidable earthworks. Connelly rightfully blames Polk for "his failure to make a personal reconnaissance of the front. It was obvious to Hill, Cleburne and Breckinridge [as well as the soldiers on the line] that the Federals on Cleburne's front and on Breckinridge's left front were entrenched behind heavy log fortifications. That morning about 7:00 in a message to Polk, Hill had warned of this." To remedy the situation, Hill moved the brigades of General Adams and Stovall, of Breckinridge's division, to the far right beyond the Yankees' works in preparation for a flank attack.[29]

The second problem was that the Confederate force on the right was inadequate to begin with. This was Bragg's oversight. In fact, the right had been insufficiently manned the day before as well due to Bragg's misunderstanding of Rosecrans's position; he had no idea that Rosecrans had moved his line farther to *his* left, as evidenced by Bragg's September 19 orders which "sent no strong force to the right, *as Polk had advised as early as the seventeenth.*" If he would not listen to Polk, the day's results should have told Bragg something: "Earlier in the evening [of the 19th] Polk had sent a courier to Bragg asserting that Rosecrans' main army seemed concentrated in front of the Rebel center-right…. Yet Bragg did not take heed and readjust his plans."

Now on the 20th Bragg still failed to reinforce the right sufficiently to take on the strongly fortified, numerous foe at Polk's front, commanded by the formidable General George Thomas. It was D.H. Hill who discerned the problem and did what he could with what he had. Connelly explains that once the attack began, the "two right brigades, judiciously placed to overlap the Federal fortifications, indicated what might have been done had Bragg or Polk placed power on the far right." Now Adams and Stovall flanked the Federal line!

> Shortly after 10 a.m. Bragg had in effect seized one line of retreat to Chattanooga, had flanked the Federal left, and was menacing the Glen-Kelly Road and subsequently the Dry Valley Road to Chattanooga. But Adams and Stovall received no help and gradually were pushed back across La Fayette Road.

One would conclude from this that Polk was remiss for failing to send in timely reinforcements to augment the initial success. However, Larry Daniel disagrees that Polk was entirely to blame, offering a more nuanced criticism:

> Historians have criticized Polk for not having Walker's Corps in position to support Breckinridge, but they are incorrect. Polk belatedly brought up Walker's 4,600 or so men … but they advanced in line of battle rather than in column, slowing the response.

The overarching conclusion is that the manpower Bragg assigned to the right did not match the expectation placed upon that sector in his battle plan.[30]

Polk can rightfully be faulted for some degree of tactical error, and predictably the attack on the right failed to accomplish its goal of sweeping southward down the Federal line in proper synch with Longstreet's advance. Some analysts attribute the failure to Polk's delay earlier in the morning. After all, Bragg ordered the attack to begin at "day-dawn," and sunrise occurred at 5:47 a.m. that day, but the actual advance did not take place until around 9:30, almost four hours late. In his mind, Bragg's own high hopes for the entire war effort were dashed by the delay; he actually claimed "that but for the loss of those precious hours, 'our independence might have been won.'" Even his sympathetic biographer Judith Hallock admits this statement to be "unrealistic." She also correctly contests the notion that Longstreet was held up by Polk's delay:

> When the attack finally began on the right, Longstreet had not completed his arrangements, so it is probable that Bragg's plan for the fight to be taken up successively from the right to the left would not have been executed properly, even if Polk had not dawdled.

In her enthusiasm for her subject, however, Hallock then goes on to credit *Bragg* with Longstreet's triumphant break through the Federal lines:

By the time Longstreet felt prepared, Bragg had already ordered units of the left wing to attack thus setting in motion the advance that broke the Federal line, long credited to Longstreet.... Bragg's timing proved perfect: a gap had inadvertently been created in the Federal line at the precise time and place the left wing attacked.

This sequence skips over a few crucial details. The "units of the left wing" that Bragg ordered forward (actually, he sent his mendacious aide, Pollock Lee, to the front to issue the order) were Stewart's division, which advanced around 11:00, before Longstreet was ready on his left, and were quickly thrown back. Thus, Stewart's attack in no way ushered in Longstreet's advance. It is inaccurate to attribute Longstreet's breakthrough to Bragg's perfect timing, as Longstreet's 11:30 advance was not linked with Stewart's attack.[31]

The point in relation to Polk is that not only did his delay that morning *not* hold up Longstreet, but the overall tardiness, both on the right and Longstreet's on the left, actually turned out to be quite

Major General Daniel Harvey Hill won a victory in one of the first battles of the Civil War, at Big Bethel in Virginia. He served in Lee's army during the Seven Days, but was transferred to North Carolina for a time and missed Second Manassas, rejoining Lee for the Maryland Campaign and Fredericksburg. A brother-in-law of Stonewall Jackson, he was well known for his hatred for Yankees and his sarcastic, irascible nature, possibly the reason for his transfer to Bragg's army where he took command of Hardee's corps. After Chickamauga Bragg dismissed Hill along with Polk, Hindman and others (Library of Congress).

fortuitous. Had everyone been ready at dawn, various portions might have met with success or setback—but then *Longstreet's advance would not have occurred at precisely the moment that a gap opened up in the Federal line on his front.*

Furthermore, Polk's attack, in spite of justifiable criticism for being made in a piecemeal fashion and ineffectively managed, drew reinforcements from the Federal right, directly resulting in the fatal Federal gap:

Thomas managed to check Cleburne and other Rebel units which assailed him, chiefly because Polk insisted on sending them in piecemeal, but the Union corps commander was concerned enough to call for help from Rosecrans. Rosecrans responded by pulling units from his right and sent them to Thomas. The arrangement led to Rosecrans's undoing. Because of a mixup, an entire division was withdrawn from Crittenden's front just as Longstreet ordered his massed brigades forward.[32]

Therefore, in spite of all the recriminations for Polk's delay in attacking, the matter of timing actually worked out dramatically well for the Confederates. As Connelly tells it, Bushrod Johnson, commanding Longstreet's lead division, "smashed the Federal line. Suddenly, in one of the war's most notable scenes of panic, the entire Union right collapsed, and retreated."[33]

"A Barren Victory"

By mid-afternoon much of the Union line had disintegrated except at its northern end where General George Thomas rallied his and other units in a strong position on Snodgrass Hill. General Gordon Granger, posted on the army's far north in Rossville, marched his men on his own initiative southward to reinforce Thomas. Their advance, led by James Steedman, was spotted by D.H. Hill who thought they were moving to attack the Confederate right wing. After being battered the day and evening before and again that morning, Hill's men on the far right were not battle-ready and he asked Polk for reinforcements. Polk

Lieutenant General James Longstreet, known as Lee's "Old War Horse," commanded the First Corps in most of the major battles of the Army of Northern Virginia except Chancellorsville when his force was on detached duty in southern Virginia. In the fall of 1863, leaving behind Pickett's shattered division, Longstreet went west to reinforce Braxton Bragg and at Chickamauga spearheaded a spectacular breakthrough of the Federal lines resulting in a major victory for the Army of Tennessee. He was not long in perceiving Bragg's dysfunctional leadership, and conspired to have Bragg removed. Instead, he was ordered away to attack Knoxville (unsuccessfully), and after wintering in East Tennessee rejoined Lee in time to play a decisive role in the Wilderness Campaign. After suffering a grave wound, he spent a long convalescence near Augusta, Georgia, where he attended the funeral of Leonidas Polk (photograph by Mathew Brady, Library of Congress).

ordered Cheatham's division to Hill, but no attack ensued as Steedman continued on toward Thomas. Meanwhile Confederate forces under Bushrod Johnson and others advanced from the south to attack Thomas's position.

Polk's command on the right had lain relatively dormant for some hours. They faced a Federal line at Kelly Field, and around 2:00 Bragg had ordered Polk to attack. However, Hill fearing for the right flank pulled Cheatham out of his initial position, and although this should not have affected the execution of Bragg's order—in fact, it could have aided it—concerns over the resultant gap between Cleburne's and Breckinridge's divisions took away any initiative to advance. The underlying problem was likely an argument that had flared earlier in the day between Polk and D.H. Hill. With that tension still unresolved, by this time in the afternoon General William H.T. Walker, who by nature was even touchier and more prickly than Hill, came into the fray when he and Hill had words. Then Polk had to settle a disagreement with Hill over the troops' dispositions. A captain who heard their exchange years later disclosed that Polk walked away from Hill muttering under his breath, "That is the most pig-headed General officer I have ever had to deal with." Some off-and-on attacks erupted from both sides at Kelly Field, but the Federals maintained their lines, allowing for Thomas's build-up on Horseshoe Ridge.[34]

The fight against Thomas was mostly Longstreet's, but as the afternoon went on he looked increasingly to Polk's wing for support. Finally around 4:00 the fight at Kelly Field flared up again. Polk had become frustrated with D.H. Hill's recalcitrance and ordered Cleburne to close up the gap that stymied Hill. The ever-canny Cleburne first took a harrowing reconnaissance ride and saw that a surgical artillery strike was needed. He called up Captain Henry Semple who opened up his guns with great effect, and along with other cannon fired from Poe Field the barrage catalyzed the Federals' withdrawal from Kelly Field, some running "a gauntlet of concentrated fire from the enemy's artillery" while others "left the field as if on parade."[35]

Polk's nephew, brigade commander General Lucius Polk, advanced as Federals continued their retreat. Captain Peter Simonson's 5th Indiana battery, destined to fire the shot that would kill Leonidas Polk the following year, left behind a gun that had been struck by Confederate artillery. When Lucius Polk's brigade charged, the orderly Federal withdrawal turned into a rout. Cheatham's division stepped up to prepare to join the charge, and at that point Leonidas Polk rode up and conferred with Cheatham and George Maney, one of his brigade commanders. Here ensued a scene evincing the tenderness with which Polk was regarded by his men, as related by Sam Watkins, 1st Tennessee:

> "Say, General, what command is that which is engaged now?" someone asked from the ranks. General [Polk] kindly answers, observed Watkins, "that is Longstreet's corps. He is driving them this way, and we will drive them that way, and we will crush them between the upper and nether millstones." Turning to General Cheatham, he said, "General, move your division and attack at once." Cheatham, to give the boys a good send-off, says, "Forward, boys, and give them h—l." General Polk also says a good word … "Do as General Cheatham says, boys." (You know he was a preacher and couldn't curse.)

When Maney's brigade advanced, Sam Watkins "remembered how he and the rest of the regiment, 'with one long, loud cheering shout … press right up to their breastworks and plant our battle flag upon it. They waver and break and run in every direction.'"[36]

The Battle of Chickamauga ended the evening of September 20 with a spectacular Confederate victory, and the Southern army roared a spontaneous cheer across the bloody fields. Polk ordered his aide Lt. Spence to ride his lines, then proceed to Bragg and report on their dispositions. Spence returned to Polk with a summons from Bragg to his headquarters. Bragg also asked for Longstreet but the lieutenant was unable to locate him.

Brigadier General George Maney was the only brigade commander who served in Polk's Corps throughout all four of the major battles: Shiloh, Perryville, Murfreesboro, and Chickamauga. During the battles of Atlanta he commanded a division under Hardee but was not promoted to major general. After the war he became a Republican and was appointed to various diplomatic posts in South America (Wikimedia Commons).

Once Polk reached Bragg's headquarters after a difficult ride, it was midnight or perhaps 1:00 a.m. Spence was also present, as was Governor Isham Harris of Tennessee who had been acting as a volunteer aide to Bragg. According to Harris, "the Commanding General would not believe the Federals had been beaten but insisted that we were to have a harder fight the next day." Contrary to his later claims, at this point Longstreet also believed that the enemy remained in their front. However, Polk advised Bragg that the enemy had fled and, according to Lt. Spence, Polk was "in favor of moving forward at once."[37]

General Liddell also believed that the enemy had withdrawn altogether and sent scouts out that night to verify their departure. First thing the next morning Liddell reported his findings to Polk, who ordered him farther forward to ascertain the whereabouts of the Yankees. However, before he could proceed General Bragg approached, and while waiting for his superiors to conclude their conference Liddell sent out scouts for the additional reconnaissance. D.H. Hill was also busy seeking the location of the enemy, and none were found more than a mile distant. Meanwhile Bragg fretted over the condition of his army and ordered no pursuit of the retreating Federal army.[38]

General Nathan Bedford Forrest performed a reconnaissance of his own, and much has been made of his insistent reports to Bragg that the way was wide open for the Confederates to roll over the enemy whom he reported to be in a state of chaos. As Forrest was attached to Polk's command at this time, it was the latter to whom the cavalryman addressed his messages. David Powell has presented a thorough study of the fallacy behind some of Forrest's reporting. The truth was that Thomas had his force well-fortified in a formidable line at Rossville. Powell concludes: "The Federals had disengaged successfully, and now held Rossville in sufficient strength to make a frontal attack there unpalatable."[39] Meanwhile, Forrest grew sorely frustrated at Bragg's reticence to advance on Rosecrans, and according to some accounts he confronted Bragg in a rage. Whether or not that actually occurred, Forrest transferred out of Bragg's army shortly thereafter to operate behind enemy lines in Tennessee and Mississippi where during the following year he would play a crucial role under Polk.

Although a *portion* of the Federals had "disengaged successfully" and fortified at Rossville, it was undeniable that Rosecrans's army as a whole had been defeated and driven from the field, leaving thousands of wounded (and entire hospitals) behind. For once Bragg had won an epic victory, yet from all reports he could not grasp that it was so. Perhaps still stung by the repercussions from his premature declaration of victory at Murfreesboro, he was wary of heralding his triumph now. Or he might have been overcome by a state of mind described by historians Scott Bowden and Bill Ward, in which a general is irrationally incapacitated by disbelief in his victory. Bowden and Ward list a number of commanders in ancient and modern times who fell victim to this phenomenon.[40] Whatever the explanation, many of Bragg's subordinates chafed at his half-measures following the battle, and in particular his failure to reap the fruit of the Southern army's bloody victory.

Meanwhile, Rosecrans's army took refuge in Chattanooga and both sides went into recovery mode, counting and tending to their casualties. Within days Bragg's army took position in a semi-circle along the heights and valleys south and east of Chattanooga. By that time the Army of Tennessee's familiar, old pattern of bitter internecine conflict reared its ugly head.

Bragg's After-Battle Ax

While the dead were being buried (including, sadly, Polk's trusted and loyal aide, William B. Richmond), the wounded shipped off to hospitals in Marietta and

Atlanta, staggering casualties tallied, and captured arms and supplies inventoried and allocated, Bragg set about his usual after-battle routine of punishing subordinates and fingering scapegoats. In this case the syndrome strikes one as most bizarre and inappropriate: an altogether strange reaction to his army's triumph! A general's blaming and branding scapegoats is perhaps understandable after a *loss* but what leader attacks his subordinates following a resounding win? Perhaps this preoccupation explains Bragg's failure to follow up on his victory at Chickamauga. Rather than rapid, proactive pursuit of a beaten foe, he threw his energy instead into warring against his own side. He certainly wasted no time at it, nor did he exercise restraint this time around, but plotted a wholesale purge. *Less than 48 hours* after copious blood had been spilled on the battlefield, Bragg targeted Polk, ordering him on September 22 to report immediately with an explanation of his "failure to attack the enemy at daylight on Sunday last." He repeated the demand on September 25, when he also sent an angry letter to President Davis berating Polk and others.[41]

From all reports, Bragg cared for the wounded, but what kind of man could be so callous immediately following the carnage of Chickamauga, that all he could think of was misplaced vindictiveness and his own petty vindication? During a window of opportunity when bold vision and decisive action were crucial to securing victory, Bragg instead burned with vitriol against his own lieutenants. Yet historians sympathetic to Bragg treat this entire episode as though it were perfectly rational and justifiable.

However, Bragg's staff and supporters actually on the scene did not see it that way. Just as Buckner and others had pleaded with Bragg to let go of his vendetta after Murfreesboro, chief of staff William Mackall and General Liddell tried to deflect Bragg's ire and persuade him to make peace with his lieutenants following Chickamauga. Liddell reported, "To my distress, his mettle was up and beyond the control of dispassionate reason. He said with emphasis, 'General, I want to get rid of all such generals.'"[42]

Mackall by this time had astutely assessed Bragg's nature and character. He was mystified, however, by his superior's habit of reacting vindictively after engagements, especially in the wake of victory. "If Bragg carries out his projects, there will be great dissatisfaction. I have told him so, but he is hard to persuade *when in prosperity*, and I do not think my warning will be heeded until too late." Mackall perceived a pattern. Bragg was on another rampage and it had become clear by now that he, rather than the objects of his rage, was the source of the problem. Mackall discreetly resigned as chief of staff shortly thereafter and went on to serve with Joseph Johnston in Mississippi.[43]

To the first victim of Bragg's inquisition, Leonidas Polk, Bragg forwarded accusatory questions regarding the reasons for his delay in attacking on the morning of September 20. Upon receiving his detailed reply, on September 28 Bragg peremptorily suspended Polk from command, as well as General Hindman for his failure at McLemore's Cove, and ordered both to Atlanta. Thus began a long, sad saga which again begged President Davis's personal intervention to salvage the troubled power structure of the Western army. During the time that Davis traveled in person to nurse the ills afflicting Army of Tennessee high command, back in Richmond Secretary of War James Seddon decried the unfruitful outcome at Chickamauga: "What matter victories however unless they are improved. So far we seem to have reaped in our Harvest of Death only barren glory." In the same letter he references "Bragg[']s unwise suspension of Polk."[44]

Polk's dismissal generated a wave of ardent protest from the public. "[T]he news of his suspension created an uproar," according to Connelly. A young diarist in Macon, Georgia, LeRoy Gresham, recorded his thoughts. Fifteen-year-old LeRoy was confined to his home due to a childhood injury and the subsequent onset of disease. An astute observer of the war, he reflected on the army's predicament immediately after Chickamauga: "Rosecrans has been reinforced and is unassailable. Meanwhile Bragg has taken this emergency to quarrel with his officers: Polk, Forrest and Hindman [are] all under arrest." Even a teenager could perceive Bragg's folly. Two days later on October 7 he wrote: "Bragg has commenced to shell Chattanooga. It is generally conceded that he will be in Central Ga. this winter. Some folks declare he is losing his reason."[45]

Polk was offered accommodations in the comfortable Atlanta home of John Sidney Thrasher. Later, in November, General John Bell Hood came to Atlanta during his recuperation after his leg was amputated in a Chickamauga field hospital, and Polk offered his cozy quarters to the wounded Texan. For this kind gesture, Hood later wrote that he "had grown to love [Polk] with my whole heart."[46]

Meanwhile, distressed over Bragg's failure to capitalize on the army's victory at Chickamauga, a number of high-level commanders remaining with the Army of Tennessee met secretly and produced a petition signed by twelve corps and division commanders urging, albeit in the utmost of polite language, Bragg's removal. Even though the petition was never officially submitted, this near-mutiny came to the attention of Richmond. Davis sent his aide, Colonel James Chesnut, to Chattanooga to try and sort through the difficulty. On his way to army headquarters, Chesnut stopped in Atlanta to meet with Polk. Echoing other detractors, Larry Daniel has Chesnut falling under the mesmerizing magnetism of Polk who, he claims, "easily won him over with his charming ways. The colonel … quickly fell in line with Polk's version of events." However, Mary Chesnut's diary casts doubt upon the notion that her husband was so pliable. True, he told his wife that he perceived Polk, upon this first personal encounter with him, to be "a splendid old fellow." But rather than evidence of Polk's working some kind of magical manipulation upon Chesnut, perhaps this was simply his impression. Mary goes on in her diary to offer her independent opinion of the endless grappling among "Bragg and his generals. I think a general worthless whose subalterns quarrel with him. Something wrong with the man. Good generals are adored by their soldiers. See Napoleon, Caesar, Stonewall, Lee, &c. &c."[47]

Upon uncovering the drastic dysfunction in Bragg's command, Chesnut sent a message that the situation required the immediate intervention of Davis himself. Thus the president traveled to Atlanta first to confer with Polk, then visited army headquarters in an attempt to mediate the disputes and restore order. The president insisted on a bizarre, face-to-face meeting among Bragg and the petitioners, in the fashion of a 1960s encounter group. Everyone had his say, but no happy breakthrough occurred.

Perhaps in attempting this confrontational meeting among antagonists, Jefferson Davis imagined himself like unto Admiral Lord Nelson legendarily summoning the squabbling captains of his fleet before the Battle of Trafalgar and ordering them to clasp hands. Placing his own hand atop the mass, he pointed to the sea with the other and exclaimed, "Gentlemen! Yonder is the enemy!" But the Army of Tennessee possessed no such enlightened leadership; as Bragg had so often demonstrated, he desired no resolution, but seemingly gloried in conflict: jumping into it, prolonging it, and often originating it—but not through any sinister motives. In the words of Lanny Smith, author of a magnus opus on Murfreesboro, it was a matter of "Bragg just being Bragg." One gets the sense that if Bragg was not fighting against someone externally, then he was fighting someone internally. Purely and simply it was fundamental to his nature, and went no further than that. Braxton Bragg's combativeness arose not out of hatred or evil but simply a heightened energy level. His over-animated psyche emitted a kind of natural belligerence that others often misinterpreted by taking personally and (understandably) taking offense.[48]

If the fight at the root of Bragg's soul did not spring from evil, nevertheless he was not free and clear of guile, as evidenced on several occasions—for example, the duplicity of his Murfreesboro battle report. But even the method he employed there demonstrates an essential innocence on his part: if Bragg could only have a *correct* report from the artillerist Felix Robertson, then his recriminations against Breckinridge and others would be justified.

Such an understanding of Bragg's underlying purity of motive, belying his bellicose behavior, could explain Davis's reticence to remove the general commanding. It almost seems as though Davis, like Bragg, sought no resolution to the conflict roiling the western army. In spite of patiently listening to each general's viewpoint at his impromptu therapy session, he hardly entertained any notion of relieving Bragg—perhaps because he believed him essentially innocent. Years in the political arena would have given him a keen instinct for sinister motives, and he found none in Bragg. But by this time Davis should have accorded greater consideration to the *practical effects* of Bragg upon his organization. Everyone had been through this exercise more than once, and by now the general's internal intentions should have been deemed irrelevant. What counted were the inevitable, repeated results, the dire consequences, of Bragg's antagonistic nature upon the key people around him. It could also be true that the president retained Bragg because of his many talents and assets, but in the position he currently occupied they were being misapplied—exactly what Polk had argued many months before.

Davis did, however, insist that Bragg drop his allegations of disobedience and neglect of duty against Polk, although the latter, never reticent to defend himself when wronged, preferred for the charges to remain so that he could contest them in a court of inquiry. Davis hoped to restore Polk to his command under Bragg, but that was satisfactory to neither general. When Polk vowed to resign rather than serve under Bragg, Davis granted Polk a new assignment: second-in-command under Joseph Johnston in the Department of Mississippi, a post currently occupied by William Hardee, who would be reinstated in the Army of Tennessee, now to command Polk's corps. Along with his orders to return to Bragg, President Davis called upon the tactful Hardee to bring his graciousness to bear upon the tense atmosphere in the army's high command, in the hope that he might help to restore harmony.

Woodworth and others have cast Polk as the primary instigator of the turmoil that gripped the Army of Tennessee. It is true that Leonidas Polk had on occasion openly expressed to President Davis and other corps commanders his grave concerns regarding Bragg's fitness for army command, and after Chickamauga he even appealed to Robert E. Lee to relieve the problematic situation at army headquarters. He was certainly not the only one to cast about for a solution, and it is wrong to deem him ringleader of the mutinous petitioners (as Bragg believed him to be). By that time Polk was no longer even present with the army, yet the unraveling continued unabated.

It is significant that Polk's banishment had no effect of quelling the disquiet within the army's high command. His detractors would argue this was because Polk's influence had been so poisonous that it outlasted him, but even had Polk engaged in the degree of machination that such critics claim, it could endure only for so long. Polk was now out of the picture, while new actors such as Longstreet had appeared on the scene. In fact, Longstreet's arrival as recently as September 20, and his active involvement in the dissension against Bragg, should refute any notion of Polk's "pernicious influence." Polk left the army for Atlanta on or about September 29—could he have so thoroughly corrupted Longstreet in only nine days? Even supposing Master Puppeteer Polk had manipulated the minds of his marionettes now calling for Bragg's removal in his absence, it is difficult to imagine the stolid, impervious Longstreet falling so readily under his sway. Instead, Longstreet observed for himself the obvious dysfunction and *independently* reached the same conclusion as the others. Sadly, the same melodrama was playing out yet again, and the common denominator throughout was none other than Bragg. The truth was that even as Polk's hypothetical impact waned, new fires broke out and each general dreaded that his head would be the next to roll.

On November 7, 1863, Leonidas Polk departed Atlanta for Enterprise, Mississippi, for his new assignment.

Relieving Polk Brought Bragg No Relief

If those who blame Polk are to be believed, his departure should have corrected the personnel problems plaguing the Army of Tennessee. Instead, the turmoil in Bragg's army only grew worse. In the wake of Bragg's surviving as commander through yet another personnel crisis, D.H. Hill was the next scapegoat to fall under Bragg's ax. Meanwhile Longstreet posed a constant challenge to Bragg's leadership and resisted his directives, although directives came few and far between as Bragg gave little attention to strategizing against the Yankees. Instead he targeted his enemies within the army, and resorted to his favorite tactic: the sweeping purge. This drastic remedy again got the attention of the young Macon diarist LeRoy Gresham, who in his entry of November 20 grimly tallied Bragg's victims: "Longstreet is in Knoxville! ... Generals Cheatham, Buckner, Polk, D.H. Hill, Forrest, [and] Hindman have been ordered away from the Army of Tennessee since Chickamauga."[49]

But what of Bragg's predilection for purging his command of undesirables? Assuming that he remained within his authority (which was not the case with Polk; Davis reminded Bragg that it was unlawful for him to dismiss a lieutenant general outright), should not an army commander be free to prune perceived deadwood from his operation? One might argue that Lee did the same following the Seven Days' battles when Holmes, Magruder, Huger, Whiting, and D.H. Hill (who was not permanently transferred out of Lee's army until after Fredericksburg, but fell out of grace during Seven Days) were quietly dispersed to distant theaters. However, the difference between the two generals' approaches is instructive. For one thing, Lee imposed this kind of wholesale turnover only once, early on after assuming command; he did not make a habit of it. Thereafter Lee mostly worked with what he had, and generals like Richard Ewell were relieved few and far between. Secondly, Lee was discreet in replacing generals, rather than demonstratively punitive by bringing charges for poor performance, for example. Lee's motive seemed to be *team building* rather than tearing down; he was choosing people with whom he perceived that he could best work. Otherwise Stonewall Jackson would have been the first to go, based on his dismal showing during the Seven Days.

One might argue that Lee had an advantage over Bragg by virtue of having more clout in Richmond, and that Lee's "dumping ground" for unwanted generals was usually the West which thereby suffered in comparison to the talent pool that Lee enjoyed. These arguments do not hold up under scrutiny, however, where Bragg's army is concerned. None of the generals that Lee exiled went to the Army of Tennessee except for D.H. Hill, and he not until 1863 just before Chickamauga (then exiting shortly thereafter). Furthermore, Bragg had plenty of talent that he failed to utilize. Patrick Cleburne was easily one of the finest generals in the Confederacy. Bragg was well aware of his ability; he once advised D.H. Hill to "consult Cleburne, who is cool, resourceful, and ever alive to a success." But Cleburne never rose above division command, likely because he remained on Bragg's blacklist beginning with his vote of no-confidence after Murfreesboro. Additionally, a future, capable corps commander of Lee's army had been posted with Bragg early in the war. Richard Heron Anderson served under Bragg at Pensacola in 1861, but became an early scapegoat of his commander following a Yankee incursion into the harbor while

Confederate officers allegedly indulged in a New Year's Eve celebration. The matter was resolved by Anderson's transfer to Virginia.[50]

Not only did Bragg "get rid of all such generals" following Chickamauga, he dismantled the army's organization as well, and not with the aim of streamlining for efficiency, but to break up blocs of perceived opposition, particularly those from Kentucky and Tennessee. Connelly describes the deleterious effect on the army and the Southern cause:

> The two months of feuding with other officers had prevented Bragg from giving rightful attention to military duties.... During October and most of November, Bragg lacked a general strategic plan.... This lack of planning and the amount of time expended on the army's command problems led to disastrous results.[51]

Indeed, Bragg's ill-advised distraction with personnel matters contributed heavily to his army's calamitous rout at Missionary Ridge that November.

Subsequent events and outcomes demonstrate that Polk and the other officers

Major General Patrick Cleburne, a native of Ireland, was one of the most talented generals in the Confederacy. That he did not attain command above the division level represented a loss to the South largely attributable to Bragg. Two actions incurred Bragg's disfavor: the first was Cleburne's vote of no confidence in reply to Bragg's first circular letter; the second was Cleburne's studied recommendation submitted in January 1864 that the army enlist and train slaves in exchange for their freedom. Bragg was working in Richmond as military adviser to President Davis when the latter came across his desk, and gloated that "the Emancipation project of Hardee, Cheatham, Cleburne & Co.... will kill them" (Hallock, *Braxton Bragg*, 180) (Library of Congress).

were right: Davis should have reassigned Bragg—preferably earlier, but certainly during the interval after Chickamauga when his command structure imploded upon itself. Bragg had come very close to removal once before, in March 1863, when President Davis ordered Joseph Johnston to dispatch General Bragg to Richmond and assume command of the Army of Tennessee. That did not come to pass, however, after Johnston arrived and found Bragg at the bedside of his critically ill wife. By the time she recovered, Johnston had fallen ill himself and Bragg retained his command.

When worse strife erupted after Chickamauga, Davis surely saw the same pattern repeating itself and should have known that all would not end well. Instead, he clung to the hope that, if retained, Bragg would put aside his vendetta. "The President held consistently to a naive conviction that every Confederate would put aside personal considerations and grievances stemming from past events and cheerfully cooperate in the cause."[52]

Even had he considered removing Bragg, a secondary problem for the president was the question of who should replace him. A creative solution to this dilemma might have been Longstreet. After he and Lee had clashed over strategy at Gettysburg, the Old War Horse was likely looking for greener pastures. He craved a separate command; he was at hand and had already made himself at home in the Army of Tennessee; and he was actively formulating strategic proposals for the West. The subsequent course that events took for Longstreet, including the failure of his advance upon Knoxville and the trying, fruitless sojourn in East Tennessee throughout that winter, suggests that he was not being well utilized. It is true that shortly after reuniting with Lee's army in May 1864 he conceived a brilliant flank attack during the Battle of the Wilderness which would not have happened had he been away commanding in the West, but its potential was cut short when he was grievously wounded. After an extended recovery, he served Lee effectively during the long siege outside of Richmond and Petersburg. Nevertheless, it is conceivable that Longstreet's gifts might have been better realized at the reins of the Army of Tennessee.

Such speculation is inconclusive at best. But Longstreet was not the only general whose talents were misdirected. Bragg's abilities clearly resided in the area of organization and administration, not field command. Polk had reached this conclusion some time before, and wrote his views to Davis by letter dated March 30, 1863, extensively quoted in Chapter 6.

For two months following Chickamauga the Army of Tennessee, with Bragg still at its head, maintained a vigil from the heights above Chattanooga. Initially Bragg thought to starve the Federal army out of the city, but then General William "Baldy" Smith contrived a means to restore the Yankees' commissary and succeeded in opening their "Cracker Line." Bragg seemed to have no other strategy. No longer a siege, he nevertheless remained in place with little thought or effort toward improving the Confederate works. Many believed Missionary Ridge and Lookout Mountain naturally impregnable, while others worried over the army's inactivity as Federal reinforcements arrived weekly. Even Bragg ultra-loyalist and staff surgeon Dr. T.G. Richardson urged the commanding general to resign during this interval, and referred to the army's situation above Chattanooga as "this most incomprehensible position."[53]

Bragg finally did resign from command of the Army of Tennessee, but not until the aftermath of its tragic defeat on Missionary Ridge in late November 1863. The army's dramatic rout was perhaps inevitable: as Lee had written recently after his Gettysburg defeat, "Once a leader lost the confidence of his men, 'disaster must sooner or later ensue.'" And indeed, disaster ensued. To Bragg's credit, he tried valiantly to rally his men as they streamed down the back side of Missionary Ridge. Amidst heavy fire he jumped off his horse to grab a Florida regiment's battle flag that had fallen to the ground. "Bragg, thought an observer, may be a tyrant to his men, yet he still is 'a brave old soldier.'"[54]

Again, as he had done after other debacles, Bragg framed a scapegoat. This time he blamed Breckinridge, claiming he was drunk for three days before, during and after the battle of Missionary Ridge. However, the record refutes this accusation, as evidenced by the fact that Bragg followed Breckinridge's advice offered in a council of war the night of November 24. During that meeting Hardee proposed an overnight withdrawal, but Breckinridge insisted on maintaining the position. "If the army 'couldn't fight here with such advantage of position, they couldn't fight anywhere,'" he declared. Bragg chose Breckinridge's course over Hardee's. Would he have heeded the counsel of a drunken man?[55]

Interestingly, although he proffered his resignation following the inglorious rout, Bragg was stunned when it was promptly accepted, perhaps another manifestation of his incongruous optimism. After leaving the army, he sojourned at Warm Springs, Georgia, for some therapeutic rest and recuperation with Elise, Dr. Richardson and other staff members. In February 1864 Davis named Bragg to a position in Richmond that suited him well. As military adviser to the president he served as *de facto* chief of staff of the Confederate Army and, significantly, had a hand in administrative and logistical matters. The job favored his talents, and for the most part he performed admirably. However, many were mystified and indignant at Bragg's apparent promotion after the drastic failure at Chattanooga. Others saw it more cynically. The general's former chief of staff William Mackall wrote to his wife, "Bragg is humbugged by the President and is in 'honorable exile.'"[56]

In Richmond Bragg's health and mental state stabilized and he mostly refrained from stirring up new quarrels, although old ones with his former army comrades flared up from time to time. He enjoyed a cordial relationship with Josiah Gorgas, chief of the Confederate Ordnance Bureau and like Bragg a superior administrator and staunch devotee to the cause. The Braggs regularly played whist with Gorgas and his wife. However, even during this time of relative equilibrium Bragg's erratic personality occasionally surfaced. Gorgas wrote of him in April 1864: "His views are so startling & decided that I am tempted to think him *a little cracked.*"[57]

If there is any proof of Bragg's talent for a desk job as opposed to field command, it is demonstrated by his return to the field in October 1864 when Davis dispatched him to Wilmington, North Carolina. There the Union army and navy launched a joint attack on Fort Fisher in late December 1864, but defeated themselves under the poor leadership of General Benjamin Butler with some help from the harsh winter weather along the North Carolina coast. An overly elated Bragg saw this stroke of good luck as a well-earned "victory," ignoring warnings from the fort's commanders that the Yankees were certain to try again. Bragg even staged a celebratory parade in Wilmington, another example of his "unfortunate way of announcing his successes" prematurely, as observed by his eldest brother John. Bragg's glee rendered him ill-prepared for the inevitable return of the Federal fleet in January 1865, and he fell back on his old pattern in the face of the enemy: indecision, fretfulness, and inaction, followed by defeat.[58]

On January 15, as his beloved bastion endured the most intense naval bombardment in history and land invasions from two sides, Fort Fisher's engineering genius General Chase Whiting implored Bragg to order up Hoke's brigade, which had been sent to Wilmington from Virginia to reinforce the fort. In the midst of Whiting's repeated, desperate pleas, Bragg messaged him that

"Hoke is moving on enemy, but I am confident you will repel him with your infantry." However, Hoke had no orders at the time to attack…. Whiting wired another plea to Bragg: "The enemy are about to assault; they outnumber us heavily…. Attack! Attack! It is all I can say and all you can do." Bragg was not yet stirred to action.

The crisis stymied Bragg, and Hoke's men remained on standby until belatedly ordered to advance, then erratically recalled before they made contact with the enemy. Fort Fisher, guardian of the sole remaining port of entry into the Confederacy, fell to General Bragg's incapacity as much as to the Federals. Bragg remained in Wilmington for five weeks afterward and, as in the past, obsessed over what newspapers had to say about the Fort Fisher disaster. Again he repeated his pattern of pressuring an officer, in this case General Hoke, to self-incriminate, still nursing his resolve "no longer to bear the sins of others." But of course in his mind *all* sins were unquestionably the responsibility of others.[59]

General Bragg commanded

Brigadier General Josiah Gorgas was the superlatively talented chief of ordnance for the Confederate States Army. While the army suffered chronic shortages of food, clothing, shelter and other necessities, under his leadership the supply of arms and ammunition was invariably dependable. He energetically established Southern armament manufacturing centers and arranged to import as many arms from overseas that could be run by the blockade. Gorgas and his wife enjoyed quietly socializing with Braxton and Elise Bragg in Richmond, but nonetheless he confided to his diary that he sometimes found Bragg "a little cracked" ("Gorgas, Josiah," House Divided: The Civil War Research Engine at Dickinson College).

the Department of North Carolina forces in the last major battle of the Civil War at Bentonville, North Carolina. Here he committed another of his trademark field blunders. General Hoke spotted a "golden opportunity," a gap in his front asking to be exploited. Even though Bragg was not even present on the field at that time, just as at Perryville he disregarded the judgment of his subordinate on the ground and ordered Hoke to make "a full frontal assault. Though he knew it was a mistake to do so, Hoke complied with Bragg's orders" resulting in tragic waste of life. The overall commander, Joseph Johnston, later noted that as the battle unfolded "Bragg's nervousness ... was very injurious." Bragg simply lacked the gift and temperament for field command.[60]

Perhaps it is Davis's fault that Braxton Bragg was not better utilized for the Confederacy all along. Davis kept Bragg in command of field armies for too long, and similarly stood by an incompetent commissary general throughout almost the entire war. Many men suffered debilitating hunger and deprivation as a result. Bragg in this position would have speedily transformed the department into a squared-away, efficient operation, especially if given ancillary power over the railroads as was General Haupt of the Union. At least Bragg should have been transferred to his advisory position earlier in the war. As it was, once in Richmond he was able to alleviate considerably the troops' suffering by threatening the railroad presidents, bullying them to prioritize freight over passengers and thereafter transport many more tons of supplies to the front. And as always, in his administrative position he made it a priority to address the needs of hospitals. Polk was right in urging Davis to transfer Bragg to Richmond, but for so long the president would not listen. Had Bragg been in his administrative position at the capital earlier, it would have relieved Davis of considerable burden and stress, and the Army of Tennessee might have achieved the victories that its brave, valorous fighting men deserved.[61]

CHAPTER 9

Independent Command in Mississippi

In the wake of Bragg's spiteful dismissal of Polk, President Davis shuffled generals, landing Polk in Mississippi as second-in-command over Joseph Johnston's department. On November 13, 1863, Polk arrived in Enterprise, Mississippi, to replace General Hardee who gladly returned to the Army of Tennessee. Polk's first task was a continuation of Hardee's primary duty: receiving and reorganizing the stream of paroled and exchanged prisoners who had been captured at Vicksburg and Port Hudson in July.[1]

As a result of Bragg's disastrous defeat at Missionary Ridge and his subsequent resignation, in December Joseph Johnston was called away from the department to take command of the Army of Tennessee. The bitter discord surrounding Bragg's leadership, which consistently generated polarization and even paralysis in the army's operations, was finally through. Polk had long lobbied for Davis to face the truth of Bragg's ineptitude for that particular position, but the end finally came when Bragg himself submitted his resignation following the debacle outside Chattanooga. Johnston was ordered to Dalton, Georgia, on December 13, and Polk inherited the helm of his department in Mississippi.

Polk renamed his command the Department of Alabama, Mississippi, and East Louisiana with headquarters in Meridian, Mississippi. His forces consisted of two infantry divisions led by generals William W. Loring and Samuel G. French, totaling approximately 6,000 troops (a number steadily increasing from the remustering of exchanged prisoners). In addition, Polk reorganized the cavalry under General Nathan Bedford Forrest and General Stephen D. Lee, designating a boundary line running through Prentiss, Mississippi, north of which Forrest would operate while Lee's cavalry patrolled to the south. Polk also ordered General French to go to work repairing damaged track and bridges of the Southern Railroad in the vicinity of Jackson, which the latter set about diligently to accomplish.[2]

In early January 1864 reports from various sources came into Polk's headquarters of a pending naval attack on Mobile. Polk aided General Dabney Maury, the commander at Mobile, in implementing an intensive program of shoring up fortifications, and sent two brigades previously loaned to the army in Georgia, now returned by the president's order, to reinforce the Mobile works. No sooner was all of that accomplished than the threat along the Alabama coast subsided, and a new crisis loomed on the western horizon: General William Tecumseh Sherman was assembling an army of invasion.³

Sherman's "Meridian" Campaign

After Grant's victory at Vicksburg in July 1863, won with his trusted comrade-in-arms Sherman at his side, the Union commander looked to Mobile as his next logical conquest. From there Federal forces could penetrate into the heartland of Southern war industry at Selma, then aim eastward at the multifaceted martial production and distribution facilities in Georgia. However, that summer Washington had different political agenda and goals. Nonetheless, as author Buck T. Foster demonstrates, Grant's ambition to take Mobile in 1863 was the genesis of Sherman's Meridian campaign of February 1864:

> Grant did not secure permission to attempt a capture of Mobile.... [although] the importance of the city never left his mind, and he hoped that Sherman would have an opportunity to attack the city later on. As early as August 1863, therefore, Sherman had begun to make plans for a move against Meridian.⁴

In his usual frenetic manner, Sherman devoted much thought and effort toward planning the march eastward from Vicksburg. "He ordered a map containing his intended route. The map included information on Meridian in Mississippi as well as Demopolis and Mobile in Alabama." *From the beginning the ultimate objective was never Meridian, but points in Alabama, ultimately Mobile.* However, Sherman's plans were temporarily waylaid by Bragg's victory at Chickamauga, after which Federal reinforcements, including Sherman and his Army of the Tennessee, marched to Chattanooga and helped win Grant's victory there in November 1863. Even then, Sherman continued to focus on his move across central Mississippi. "While in Tennessee in mid–November, Sherman ... wrote to [Union general in chief Henry] Halleck that a force should hit Meridian and Selma."⁵

The Federal win in Tennessee opened the way for new ventures, but Grant still clung to his cherished scheme to go after Mobile and the desirable fruit that victory there would yield. "Grant had written Halleck that he would like to try a previously considered movement to capture the port of Mobile, Alabama. As Grant saw it, whether Mobile fell or not, this would open the prospect of a campaign that would move his forces east from the Mississippi River into Alabama." On December 21, 1863, Union brass met at Nashville to plan their next move. Although once again Grant urged the importance of taking Mobile at this juncture, again he was thwarted by Washington. Thereupon Grant delegated to Sherman this aspect of his grand plan, and the latter pulled out his previously acquired maps to work on the operational specifics:

> It was not until January that Sherman, for the first time, outlined his exact intentions. He planned to gather as many infantrymen and artillerists as the region could spare and move

from "Vicksburg direct on Demopolis or Selma" while a significant cavalry force moved from Memphis until it reached the Mobile and Ohio Railroad. The cavalry would travel down the railroad to Meridian, where it would meet with Sherman's main force. This action, he explained, would ... "endanger the loss of Selma, and perhaps Mobile."[6]

Grant approved Sherman's plan and wrote Henry Halleck in Washington that he had ordered Sherman to advance upon Meridian, destroy the railroads there, and move on to Mobile provided his force at hand was adequate to the task. To reassure the cautious Halleck, Grant outlined in his missive a safety net, noting that Sherman would return to Vicksburg after his destructive work at Meridian "unless the opportunity of going into Mobile with the force he has appears perfectly plain.... Sherman will be instructed ... to take no extra hazard of losing his army."[7]

In February 1864 Major General William Tecumseh Sherman embarked on an expedition of destruction across central Mississippi. His objective was to march into Alabama to attack the important war manufacturing center at Selma, and if possible go on to capture Mobile. His plan depended on a rendezvous in Meridian with a specially outfitted cavalry force sweeping down from the north—but when it failed to appear Sherman marched his men back to Vicksburg (Library of Congress).

Foster, however, contends that Sherman did not consider Mobile a realistic objective. On January 28 the general wrote his wife that "he 'would be tempted to try Mobile but as it is,' he would only attempt to take Meridian and Demopolis and possibly Selma." Sherman had wired his own message to Halleck and Grant, omitting mention of Mobile: "by the 24th I can make up a force of 20,000 men to strike Meridian, and it may be Selma." Despite Foster's contention that he had ruled out Mobile, Sherman nonetheless continued to give it lip service as a possible objective. And he definitely intended at least to fulfill Grant's desire "to move into the interior of Alabama" with Selma squarely in his sights. Sherman elaborated on his intentions in a letter to General Nathaniel Banks, commander of the Department of the Gulf in Yankee-occupied New Orleans. Among his aims, he explained to Banks, was to destroy "the only link between Mississippi and Alabama and Georgia[,] ... the single track railroad from Meridian, Mississippi, to Selma, Alabama."[8]

Sherman's infantry advance from Vicksburg was to be coordinated with a large cavalry force launched from Memphis under General William Sooy Smith. Sooy Smith would assemble at Collierville, Tennessee, set out on February 1 toward the Mobile and Ohio Railroad at Okolona, Mississippi, then follow the rails to Meridian where he would unite with Sherman by February 10. This line of march would penetrate territory defended by the formidable Confederate cavalry commander Nathan Bedford Forrest, but Sherman trusted his meticulous preparations: "Sherman believed that Sooy Smith would outnumber Forrest almost two to one." Indeed, Sherman held high hopes for his cavalry leader; he "wanted Sooy Smith to obliterate Forrest's command on the way to Meridian if the opportunity presented itself." At the very least Sooy Smith's "force of 7,000 men would move southeast to Okolona, brushing aside any Confederate cavalry that they came across."[9]

Meanwhile at Polk's headquarters in Meridian, the first inkling of Sherman's scheme came courtesy of Forrest: "As early as January 11 one of Forrest's scouts reported that an advance into Mississippi was being planned. Forrest rushed the information to Polk." The most likely objective of the move, Polk reasoned, was Mobile, and indeed his conjecture was correct in the larger strategic sense. Sherman's column departed Vicksburg on February 3. The question was, what were Sherman's intermediary destinations?[10]

Not fathoming that Sherman would advance without a fully operational supply line, virtually unheard of before then, Polk ordered Stephen Lee to destroy the railroad west of Jackson. To division commander William Loring, Polk telegraphed that he "detain the enemy as long as possible from getting into Jackson." The problem was that Sherman, unexpectedly unencumbered without the usual long supply train, marched at record speed and had already reached Clinton, ten miles west of Jackson, by February 6.[11]

Polk was bringing reinforcements from Mobile as rapidly as possible. Even so, his major problem was the disparity in numbers between his available force and the juggernaut heading in his direction. Sherman marched with at least 20,000 infantry, according to Ben Wynne; French and Loring numbered the force at 25,000. Foster gives this number as well, counting the 5,000 cavalry and artillery accompanying Sherman's main column. Connelly sets the Union number at 35,000, apparently derived from the figure stated by Joseph Johnston from his command post at Dalton, Georgia, thus not reliable.[12]

The numbers for Polk's available force are even more unclear, partly because his strength remained in flux with reinforcements from Mobile coming and going and detached brigades returning from the Army of Tennessee. Connelly characterizes Polk's "infantry force of 9,000" as "feeble." This number, derived from Polk's February 9 report to the War Department, includes "1700 exchanged prisoners imperfectly organized." Polk's two divisions had both been greatly reduced. For example,

Loring's division, previously composed of seven brigades, in February 1864 counted only three brigades present in Mississippi. French's division was one brigade short of its usual three; the absent brigades from both divisions had earlier transferred to the Army of Tennessee, although arriving too late to reinforce Bragg at Chattanooga. The only figure with any reliability is provided by French himself; he states he had 2,200 on February 1. In spite of its reduced status, Foster quotes a report of Union general Hurlbut that Loring's division numbered 6,000, consistent with Polk's February 9 report. Foster's own separate counts for Polk's two divisions add up to 8,200; yet, incongruously, Foster also claims that Polk, "without adequate reinforcements" had "twelve thousand infantry in Mississippi." It is difficult to understand his derivation, unless he simply doubled the 6,000 number for Loring, assuming French's force to be of equal strength. This estimate can be safely disregarded as Foster seems to have difficulty with consistency in numbers: reporting, for example, Polk's "promised reinforcements from Mobile" at 6,000 in one instance and 2,000 at another. Perhaps this discrepancy simply illustrates the fluidity of Polk's numerical strength.[13]

Weighing all of these estimates, no one disputes that Polk was significantly outnumbered, and it seems fair to conclude by more than two to one. In spite of the disparity the Confederates offered constant resistance, contrary to many historians' assertions that Sherman swept across Mississippi encountering little to no opposition. Actually, numerous fights occurred along the way involving delaying actions, battle lines, and considerable casualties. On the morning of February 4 General James McPherson's column encountered an 800-strong line of cavalry under Wirt Adams's command on the old Champion Hill battlefield. McPherson advanced a 2,000-man line which steadily drove the Confederates back but necessitated fighting for the remainder of the day. The Yankees described a brave drama likely starring General Adams himself:

> Not long after McPherson arrived, a Confederate officer on a white horse came riding hard across the field.... The horseman came within "easy range, coolly drew his revolver" and fired at the Union officers. The shot ricocheted off a tree branch and rolled "harmlessly" across the ground. Some of the blue-clad soldiers returned fire, at which time the officer shouted: "You may shoot, you damn Yankees, but you can't hit me anyhow." The rider quickly turned his horse and rode hard for the opposite side of the field with Federal bullets flying after him. No shot hit its target, and the white horse carried its rider out of musket range and into the Confederate lines. For the rest of the day, as the Federals advanced, they could see the officer riding wildly up and down his lines, waving his sword violently and encouraging his men. Union officers fired shot after shot, but the officer remained uninjured.... Late that afternoon, the Federals came across the white steed lying dead by the side of the road. When they inquired about the horse's owner, nearby citizens said that they thought it belonged to Wirt Adams.[14]

After the Yankees entered Clinton, bands blaring and banners billowing, they ran into a "fierce" skirmish two miles east of the town. This engagement impressed the Yankee combatants, one describing widespread admiration for Confederate maneuvers:

> At this junction I witnessed one of the most beautiful and interesting sights I had ever seen.... The enemy ... had here massed their entire cavalry force in an immense cotton field and clearing.... A battery was hastily brought forward and opened upon this dense mass of the enemy effectively but without producing panic or confusion. Their perfection of discipline, graceful movements and apparent ease with which they formed into columns of divisions at a trot, and left the field before we could bring our infantry forward, was a sight which elicited the hearty applause of our men.[15]

That evening Iowa soldiers stormed the earthworks protecting the capital city of Jackson. A race ensued as the evacuating Confederates rushed to cross the Pearl River, detaching their pontoon bridge to prevent the Yankees from using it. They only half succeeded: cutting the bridge from its moorings and hacking and chopping at the pontoon boats while under fire from the banks, the Rebels eluded the Yankees' pursuit, but within a day and a half the Northerners were able to repair the broken-up bridge and appropriate it for their own crossing. Meanwhile the Yankee army set about wreaking massive destruction upon Jackson. This was the third time since the war began that the Yankees looted and burned the capital city, and they spared nothing.

> "Nearly all of the large buildings here have been burnt," an Illinoisan commented, and "there are a good many buildings being burnt today, and the Soldiers are doing a big business of the foraging line." "It was a heap of ruins," another soldier wrote.[16]

Modern historians, apologists for Sherman, go to great pains to lecture repeatedly that he ordered only the destruction of "public property." If that is so, the taxpayers of Mississippi (and other regions later victimized by Sherman's hard war raids) apparently expended state funds on goods of a surprisingly personal nature, such as "furniture of every description, from rocking-cradles to pianos, clothing, books, in fact almost every article of domestic utility and ornament." Federal soldiers' diaries and accounts belie any claims of a "public property" policy, as these writings extol the extensive burning of private homes and belongings. Unconvincingly, the same Sherman apologists invariably accuse Confederates of the lion's share of pilfering and destruction. If that was the case, then Rebels must not have been very thorough at their thieving, for it seemed that vast quantities of their countrymen's property escaped their notice only to fall into the hands of the enemy.[17]

The following day the Union army left behind the ruins of Jackson and marched toward Brandon. McPherson's corps saw to it that tiny Brandon met a fate similar to the capital city. "The town all laid in ashes. Great destruction of property," one soldier wrote. Another employed a Biblical metaphor: "Brandon purified as by fire."[18]

The Confederates meanwhile made their way to Morton, where they entrenched and assumed a battle formation. Once the Federals approached, so close were the lines that Union soldiers enjoyed the music of Confederate bands. At this place Foster states that Sherman "plan[ned] for a pitched battle the following day." He was not the only commander preparing for combat. Confederate general French records on the 8th that "Loring placed the whole force present at my command to face about, form line of battle, and give the enemy a fight.... We held a good position and the troops were in fine spirits, but the enemy would not attack us."[19]

In spite of the Confederates' offering battle, Wynne unaccountably contends that "Polk's infantry ... could offer no resistance." Foster similarly dismisses the Confederate army as having "little chance of a victory against such overwhelming odds. Sherman had seen to it that only a conventional attack would prove any threat to his mission, and the Confederates were incapable of launching one." Apparently, neither was Sherman inclined to attack the Confederate infantry as it faced him in line of battle, but there was a cavalry fight that day. Interestingly, at Morton an Iowa soldier, huddled with comrades around a fire, voiced his understanding of his army's purpose: "By this time it became apparent that we were on 'Uncle Billy Sherman's raid toward the heart of the Confederacy. We were bound for Alabama or Georgia; possibly Mobile [or] Savannah; certainly Selma." By now even the rank and file grasped that their ultimate objectives lay beyond the borders of Mississippi, in the Confederate stronghold of Alabama—"*certainly Selma.*"[20]

Not only did the campfire strategists of Sherman's army expect their march to extend beyond the eastern boundary of Mississippi; Confederate commander Leonidas Polk anticipated the same. His only question was whether Sherman would veer southward from the Southern Railroad in a direct path for Mobile, or remain on a due-east course into Alabama, the route to Selma. Polk's on-again, off-again worrying over Mobile resulted in some back-and-forth shuffling of brigades to and from the coastal batteries on slow, rickety railroads. When one of Sherman's two columns took a southward turn before reaching Morton, Polk became convinced that it meant the wing would cut a diagonal path cross-country toward the Mobile & Ohio Railroad south of Meridian, then follow it on to Mobile. Thus, for a time Polk believed Sherman would bypass Meridian in favor of a more direct route to Mobile. His subordinates disagreed; Stephen Lee, for example, remained convinced that Meridian was Sherman's initial target.[21]

In keeping with Sherman's later self-congratulatory writings of his campaign, Buck Foster makes much of Polk's "confusion" over the objective of Sherman's advance, and takes the opportunity to charge the Southern commander with "miscommunication and poor leadership." But in fact, Polk drew his conclusions by applying military logic to Sherman's movements. Polk suspected that Sherman ultimately aimed for Selma or Mobile—and indeed Selma was the intended destination, while Mobile remained a possible ultimate goal in keeping with orders of his superior, General Grant. Later, not having reached either, Sherman conveniently redefined his objectives even as he gloated over "completely confus[ing] his enemy.... When he arrived a few miles from Meridian and understood that his feints continued to keep Polk guessing, he was astounded at their success." What Sherman later deems "feints," at the time may have been more accurately termed "keeping his options open." Virtually every historian in analyzing Sherman's Meridian campaign refers to it as a dress rehearsal or practice or learning exercise portending his March to the Sea through Georgia. It is important to remember, however, that during much of his Georgia tramp Sherman likewise refrained from deciding his final destination, which ultimately turned out to be Savannah. There, too, he "kept his options open" as to whether he would end up on the Gulf Coast, perhaps Mobile; head north for the huge, vital Southern powder works of Augusta; or conclude his raid through Georgia at Savannah. Now in Mississippi Sherman also managed his march in a similarly fluid manner—with Meridian as the immediate destination, but always with an eye for "the opportunity of going to Mobile," in Grant's words. Therefore Polk cannot be entirely faulted if he was confused, for Sherman's own aims remained indefinite and open, dependent upon circumstances.[22]

After Sherman declined any frontal attack against the enemy at Morton and the Confederates retreated to Hillsboro, the Federals promptly pillaged and burned the former town. Then on February 10, after skirmishing with the Confederate rear guard, they repeated their destructive rampage in Hillsboro. "'Most of the town was burned up,' a fellow commented. 'I could not help pitying many women and children who were thrown outdoors.'" "The town is in flames," a member of the Ninth Indiana noted in his diary.[23]

The following day a single Confederate cavalry regiment "stubbornly battled" four Union regiments, "burn[ing] bridge after bridge before the Union cavalry." Lake Station was the next victim of the incendiary Yankees, and after only a brief occupancy the evening of February 12, Decatur followed. Near Decatur Sherman came close to being captured in a wayside house where he stopped for a few hours' rest. In retaliation for his scare, the structures in Decatur that had survived its first burning were thoroughly obliterated. "Most of the town burned during the night," and Foster lamely adds, "causing some of the Union division commanders to order their men to cease such excessive actions.... Although the officers issued warnings, the men continued pillaging, robbing, burning and shooting. 'I heard of none being even arrested for it,' the same fellow concluded."[24]

After their wanton destruction of Decatur, the last leg of the Federals' march would bring them to their first objective: Meridian. The importance of this point lay not only in the potential for great destruction and deprivation that could be wreaked there upon the Confederates, for whom the town served as a major depot. More important to the long-range goals of the raid, this was the appointed site for the rendezvous with General Sooy Smith's cavalry force making its way southeastward across upper Mississippi. Already Smith was late according to the original schedule. He was to meet Sherman at Meridian on February 10, but then Sherman himself was also running a few days late. Nevertheless, even as his columns neared Meridian, Sherman continued to look ahead optimistically to what he and Smith together could accomplish beyond the Mississippi border: "If William Sooy Smith's cavalry force reached him at Meridian, he could continue into Alabama and break the railroad at Demopolis or Selma." Sooy Smith's 7,000-man cavalry was the key to further operations, but for the moment while he awaited Smith's arrival Sherman focused on Meridian and the damage he could accomplish there to set back the Confederate cause.²⁵

In the meantime Polk was hardly sitting back waiting passively for Sherman to burst in on Meridian. The town, a major railroad junction, contained vast and valuable equipment and stores, and Polk supervised a massive, systematic salvage operation to prevent their falling into the hands of the enemy. "All stores and all at Enterprise 'except corn in the shuck' were saved. All shop tools and rolling stock 'except eight or ten cars' were likewise moved to safety." In little time Polk accomplished "the removal of an estimated $12,000,000 in military property, south to Mobile or east to Selma, together with the rolling stock of the three railroads, so that when Sherman marched in on Valentine's Day he found the warehouses yawning empty and the tracks deserted in all four directions." Without sufficient numbers to defend Meridian, Polk had withdrawn his infantry and trains on February 14, hours before Sherman marched in. The Southerners moved eastward across the border to Demopolis, Alabama, where they formed in a strong position to block Sherman's anticipated advance, and awaited reinforcements finally on the way from Johnston's army in Georgia.²⁶

Sherman was reportedly "furious at the loss" of Confederate property successfully removed by Polk, and "he put the blame on Smith, who should have arrived four days ago, in time to prevent the removal of spoils, but who had neither come himself nor sent a courier." In the meantime, "though the military property had been hauled away, the facilities were still there, and there was civilian property in abundance," and Sherman put his men to work destroying the town with tools brought in specifically for that purpose. What could not be torn down was burned. After five days, pronounced Sherman, "Meridian … no longer exists." As his men wreaked havoc, Sherman fumed over the non-appearance of Sooy Smith. "'It will be a novel thing in war,' he complained testily, between puffs on a cigar, 'if infantry has to await the motions of cavalry.'"²⁷

And just where was Sooy Smith? Polk had ordered Stephen Lee's cavalry to join Forrest's in blocking Smith's march through Mississippi, and the Southern horsemen had proven more than successful in that aspect of their mission. Polk had urged even more: "he had hopes of destroying that arm of the Federal force.… It was of the 'highest consequence' that this cavalry force be destroyed. If this could be accomplished Sherman's whole army 'must come to a bad end.'" Polk was not the only general nurturing hopes with regard to Smith's cavalry expedition; Sherman too held great expectations of Sooy Smith, expressed while outlining Smith's assignment and instructing him on how to outfit his force. Sooy Smith's command included a division under General Benjamin Grierson, who had overseen the successful raid throughout Mississippi and Louisiana in April 1863 which diverted Southern cavalry from Grant's maneuvers around Vicksburg and destroyed millions of dollars' worth of Southern property. During that expedition, however, because most of the regular Confederate cavalry had been transferred to Bragg's army, Grierson faced nothing more than home guards, state militia, and convalescents turned out of hospitals and lined up along the main streets of Mississippi towns.[28]

Now, however, the infamous Nathan Bedford Forrest stood in the path of the Federal horsemen, albeit with less than half the number of his Northern foe and far less effectively armed. Outnumbered as he was and uncertain of Smith's—or for that matter Sherman's—plan, Forrest could not attack outright; instead, for several days he maintained a parallel, southeastward track, monitoring Smith's progress and staying alert for opportunities. Detachments from Forrest's main force skirmished with the Federal cavalry at Prairie Station and Aberdeen. Once Smith reached the Mobile & Ohio Railroad the Yankee scenario became clear and Forrest set a typically wily trap to envelop the Federal force. Faced with this level of maneuvering and awed by Forrest's reputation,

Brigadier General William Sooy Smith was an accomplished engineer, but as a cavalry commander he was no match for Nathan Bedford Forrest. He never made his rendezvous with Sherman's infantry in Meridian, but when routed at Okolona his horsemen fled precipitously back to Memphis, even though his force outnumbered Forrest's more than two to one. Sherman was disgusted with the cavalry, writing his wife that he was "ashamed of them" (photograph by Jefferson T. Upson, Library of Congress).

after a fight at West Point Smith suddenly and unexpectedly opted to turn around and go back to Memphis, abandoning his scheduled rendezvous with Sherman. Forrest pursued and on February 22 a "major engagement took place at Okolona, where the Confederates drove the federals into a full retreat" and the Northerners abandoned five guns. A subsequent fight near Pontotoc lost the Federals another gun. There broken-down horses forced Forrest to break off his pursuit, but Sooy Smith kept running all the way back to Memphis. "Sherman was livid, and later chastised Smith for failing to follow orders."[29]

Sooy Smith made his U-turn on the same day that Sherman took a U-turn of his own back to Vicksburg, and thus "abandoned his proposed advance on Selma." Not only did the Federal commander find himself stood up by his cavalry ("*If* William Sooy Smith's cavalry force reached him at Meridian, he could continue into Alabama"), but had he continued on his own he would also face Polk's formidable line of infantry drawn up at Demopolis, with reinforcements from Cheatham's and Cleburne's crack divisions already in Alabama moving rapidly to join Polk.[30]

Using words eerily foretelling his March to the Sea through Georgia, after returning to Vicksburg Sherman boasted publicly of his grand success in cutting "a swath of desolation fifty miles broad across the State of Mississippi which the present generation will not forget.... I could have gone on to Mobile or over to Selma, but without other concurrent operations it would have been unwise." However, privately to his wife Ellen, Sherman "confessed his regret that Smith's non-arrival had prevented him from applying what his foes were calling 'the Sherman torch' to Alabama." He declared to Ellen his disgust with his cavalry: "I am ashamed of them."[31]

Polk's Primary Accomplishment: Saving Selma

Polk directed his cavalry to stop Sooy Smith, and their success cut short Sherman's adventure and prevented his plunging toward further destruction and conquest in Alabama, whether Selma or even Mobile. As early as February 6, Polk ordered Forrest to "move down with the greater part of your force to Grenada, and to hold yourself in readiness," although at that time Polk projected that cutting the enemy's supply line and communications would be Forrest's primary tactical goal. Several days later, however, Polk had a clearer picture of the situation. Based on Forrest's report deducing that the large Federal force moving "from Collierville to Pontotoc [to] strike the Prairies and Mobile and Ohio Railroad" was the primary threat facing him, Polk understood the scope of Sherman's thrust. Their concurrent operation resulted in Forrest's halting Sooy Smith at Okolona, which in turn arrested Sherman. Yet most historians overlook Polk and Forrest's accomplishment, even going so far as to revise Sherman's own intent. To his credit, Buck Foster, never failing to praise Sherman's great success, at least acknowledges that Forrest stymied the Federal commander's original plan to move into Alabama. Brian Steel Wills also openly discloses that, after Meridian, "Sherman then expected to seize Selma, Alabama, with its arsenals and foundries, before proceeding to Mobile, Alabama."[32]

In contrast, Ben Wynne omits any mention at all of Sherman's designs on Alabama, instead—incredibly and illogically—insisting that Sherman intended all along to turn around at Meridian. Supposing that was so, what need had he of his awaited cavalry reinforcements, if he planned nothing more after Meridian than to countermarch through territory already exploited and subjugated? Wynne creatively and deftly explains it: "After destroying Meridian, Sherman planned to march his men back to Vicksburg *with Smith's horsemen leading the way.*"[33] So in this scenario,

Sherman rounded up and outfitted 7,000 cavalry and dispatched them separately upon a 200-mile march for the sole, ultimate purpose of providing him a *grand escort* for his return march across central Mississippi! This assertion defies logic and common sense, yet there it is: the Sherman apologia that modern readers of Civil War history are force-fed. Under this scenario, his work done, *Sherman intended all along* nothing more than simply to turn around at Meridian! As always Sherman had everything under perfect control in every particular.

The reader is left to draw his or her own conclusions as to that line of thinking, and then consider the short- and long-term ramifications of Sherman's march across Mississippi in February 1864. Diarist LeRoy Gresham, now 16 years old, concluded that Sherman's Mississippi mission "accomplished nothing but the destruction of some property and the humiliation of a few defenseless women and old men." Indeed, the Macon, Georgia, teenager would find himself similarly impacted by Sherman before the year's end. That Sherman developed a template which he later utilized in his March to the Sea cannot be doubted. An analogy could be made that Mississippi represents the conception, and nine months later in Georgia the birth, of Sherman's unique contribution to the annals of warfare.[34]

Historians make much of the connection between the two raids, but what of Mississippi considered on its own merits? After the fact Sherman touted the destruction of Meridian as his primary accomplishment of the expedition, and demoralization of the state's civilians (and by extension, its fighting men) a close second. As to the latter, no doubt the February operation did contribute to many Mississippians' distress over their condition; Forrest himself warned of this after his own tour through the countryside. But it is also true that Mississippi was *already* considerably demoralized; Polk found this when he first arrived at his new departmental command back in November 1863. So disheartened did he find the troops at Enterprise around Christmas, that he "had them formed in a huge square, and … mounted a table in the center and delivered them a two hours 'Stump Speech,' after which he was applauded with 'three cheers.'" Mississippians had good reason to feel discouraged with Natchez and Vicksburg occupied and their capital Jackson twice burned by the Yankees even *before* Sherman's third fiery visit during his march to Meridian. Civilians and soldiers alike suffered terrible deprivation, breakdown of law and order, and loss of life and fortune.[35]

What of Sherman's thorough destruction of the railroad junction and ancillary facilities at Meridian? He claimed that his men's work there would render the depot's usefulness to the Confederacy forever ended. One Sherman-admiring historian hyperbolically credits the Meridian campaign with "the destruction of the Confederate war making capacity." This statement is wholly untrue. Thanks to Polk's earlier efforts at retaining the excellent service of Major George Whitfield, who was by this time in the process of transferring to the Confederate Railroad Bureau, the Mississippi rails were quickly restored. Expertly aided by L.J. Fleming, Superintendent of the Mobile & Ohio Rail Road (whom Whitfield "pronounced 'the best railroad worker in this or any other country'"), Whitfield saw that the roads were repaired with remarkable speed. On May 2, 1864, Fleming wrote to Polk reporting on the success of the railroad repairs. Behind it all, Polk's undaunted optimism was the force driving Mississippi to recovery:

> Polk took no such gloomy view of the prospect. Though he could scarcely deny.... Sherman's boast of having "made a swath of desolation fifty miles broad across the State of Mississippi ...," he did not agree with his adversary's further assertion that the east-central portion of the state could be written off as a factor in the conflict. "I have already taken measures to have all the roads broken up by him rebuilt," the bishop notified Richmond two days after the raiders turned back in the direction they had come from, "and shall press that work vigorously." Press it he did.... [W]ithin twenty-six days he had the Mobile & Ohio back in operation.... The Southern took longer, mainly because of administrative complications, but within another five weeks it too was open, all the way to the Pearl [River].

It was this kind of energy that no doubt contributed to Polk's being designated "the most enterprising and successful Civil War railroad general." Southerners had suffered railroad rampages before and this time was no different; intrepidly they picked up the pieces and expeditiously repaired the damage.[36]

To the Confederacy as a whole, the most important and crucial ramification of Sherman's march was Polk's saving Selma, Alabama, from the Yankees. Had General Polk not correctly perceived that blocking Sooy Smith's cavalry was the key to stopping Sherman, the latter made it clear that he would have continued into Alabama with Selma his likely target. As it happened, without his formidable cavalry reinforcement, and knowing that Polk's infantry, with sizable reinforcements on the way, stood entrenched outside of Demopolis, Sherman did not dare continue on and risk his army. Instead, he opted for Grant's safety net, as previously outlined to General-in-Chief Henry Halleck: declaring victory and returning westward to Vicksburg.

Polk rightfully pronounced his own satisfaction with what he was able to accomplish in the face of a foe vastly outnumbering him; characteristically, he likened his situation to the Biblical disparity between David and Goliath. Newspapers in Alabama gladly celebrated their salvation from the hard hand of William T. Sherman. A Demopolis paper carried the headline SHERMAN DEFEATED AND HIS CAMPAIGN BROKEN UP in its February 24, 1864, issue. Well did its editors know that their printing presses would have been demolished had Sherman made it to their town.[37]

Polk's movements, both in the use of his own cavalry as well as his infantry, gained for the Confederacy fourteen additional months for Selma's industrial complex to crank out and expand its armaments and naval production. It is almost impossible to exaggerate the importance of Selma, Alabama, to the Confederacy. "At Selma the naval foundry built ironclads for the defense of Mobile. Half of the cannon and two-thirds of the fixed ammunition used by the South in 1864 and 1865 were reportedly made at Selma."[38] Had Selma fallen to the Yankees, the overblown attribution to Sherman of "the destruction of the Confederate war making capacity" might have come closer to the truth. As it was, though, Selma continued operating its iron furnaces, rolling mills, powder mills and arsenals, contributing vast amounts of ordnance to the war effort for another 14 months—undeniably a major factor in extending the life of the Southern Confederacy.

It is interesting to note historians' characterizations of Polk's overall performance, in light of his actual accomplishment of saving Alabama, especially Selma, from Sherman's destructive reach. To begin with, almost universally the impression is given that Sherman met absolutely no resistance in his march eastward. In his only sentence describing the movement across 150 miles of central Mississippi, Charles Bracelen Flood contends, "just the news of Sherman's advance, which was blasting aside every enemy in its way, convinced Confederate general Leonidas Polk to give up Meridian without defending it." No mention is made of the numerous cavalry fights, the Southern infantry taking a stand at Jackson and Morton, or the successful removal of vast stores at Meridian—instead, in his version the Southerners simply slunk away from Sherman's path. Wynne creates a similar impression in *A Hard Trip*, his study of the 15th Mississippi Infantry Regiment: "Polk's entire infantry fell back to the east, retreating through Meridian into Alabama.... During the course of the expedition across central Mississippi, ... the Confederate infantry had not fired a shot in opposition."[39]

Union soldiers actually fighting their way across the state experienced it quite differently: they took plenty of shots! General French, Polk's infantry division commander, saw it differently too; as his men stood eagerly awaiting battle outside Morton, numerous bullets were fired by skirmishers he sent forward, only to have the Yankees decline battle. At Jackson as his men narrowly managed their crossing of the Pearl River under fire, Mississippi sharpshooters fired in return. The Rebels hardly rolled over and played dead during Sherman's march; instead, they expended plenty of ammunition.

Similarly, Forrest's accomplishment in holding back Sooy Smith is cavalierly dismissed by Ben Wynne: "the Union cavalry's departure from the area did not have much of an effect on Sherman's march to Meridian." In fact, Sooy Smith's retreat had a dramatic and decisive effect on Sherman's march by stopping him cold in Mississippi. As the young Georgia diarist LeRoy Gresham accurately assessed it: "The retreat and disappointment of Sherman is owing to the bravery and daring of Forrest, who fought and routed the cooperating column of cavalry, although they were 3 to his 1." Had Sooy Smith's cavalry joined Sherman, the destruction of Meridian would have been only a warm-up to the havoc Sherman could have wrought upon the ironworks and factories and arsenals comprising a veritable industrial corridor through central Alabama.[40]

Finally, historians even go so far as to blame Confederates for the losses inflicted on them by the Union: "While much would be made in future years of abuses by Sherman's 'thieving Yankees' as they crossed Mississippi, the Confederates stripped Meridian of everything that could be carried away, regardless of who it belonged to, as they left the city." Strange, after Confederates had allegedly taken "everything," the Yankees seemed to find plenty of personal property to plunder and burn. Historians who expend much breath and ink minimizing and justifying Sherman's tactics of destruction and starvation then turn around and accuse Confederates of being the true perpetrators. In the same vein, a University of Georgia history professor in an interview aired by NPR assured listeners that it was "probably Confederate guerrillas" who actually burned Atlanta rather than the Yankee army that by then overran and occupied every inch of the city, having evicted almost all of its citizens, even the elderly and ill. Hard to imagine how guerrillas eluded capture while managing to cross heavily guarded lines, and then set widespread fires, all the while escaping the notice of Union provost marshals in an occupied, fortified city! (It is also difficult to understand how academic historians, presumably advocating for the "right" side, believe that anything is made right by untruth.)[41]

Perhaps the crowning touch in rewriting the history of Sherman's February 1864 march through Mississippi has been accomplished by the name conferred upon his operation. "Meridian Campaign" is truly a misnomer. Numerous sources, primarily Sherman's own writing, show that Meridian was not at all the object of the campaign, but merely a meeting place. Although the Mississippi town was in fact the farthest point reached by Sherman's army, he marched with points in Alabama as his intended destination. Perhaps a more accurate name would be "Sherman's Failed Selma Campaign."

Commanding Nathan Bedford Forrest

That Polk successfully turned back Sherman rested largely upon the ability and determination of Major General Nathan Bedford Forrest. Aided by the diligent intelligence gathering of Forrest, Polk discerned Sherman's overall scheme and crafted his defense using Forrest to apprehend the Federal cavalry before it could unite with Sherman's infantry. The tactics employed in accomplishing this purpose were uniquely Forrest's. Many books have examined Forrest's fine work leading up to his victory at Okolona. What goes untouched by historians is the harmonious cooperation that Forrest willingly offered Polk.

Harmonious cooperation from Forrest was never a given. Not one to suffer fools or tolerate men of lesser commitment and willpower than he, Forrest functioned best in independent operations. From the beginning of the war he asserted his personal vision, determination and native ability. At Fort Donelson Forrest contemptuously condemned the commanding generals who determined to surrender, and cut out the following morning with a contingency of men who trusted him to lead the way. At Shiloh he chafed under his orders to guard a quiet creek, and on his own initiative took off with his men for the hottest part of battlefield. That night he independently reconnoitered behind Union lines and pleaded with his superiors to take heed that Union reinforcements were arriving on the field. Later he refused to serve any longer under Wheeler following a conflict, and similarly demanded to be released from Bragg's command. Forrest was not by nature a submissive subordinate.

However, he seemed to serve seamlessly under Polk during this stressful season in Mississippi. Of course they already had a working relationship, as Forrest had earlier been attached to Polk's command during the Kentucky Campaign and at Chickamauga. Never had any known discord rippled their relationship, and Forrest's communications with Polk were invariably respectful and deferential. The underlying reason for this was likely Polk's leadership style. As previously noted, the bishop employed a kind guiding hand. He responded to his subordinates' concerns and skillfully mediated disputes that arose among them. For example, in March 1864 Forrest clashed with his brigade commander General James Chalmers, and promptly dismissed him. Polk considered the matter carefully and after consulting Richmond, "returned [Chalmers] to command within the month, the dispute apparently resolved because it did not arise again." In another incident during the pressing days leading up to Sherman's rampage through central Mississippi, an officer appeared at headquarters with orders to arrest men serving under Forrest who had deserted prior infantry posts. Just then Polk and his subordinates were scrambling to ready their commands for Sherman's advance. Polk attempted to head the matter off, but the officer insisted on confronting Forrest right then. Forrest threatened to quit over this untimely intrusion upon his command, but Polk again smoothed the matter over and no more was heard of it.[42]

Lieutenant General Nathan Bedford Forrest, "Wizard of the Saddle," served under Polk briefly during the Kentucky campaign, at Chickamauga, and again in Polk's Department of Alabama, Mississippi and East Louisiana. Forrest was a brilliant cavalry strategist, tactician and leader of men, but not known as a submissive subordinate. He resolved never again to serve under Wheeler and Bragg, reportedly almost coming to blows with the latter, but relations between him and Polk were always marked by mutual respect, cordiality and cooperation (Brady-Handy Photograph Collection, Library of Congress).

Polk's ability to work successfully with Forrest demonstrates that aplomb and diplomacy were foremost qualities of his leadership. In addition, their relationship serves as evidence of Polk's authenticity of character, for Forrest was one to size up a man and discern any pretensions or duplicity, and finding any, reject him outright.

Jones County

After Sherman made his U-turn at Meridian and returned to Vicksburg, General Polk faced numerous problems in his department in addition to restoring the railroads. One crisis demanding immediate attention was the increasing violence perpetrated by bands of Confederate army deserters in southeastern Mississippi. This isolated area with its low population density and extensive swamplands provided a haven for deserters, whether local residents returning home without leave or soldiers from elsewhere hiding there to evade Confederate authorities.

Deserters' and stragglers' reasons for shirking their duty varied, but they fell under two broad categories. First, by this time many men had grown disillusioned with the war and the prospects for Southern victory. They had long since tired of fighting, retreating, starving, entrenching, and endless marching. Perhaps some felt after seeing so many comrades die that quitting provided their only assurance of survival. A more specific motivation for desertion in Mississippi at this particular time was General Polk's falling back to Alabama as Sherman's forces rampaged across the state in February. The temporary move beyond the state border "greatly demoralized thousands of Confederate soldiers from southeastern Mississippi, many of whom stayed behind to protect their families when Polk retreated behind the Tombigbee River."[43]

Quite a legend grew up surrounding the gangs of deserters in and around Jones County, Mississippi—just about all of it false. The story began with a July 1864 article in a Unionist newspaper operating in the Yankee-occupied town of Natchez. As argued by the late Rudy Leverett, the story was likely never intended to be taken seriously. Newspapers at that time routinely ran articles full of hyperbole and tongue-in-cheek claims. This particular column was probably intended as a kind of parody expressing Northern disdain for quaint backwoods Southerners and their secessionist cause. According to the article, Jones County, thereafter to be known as the "Republic of Jones" (complete with head of state, cabinet and congress), had seceded from the state of Mississippi, and by extension the Confederacy.[44]

Leverett shows how the story was picked up and repeated as though fact by historians, notably a Harvard professor in 1891. Although the account is riddled with factual errors and inaccurately conflates people, events and dates, it continues even to this day in the Civil War lexicon; for example, Ken Burns presented the legend as fact in his documentary on the Civil War. The truth is that no "secession" was enacted or otherwise took place in Jones County.

Through the years writers have used the circumstances in Jones County to fit their particular agenda. Recent authors and movies have re-invented Newton Knight, the cut-throat leader of one of the deserter bands, as a principled Unionist and civil-rights advocate. Even Polk biographer Huston Horn makes this mistake, painting Knight and his gang as "champions of the black people in their midst." In the Manichaean mindset which currently predominates in Civil War history, the Confederacy was by definition on the side of evil, and since the ringleader resisted the Confederacy he is portrayed as good and motivated by the highest principles. Nothing could be further from the truth; before the war this outlaw, while still a minor, committed his first homicide, his victim a slave boy. The next person to die at his hand was his brother-in-law.[45]

A thorough, de-romanticized treatment of this convoluted tale of fugitives hiding out in Jones County can be found in Rudy Leverett's *Legend of the Free State of Jones*. Behind all of the falsehoods, it is an undisputed fact that the deserter camps in southeastern Mississippi and their escalating depredations against helpless civilians, Confederate personnel and facilities quickly got the attention of Leonidas Polk, and he set about to remedy the situation.

On February 7, 1864, Polk ordered a detachment of cavalry from Mobile to deal with the deserters in Jones County; however, this expedition was delayed for the obvious reason of Sherman's lightning-like appearance along the Southern Railroad through the heart of Mississippi. Polk's picked force remained in Mobile given the uncertainty of Sherman's destination; they finally set out for Mississippi on March 2. Colonel Henry Maury, commander of the expedition, wrote a report dated March 12 stating his success in taking a number of prisoners and scattering other outlaws away from their points of concentration. Complaints soon came in from other parts of southern Mississippi and across the border in Louisiana where the runaways who eluded capture had fled. Four deserters who violently resisted arrest were hanged.[46]

Polk also elected to send an infantry force, comprising the 6th and 20th Mississippi, to contend with deserters in Smith County on the northwestern boundary of Jones, under a trusted leader selected by Polk: Colonel Robert Lowry, future governor of Mississippi. During the course of his work, Colonel Lowry's men also entered Jones County where outlaws of Newton Knight's deserter gang fired shots at a small contingent of Lowry's force resting on a porch, killing a sergeant, mortally wounding a lieutenant, and wounding a corporal. The perpetrators of that act were executed, as well as two others who ambushed a party of the Confederate infantrymen. Overall, Lowry brought in hundreds of deserters; around 1,000 returned to their commands under the umbrella of a pardon with a short deadline issued by General Polk on April 16. A total of seven were executed during Lowry's operation.[47]

Notably, none of the Confederate forays into southeast Mississippi to confront the desertion crisis found any semblance of governmental or official organization, not even a united front, among the deserters, contrary to popular tales. There were no articles of secession, no pretense at any government, no "Republic" or "Free State" of Jones or other such entity. Instead, these fugitives from the army operated in small bands with loose ties to one another. Nevertheless, during ensuing decades the wartime events which had taken place in and around Jones County, Mississippi, continued to generate exaggerated and false stories, probably reflective of Americans' fascination with and glorification of outlaws—assigning to them, in the Robin Hood tradition, lofty motives, but lacking any connection to reality.[48]

Lowry remained in the vicinity of Jones County until early May when Polk's army moved to northern Georgia to take part in the Atlanta campaign. Once his mission was concluded, deserter activity in the area was brought to a standstill for many months afterward. Polk could rightfully "take credit for re-establishing the ascendency of the civil power in the courts" and restoring law and order throughout his department.[49]

Colonel Robert Lowry was hand-picked by Leonidas Polk to lead an expedition into Jones County, Mississippi, and surrounding areas to round up deserters who were terrorizing the residents with crime and lawlessness. He commanded the 6th Mississippi Infantry at Shiloh, and during most of the 1880s served as governor of Mississippi ("Lowry, Robert Gadden Haynes," House Divided: The Civil War Research Engine at Dickinson College).

King Cotton

Another side issue that General Polk had to contend with as commander of a department in the vicinity of the Mississippi River was the question of cotton. In the West and Trans-Mississippi, the presence of large amounts of cotton influenced the war policy of both sides. As Federal forces penetrated this area, Northern civilians followed to take advantage of the opportunity to obtain and ship cotton, at huge profits, to waiting New England mills. More than a few U.S. Army officers succumbed to the temptation of greasing their own palms in this unsavory commerce. The situation gave rise to corruption on a massive scale, and many grew rich.

Finally, in 1863 the United States government legitimized this lucrative cotton trade

Chapter 9. Independent Command in Mississippi

through the Captured and Abandoned Property Act, which essentially defined all Southern property as fair game:

> The Treasury Department was responsible for its collection or administration. This led to a great proliferation of the department's bureaucracy.... The full extent of fraud perpetrated by these swarms of agents will never be known. In corrupt collusion with army officers, they got up expeditions whose sole purpose was to capture cotton.[50]

Sometimes Confederate authorities were even able to use stores of cotton to manipulate the movement of Federal forces. Apparently Leonidas Polk engaged in this cotton strategy from time to time. While in command of the department in Mississippi, he directed a subordinate: "See that the Yankees get cotton now and then, but not faster than suits our purposes."[51]

Chapter 10

The Atlanta Campaign

During April 1864 Polk moved a significant portion of his force into northern Alabama in response to a Union build-up along the Tennessee River in that state. Again a possible thrust upon the industrial assets of central Alabama appeared imminent, but by the end of the month Forrest reported the Federals instead moving *en masse* to Chattanooga. A significant change in Union command had Grant in Washington assuming the post of general-in-chief, while Sherman was named commander over an army group composed of the Army of the Cumberland, Army of the Tennessee (the force in transit reported by Forrest), and Army of the Ohio. This sizable host mobilized in Chattanooga as one prong in Grant's overall plan of attacking the Confederacy on several different fronts. Sherman's object was to defeat the Army of Tennessee, Bragg's former army now under command of General Joseph Johnston. Sherman would direct his march along the Western & Atlantic Rail Road which ran between Chattanooga and Atlanta.[1]

On May 2 Sherman opened his Atlanta Campaign by attacking Joseph Johnston's force at Dalton, Georgia. Fully aware that he was greatly outnumbered by Sherman, Johnston called for reinforcements. In response Adjutant General Cooper in Richmond wired Polk: "The President directs ... that you move with Loring's division, and any other available force at your command, to Rome, Ga., and there unite with General Johnston to meet the enemy." On May 4 Johnston also sent dispatches directly to Polk calling for at least a division to be sent immediately to Rome. He soon followed up with a thanks for Polk's prompt attention to the matter, as Polk had notified Johnston on May 7: "Not a moment has been lost in complying with your wishes, since the receipt of your first dispatch of the 4th."[2]

Polk left General Stephen Dill Lee in command of his department and transferred the bulk of his troops eastward, the Army of Mississippi consisting of French's and Loring's divisions of 10,000 infantry and 4,000 cavalry. Polk also ordered a division commanded by General James Cantey brought up from the Mobile garrison. Transportation deficits and delays bedeviled the movement of Polk's force. Locomotives and cars were hard to come by, and the railroad terminated at Blue Mountain, Alabama; from there the army had to march to Georgia over terrible roads through rough terrain. Cantey's men, however, were able to travel the entire way by rail from Mobile.[3]

Bragg, now established in his advisory position with the War Department at Richmond, once again occupied a position of superiority over Polk. At this time, "always happy to squelch Polk," Bragg revived the spirit of their former association. As Polk struggled on the ground to move his army toward the emergency in Georgia, from his desk Bragg antagonized Polk, exacerbating the ordeal with prolonged, written argument in which he accused Polk of sending too many men to Johnston. Bragg was reverting to his old pattern, again charging Polk with acting against orders; as he sarcastically put it, neither he nor the president could locate such orders after a thorough search.[4]

Historian Larry Daniel agrees with Polk's present-day antagonist, Steven Woodworth, that Polk was once again guilty of flaunting orders by sending "so large a force" to Johnston. Woodworth further asserts that "the Bishop's 'self-willed twisting of orders' angered the chief executive." However, Polk shot back at Bragg a whole sheath of dispatches showing that he was in fact acting under orders, with the orders in question coming from General Cooper himself. Bragg and the president apparently neglected to include the adjutant general's office in their "thorough search"! Seemingly the right hand did not know what the left hand was doing in the Confederate War Department, or perhaps Bragg forgot that he was not the only one in charge at the bureau. Polk persevered through the persecution as his army made its way eastward to face Sherman again, soon to play a crucial role in checking his old adversary.[5]

May 16 found General French in Rome, Georgia, awaiting the arrival of one of his brigades. On that date some of his advance troops skirmished with a Union force outside of the industrial city. Afterwards French was ordered to continue moving east to join the main body of the combining armies. By then a battle had been fought at Resaca, Georgia, where Polk had arrived on May 11 with Loring's division.[6]

Resaca

When Polk personally rode into Resaca he assumed overall command of the forces there, consisting of components of his own and Joseph Johnston's army. Until his arrival General John Bell Hood had been in command. Hood's corps was positioned to oppose General James McPherson's Army of the Tennessee which had made its way through Snake Creek Gap to Resaca. Two days before Hood's corps arrived, however, the only Confederates present to defend the town and its Oostanaula River crossing were Cantey's division, the troops Polk called up from Mobile. They had arrived there in the nick of time.[7]

While the huge, ponderous Army of the Cumberland engaged Johnston at Dalton, Sherman had sent McPherson on a stealthy march southward, hidden by Rocky Face Ridge, to reach Johnston's rear and cut his supply line, the Western & Atlantic Rail Road. On May 9 McPherson debouched out of Snake Creek Gap, which

Johnston unaccountably left unguarded. But Johnston was not entirely remiss in covering his left flank; it was he who ordered Cantey to Resaca "at once" from Rome, on May 5. And it was Polk's foresight and initiative that got them to north Georgia in the first place. After faulting Polk for bringing up so many reinforcements, Larry Daniel admits that "Cantey's Brigade [sic], 2,100 strong, ... had *opportunely* arrived from Mobile the night of the seventh." But he leaves unsaid that they were only present thanks to Polk, and in spite of Bragg's haranguing him over transferring "so large a force." Thus, Cantey's small division, the first of Polk's reinforcements to arrive in Georgia, stood virtually alone to defend Resaca as the XVI Corps of McPherson's army probed through the gap. "Cantey responded with a determined fire from the fortifications" (built earlier by Johnston to protect the river crossing at Resaca). Throughout the afternoon of May 9 the Mobile artillery fired upon the Union forces as they slowly advanced and maneuvered into position, nearing the railroad. The strength of Cantey's stout resistance convinced McPherson, unsure of what force he faced, to order his men back to the protection of Snake Creek Gap.[8]

Polk's smallest division, in the right place at the right time, successfully secured Resaca against an entire Union corps! Bragg had argued vehemently against Polk's depleting the Mobile garrison in order to transfer these troops to Johnston. Over Bragg's objections Polk had already transferred too many men in Loring's and French's divisions, and from the vantage point of his Richmond desk Cantey's additional division represented overkill. Yet, the fact that the Mobile garrison was able to reach North Georgia quickly by railroad was the contingency that saved Johnston's vital rail communica-

Brigadier General James Cantey, commander of a small division garrisoning Mobile, acted expeditiously when Polk ordered him to Georgia to reinforce Joseph Johnston's Army of Tennessee. From Richmond Bragg badgered Polk for sending so large a force, even wrongly accusing him of flouting orders, but Polk's action saved Johnston's army from being cut off before the campaign had barely begun ("Cantey, James," House Divided: The Civil War Research Engine at Dickinson College).

tions. The Army of the Tennessee's surprise penetration through a mountain defile had threatened not only little Resaca, but the Western Confederacy. As he had turned back Sherman at Meridian, Polk again survived a meeting of David and Goliath.

For two days Polk's Mobile division was left in Resaca without support while Johnston puzzled over Sherman's intentions. Cantey's intrepid stand granted Johnston time to concentrate sufficient force at Resaca before battle opened in earnest there five days later. Had McPherson pressed his advantage initially, the Atlanta Campaign might have been over barely after getting underway. Sherman ruefully recognized the import of McPherson's over-caution; on May 12 he rode to Snake Creek Gap and chided McPherson, "Well, Mac, you have missed the opportunity of a lifetime."[9]

Finally, on May 11 Johnston sent Hood's corps to Resaca to aid the beleaguered Cantey. Shortly after Polk arrived at Resaca late that afternoon, he and General Hood rode north together to meet with Johnston at his

Major General James B. McPherson, Sherman's favored subordinate, was beloved by all the Union army and many "Old Army" Confederates as well. Sherman sent McPherson on the first of his many flanking maneuvers of the Atlanta Campaign, to cut Johnston's line of communications, the Western & Atlantic Rail Road. Because Polk had ordered James Cantey to move his small division by rail from Mobile, that lone force was at Resaca in time to hold off McPherson's entire army as it advanced from Snake Creek Gap. Sherman later chided the overcautious McPherson for missing an "opportunity of a lifetime" (photograph by Mathew Brady, National Portrait Gallery, Smithsonian Institution).

headquarters in Dalton. John Bell Hood had recently returned to duty after several months' recovery from the loss of his leg at Chickamauga. As he rode with Polk, Hood expressed a desire to be baptized. Polk reprised his role as Episcopal cleric and performed the rite that very night at Dalton army headquarters. A Hood aide recounted: "There stood the battered old hero (barely thirty years old). There the

Warrior Bishop Polk. And there stood your humble servant, with a flaring yellow candle in one hand and a horse bucket of water in the other." Polk's aide and son-in-law William Gale described the ceremony as "most imposing."[10]

By the time of the main Battle of Resaca on May 14, most of Johnston's army had arrived and taken position around the town. Loring's division of Polk's Army of Mississippi (now a *de facto* third corps of Johnston's Army of Tennessee) occupied the position closest to the village of Resaca, on the Rebels' left. (French's division remained in Rome.) Hardee's corps extended northward from Polk's line, and Hood's corps occupied the far right of the Confederate position, bent to the right so that it faced north.

On May 14 Polk faced a fight in his sector that he could not win. Two of Cantey's advance regiments occupying low hills were swept off of their eminence by two brigades of Logan's corps, and Polk, realizing that the hills must be retaken in order to deny the artillery advantage they afforded the Federals, ordered multiple attacks attempting to regain the heights. A Union battle report described how battle lines from Cantey's and Loring's divisions "advanced to within thirty yards of our line before they were checked, and then only falling back to reform and renew the attack, threatening my right flank. They were again repulsed, and again rallied for another onset." Polk's men continued valiantly to storm the position, even fighting into the night. A barn had been set afire to aid visibility after dark, but the Confederates could not drive Logan's Yankees from the hills.[11]

While Polk understood the vital importance of the heights, Philip Secrist explains that Sherman failed to take advantage of the hard-won elevation which he could have used as a staging area for an attack on the Confederate position "and almost certain destruction of the Confederate army." Instead, Sherman limited his thinking to the defensive and "spen[t] the next day entrenching artillery on the newly-won hills." Therefore, although his loss of and failure to regain the eminence could be deemed a failure on Polk's part, the dire consequences that might have ensued did not materialize.[12]

As it turned out, rather than attack the Rebels from the advantageous hill or any other position, Sherman found a way to flank Johnston's army by crossing the Oostanaula River. At that point it became necessary for the Confederates to fall back in order to prevent the enemy from gaining Johnston's rear. Polk covered the army's retreat and afterwards destroyed the bridge over the river.[13]

Cassville

As the army moved past Calhoun, Johnston may have passed up his best opportunity of the entire Atlanta campaign to stop Sherman's advance. Connelly argues that on May 16 Johnston

> was in an excellent position to strike Sherman's army while it was crossing the Oostanaula.... Hardee's corps was skirmishing with that portion which had crossed west of Calhoun....

Johnston might have held that portion of Sherman's army on the north bank while striking at that part isolated west of Calhoun.

Presumably Polk recognized the opportunity, as his "son-in-law and aide-de-camp, Colonel W.D. Gale, recorded in his diary on May 21 that 'we ought to have fought near Calhoun.'"[14]

Nevertheless Johnston passed on Calhoun, continuing southward where he formulated a plan to attack Sherman's divided army as it approached the town of Cassville. On May 17, while the army prepared to assume a battle stance there, command headquarters was the scene of another religious rite involving Joseph Johnston, who

> stood as the next in line to receive Bishop Polk's administration of Holy Baptism. Lydia Johnston, the general's wife, had taken note of John Bell Hood's previous sacramental alteration and, "full of all the sympathy of a loving, earnest wife," ... had now besought the bishop to perform the same rite for her husband. The soldier-husband had acquiesced. A little better organized than the rushed tin-basin baptism given John Hood, the ceremony had suitable light and ambience provided by a crucifix candlestick from Polk's field communion set. Among the witnesses now were Hood and Hardee and Johnston's chief-of-staff, Brig. Gen. William W. Mackall.[15]

That same night Johnston's army moved into position with Polk in the center (French's division now having joined him) while to his left Hardee faced the Kingston road along which part of the Union army approached. Hood was positioned to the right, where he was expected to attack the left flank of the Yankee army, Schofield's Army of the Ohio marching on the Adairsville road, whereupon Polk would attack to his front. Fortifications completed, the Southern army was primed for victory. During the morning of May 19 Johnston addressed the troops with stirring words. Women and children had been ordered out of town and field hospitals prepared to receive the wounded.[16]

Hood was to open the battle, but as the sun rose high in the sky no sounds of firing could be heard. Johnston dispatched to the front line a staff officer who surprisingly found Hood in retreat. Hood's staff had reportedly come upon enemy cavalry unexpectedly advancing upon his rear along the Canton road. Without informing Johnston, Hood had already withdrawn. The plan had gone awry, and Johnston therefore regretfully canceled the attack.[17]

Looking for the next opportunity to engage the enemy, Johnston moved his army to a ridge south of town and again assigned the right to Hood, Polk the center, and Hardee the left. Johnston believed the position "the best I saw occupied during the war," but his subordinates disagreed. However, exactly which of his lieutenants initiated the dissension was contradicted among competing recollections and has come under question in subsequent writings.[18]

At issue was the alleged vulnerability of a section of the Rebels' line to possible Union artillery fire from a ridge fronting their position. A meeting took place that evening among Polk, Hood, Johnston, French, and Hardee, with various staff officers present as well. According to Johnston's post-war account, Hood took the lead in urging Johnston to abandon the line—in fact, retreat across the Etowah River. Yet Hood later alleged, in *his* post-war memoir, that Polk allied with him in advocating *not a retreat* but an *offensive*. General French cast doubt on Hood's version with his claim that Hood strongly argued that "his and Polk's line were so enfiladed by the Federal artillery that they could not be held." He added, "Polk was not so strenuous. Johnston insisted on fighting." These are important points, for later it was revealed that Hood had been surreptitiously sending a series of letters to Richmond complaining of Johnston's repeated retreats and claiming that the commander turned a deaf ear to Hood's constant calls for more aggression against the Yankees. It would not behoove him, therefore, to go down in history having advised Johnston to retreat. But that is what he did, according to French, who states that Johnston's version as recorded in his memoir was substantially correct and Hood's account in his posthumously published book, *Advance and Retreat*, was inaccurate. French insisted that Hood "made no reference to being in a good position for acting on the aggressive and making an attack." (Hardee, who arrived late to the meeting, concurred with French's version.)[19]

French went on to imply that Polk was not as disinclined to fight, if at all, as Hood and others have made him out to be. "I regret that this fabulous *Picayune* article [one of the postwar accounts of this episode], emanating in New Orleans, was ever written on account of Gen. Polk. It made him appear to be a weak man."[20] But by that time Polk no longer lived to defend himself or correct the record as to his position in the affair. Therefore others found it convenient to claim him as an ally— or to lay blame at his feet.

Cassville presents a classic case of how contrasting versions of an event can confound historians. New research is currently emerging on the Cassville controversy that casts new light on the arguments offered by all sides. Author Robert D. Jenkins, Sr., has discovered, among other factors, a glaring omission on the part of Confederate cartographers which played a key role in the confusion surrounding Federal positions on May 19. Jenkins postulates that Johnston's cancellation of the highly anticipated attack can be blamed partly on faulty maps of the Cassville road network, a blindness afflicting his subordinates as well as historians examining the affair down to the present day. The author does not maintain neutrality amidst the charges and counter-charges brought by the participants, however; instead, his findings decidedly convict Johnston and exonerate Hood. Jenkins's work, not yet published as of this writing, is highly anticipated as a clarification of what went wrong at Cassville.[21]

New Hope Church

Whatever was actually said at the meeting or recorded in subsequent accounts, in the end Johnston ordered yet another retreat. The Army of Tennessee crossed to the south of the Etowah River and assumed a strong position at the Allatoona railroad cut, anticipating that Sherman would attack there. However, Sherman was acquainted with the territory, having been posted farther down the railroad in Marietta as a young officer, and made sure to avoid the Allatoona trap. Awaiting him in vain, the Confederate army, from privates to generals, gathered on a Sabbath morning for divine services conducted by newly ordained the Reverend Bakewell of Louisiana, and overseen by his bishop, General Polk. Indeed, the deep railroad cut of Allatoona provided a cathedral-like setting with its sheer, soaring walls. Newly baptized Johnston and Hood worshipped alongside one another that day.[22]

Learning that the Federals reportedly crossed the Etowah far to the west, Johnston ordered his army in that direction to block Sherman, now separated from his rail supply line, from moving yet again around the Rebels' flank. Thus, the two armies came to square off against one another for nearly two weeks along the Dallas–New Hope Church line.

The fighting here reached truly terrible proportions. Incessant firing and sniping compelled soldiers to remain confined in miserable, muddy trenches. While hostilities were exchanged across the lines day and night, three separate, pitched battles erupted along the position. The first major fight occurred at New Hope Church on May 25 when Union general Joseph Hooker's corps slammed into Hood, with A.P. Stewart's division receiving the brunt of the attack. Some of his men even took cover behind gravestones in the church cemetery. In spite of Stewart's declaring to Johnston, "My own troops will hold the position" (which they did), a contingent of Polk's corps were sent forward in support. As the battle raged, thunder and lightning added to the din.[23]

The following day saw much shifting of troops through the thick woods and broken terrain near Dallas. Johnston ordered Polk's corps to extend northeastward in response to a perceived Federal movement in that direction. Upon discovering that the Federals had extended even beyond Polk's right flank, Cleburne was transferred to the right of Polk on May 27, a day which ended in a fierce battle against Cleburne's division which had not had time to entrench properly but nevertheless soundly defeated parts of two Federal corps. This engagement, known as the Battle of Pickett's Mill, ended with a violent counterattack at night by Lowrey's brigade of Cleburne's division.[24]

The day after the battle a Confederate soldier described the scene in a ravine in front of his line: "The field looked as though a great blue carpet had been spread out over the ground. Dead men were every where; they lay in solid lines just as they fell and in many places were in heaps." Polk, along with Johnston, Hardee and Hood rode over to view the scene as burial details engaged in their gruesome work and hungry Confederates rummaged through haversacks of their dead foe. One was delighted to find "surenough coffee."[25]

The third and final battle along the New Hope Church line took place on the Confederates' far left in front of Dallas with an attack upon well-entrenched

Yankees, and turned out to be as much a disaster for Johnston as Pickett's Mill had been for Sherman. Then that night Hood proposed a flank attack to the east beyond Pickett's Mill, and led his troops in the darkness behind and past the Confederate right, obligating Polk's corps to extend eastward to fill the part of the line vacated by Hood. After an all-night march "along the crookedest roads to be found, across streams, up hills, down in ravines," the attack was cancelled upon discovering the Yankees had "crossed the creek at Pickett's Mill and thrown up fortifications." Hood, the self-styled champion of aggression, had backed down again from a proposed attack. "For the third consecutive time, Johnston called off a planned assault on Sherman upon Hood's advice."[26]

Pine Mountain

Several days later as Sherman sidled back toward the railroad, the Confederates moved southeastward to a new line laid out by Johnston's engineers. The position stretched for ten miles and was anchored upon three prominences: Lost Mountain on the left; Pine Mountain in the center, where the line extended forward in a salient; and Brushy Mountain to the right, across the railroad. This line proved too long and thin, especially at the segment in front of Sherman's greatest concentration at the railroad. Johnston tightened and readjusted his positions; this move left only Bate's division atop the Pine Mountain elevation, still forward of the main line.[27]

Not truly a mountain, perhaps more accurately a knob, Pine Mountain nevertheless rises dramatically over the surrounding land of rolling hills, creeks, forests and ravines. It stands as an isolated remnant on the far-flung southern fringe of a mighty, majestic, ancient mountain range of which the Appalachians remain as a mere trace worn down by eons of erosion across the oldest land mass on the earth's surface. Four years earlier a distant, parallel ridge of the same range had been crowned by Leonidas Polk's hope and dream, the culmination of his life's work as a bishop of God's Church on earth: the site of an unrealized university that he consecrated upon a mountaintop flattened through the ages.

Dwarfed by Kennesaw Mountain seven miles to the east, Pine Mountain's surprising elevation nonetheless challenges a climber. General Polk left his faithful horse Jerry below and climbed the height on foot the morning of June 14, 1864, along with generals Johnston, Hardee, and his cavalry chief, William "Red" Jackson. By this date Polk had established his headquarters well to the rear, in the house of the Hardage family a mile west of Kennesaw Mountain. There, on Saturday, June 11, Polk provided a beef barbecue for his entire corps. The rainy Sabbath morning following, Bishop Polk intoned the Holy Eucharist mass for his staff, the Hardage family and other visitors wishing to partake of precious sacred moments in a season of strife and war. That afternoon, Leonidas retrieved his copies of a booklet by Dr. Charles Quintard titled *Balm for the Weary and the Wounded.* Polk had received them a

Polk's communion vessels that he carried with him throughout the war. On Sunday, June 12, 1864, at his headquarters near Kennesaw Mountain, he administered communion for the last time. His hosts, the Hardage family, along with staff members and others from the army, partook of the sacrament that rainy morning (photograph courtesy the Sewanee Chapter, The Leonidas Polk Memorial Society, used with permission).

week earlier, the first copies off the press, and by now had read in entirety the compiled quotations, poetry, Scriptures, hymn lyrics, prayers and short essays. For several quiet moments that gloomy afternoon, he inscribed and dated three copies as gifts to William Hardee, Joseph Johnston, and John Bell Hood. Recalling the day that he witnessed Braxton Bragg's baptism and confirmation, he also inscribed a copy to be sent to Bragg in Richmond, speaking a blessing over it upon the man who had harbored such ill will toward him—an act of forgiveness in accordance with the Savior's teaching, and an acknowledgment that together they waged a greater struggle against a common enemy.[28]

Now, just two days later the opportunity arose to present the edifying tracts to his compatriot commanders, for Johnston had summoned each of them atop Pine Mountain to survey the Federals' lines and evaluate whether the forward position should be abandoned. Warnings had reached headquarters that Bate's division and its valuable artillery on the height had come under increasing fire from three sides and was in potential danger of being cut off from the army should the Yankees manage to work around to its rear.

Rain had fallen steadily for 10 days, but the sky shone clear that Tuesday morning when the ranking generals of the western Confederate army, accompanied by staff officers, met at the foot of Pine Mountain and began their ascent. So bright seemed the sky after days of gloom that soldier Sam Watkins's description of a fateful day of battle two weeks hence (quoting from Deuteronomy 28:23) could be said of this morning as well: "[C]lear and cloudless, the heavens seemed made of brass, and the earth of iron."[29] Indeed, decades later the skilled Atlanta artist and historian, Wilbur Kurtz, would paint the scene atop Pine Mountain this day, depicting the sky in a hue of burnished brass. And the earth was truly encumbered of iron: ordnance spewed from cannon of vast armies contending over this soil.

For the past days Polk's heart had felt uncharacteristically heavy, but the bright sun surely lifted his spirits as he climbed the height. He felt against his chest, in his coat pocket, Quintard's booklets which he intended that day, perhaps as they lunched, to present to Johnston and Hardee; he would search out Hood following the morning's reconnaissance. The view atop the mountain was spectacular; its elevation was sufficient to produce an atmospheric effect which he had observed before atop Sewanee Mountain, causing the valley below seemingly to ripple and seethe like swells on the surface of the sea. Here the land indeed seethed and swelled— with swarms of Union troops. The position proved perfect for assessing the enemy's strength—too perfect, for it placed the generals in peril as they stood on the works gazing down through field glasses on this rare, clear day, in full view of Union gunners below busy sighting their artillery, as well as General Sherman standing alongside General Oliver Howard studying the summit and noting the coterie of fearless, gray-uniformed officers above. "How saucy they are!" Sherman remarked to Howard, and ordered his nearby artillery to induce the officers to take cover. The order was duly transmitted to Captain Peter Simonson's 5th Indiana battery.[30]

Meanwhile in the Confederate works high above, Rebel artillery crews nervously watched the generals expose themselves to the danger below. Accustomed to constant, accurate firing upon their works, they prayed the commanders would quickly conclude their examination of the surrounding countryside and take cover from fire that they knew would be hurled in their direction any second. Colonel William Dilworth, commander of the Florida Brigade of Bate's division, pointed out the obvious, that the generals were "sure to attract the fire of the enemy," and urged them to move farther to the rear. No sooner had he spoken than a puff of smoke popped from a cannon below.[31] Johnston walked off in one direction and Hardee the other as the shell screeched overhead. But General Polk paused. Facing northwest and forgetting the Yankee army below, for just a couple of seconds he gazed in the direction of another mountaintop where his beloved university would come to being. Perhaps he recalled the consecration day upon yonder height almost four years ago, crisp and autumnal then, not unlike this unseasonably cool June day—and standing here high above the valley below evoked the feeling of that past occasion when he smote the cornerstone in God's name. Perhaps those were Polk's thoughts as he stood atop Pine Mountain, serene under fire as always, arms folded. And like Moses, he was destined to view the Promised Land only from a distant mountaintop, not living to see his people inherit it.

A second and then a third shot fired from the cannon below, and suddenly Polk's magnificent frame was felled by a three-inch Hotchkiss shell. As Johnston later wrote to Quintard, "a cannon-shot crashed through his chest, and opening a wide window, let free that indomitable spirit." Perhaps in the manner of the terrible earthquake which rent the land following his Savior's crucifixion, after Polk's instantaneous death

> [a] fierce bombardment followed ... the enemy poured "a perfect deluge of shot and shell." The Yankee guns "sent up to us one prolonged deafening roar, from what seemed to us at least a hundred guns! The sides of the mountain trembled."[32]

That very morning Dr. Quintard, serving as rector of the Church of St. Luke's in Atlanta in addition to his army duties, sent a telegram to Polk offering to visit soon and administer communion at his headquarters. A return wire shocked Quintard with the news of the bishop's death and instructed him to receive the body at the Atlanta train depot. Quintard described the events that followed:

A monument to Leonidas Polk sits atop Pine Mountain at the very spot where he was killed (photograph by the author).

> On reaching Atlanta the body of the dead Bishop and General was escorted to St. Luke's Church, and placed in front of the altar. He was dressed in his gray uniform. On his breast rested a cross of white roses and beside his casket lay his sword. Throughout the following morning, thousands of soldiers and citizens came to pay their last tribute of affection. At noon.... I held funeral services and made an address.[33]

A young girl living in wartime Atlanta, Sallie Clayton, recounted the day of Polk's funeral service in her memoirs written years later:

> Sallie Clayton remembered the occasion as "one of the saddest" in

the city's history, and she added that "the good old Bishop's death seemed a personal loss to everyone who looked upon his bloodless face that day." [M]any who stopped at the open casket shed a tear or deposited a "leaf, or flower, or twig" on the "flag that draped his remains." With astonishment, Clayton recalled that "it was the first and only time in some years to come that flowers were used in Atlanta" during a funeral.... Clayton observed that "the beauty of the morning seemed a mockery to the gloom and sorrow of Atlanta that day."[34]

Quintard continued with his narrative of the journey of Polk's remains to the burial place:

> The body was then escorted to the railway station by the dead General's personal staff.... At Augusta the body remained two days at St. Paul's Church and lay in state at the City Hall until St. Peter's day, June 29, when the final rites were held at St. Paul's church. The burial was in the chancel of the church.

General James Longstreet, convalescing in Augusta from his wound sustained at the Wilderness, attended the burial service.[35]

Joseph Johnston, moved to tears by Polk's death, composed a solemn tribute to the bishop-general to be read to the Army of Tennessee:

> You are called to mourn your first captain, your oldest companion in arms. Lieutenant General Polk fell to-day at the outpost of this army—the army he raised and commanded, in all of whose trials he shared, to all of whose victories he contributed. In this distinguished leader we have lost the most courteous of gentlemen, the most gallant of soldiers. The Christian, patriot, soldier, has neither lived nor died in vain. His example is before you; his mantle rests with you.[36]

It seems fitting that Polk died atop a mountain, bearing near his heart spiritual words of comfort to edify his comrades (discovered later on his body, spattered with his blood). One bygone, similarly clear day Leonidas Polk the bishop ascended a distant mountain to incarnate a vision, implanting the ovum of higher truth and learning into the womb of Southern soil and culture: spirit enlivening earth. For years he had battled to effect such a union, but atop Pine Mountain he battled for the land alone, for nationhood, the very survival of his cherished, newborn country—a war ultimately lost. Nonetheless, on June 14, 1864, upon an eminence overlooking his foe ever entrenching and encroaching over Georgia's red-clay hills, Leonidas Polk the general was thereafter relieved of duty.

Although no power on earth could salvage the cause of the Southern Confederacy for which Leonidas Polk sacrificed his life, the Reverend Quintard would carry on the work of establishing The University of the South at Sewanee. In August 1867 a cornerstone was laid for the college chapel, St. Augustine's Church, replacing the marble block dismantled and destroyed in 1863 by the 26th Illinois Cavalry. Polk's dream finally came to fruition when the university opened its doors in September 1868.[37]

Chapter 11

Historians' Negative Portrayal of Polk

Bishop-General Leonidas Polk lived out his principles and convictions with discipline and serenity: exhibiting reverence toward God and his church, and exercising kindness, compassion and tolerance toward the people around him. In response, the soldiers under his command loved him ardently. Sam Watkins, in his acclaimed memoir of service with the First Tennessee Infantry, repeatedly notes Polk's care and openness toward his men. "His soldiers always loved and honored him," wrote Watkins. Lieutenant J. Litton Bostick, aide-de-camp to General Govan, a brigade commander in Cleburne's division, wrote home of Polk following his death, "There was not a more gallant man in the army."[1]

Even some who initially had reservations concerning the bishop were won over by his grand sublimity. A Louisiana major serving under him, Edward G.W. Butler, Jr., a family friend of the Polks before the war, wrote his mother from Columbus that the army had "no confidence in neither" Polk nor his second-in-command, Gideon Pillow. Yet following Polk's tender ministrations to Butler as he lay dying from wounds sustained in the Battle of Belmont, the young officer declared Polk to be "one of the noblest men God ever made." A witness to that scene was Margaret McLean, wife of Major Eugene McLean who served as Polk's (and later Bragg's) quartermaster, daughter of eminent Union general Edwin "Bull" Sumner, and friend and confidante of diarist Mary Chesnut. She too initially disapproved of Bishop Polk's taking up the sword, describing her "revulsion of feeling" over the matter. However, after interacting with him extensively during her husband's assignment, Margaret grew to admire Polk immensely and firmly endorsed his change of vocation, deeming him "the right man in the right place." Some held onto their disapprobation of a bishop taking on a combat role, but most of his contemporaries held Polk in high esteem.[2]

In the decades following the Civil War, General Polk was similarly viewed in a favorable light among Lost Cause essayists and historians (never reticent to argue over and assign blame for the South's defeat), and his son's two-volume biography was widely read and appreciated. Polk was hailed as "a military hero and model of Christian character" to generations of Southern schoolchildren in the quaint past when Civil War curriculum covered generals and campaigns.[3]

While almost all writers concede Polk's personal popularity with his troops, over the years the general's favorability rating has plummeted dramatically. This shift cannot be attributed solely to the trend in Civil War historiography de-emphasizing the military aspect in favor of civilians' (particularly women's and slaves') experiences and political/social issues. Generals, with the exception of two or three, no longer command much attention in academia, and Southern generals in particular are universally depicted as evil, incompetent, or inane. (Nevertheless, scholars continue to write books and give lectures on the battles and leaders of the Civil War in response to public demand.)

Even given academic frowning on the study of ranking military figures, Polk stands almost alone in the degree of vitriol that arises upon the mention of his name. Indeed, there seems to be an unspoken, official duty on the part of Civil War writers to issue some version of an up-front, obligatory disclaimer condemning Leonidas Polk, even if in the remainder of their work his actual performance proves positive (the author in question never overtly admits this), or at least incongruous with such demeaning characterization. Below are three examples, not even from rabid denunciators of Polk but even-toned, neutral authors:

> *David Powell:* With the war's arrival, President Davis offered [Polk] a general's commission.... It was one of Davis's more unfortunate decisions.
>
> *Kenneth Noe:* ... the genial but pompous and often incompetent Bishop Polk.... Unfortunately for Bragg and for the Confederacy as a whole, Polk remained a great favorite of Jefferson Davis.
>
> *Albert Castel:* Shortly after the war began in 1861, Davis appointed [Polk] a major general. It was a mistake.... [H]e proved at best mediocre, at worst execrable, as a military leader.[4]

Other authors who habitually employ a stringent, partisan tone appear to relish anti–Polk rhetoric. Consider below some examples of more extreme denigration of Polk.

> *Richard McMurry:* Leonidas Polk, the senior lieutenant general in the West, was a troublemaker of the first magnitude and an officer of demonstrated incompetence. He had mishandled his troops in many battles and disobeyed orders in several others.... [Polk] contributed much to the steady stream of failures that characterized Confederate command in the West.

While most of McMurry's accusation references events preceding the subject of his book (the Atlanta Campaign), still it is interesting that he lambastes the general using such sweeping subjective statements—yet in keeping with the typical pattern, in the body of his narrative Polk comes across neutrally at worst, and in one instance he actually credits Polk with timely reaching Resaca:

> Fortunately for the Rebels, the leading units of Polk's reinforcements from Alabama reached Resaca that day, as did Polk himself. Johnston instructed Polk to have all his men move on from Rome to Resaca as fast as possible.[5]

Thomas Connelly's treatment of Polk is even more incongruous. He spares no invective when introducing Polk to the reader in the first of his two volumes on the Army of Tennessee:

[Polk] could be stubborn, aloof, insubordinate, quarrelsome, and childish…. Polk would treat his superior officers in a manner that smacked of insubordination. Until his death in 1864, the bishop often chose to obey his commander only when it pleased him to do so. Yet throughout his career in the Army of Tennessee, Polk had a remarkable ability to evade the blame for situations that were the result of these flaws in his character. With such a personality and with amazing abilities to escape responsibility, Polk in 1861 was the most dangerous man in the Army of Tennessee.[6]

These are strong words, indeed: "the most dangerous man in the Army of Tennessee"! Inexplicably, Connelly lists three sources in his footnote to this scathing denunciation of Polk, all well-known, first-person memoirs: Fremantle's diary, Moxley Sorrel's *Recollections of a Confederate Staff Officer*, and Sam Watkins's *Company Aytch*. Because Connelly cites these informants, a reader would assume their writings correlate with the derogatory views expressed in this paragraph. However, all three contain only glowing, admiring reports and descriptions of Polk, not only at the page numbers listed, but in *every reference to Polk* made throughout the works in question! It is a mystery how Connelly derived his demeaning diatribe from the citations he lists in support of his conclusions. Passages from those very pages follow:

Sword Over the Gown. This 1900 painting of Leonidas Polk by Eliphalet F. Andrews depicts three primary areas of his accomplishments and legacy: spiritual (Episcopal bishop of Louisiana); military (USMA graduate and Confederate corps commander in the American Civil War); and educational (founder of The University of the South in Sewanee, Tennessee). In all of his endeavors Polk was universally beloved and esteemed. Colonel Basil Duke described him as "one of the finest specimens of the ante-bellum gentleman I ever saw" (photograph courtesy the Sewanee Chapter, The Leonidas Polk Memorial Society, used with permission).

> *Fremantle:* Lieutenant General Leonidas Polk, Bishop of Louisiana, who commands the other *corps d'armee*, is a good-looking, gentleman-like man with all the manners and

affability of a "grand seigneur." He is fifty-seven years of age—tall, upright, and looks much more the soldier than the clergyman.... He is much beloved by the soldiers on account of his great personal courage and agreeable manners. I had already heard no end of anecdotes of him told me by my traveling companions, who always alluded to him with affection and admiration. In his clerical capacity I had always heard him spoken of with the greatest respect.

Sorrel: It was a lasting regret that I had no more than a passing glimpse during these operations [Chickamauga] of the distinguished soldier, Lieut. Gen. Leonidas Polk, second in command of Bragg's army. A pure and lofty character, nothing but the most self-sacrificing, patriotic convictions, and the almost peremptory wishes of the Executive had led him to lay down his great Episcopal station and duties and take to arms. His training at West Point had well prepared him for the stern efforts in the field awaiting Southern men. Throughout his army career he was never without a desire to put by his sword and take up again his dearly loved people, his Bishop's staff.... But the President, holding him in the highest esteem and confidence, insisted on retaining him in the armies of the Confederacy. He could not but yield. Of commanding presence and most winning address, he served with distinction and renown. While suffering at the hands of Bragg treatment unjust and harsh, he on the other hand had won to himself the abiding affection and confidence of all officers and men whom he commanded.

Watkins: Every private soldier loved [Polk]. Second to Stonewall Jackson, his loss was the greatest the South ever sustained. When I saw him there dead, I felt that I had lost a friend whom I had ever loved and respected, and that the South had lost one of her best and greatest generals. His soldiers always loved and honored him.... "Bishop Polk" was ever a favorite with the army, and when any position was to be held, and it was known that "Bishop Polk" was there, we knew and felt that "all was well."

One would find it difficult to compose more praiseful testimony than that found in these three passages, yet strange to say, Connelly cites them as evidence of his denigration of Polk![7]

Furthermore, Connelly not only contradicts the viewpoints of these primary sources, but his own analyses in both of his volumes belie his introductory Polk-bashing. As examined in Chapter 7, he adjudges Polk *correct* in his "insubordination" at Bardstown and Perryville. Connelly exposes Bragg's fabricating a story to accuse Polk of neglect of duty at Chickamauga (the "breakfast myth," a lie which numerous authors pass on as truth to discredit Polk). After faulting him for tardiness, Connelly points out that Polk's late attack on the morning of September 20 in fact turned out to be fortuitous as Longstreet was not ready to advance; thus, had he been on time Polk would have advanced alone without support on his left. Later authors echo Connelly's *attitude* against Polk while ignoring these factual points in his favor set forth in the body of Connelly's masterful works. Connelly seemed to harbor a personal dislike or prejudice against the bishop, but to his credit kept it from sullying his hard analysis of actual events on the field.[8]

Steven Woodworth does not confine his disparagement of Polk to the first pages of his works; instead, throughout he twists just about everything into an indictment against the bishop. Many examples have been cited here, and it would be a lengthy, tiresome task to address his numerous accusations point-by-point. It must be noted that Woodworth has attained considerable prominence in the community of Civil

War historians, and aided by the truth that negativity is highly contagious, he has had an unfortunate influence on the prevailing treatment of Leonidas Polk.

Below follows an examination of some specific points of criticism leveled against Polk by historians, and the names of Connelly and Woodworth will come up again. But as to the general trend against Polk over time, an interesting case in point is historian James McDonough. In his early book *Shiloh: In Hell Before Night* published in 1977, he portrays Polk in a largely neutral light. The closest the author comes to a negative characterization of the bishop in that book is his reference to A.S. Johnston's "strong-willed subordinates such as Polk." Otherwise, he ridicules Bragg's accusation that Polk personally plundered civilians, and only mildly blames Polk for retreating to Cheatham's distant camp site following the first day of battle.[9]

Seventeen years later, when his *War in Kentucky* was published in 1994, McDonough's tone had completely changed. First, he features Mrs. Bragg's sniffing to her husband, upon Bragg's promotion to full general, that "this relieved him 'from obeying the commands of our vain glorious Bishop [Polk].'" Then he aligns with Woodworth's hyperbole over Polk's taking Columbus, Kentucky, calling it "one of the most decisive catastrophes the Confederacy ever suffered." He contributes his own absurd claim that the "violation of Kentucky's neutrality ... drove Kentucky into the arms of the Federals" (even though Kentucky was already firmly in the embrace of the United States government, as previously examined), and concludes, "[Polk] began the war badly and never showed any notable improvement." In addition to coming down heavily on Polk for his "disobedience" at Perryville, he furthers the doctrine propounded by Bragg's biographer McWhiney that Polk's decision not to march toward Frankfort from Bardstown (which, had he done so with the bulk of Buell's army bearing down on him, would have courted disaster) "cost the Confederates a victory."[10]

What a change a few years made in James McDonough's treatment of General Polk! The discrepancy cannot be explained by surmising that McDonough deemed Polk's performance acceptable in the early days at Shiloh, thereafter to decline—for he reaches back with his revised assessment to the even earlier days of Columbus (Polk "began the war badly"). In the 1970s Polk passed the author's inspection, but by the 1990s his generalship stank. What changed? By that time McDonough had apparently fallen in line with the Woodworth school of wanton Polk-bashing. This kind of extreme polemic stance does not enhance our understanding of history but detracts from it, and lowers the standard to an open-season targeting of certain historical figures fingered by a few influential and vocal historians. Perhaps this phenomenon simply parallels the polarization which has increasingly poisoned public discourse during the same passage of time.

What is interesting about Woodworth's attacks on Polk is that he concurrently defends Bragg to a degree that renders Braxton Bragg almost unrecognizable. Bereft of support from his scheming subordinates, Bragg assumes the role of pitiable, suffering victim. The general himself would scoff at this image and resent it intensely—but surely would embrace Woodworth's pre-supposition that he was right on every point. From there the historian-advocate and his followers build a case against the beleaguered commander's alleged antagonists, primarily Polk, based on Bragg's self-absolving allegations. The problem is that there is no objectivity in this approach. It does not lead to truth but produces only a one-sided viewpoint, much like a lawyer arguing on behalf of his client regardless of innocence or guilt. The case for Bragg brought by his "lawyers" essentially centers on two episodes: the Perryville orders culminating in Bragg's April 13, 1863, circular letter and revised Perryville report; and Bragg's dismissal of Polk following Chickamauga. In both instances the basic charge against Polk is his alleged disobedience of orders.

In taking Bragg's side historians overlook the commanding general's underlying motives which in fact cast much light on his accusations and ongoing squabble against Polk. Consider again Bragg's resolution in his letter to Jefferson Davis of February 27, 1862: he would no longer bear others' sins, only his own. But did Bragg ever comply with the second clause by acknowledging any wrongs on his part? Had he done so, he might have conceded that his orders were faulty, both at Perryville where they were not in accord with the situation on the ground, and at Chickamauga with its eleventh-hour army reorganization and difficulties of terrain and darkness which hindered Bragg's orders from ever reaching some intended recipients. Certainly Polk also made mistakes at both locations: lapses of communication at Perryville and Chickamauga, and faulty troop movements at the latter. But rather than examine the issues and improve his operation, Bragg stormed ahead with charges and even dismissal while entertaining no defense. From all of this it is clear that under Bragg's new policy he would *not* bear only his own sins, but in fact he would bear *no* sins—and beyond that, *others* would heretofore bear *his* sins. What is evident in all of this is a classic persecution complex taken to the next level—that is, implicit in Bragg's revelation that he would no longer bear the sins of others, is a declaration of transition from *persecuted* to *persecutor*. And behind every persecution complex is a messiah complex. One sees evidence of this in Bragg's correspondence and complaints regarding his fellow generals: no one was good enough, none measured up to his standards—he was "*the only one*" in his own mind and that of his wife. By going along with this scenario, historians participate in General Bragg's delusions of infallibility and his resultant habitual scapegoating. It has become as much a pattern among them as it was at Army of Tennessee headquarters.

The truth has been turned around. Rather than acknowledge that Bragg was the attacker starting with the snarky letters to his wife before Shiloh and continuing right up to the public censure of Polk following Chickamauga and beyond—indeed, until Polk's death—authorities now unquestioningly depict Polk as the aggressor out to get Bragg. Larry Daniel stands out as a rare honest analyst on this point by admitting that, as early as before the Kentucky Campaign, it was in fact Bragg who "did everything in his power to be rid of Polk." But many others fall in line with the caricature of Polk plotting and conniving to depose Bragg. In his book about a battle not even involving Polk, author Eric Jacobson describes the situation after Chickamauga:

> [A] number of the general officers in the Army of Tennessee staged a near mutiny. The anti-Bragg crowd practically accused the commanding general of treason, claiming that he was inept and unfit to command. Chief among his persecutors were James Longstreet, Daniel Harvey Hill, and Leonidas Polk, and the harder they attacked Bragg the more virulent his responses became.

Jacobson's listing Polk with Longstreet and Hill is highly misleading, as their petition for Bragg's relief (which did not even come close to accusing him of treason) was drafted *after* Polk had departed the army. So when did Polk "attack" Bragg? Was it his March 30, 1863, letter to President Davis—written behind Bragg's back, it is true—in which he extolled Bragg's "talent of organization and discipline" which "could be of service to all the armies of the Confederacy," and recommended him for promotion to equal General Samuel Cooper, ranking general of the Confederate army? Was it his truthfulness when summoned to Richmond or questioned by Johnston during the latter's investigation of the conflicts roiling the army? Was it his investigation on behalf of General Breckinridge of the duplicity of his own subordinate's battle report? Was it in sharing concerns with fellow generals when their commander's soundness of mind and body came under question? During these latter instances Polk discussed Bragg's problematic style of command, but also defended Bragg on some points and invariably argued on behalf of Bragg's strengths. Polk did not "attack" Bragg, whether overtly or subtly, but he often found himself parrying Bragg's habitually lashing out at him and other subordinates. To read Jacobson's account, however, one would infer that Bragg's role was limited only to his "responses" to his mutinous subordinates.[11]

Historians charge Polk with harboring an evil animus toward Bragg. But evidence is lacking of any such antipathy on Polk's part, at least not before Bragg kicked Polk out of the army. Until then he showed restraint even when voicing his concerns over Bragg's erratic behavior. In fact, in spite of the clashes that arose between them, the bishop on occasion expressed in his correspondence feelings of camaraderie and care for his commanding general. For example, in a letter to his daughter of April 6, 1863, he tenderly reported on the health of Bragg's wife, noting that she suffered a relapse but "is said to be getting better again." That same month he wrote his wife of General Bragg's visit to his Corps. He reported with no hint of detraction that Bragg stayed with him all day, and related a lighthearted incident among the officers present involving some kind of difficulty over affixing spurs to boots. He ended the letter with a P.S.: "I had a grand review … of all my corps. Genl Bragg + staff present + highly pleased." Even though this letter was written at the same time that Bragg was targeting Polk through his second circular, the bishop nevertheless aimed to please his commanding general and conveyed his pleasure in having done so. Finally, in Polk's August 1863 letter to Kenneth Rayner deploring the public drift in North Carolina toward Unionism, he states that he heard of it from General Bragg, indicating that the two generals commiserated over current issues in which they agreed. If Polk was seething with hatred for Braxton Bragg, one would not know it from his letters. A tone of hostility only appeared after Bragg wrongfully dismissed him from the army, which would seem understandable.[12]

So, in the absence of written evidence, how do Polk's detractors back up their claims that he hated Bragg to the very depths of his soul? William Glenn Robertson, in Volume One of his Chickamauga study, offers a clever explanation for the absence of corroboration in the record: "Slyly, Polk," he claims, "avoided expressing anti-Bragg views in writing."[13] How, then, is the historian to conclude that he held such views? Under this theory, in his day Polk apparently had everyone fooled. Despite the fact that no contemporary person who actually knew Polk left any observations of this deep, dark side delineated by Robertson and others, we are supposed to take their word for it.

Historians would also have us believe that Polk, Hardee and others repeatedly and obsessively communicated among themselves and gathered for secret sessions to criticize and conspire against Bragg. During the time of acute crisis in army command, particularly after the April 13 circular letter, there was assuredly alarmed messaging among Bragg's subordinates. Hardee and the others immediately informed Polk that Bragg was framing him. This was not a recurring habit, however. If so, one would imagine that after Hardee left the army for Mississippi, he and Polk would continue to engage in their favorite pastime of bashing Bragg. But in their correspondence Bragg was not even mentioned; they did, however, engage in some mild criticism of Joe Johnston. The accusations and innuendo against Polk as incorrigible Bragg hater and conspirator extraordinaire simply do not seem justified by the record, but instead appear to be a matter of speculation or opinion which by rote repetition and magnification have hardened into an assumed habit among historians.[14]

Thankfully, just when there seems to be no limit to the acerbity heaped upon Polk and others whom it is fashionable to ostracize, a new wave of historians is appearing. Exemplified by Dr. Timothy Smith, they abstain from the stridently partisan approach, instead employing a more even, composed tone. Rather than hurl blame, Smith starts with the premise that participants mostly performed their duty in good faith and as best they could. Smith examines events unencumbered by prejudicial doctrine, and—lo and behold!—unexpected truths come to light. Others have come forward as well to question and push back against accepted slander, including William Glenn Robertson featured in the excellent collection of essays, *Gateway to the Confederacy*. However, Robertson seems lately to have undergone a dramatic conversion. In his recent book, *River of Death: The Chickamauga Campaign, Volume One: The Fall of Chattanooga*, he comes across as the most strident of Polk detractors. In a bewildering departure from the reasonable tone of his past writings, he resorts to factual falsehoods and unfounded, exaggerated opinion regarding Polk and Bragg which unfortunately detract from the integrity of his superlative and otherwise admirable Chickamauga project.

Chapter 11. Historians' Negative Portrayal of Polk

First, Robertson belittles Polk's religious awakening at West Point by repeating some of the standard distortions: his religious conversion happened only as fallout from the "minor scandals in his third year," and he passively "came under the influence of the academy's chaplain, Charles McIlvaine." Robertson then charges that after graduating from West Point in 1827, Polk indulged in "several years of adolescent wandering." This is patently false. It is true that Polk travelled during his three-month, earned furlough, touring several northern cities and energetically examining centers of innovative technology, then reconnecting with family in Tennessee. He spent the following year running his father's extensive farming operation. While the latter traveled in Europe, Polk took charge of planting, harvest, structural repairs, and marketing and transporting of crops. The next spring he became engaged to Frances Devereux and studied Hebrew in New York to prepare for seminary, which he entered that fall in Virginia. While completing his course of study, Polk met with two presidents, served church mission and building programs, and cared for a brother then dying of tuberculosis. Upon his ordination in 1830 he married, conducted his brother's burial service, and assumed the leadership of a parish whose rector departed on sabbatical. Rather impressive accomplishments to be dismissed as mere "adolescent wandering"![15]

Robertson also misrepresents the circumstances surrounding Polk's entering the Confederate Army in 1861. He states that Polk "offered his services to the Confederacy as a military officer in the spring of 1861." In fact, he merely corresponded with President Jefferson Davis regarding defenses for the Mississippi River Valley, whereupon the president *invited him* to Richmond in June for further consultation. It was then that Davis unexpectedly offered Polk a brigadier general's commission, which the bishop initially declined considering his position in the church. However, after visiting Louisiana troops stationed in Virginia and counseling with Bishop Meade, Polk returned to Richmond to accept the commission offered him. At that time Davis assigned him temporary departmental command and correspondingly upgraded his rank to major general. Robertson inaccurately claims that Polk, "refusing brigadier general's rank, accepted a commission as a major general in June." The clear implication is that Polk coyly held out, angling for higher rank. Robertson expands on this innuendo, postulating Polk was displeased after Shiloh at finding "an officer formerly junior in rank [Bragg] had been promoted above him." Robertson offers no evidence or source for this assertion. In fact, Polk harbored no ambition for military rank. His heart was with his bishopric, as evidenced by his desire, repeatedly stated (and acted upon, in the form of three resignations), to return to church work as soon as possible. Yet Robertson accuses him of petty jealousy toward Bragg, and adds to this impression by implying that Polk's two attempted resignations during 1861 were motivated out of resentment toward Sidney Johnston and P.G.T. Beauregard, respectively.[16]

Throughout his book, Robertson similarly presumes to know Polk's inner thoughts and heart. He enlightens the reader that the bishop "basked in the deference his religious title afforded him" and was kindly disposed only toward "underlings who did not challenge his supremacy." Not only is the author a mind reader, but apparently he believed Polk a diviner as well, based on his sharing information with Bragg "knowing the effect it would have on the latter's deliberations." One wonders *how* Polk could have known in advance the effect of his disclosure on Bragg, not to mention how the author knows what Polk knew! But he also confidently divines how Polk *felt* as well, as in Chattanooga during August 1863 when "Polk was unworried about recent events." At least in this case Robertson does offer a single letter from Polk to his wife as evidence, but two others dated August 14 and 15 to his brother-in-law and fellow bishop, previously quoted, show that on the contrary Polk was then in a state of extreme worry "about recent events." Finally, throughout the book Robertson utilizes his magical insight into Polk's heart by repeated affirmations that Polk harbored "dislike" and "contempt for Bragg," and "despised" him. As if that wasn't deplorable enough, Polk was also "selfish," "incompetent and insubordinate," and "exceedingly self-indulgent." In contrast to the accounts of hundreds of 19th-century writers, keen and practiced observers of men who personally interacted with Polk and offered no such judgments, 160 years later we somehow know better.[17]

In the process of vilifying Polk, Robertson presents a distorted portrayal of Bragg as well. He sets the stage with a sympathetic explanation for Bragg's famously hostile personality, which he attributes entirely to his numerous health complaints: "When overcome with these maladies he was decidedly unpleasant to those around him. He quickly gained a reputation for being abrupt and severe in his dealings with others, most of whom were unaware of the cause of his black mood." (Robertson does not accord the same courtesy to D.H. Hill. While acknowledging the latter's physical maladies which more than rivaled Bragg's, Robertson refrains from similarly excusing his "extremely acerbic personality.") The problem, of course, is that Bragg was known to be "abrupt and severe" as far back as his youthful days as a cadet at West Point, before most of his physical symptoms appeared. Even Robertson quotes classmate Joseph Hooker's description of Bragg as "brusque."[18]

This is not the only instance in which Robertson overcompensates for Bragg's personality. He excuses Bragg's personal rudeness while in command of the Army of Tennessee by explaining that he was "*never* a social or convivial person." However, again back to his days as a cadet, Robertson admits that Bragg was "convivial enough to be regarded favorably by most of his peers." Whether truly convivial or not, Bragg most certainly was "a social person" throughout his life. During his Old Army service he cultivated many casual and intimate relationships, including his closest friend and fellow officer James Duncan, and he and Elise enjoyed an active social life with other officers' families at distant western posts. Even after leaving the pre-war army he maintained deep personal friendships, through correspondence and personal visits, with fellow officers including William Sherman, George Thomas and Henry Hunt. During the war while posted in Richmond, Bragg and Elise abstained from the city's excessive social scene, but regularly gathered to play whist and enjoy the company of Josiah Gorgas and his wife and others. Immediately after the war when Bragg and Elise lived for a time on his brother's Alabama plantation, he decried his social isolation. Robertson is simply wrong to predicate Bragg's harshness on a hypothetical, intrinsic anti-social nature when his lifelong behavior and inclinations show otherwise.[19]

Robertson continues his skewed depiction of Braxton Bragg by stating the general's personal prejudices as though fact: endorsing a charge of "sloth and incapacity of his officers," for example. Such a characterization may accurately describe Bragg's hypercritical view, but Robertson includes it in an objective list of the general's tribulations. However, this merely serves as a lead-up to Robertson's ultimate agenda of portraying Bragg as innocent victim. Beleaguered by backstabbing subalterns, poor Bragg found himself "left alone among his enemies" (*not* the Federal ones). Perhaps it should not be surprising, given the current academic culture in which victimhood is synonymous with righteousness, to see Bragg cast as a martyr by way of justifying his vendetta against Polk. Truly it is novel, however, to find the overused virtuous victim archetype applied to so unlikely a beneficiary as a Confederate general![20]

According to Robertson, Bragg bore no responsibility for the conflicts riddling his command; instead, the "primary source of that army's dysfunction lay … with its senior tactical commanders and their relationship with the commanding general." *Their* relationship with *him*—as though Bragg had no input or effect upon such relationships! Yet Robertson repeatedly insists on Bragg's blamelessness. For example, he blames Breckinridge solely for falling out with Bragg, but conveniently omits any mention of Bragg's inflammatory Murfreesboro battle report which contained such blatant attacks on Breckinridge's performance and honor that it spread uproar in Richmond and throughout the entire Confederacy.[21]

In addition to victimhood, Robertson offers additional unlikely characterizations in his attempt to burnish Bragg's image. Most startling, he credits Bragg with "magnanimity" toward his subordinates. That is one quality rarely associated with the general! In addition, Robertson portrays Bragg's issuance of his circulars of January and April 1863 as "naive." Most assuredly, Bragg did not "naively" draft the circular letters (especially not the second one); he did so willfully against the advice of his staff and others who begged him to desist from his campaign of aggression against his own lieutenants.[22]

The truth is that it was Bragg's inherent nature to generate conflict throughout his life; indeed, he thrived on it. In his early army days he picked fights with superiors and even put himself in legal jeopardy by publishing confrontational articles criticizing the command hierarchy. To his close friend James Duncan he explained his compulsive combativeness: "I feel I can never rest without some excitement." It is simply impossible to reconcile Bragg's lifelong and well-documented habit of courting controversy with Robertson's portrait of him as a naive, innocent army commander treacherously bullied by Polk.[23]

Keeping in mind Bragg's natural predilection for conflict, one can see the inaccuracy not only with which Robertson describes the general, but also in the way he interprets his relationship with Leonidas Polk. Throughout *River of Death*, Robertson repeatedly insists that it was Polk who initiated hostilities and was the "original source of friction." As already thoroughly examined, the record does not support this thesis. But Robertson attempts to conjure up some evidence (which he admits is "purely circumstantial," i.e., non-existent) by introducing a novel theory: the "relationship between the two was strained from the beginning" because Polk held a "class bias" against Bragg. The bishop's supposed snobbishness originated with his own mother and wife and their privileged familial ties to the vicinity of Bragg's hometown. "[T]he Polk women could hardly have been unaware of Braxton Bragg's pedigree," Robertson declares, "and no doubt made it known to the bishop." Robertson authoritatively concludes that Polk's perception of Bragg as his social inferior rendered "the relationship between the two men adversarial from the moment Bragg assumed command of the army." This notion is nothing more than fantasy. Speculatively bringing wives into the mix is doubly absurd when one considers the *actual* correspondence between Bragg and his wife in which Elise from the beginning of the war more than amply demonstrated her disdain and outright hostility toward Polk![24]

But Robertson is nothing if not thorough in his unfounded accusations. He paints Polk as the guilty party by dropping a provocative explanation for Bragg's disapproval of Polk: the bishop's "sybaritic habits alone disqualified him in Bragg's eyes." *What* sybaritic habits, one wonders, but the author does not elaborate; he simply leaves the reader with an unspecified, distasteful blemish on Polk's personal character.[25]

Using another vague dig, Robertson implicates Sidney Johnston as having had some undefined issues with Polk: "By making Bragg his chief-of-staff, Johnston could bypass the amiable but inefficient Polk."[26] Such subtle aspersions served up in succession have a cumulative effect, with the author bypassing evidence or explanation.

Probably the most egregious misrepresentation made by Robertson with regard to Bragg's issues with Polk pertains to Bragg's second controversial letter circulated among his subordinates in April 1863. Robertson skirts the true nature and intent of the letter altogether, by explaining that Bragg "drafted a long review of the Kentucky campaign, *discovering in the process* that Polk, Hardee, and their subordinates had willfully disobeyed his orders in October 1862."[27] The author's sly rendition of this affair stands as his most unfounded accusation of Polk. Bragg did not innocently "discover" disobedience while writing an innocuous "review." In fact, from the beginning of "the process" Bragg *set out to prove* Polk's "disobedience." While *initially* compiling material for his report, before writing had even begun, Bragg demanded that other army commanders fork over incriminating evidence against Polk (and incidentally, themselves). Robertson's treatment of this affair demonstrates the fallacy of historians' taking Bragg's stance as objective truth, overlooking the obvious fact that Bragg was undeniably engaged in a full-blown vendetta.

Robertson goes the way of other Polk detractors by referring to Polk's correspondence with Jefferson Davis solely as seeking Bragg's *removal*. As previously shown, reading the entire letters reveals that Polk heartily recommended Bragg for *promotion* to a position of army-wide leadership in Richmond. Indeed, Polk's advice was wise, for Bragg offered arguably his best service to the Confederacy when President Davis finally called him to just such an office one year later.[28]

Finally, Robertson blithely blames Polk for Bragg's failures in the field. It was Polk's fault that Bragg lost Middle Tennessee following Rosecrans's Tullahoma Campaign in June 1863, and Polk was similarly to blame for Bragg's refusal to advance against Rosecrans that August.[29] It is a pity that Polk was dead by the time Bragg returned to field command at Wilmington, North Carolina; otherwise, Robertson might have blamed the bishop for the fall of Fort Fisher!

William Glenn Robertson's severe condemnation of Polk in *River of Death* is disheartening, for it represents a departure from principles he so wisely laid out in the essay "A Tale of Two Orders," previously cited. In that piece he defends Polk and decries "single-minded blame heaped upon him," specifically with regard to events at Chickamauga—but the principle applies generally. "It is dangerous for historians to ascribe simplistic motivations to individuals," he proclaims, yet in *River of Death* he commits the same offense that he himself previously condemned.[30]

Hopefully, the extremist, insult-ridden style of writing history has nearly run its course. Hyperbole, targeted sarcasm and false characterizations do not render a story more interesting (and any writer resorting to them should make doubly sure of accuracy). History is sufficiently fascinating on its own without later observers inflicting their own agendas upon it. If we can refrain from doing so, perhaps General Patton Anderson's lament to his wife, "Who will ever write a *truthful* history of the War?" will finally be resolved.[31]

Were Polk and Jefferson Davis Lifelong Friends?

A common claim made by those who impugn Polk's military service is that he came by his position in the Confederate army solely by virtue of a longstanding friendship with Jefferson Davis. David Powell states categorically that "[Polk's] principal military qualification was that he was a friend and classmate of Jefferson Davis." Polk was indeed a classmate of Davis's at West Point, and Cadet Davis named Polk as one of "the set" with whom he associated at the Academy, which also included Albert Sidney Johnston, Polk's roommate. However, Polk was not so tight a friend at West Point as to accompany Davis on his surreptitious drinking outings at Benny Haven's or his numerous other demerit-racking shenanigans![32]

More significantly, *Polk and Davis never kept in touch at all after graduation from the military academy* until the outbreak of the Civil War. Yet historians imply otherwise. Earl Hess states that they had "an *enduring* personal friendship" and that

Polk "had *always* benefited from his friendship with Davis." Woodworth also makes much of the connection as a source of benefit to Polk, although he acknowledges that the two had not maintained any contact after their cadet days. William Glenn Robertson makes no such admission, calling Polk "a friend of Jefferson Davis from their time together at West Point" and accusing Polk of "privately exploit[ing] his friendship with Davis." McMurry refers to "Polk's *long* friendship with Jefferson Davis." Even though many would agree that friendships formed in college retain a certain immortal quality, characterizing the relationship as "long" and "enduring" implies that it continued over the years, which was not the case.[33]

Undoubtedly Polk's West Point friendship with Davis was a factor in the general's commission awarded him in June 1861. It is well known that Davis put great stock in a West Point education. But what surely counted more were Polk's achievements and reputation built up during the intervening years, the urgings of influential people from the Mississippi Valley whose interests Polk represented during his trip to Richmond to confer with Davis, and the favorable impression he made upon Davis during these meetings.[34]

Was Polk a Conniving Underminer?

A frequent and severe charge leveled by historians against Polk concerns his role in the command conflicts of the Army of Tennessee. Steven Woodworth brands Polk "the chief source of the backbiting and criticism that would eventually undermine Bragg's effectiveness." He paints Polk as an evil-hearted ringleader corrupting naive, suggestible officers such as Hardee, Buckner, Breckinridge and others who, solely through being contaminated by Polk, turned against Bragg themselves. Similarly, David A. Powell, in the opening pages of his Chickamauga study, Volume II, proclaims: "Polk's pernicious influence was the genesis of the current discontent seething within the Army of Tennessee."[35]

While it is true that Polk would adamantly defend himself (or another) when unfairly judged or accused, he simply did not exhibit the malice ascribed to him by Woodworth, Cozzens and Powell. However, as evidenced by Bragg's correspondence, from the beginning of their association Bragg nurtured an active, bitter dislike for Polk. Nevertheless, many authors portray Polk and his alleged co-conspirator Hardee as the perpetrators of persecution against Bragg.

But what of Polk's handful of letters to Jefferson Davis in which he expressed concerns over Bragg's fitness for army leadership and field command? Historians paint this as glaring evidence of a sinister side to Polk, revealing him to be an intriguer extraordinaire transplanted from some medieval European court. They would have readers believe that Polk singularly stands apart in the annals of military insubordination. But is this a valid characterization?

In fact, the kind of communication that Polk forwarded to Richmond happened frequently on both sides. A thick tome could no doubt be compiled of multiple letters of complaint to both Davis and Lincoln from officers unhappy with their commanding generals. Some took their campaigns beyond letter-writing; Joseph Hooker, for one, is well known to have made the rounds in Washington lobbying congressmen against both McClellan and Burnside while serving under them.

A notable example on the Confederate side took place in April 1862 when two Richards, generals Taylor and Ewell, conspired against Stonewall Jackson. Both felt frustrated by Jackson's secretive strategizing which drove Ewell to conclude that the commanding general was likely insane. He urged Taylor to argue their case before Jefferson Davis in Richmond. Taylor knew he would have a ready audience with the president by virtue of a special relationship: Davis was his brother-in-law. (Years earlier Taylor's sister Sarah had been married to Jefferson Davis for mere months before she died of malaria.) Taylor traveled to Richmond and voiced his concerns to Davis and Secretary of War Judah Benjamin, requesting that they replace Jackson or at least supersede him with a sane superior. Taylor even had the audacity to suggest such a commander: General James Longstreet. He was persuasive enough that Davis agreed to transfer Longstreet to command in the Valley, but Lee intervened and the move was cancelled. Had Taylor and Ewell's intrigue succeeded, Jackson's brilliant Shenandoah Valley Campaign would never have happened![36]

This episode shares some of the same elements for which historians excoriate Polk. In the same vein as their allegation that Polk capitalized on a long-term friendship with Davis, Taylor had the ready ear of the president thanks to a special relationship from years past. Like Polk, Taylor raised concerns about his commanding general, calling into question his mental competence. The difference is that Polk suggested a more appropriate position for Bragg which amounted to a promotion and ensured greater influence over the army, while Taylor called for a replacement who would outrank Jackson and thus deprive him of further control. In spite of the potentially detrimental, even devastating, effect on the Southern war effort that Jackson's removal would have caused, historians condemn neither Taylor nor Ewell for their intriguing. Instead, the incident is routinely reported in a non-judgmental, incidental manner, and never do historians brand Richard Taylor a backbiter or a troublemaker, at least not with regard to Jackson—Kirby Smith might be a different story. But even in the latter case, rather than condemn him they debate the merits of Taylor's disagreements with his superior.

Similarly, Hood's undermining correspondence behind the back of Joseph Johnston during the Atlanta Campaign is generally tolerated, even justified, by certain historians including Richard McMurry, Stephen Davis, and (not surprisingly) Stephen Hood. Rather than condemn him, Larry Daniel leaves Hood's motives open to question and partially blames Richmond, but never fails to view Polk's correspondence with Davis in the worst possible light.[37] One might question why Polk is so roundly castigated and his offenses magnified while others are given a pass for the same behavior. The truth, of course, is that this kind of thing happened all the time, and thus it becomes clear that the charges against Polk arise not from his actions but rather out of some manner of personal prejudice against him.

An interesting, recent turn in the ongoing effort by historians to deny that Bragg actively harbored hostility toward Polk, appeared in Larry Daniel's book, *Conquered: Why the Army of Tennessee Failed.* He recounts Richard Taylor's August 1862 visit to Bragg's headquarters in Chattanooga and the commanding general's unrestrained lambasting of one of his generals. (The conversation is quoted in full in Chapter 6.) In spite of Taylor's polite redaction of the injured party's name, historians are virtually unanimous in concluding that it was Polk whom Bragg pilloried so severely. But Daniel suggests an alternative victim of Bragg's fury: General Samuel Jones. Perhaps it is necessary to designate another general as the recipient of Bragg's dinner denouncement, to preserve the prevailing theory that Polk, rather than Bragg, was the source of their hostility. But Samuel Jones? An interesting exercise would be to look into what a stretch it is to attempt to fit him into this scenario.

Major General Samuel Jones began the war in his native state of Virginia, serving on Beauregard's staff during First Manassas, then taking command of Bartow's mostly Georgia brigade after the latter's death in that battle. He subsequently rotated around the Confederacy, serving under Bragg for two months in Pensacola, then commanding the Departments of East Tennessee; Western Virginia, for which he is most known; and South Carolina, Georgia and Florida ("Jones, Samuel," House Divided: The Civil War Research Engine at Dickinson College).

First one needs to consider the clues offered by Taylor: "I inquired for one of his division commanders, a man widely known and respected." At first glance, the category "division commander" provides some justification for Daniel's theory that it could have been Jones whom Bragg targeted, since Polk commanded a corps rather than division. However, just prior to that time during one of Bragg's reorganizations, the army's "corps were redesignated as divisions." Therefore, Polk technically did command a division for this short while, until Bragg moved him into the nebulous position of "second in command." But Taylor could easily have been unaware of that subtlety and assumed that Polk, as one of Bragg's immediate subordinates, commanded a division.

However, a greater problem with suggesting Jones as the subject of Taylor's inquiry arises with the second clue: the man he asked after was "widely known and respected." Samuel Jones seems an unlikely candidate under this description, both generally and with respect to Richard Taylor particularly. Jones was a Virginian while Polk, like Taylor a prominent Louisianan, served as Episcopal bishop of that state—thus, both descriptors aptly applied to him. Finally, the point that irrefutably proves that Jones was not the subject of Bragg's rant took place after the dinner party, when Taylor privately asked Bragg with whom he would replace the offending general. Although it is unclear where Jones was stationed at precisely the time of this conversation, he was not then serving under Bragg's command—so how could Bragg replace him? It is true that Jones and Taylor had both served two-month stints under Bragg at Pensacola, but not at the same time. For all these reasons, it is hard to imagine why Taylor would have had a keen interest in General Jones. To be fair, by leaving unnamed the subject of Bragg's wrath, General Taylor left the matter open to speculation. Daniel should certainly be credited with creativity in redirecting Bragg's mealtime maelstrom away from Polk to an innocuous, obscure general like Samuel Jones, thus absolving Bragg of rudely attacking the bishop in public.[38]

The undeniable truth is that Bragg at times expended more energy fighting and punishing his own army than the enemy. This behavior assumed the form of a repeated pattern which Bragg compulsively followed against the advice of supporters. In addition to the numerous occasions when he turned his ire upon individual subordinates, there were four episodes that stand out involving *multiple* officers, thereby undermining overall army function. The first was Bragg's January 11, 1863, circular letter, which generated considerable controversy reaching all the way to Richmond. Nevertheless, Bragg managed to stay in command in spite of his misstep in writing the highly irregular letter in the first place, but more importantly stating his intent to resign and then not following through with it. The second controversy erupted when Bragg issued his April 13, 1863, letter accusing Polk and eight officers of disobedience of orders in the lead-up to the Battle of Perryville. The third crusade against Bragg's subordinates came after his victory at Chickamauga when he dismissed Polk and Hindman, with others lined up on the chopping block. On this occasion Longstreet, an outsider to the army's history of intrigue, joined in because he saw Bragg as an unfit and destructive leader. Again Richmond was brought into the imbroglio and this time President Davis even made a personal visit. And again Bragg survived the intervention, only to follow up with his fourth bout of scapegoating officers, resulting in the dismissal of D.H. Hill, demotion of Simon Buckner and William Preston, and banishment of Longstreet from the army to conduct an independent campaign in Knoxville.

Interestingly, the second, third and fourth incidents came after Bragg *won in some way*, whether prevailing in an actual battle or retaining the support of President Davis. Undeniably, all were conceived in his mind and initiated and carried out by him. Bragg cannot be construed as a passive player, an unwitting victim, or a mere responder in any of these scenarios. Indeed, he played the role of antagonist. He was in charge and he made the choices. Yet historians persist in the view that Bragg was somehow on the defensive when it came to his subordinates. For example, Earl Hess, referring to both Polk and Hardee, makes the blanket statement: "The results *of their attacks on Bragg*, and of Bragg's unwise counterattacks, were ruining the field effectiveness of the Confederacy's main army in the West." Again one must ask, what attacks? By overreacting to criticism in a newspaper, any attacks were carried out by Bragg, unless one considers the votes of no confidence *solicited by Bragg* an attack. These men were forced onto the defensive by their commander, and it was only natural that some put their heads together about Bragg's erratic behavior and had something to say about it to Richmond. It is also inevitable that their relationship with and respect for Bragg would be damaged by his ill-advised stabs at his subalterns.[39]

Historians attribute to Polk sole responsibility for the rancor in the ranks because they apparently believe that by some compulsion or moral flaw within his inherent nature he cultivated intrigue and discord. The language they use to describe his unbecoming, underlying treachery is sometimes exceedingly elaborate and entertaining. David Powell ranks highest in this category with his phraseology that because of Polk's "penchant for Machiavellian political maneuvering," he "took to behind-the-scenes intrigue like a Medici pope"![40] All of this is offered up to the reader as unquestioned doctrine.

Yet one might ask, if Polk was truly such an incorrigible intriguer, why did he not continue the same behavior under Joseph Johnston? It would logically follow, based on these characterizations of Polk as an inveterate schemer, that he would exhibit the same traits and attitudes regardless of who commanded over him. Indeed, most of the officers whom he supposedly influenced (even after departing the army) to sign the petition for Bragg's removal, in addition to General Cheatham who did not sign, continued to serve in the Army of Tennessee after Bragg's resignation. Surely with such a sullied, discontented gang in place, upon returning to the Army of Tennessee in 1864 Polk would have rekindled the conniving cabal that he supposedly savored. But he did not. In fact, Polk delighted in the harmonious relationships among the upper-echelon generals under Johnston. Similarly, if Polk was the source of the problems in the Army of Tennessee, then should not such problems have diminished upon his departure? Yet this was not the case, as William Gale reported in a letter dated October 31, 1863, to future brother-in-law William Huger: "I learn that so far from having confidence restored among his General officers, that the discord is on the increase." According to Polk's detractors, he undermined the effectiveness of Braxton Bragg as army commander. Yet Bragg's most inglorious defeat which stands as prime evidence of his ineptitude as a leader, occurred at Chattanooga on November 25, 1863, fully two months after Bragg dismissed Polk from the army. Even in his absence, was Polk somehow responsible? The truth, as Polk had clearly discerned a year and a half before, was that Bragg's talents lay not in field command or army leadership—and he amply demonstrated it all by himself on the slopes of Missionary Ridge.[41]

Another drawback to the theory of Polk as the power-mad plotter is that usually such intriguers harbor an ulterior motive behind their Machiavellian schemes. They desire something for themselves: power, money, position, or at least the gratitude and favor of another who through their machinations attains power, money, and/or position. Yet no such motive can possibly be asserted by even the most virulent Polk critics. Unquestionably he did not covet command for himself. Nor did he stand personally to benefit in any way by Bragg's removal. There simply is no conceivable reason that Polk would have embarked on the course attributed to him by numerous historians, who notably fail to offer any motive or rationale for it. Thus, by way of explanation, they invent an undefined, internal evil emanating from Polk's soul that infected the entire army. It is really a fantastic storyline that self-perpetuates so long as it goes on unquestioned, but appears ridiculous upon objective examination.

Contrary to the portrayal by Woodworth, Cozzens, and others who have echoed their distortions, Polk did not crave disharmony and discord, nor did he have the heart of an intriguer or underminer. Virtually no contemporary voice depicts him in this manner. His motives on the few occasions that he advised Davis to relieve Bragg came out of a concern for his country, not mean-spiritedness, self-aggrandizement, ambition for Bragg's position, nor for any personal advancement or benefit to himself.

Was Polk Lazy?

Another characterization of Polk that has made the rounds of historians is that he was indolent. Samuel J. Martin claims that Polk was "too lazy to demand strict obedience from his men." Powell mentions in passing "Leonidas Polk's lackadaisical attitude toward command," and Robertson similarly refers to "the more lackadaisical Polk." Perhaps the exaggerated image of Polk as a lazy, self-indulgent man originated from a passage by General William French, one of Polk's division commanders in Mississippi and the Atlanta Campaign. The description is obviously written in a tongue-in-cheek manner and meant affectionately rather than literally:

> Gen. Polk had been an Episcopal bishop, and enjoyed the best the land afforded. The mating songs of the birds disturbed not his morning repose. The glorious sun rose too early for him to see it from the mountain top. It showed its face there at an unseemly hour. But when the "drowsy morn" was passed, and the milkmaid had drawn tribute from the cows, and the coffee-pot was steaming on the hearth, and the light rolls were hot by the fire, and the plump, fine capon, with side well lined by fat, was broiling on the coals, sending a savory odor through the apartments, the Bishop would arise, his face radiant with joy. He was a valiant trencherman, but when the repast was over he threw aside the surplice. The priest became a warrior when he girded on his saber, and sallied forth a paladin in the strife.[42]

The truth is that by nature Polk was anything but lazy. During his years as missionary bishop in the frontier West, he expended mighty effort traveling through the then-far western states and territory where civilization barely had a foothold, founding churches, raising up and organizing their leadership, and overseeing numerous new parishes. His grueling travels and travails during the 1830s through the mission field in the wilds of Texas, Arkansas, northern Louisiana and Indian Territory demanded self-discipline and self-denial. Add to that his "indefatigable energy" in almost singlehandedly initiating and shepherding the founding of The University of the South.[43]

During the early days of the war when he was well into his sixth decade of life, Polk threw himself into creating and arming the extensive fortifications along the Mississippi River and especially the bastion at Columbus, Kentucky, turning it into one of the most formidable fortifications of the Civil War. At that time he pushed Congress to fund ironclad construction, spearheaded an armory in Memphis to produce rifles, arranged for production of gunpowder from Arkansas guano caves, and called on his friend Matthew Maury to provide submarine "torpedoes" to be planted in the Mississippi River. Thereafter while in field command he was ever diligent in looking after the needs of his army and completing countless administrative tasks. During battle "he was to be seen constantly at the front, at every part of his line, supervising the progress of events with his own presence."[44]

By 1864, when General French wrote the poetical description quoted above, Polk may have slowed down somewhat. He was about the same age as Robert E. Lee, who had himself by then become encumbered by age-related exhaustion and illness after years of living in the field. But even if slightly slower and ponderous, Polk remained vigorous right up to the day of his death when he scaled Pine Mountain on foot. Always he was a mission-driven man who strove hard and thoroughly for excellence in everything he did. Indolence was not in his nature.

Can a Clergyman Make a Good Soldier?

The high position that Polk held in the Episcopal Church is perhaps a major reason for historians' negative portrayal of him. Some of the insults hurled at Polk subtly touch on his vocation as bishop: for example, Powell's comparing him to a Medici pope. Historians automatically assume Polk possessed certain personality traits which upon reflection appear to be religious stereotypes. Noe calls him "pompous" and Woodworth sarcastically inserts into his narratives of Polk such religious terms as "repentance," and phrases such as "high and mighty." Similarly, Connelly repeatedly decries Polk's "dogmatism." Robertson refers to Hardee as Polk's "acolyte," and even throws in an accusation of hypocritical display: As Wilder's artillery bombarded Chattanooga on August 21, 1863, Polk "thought it best to be seen in church that morning."[45]

Part of the problem might involve a skewed notion of what religion *is*—or at least what it was in centuries past. Larry Daniel joins with Steven Woodworth in disdaining the Christianity not only of Southerners, but of believers through the ages. Daniel explains, "The problem lay not in evangelical Southerners' literal interpretation of the Bible, according to Woodworth, but their superficial interpretation." According to these historians-turned-religious-authorities (although, admittedly, Larry Daniel was a Methodist minister), shallow Southerners supposedly had it all wrong. But exactly how do they allege the South had strayed so far from true Christianity? The problem with Southern Christians, they continue, is that "[t]he church's mission was viewed as being an agent not of social change but of evangelism and salvation." That is a startling analysis indeed: Woodworth and Daniel judge two of the essential tenets of the message and teachings of Jesus Christ to be misguided fallacy. So dismissive is Larry Daniel of the 19th-century Southern church that he could not take care to spell correctly the given name of one of its most prominent bishops.[46]

Regarding Polk, throughout his Chickamauga study David Powell pointedly refers to the "bishop-turned-general" as though his prior vocation rendered him less of a general, or even an impostor. Perhaps modern, secular historians look with disdain upon any man of the cloth and cannot take him seriously as a soldier. However, numerous pastors entered the armed services during the Civil War. A few Civil War clerics attained high rank, including General Mark Lowrey, brigade commander in Cleburne's division, although Polk stands out among even these for his ordainment as bishop of Louisiana in the Episcopal Church.[47]

Some 19th-century people similarly perceived an incongruity between the military and ecclesiastical vocations. When he accepted a major general's commission in the Confederate army, "Polk received numerous letters from clergy and laity expressing surprise or astonishment at his decision to enter military service." Biographer Huston Horn quotes the objections of many in his diocese and beyond. Some, such as Elise Bragg in a letter previously cited, deemed it an insult to the faith: "Think of the scandal to our Church." Others felt that a churchman could not possibly make a good soldier, never mind a general, an insinuation made by Bragg when he complained to President Davis in 1863, "Gen'l Polk by education and habit is unfitted for executing the plans of others. He will convince himself his own are better and follow them."[48]

Modern historians are not alone in indulging in sarcastic prejudice, humor or stereotype at Polk's expense. This was done by some of his contemporaries as well. Shelby Foote relates that Sherman relished opposing Polk in his Meridian campaign: "'As it was [Sherman] chuckled, for he always enjoyed a small joke on the clergy, 'I scared the bishop out of his senses.'" David Powell, in the first volume of his Chickamauga study, includes the anecdote of an incident that took place outside of Chattanooga in August 1863, concerning the

> almost daily bombardments by [Eli] Lilly's guns, often to the great amusement of the Union troops. "The other day," wrote one Indiana Yankee, "a deserter pointed out ... the headquarters of Gen. Bishop Polk ... and the Captain was not long in sending two or three shells through the building. The old sacrilegious reprobate vamoosed the ranch at double quick."[49]

Even one of Polk's own direct subordinates looked somewhat askance at a bishop serving in the military. His division commander General French obviously harbored stereotypes regarding the life and disposition of a man of the Church, as indicated by the passage quoted in the preceding section, even if it was not intended entirely seriously.

While some people, contemporaries of Polk as well as modern scholars, see a contradiction between serving in the ministry and military, others believed Polk's ministerial background to be an asset. Jefferson Davis, for one, seemingly viewed Polk's participation in the new nation's struggle for independence as a kind of divine endorsement of the Southern cause:

> Nothing impressed me more in the interview [with Polk] [when Davis offered him an army command] … than the confidence manifested by this great and holy man, that he had a sure correspondence with his God, and was treading in the path approved by Him.

Polk's biographer Joseph Parks comments on an exchange between Bishop Otey and Polk: "If there were still persons who doubted that a bishop should become a soldier let them look into the Holy Writ. Many times had the God of Israel sent forth his leaders into battle." Soldiers under his command embraced his clerical identity, even took comfort from it as Sam Watkins explains:

> His soldiers always loved and honored him. They called him "Bishop Polk." "Bishop Polk" was ever a favorite with the army, and when any position was to be held, and it was known that "Bishop Polk" was there, we knew and felt that "all was well."[50]

Once he committed to serve, Polk felt no further conflict regarding his military and religious callings. Although some, then and now, have questioned whether a bishop, even one with a West Point education, could possess an aptitude or inclination for army command, "Polk *always thought of himself as a soldier*—in earlier years a soldier of his country, in later years a soldier of God. 'His air of command never left him,' yet he was always aware that he himself was under command." Correspondingly, while a soldier, he never stopped thinking of himself as a bishop: "When [a] friend exclaimed in surprise, 'What! you, a bishop, throw off the gown for a sword!'" Polk replied, "'No, sir, I buckle the sword over the gown.'" Indeed, as previously described, on rare occasions during his military service General Polk donned his gown and officiated at the sacred rites of matrimony and baptism.[51]

Although untroubled within himself, an exchange between Polk and visiting English army officer Lieutenant Colonel Fremantle reveals Polk's awareness of others' misapprehensions over an Anglican bishop's fighting for his country:

> After dinner General Polk told me that he hoped his brethren in England did not very much condemn his present line of conduct. He explained to me the reasons which had induced him temporarily to forsake the cassock and return to his old profession. He explained the extreme reluctance he had felt in taking this step. He said that as soon as the war was over, he should return to his episcopal avocations, in the same way as a man, finding his house on fire, would use every means in his power to extinguish the flames, and would then resume his ordinary pursuits.

Polk left Fremantle much impressed by him both as an officer and a gentleman: he "looks much more the soldier than the clergyman.... He is much beloved by the soldiers on account of his great personal courage and agreeable manners.... In his clerical capacity I had always heard him spoken of with the greatest respect." Apparently Fremantle had no difficulty in reconciling Polk's dual roles.[52]

Was Polk Lacking as a Strategist?

A specific claim that some have advanced to cast doubt on Polk's military fitness is that he lacked the ability or inclination to formulate strategy. This perception was held even by some fellow commanders such as General Liddell: "[Polk] possessed all the requisites of a great soldier, except strategy and tactical combination." This criticism may be attributable to prejudice against a clergyman serving as corps commander, or perhaps Liddell, for all of his keen skills of observation, was not an astute judge of his fellow man—for example, he describes Beauregard as "lacking in energy," while nothing could be further from the truth! Although it is difficult to discern his exact meaning, General French hints at a similar perceived fault of Polk's by pronouncing: "As a soldier he was more theoretical than practical" (which might be expected in a West Point-trained officer short on practical experience).[53]

The record amply demonstrates that Polk showed no glaring deficit as to strategy; he constantly made sound suggestions as well as predictions of enemy maneuvers that came to pass. Early on, he foresaw the need for extensive preparations and involvement of naval forces in the defense of the Mississippi River. His was virtually a lone Confederate voice urging such a build-up, while the Union "made it a major priority." As previously noted, Polk devised the successful attack plan of the early morning at Murfreesboro on December 31, 1862. Then, in July 1863 he wrote President Davis proposing a grand concentration of Confederate forces in the West to counter Rosecrans's build-up in Middle Tennessee (although his position was not unique to him; Beauregard had long urged the same). Polk again wrote in favor of concentration as Rosecrans threatened Chattanooga later in the summer.[54]

In February 1863 Polk had penned a letter to Johnston predicting (accurately, as it turned out) Rosecrans's strategy which played out point-by-point that summer during the Tullahoma campaign. Johnston's response to Polk demonstrates that the latter's thoughts on strategy were taken under serious consideration by the department commander. Indeed, Polk's letter seems to have initiated a vigorous exchange of ideas between the two generals. In his March 3, 1863, reply, Johnston lamented that "the government does not appreciate the importance to us of holding Tennessee." He then elaborated on Polk's predictions:

> Should Rosecranz [sic] make the movements you suggest we must choose between falling back, which, I think, would be next to ruin, + taking advantage of the best opportunity his division of forces might give, to open the offensive.[55]

For Johnston to call for an offensive was indeed a rarity—not an option he habitually exercised. Surely he was stimulated by some outside influence, perhaps the ideas pouring forth from Polk's pen!

Later that summer Polk engaged in deep strategizing by correspondence with General Hardee, then stationed in Mississippi. In a letter dated July 30, 1863, he called for a grand concentration of forces under Johnston as department commander, consisting of "Genl Bragg's, Genl Buckner's forces and any others that can be spared throughout the Southwest," leaving detachments in Alabama and Mississippi "to act as nuclei around which the quotas of State Troops now being raised, should be concentrated." With state troops guarding fixed points, the strategy would be to "throw us on the line of Grant's communications, open a connexion with the Trans Miss. forces, and enable us to unite and move down on Grant with our whole Western strength." This concentrated army could alternatively attack Rosecrans "with the strongest possibility of success," and such measures could result in "repossessing Middle Tennessee and wiping out the prestige of the Vicksburg success."

On a roll, Polk poured out his higher vision touching on the army's mission:

> I confess in this campaign, I find more that is hopeful and promising than in anything that presents itself, and it is in keeping with views I have always entertained and urged in regard to the mission of the Army of Tennessee. In my judgment it is the important army of the Confederacy, and has a higher mission, and properly strengthened and well handled it will be found to have accomplished more than any other in effecting the great results, after which we are all aiming.

Polk then returned to matters at hand, noting that General Bragg "has gone for some days to Cherokee Springs" (where he sought healing from the painful, chronic conditions that repeatedly wore him down in the field), the army was "throwing up earthworks, refitting, +c." and that Hardee's "successor has taken command, and promises apparently to work harmoniously."[56] The last reference was to D.H. Hill, notorious for *not* working harmoniously with anyone—but clearly Polk was in an optimistic frame of mind at the time of this letter. It might be added that Polk's "judgment [that the Army of Tennessee] is the important army of the Confederacy" matches the opinion held by several key Civil War analysts including Thomas Connelly, Richard McMurry, Earl Hess and Stephen Davis who argue that, in spite of the greater attention focused on the Eastern Theater, the outcome of the Civil War was actually decided in the West.

During the days leading up to the Battle of Chickamauga Polk played a key role in developing the Confederate plan of attack. Earl Hess credits Polk for his contribution, albeit begrudgingly and without missing an opportunity to inject a mild insult ("for once"):

> On September 15, a council of officers agreed to move toward Chattanooga, and Bragg continued to favor that course the next day. For once Polk offered a sound plan; his corps would hold Federal attention opposite Lee and Gordon's Mill as other units crossed Chickamauga Creek farther to the right and then swung around to crush Rosecrans's left flank. Daniel Harvey Hill later praised Bragg for "superior boldness" in adopting an aggressive plan.

Ignoring the "aggressive plan" that was Polk's, not Bragg's as Hill believed, Robertson in *River of Death* accuses Polk of withholding advice on strategy out of spite. In the crisis days leading up to the evacuation of Chattanooga in September 1863, Polk "remained a passive observer only," he claims, but Earl Hess's assessment of Polk's contribution during that time period shows otherwise. It should be noted that Polk's plan of attack at Chickamauga resulted in the only major victory won by the Army of Tennessee.[57]

The following year while in independent command in Mississippi Polk demonstrated that not only could he dream up grand strategic schemes on paper, devise successful battle plans, or make valuable contributions to others' plans, but he also independently implemented sound, successful strategy in real-world situations on the ground. The finest example was his two-pronged defensive strategy implemented in February 1864, starring Forrest's force which halted Sooy Smith's cavalry while Polk's main body engaged in a fighting withdrawal before Sherman's advance through central Mississippi. Forrest, of course, devised his own tactics that sent Sooy Smith back to Memphis and stranded Sherman at Meridian, halting the Yankees' advance into Alabama. But it was Polk who conceived the overall plan, and it was pursuant to his orders that Forrest brilliantly repulsed the Yankee column. Stephen D. Lee confirms this in a 1875 letter to W.M. Polk: Lee's own cavalry was to unite with Forrest whereupon they were "ordered to crush a Federal column from the direction of Memphis." But before Lee could join Forrest, the latter had already driven off Sooy Smith. It was Polk who grasped Sherman's plan and understood that the key to stopping the Federals was intercepting their cavalry with his own. He correctly surmised that Sherman would not move into Alabama (whether Mobile or Selma) without Sooy Smith. He also realized that his meager infantry could not succeed against Sherman's numbers, but that Forrest was his strong point and his hope of deflecting Sherman's aims on Alabama. Polk was fortunate to have in his arsenal the fearless Forrest who did not hesitate to take on more than twice his numbers.[58]

After being on the receiving end of Sherman's dress rehearsal for the Atlanta Campaign and beyond, Polk gained some understanding of his adversary. He accurately discerned Sherman's future strategy of targeting Johnston's army and proposed his own movements to counter it, in a letter to President Davis dated February 28, 1864:

> [Polk saw] "that no effectual opposition could be made against Gen. Sherman ... directly to his front, but that his army might be destroyed or scattered" by Polk's forces suddenly sweeping up from northern Mississippi. They would then pounce on the vulnerable backside of Sherman's divisions [then] camped in East Tennessee and Northern Alabama.

During Sherman's supply build-up in preparation for his advance toward Atlanta, Polk had scouts reconnoitering the railroads through Middle Tennessee and pointed out vulnerabilities which could have been exploited. He repeatedly begged for permission to attack the Tennessee railroads from his position in northern Alabama. That Polk was correct in his understanding is borne out by Sherman himself, who "later wrote that 'The Atlanta Campaign would simply have been impossible without the use of the railroads' from Atlanta to Louisville. The question is whether or not Polk could have destroyed this lifeline. There is good reason to believe that he could have."[59]

In fact, rather than await the Union advance in May launching the Atlanta Campaign, Polk proposed pre-empting Sherman by invading Middle Tennessee in force: "In February [Polk] sent his own proposal that he and Johnston join in Alabama and invade Middle Tennessee…. In April … Polk reiterated his proposal." Richmond had been urging Johnston to spearhead a similar invasion, but through the impassable region of East Tennessee; Polk's plan had a greater chance of success. During this same time Polk also cast his eye across the Confederacy and formulated a bold plan to retake New Orleans and much of the Mississippi River.[60]

Finally, during the Atlanta Campaign it is likely that the notation in the diary of Polk's aide-de-camp and son-in-law, mentioned previously, originated with the general himself: that Calhoun represented a missed opportunity for successful battle during Johnston's retreat through North Georgia. According to Connelly's analysis, this conclusion was correct. These are but some examples of strategy conceived in the active mind of General Polk.[61]

Chapter 12

Polk's True Nature and Personality

So misleading is the portrayal of Polk by certain cynical academicians, it can be surprising and instructive for the truth-seeking student of the Civil War to investigate his true nature and personality as shown in his life, his writings, and the observations of people who actually knew him.

Polk was undeniably an intelligent man driven to succeed in his various endeavors. Many who exhibit this kind of drive typically possess an equal measure of impatience, especially toward fellow men not as highly endowed as they, but this was not the case with Leonidas Polk. He was ever willing to overlook a wrong, invariably patient even toward those who scorned or wronged him. Before the war he forgave at least one man who deceived and set him back financially. The forbearance he displayed in the war's early days toward General Gideon Pillow, well known to be arrogant and self-aggrandizing, and later toward General Bragg who plotted to entrap and finally dismissed him unjustly for alleged insubordination, evinces a rare long-suffering quality.[1]

A corollary to Polk's forbearance was his joyful compassion and the depth of his faith from which it arose. "He disliked the puritanical approach to religion. To him to be religious was a pleasure, not a task. A kindly smile was more effective than a stern demeanor." Perhaps nothing demonstrated his tolerance and loving acceptance of others more than his unlikely, close friendship with General Frank Cheatham. Known for drinking, cursing and gambling, Cheatham had a good heart which Polk saw beneath the coarse exterior. Biographer Christopher Losson characterized the connection between them as "akin to a father-son relationship." Cheatham's observant chief of staff described Polk as "just and generous, qualities which secured for him the love and confidence of officers and men." Some thought Polk compassionate to a fault, as exemplified by his allowing Breckinridge's exhausted men to bivouac at his headquarters rather than march on to their assigned position on the Chickamauga battlefield, contributing to the tardy attack of the next morning.[2]

Above all, Polk was ever cheerful. During the tribulations of his young adult years in contending with adversity on the mission field as well as intermittent financial setbacks, he declared himself, by the help of God, "enabled to bear up under all & carry my burden triumphantly & cheerfully inward." He exhibited such inner strength that when confronted with hardships he simply dismissed them, as in a letter to his family from his post at Columbus, Kentucky, following the South's bruising defeats at Forts Henry and Donelson. "We may have some reverses, but what of that." *What of that?* (in modern parlance, "so what?") was his stalwart answer to overwhelming tests and trials that would crush lesser men.[3]

Finally, Polk was lofty-minded, sometimes to the detriment of practicality. Author Sarah Dorsey, daughter of William Henry Allen, Louisiana, governor and brigadier general who served under Polk at Shiloh, described the latter in a manner remarkably reminiscent of Thomas Jefferson:

> Polk was a grand man, a colossal nature, both in physique and morale. He thought largely, he acted nobly—his instincts were all right and true. He had invention, imagination, policy, skill and valor of high degree—but no sense of economics—no frugality.

In fact, Polk shared a number of qualities with fellow optimist and visionary Thomas Jefferson: each man was influential in the creation of a new nation, founded a major university, oversaw the building of a substantial home surrounded by extensive agricultural operations, devised agricultural and technological innovations, and suffered periodic financial strains and setbacks. The two evinced similar political philosophies, as evidenced by Polk's quoting John Knox upon accepting his major general's commission: "Resistance to tyrants is our duty to God." A paraphrase of the same quote appeared on Thomas Jefferson's personal seal.[4]

During the war an officer serving under Polk recollected, "He was every inch a gentleman, without mannerism or assumption,—simple and innocent, yet dignified and imposing."[5] This picture may bear little resemblance to the despicable man portrayed by modern historians, but there is more than ample evidence in the historical record to support its accuracy.

Where Polk Was Wrong

To understand the man, it is equally instructive to examine where he failed during his army service, in the interest of presenting a fair and accurate picture. Polk's overall record as a Confederate commander includes some incidents during key battles in which he fell short in some respects.

First, one could argue that Polk bears at least partial responsibility for the fall of Forts Henry and Donelson in February 1862, as these locations fell generally under Polk's purview. Construction had lagged on their respective fortifications and both remained uncompleted when they were attacked, despite warnings of their vulnerability. There was some ambiguity over who was directly responsible, but had Polk applied a fraction of the energy and attention to those positions as he did to Columbus, perhaps Grant's attacks might have been circumvented or withstood.[6]

Serving under Bragg in the Army of Tennessee, Thomas Connelly correctly charged Polk with inadequately communicating with his superior concerning changes in the situation on his front and his decisions to alter orders accordingly. Bragg used this failing of Polk against him during the witch hunt following Murfreesboro, by resurrecting the incidents before and during Perryville when Polk allegedly "disobeyed" orders. Some historians continue so to charge Polk today, ignoring the fact that Bragg's order contained a clear discretionary clause. Nevertheless, Polk can rightfully be blamed for his failure fully and clearly to explain the circumstances and his reasons for diverging from the original plan. Had he done so adequately, his relationship with Bragg might not have deteriorated to the degree that it did, to the detriment of the Army of Tennessee.[7]

Polk has been condemned for sending in "piecemeal" attacks against the Round Forest position at Murfreesboro, and he rightfully bears some of the blame for the disastrous results. He frankly admitted as much. However, some historians assign part or even most of the blame to Bragg for his mismanagement of Breckinridge's division. If Polk was guilty of ordering premature and poorly timed advances at Murfreesboro, his failure was hardly unique in the annals of the war; in many instances acclaimed commanders committed their forces in a piecemeal manner, including Sherman at First Manassas, Jackson at Cedar Mountain, and Hardee at Peachtree Creek.

Polk turned out to be wrong on occasion in his predictions of the enemy's designs. For example, in August 1863 during the enemy's advance on Chattanooga, he believed that Rosecrans would cross the Tennessee River northeast of the city. Just about everyone in the Confederate command similarly misread Rosecrans's intentions, but while they were distracted by General Hazen's noisy demonstrations above Chattanooga, Union columns infiltrated the mountainous ridges to the south.[8]

During the Battle of Chickamauga Polk did not take proper care in aligning his forces, reconnoitering his front, or securing his flank on the morning of September 20. Had he effectively supported Breckinridge's initial success in reaching the enemy's rear, an early breakthrough might have been achieved on the right. Much has been made of Polk's *delay* in attacking that morning—but as noted, a timely charge likely would not have mattered, for neither was Longstreet ready to advance. Nevertheless, correcting the problems with his own line would have brought far better results to the fight in Polk's sector. Clearly Polk was not at his best at Chickamauga, but not for the reasons usually cited.[9]

Where Polk Was Right

There are undoubtedly other instances in which Polk was wrong, yet numerous occasions when he was right for which he does not receive proper credit from most historians. Some, such as Connelly, Kenneth Noe and William Glenn Robertson, have shown a willingness to examine different angles of an issue. As Robertson writes, "[C]omplex affairs, such as battles involving more than 100,000 combatants, seldom can be analyzed in such simple fashion without doing violence to the truth and unfairly besmirching the reputations of commanders."[10]

To name just a few instances, Polk was right at Bardstown, Kentucky, by not marching in the direction of Frankfort as Bragg ordered, which would have exposed his flank to Buell's entire army. Similarly, he was correct not to launch his small force at Perryville against the build-up of three Union corps. He was right at Rock Spring Church in not attacking when he discovered that the situation on his front had changed. He was right that Bragg should have been relieved of command over the Army of Tennessee well before the inevitable disaster at Missionary Ridge, clearly a result of the latter's poor leadership. In the early days of the Atlanta Campaign he was right to defy Bragg by transferring most of his force to reinforce Johnston, especially Cantey's Mobile garrison that saved Resaca. Yet for each of these, Polk has been castigated by historians such as Steven Woodworth, Peter Cozzens, and others singing in their chorus.

This is nothing new. Archibald Gracie, Jr., whose father commanded a brigade at Chickamauga, used his pen to try and correct misconceptions after that battle. In so doing, Gracie employed an apt metaphor of the "hydra-headed monster of untruth" created by historians' passing along the inaccuracies, slants and agendas of others. Not only are falsehoods repeated, but like the heads of the Hydra they regenerate and multiply and magnify (and stink!) as subsequent writers add their own adjectives and aspersions to the ongoing discourse. Ultimately, the end result bears little resemblance to the truth.[11]

Why the False Narrative About Polk?

One can speculate as to the reasons for the multiple untruths about Leonidas Polk sprouting from the Hydra's head. The study of history has become sidetracked by academics' scolding and lecturing not on what *was*, but how it *ought to have been* from current perspectives. The end result is that history now relates more to the present than the past, which is perhaps to be expected in this self-obsessed age.

The issue which sits in the center of this narrative is slavery. For many it is impossible to view a 19th-century Southern white male slaveholder as anything other than heinous and evil. By extension, anyone fighting for the Confederacy is condemned as having fought solely to uphold slavery, and the Northern armies are extolled for their war of liberation. However, the truth is always more complicated than it seems. Blacks, Indians, Union generals, and even a church owned slaves, while that most despised class, slave traders, were far more likely to be Northern than Southern. For example, slave trader Dexter Niles enslaved more human beings than anyone else in Atlanta. By the time the war came to that city, he had recently departed, leaving his vacated home to be used as headquarters for Joseph Johnston. A nearby resident related that Niles "*had come from Boston, Massachusetts,* before the war and during the pre-war growth of Atlanta. He ... turned [his land] into a slave plantation, or maybe it was a wholesale slave market. We had never seen so many dark skinned people in all our lives. Perhaps two years went by and then all at once the residence was vacated and all the cabins were bare. It was said that when it became evident that the institution of slavery was doomed these bondsmen, women and children were rushed to a slave market beyond the shores to the south of us and sold before Confederate money entirely lost its value. *Dexter Niles went back to Boston.*"[12]

Reality often belies a simple Good North vs. Bad South scenario.

The culture of the 19th century stands in stark contrast to modern America in many respects, and people are inseparable from the world in which they are born and raised. All contribute their small part to their particular generation's wrongs inflicted upon the earth and its inhabitants. How easy it is to pinpoint and condemn the sins of others and of the past; how much more difficult it is to perceive one's own wrongdoing and the collective evils of the present era—all the more so to extricate oneself from them!

One should not assume Leonidas Polk to be an evil man because of repugnant aspects of his era. It is fair, however, to examine the degree of humanity he exhibited within his given social structure. It turns out that Polk advocated for the education of slaves, worshipped in communion with them in a shared chapel on his plantation, prohibited work on Sundays, performed weddings and hosted lavish marital festivities for slaves and otherwise safeguarded their family integrity, and maintained a hospital for the health-care needs of all. The degree of devotion between black and white within the Polk family is perhaps exhibited by a near-disaster on April 12, 1861, the very day the Civil War opened. Fire broke out that night at the cottage on Sewanee Mountain where Polk's wife and daughters were staying while he journeyed through his diocese. Through heroic exertion, every member of his family was "dragged to safety by their faithful servant Altimore."[13]

Many would be surprised to know of Polk's progressive ideas (for his time) where women were concerned. As Louisiana bishop he once overturned a parish election in Baton Rouge because women had not been allowed to vote. And his original intention was for the University of the South to enroll both women and men—unheard of in that day.[14]

Perhaps historians' hostility toward Polk stems from some issue other than the institutions of his time—for example, prejudice against him for his high church position. He stands alone in the degree of recrimination heaped upon him; it seems reasonable, therefore, to propose his unique background by way of explanation. Whatever the reasons, this study attempts to challenge the excessive, undue and undeserved insult heaped upon Leonidas Polk. It does not presume to be revisionist history, as no fundamental adjustment of presuppositions or viewpoint is proposed. Rather, this is *corrective* history, for many historians err in their analysis of Polk in some key factual and interpretive aspects. Not only does the slander hurled his way, seemingly obligatory among Civil War historians, represent a fundamental wrong perpetrated against the legacy of Leonidas Polk, but the wrong extends to readers and students of history by denying them the truth of a notable life.

Chapter 13

Bragg vs. Polk

> *"Very fascinating were his manners, and that not from any art or design, but from the high-toned frankness of his nature, and the noble feelings which welled up from his soul as from a fountain of truth and purity."*[1]

Bishop Stephen Elliott described Polk's noble manners as "very fascinating." No less fascinating was Bragg in his own way, although probably not when it concerned his manners! While he lacked Polk's charisma (which hostile historians even manage to turn into a fault), Bragg had a presence, and profound impact upon those around him. He was a disciplined, moral man driven to succeed and convinced of his superior ability, yet he struggled under the burden of command. Stressful situations caused him not only mental anxiety and indecision, but exacerbation of the health problems to which he was susceptible, including boils, digestive ills and severe headaches.

Bragg's chronic ailments are one explanation offered by historians for his irascible nature. Yet these same historians blame Bragg's subordinates, whom they judge to have been far more vexatious than he, for his repeated pattern of stirring up controversy. In short, Polk, Hardee, Breckinridge, et al. drove him to it. The theory postulates disobedient, conniving underlings who willfully and constantly abused Bragg and undermined any prospect for his success. The damage done by these insubordinate upstarts was thus entirely responsible for the break-down of his command effectiveness and failure to reap the fruits of his victories.

The problem with this portrait is that it casts Bragg in the role of wronged martyr. Bragg would abhor such an image of himself going down in history. His own words ("I will no longer bear the sins of others") clearly state his revulsion toward such a role, for martyrs willingly assume others' wrongs and submit to victimhood. Bragg's approach was anything but submissive; he intended to prevail over his enemies, and prevail he did. Additionally, a martyr must be a saint, or at least not guilty of the same offenses that his persecutors allegedly commit against him. Yet on numerous occasions Bragg proved himself to be an accomplished back-stabber, at no time more than his part in relieving General Joseph Johnston just before the battles of Atlanta.

In June and early July of 1864 Jefferson Davis and his cabinet became greatly alarmed at Johnston's steady retreat through northwestern Georgia. The Yankee army marched inexorably toward the transportation and industrial center of Atlanta, and Joe Johnston appeared unconcerned—at least that was the tone his messages to Richmond seemed to convey. As Bragg's friend Josiah Gorgas recorded in his diary, "Everybody has at last come to the conclusion that Johnston has retreated far enough."[2]

Davis sent his right-hand man, Braxton Bragg, to Atlanta to investigate and report his recommendations.

> Braxton Bragg did go and see Johnston, first on the afternoon of 13 July, and then again the next day. However, Bragg did not inform the field commander of the purpose of his trip, instead choosing to tell Johnston that he was merely passing through Atlanta.

Bragg acted as though it was only a friendly visit, providing Johnston no opportunity to explain or defend his plan but slyly gathering information behind his back. Bragg also conferred with John Bell Hood who presented himself as a frustrated subordinate constantly offering proposals for aggressive action that Johnston had ignored or suppressed. Bragg encouraged Hood to write Richmond to that effect, which was hardly necessary since Hood had been doing so surreptitiously throughout the campaign. Bragg not only recommended Johnston's removal, but also advised against replacing him with Hardee (whom Bragg still considered an enemy from the old personnel wars). Instead he recommended to the president: "If any change is to be made Lieutenant-General Hood would give unlimited satisfaction, and my estimate of him, always high, has been raised by his conduct in this campaign."[3]

Thus Johnston was relieved from his command on July 17 and replaced by Hood. Bragg's influential role is especially rich since he had been on the receiving end of a similar investigation in 1863. At that time his brother officer Joe Johnston had his back, covering for him by providing glowing reports to Richmond in spite of the serious problems he uncovered in Bragg's command. And later, when *ordered* to take over Bragg's command he refused out of compassion for Bragg's anxious watch at the bedside of his gravely ill wife. Understandably, Johnston felt betrayed upon discovering that Bragg's visit to him outside of Atlanta had not been merely incidental as represented, but was made for the purpose of justifying his removal.

Incidents such as this certainly bring into question the depiction of Bragg as a hapless victim. Furthermore, historians who defend Bragg in this manner unwittingly do him almost as grave an injustice as they routinely commit against Polk. Such a scenario denies his personal strength and power—not to mention his manly honor. And it ignores an essential truth about Braxton Bragg: he bore his difficulties stoically. Although a consummate complainer and critic, Bragg was no crybaby. During times of tribulation when his physical symptoms inevitably flared up, his reaction was to *bear down all the more* on his duties, a trait which might even suggest part of the motive behind his vendetta against Polk and other scapegoats. It was his way of *bearing down on his subordinates* in much the same way that he put pressure upon himself.

Of course, this internal dynamic rendered his relationships with subordinates problematic. But it is not unusual for a commanding general to be especially demanding of himself and others; this is a trait commonly found in high-up army command. Yet most armies do not descend into the depth of dysfunction that marked the Army of Tennessee.

Why did conflict and controversy always seem to boil up in Bragg's vicinity? If it did originate with him, what was it in his make-up that acted as a catalyst inevitably to evoke tension and disputes? Obviously Bragg possessed a contentious, combative nature but, again, this would not seem entirely unexpected or especially unusual among men who choose the military as a career. Nevertheless, Bragg stood out in this regard. Although he periodically enjoyed warm friendships and throughout his life a loving, tender relationship with his wife, he seemed driven to challenge and contest others around him, especially those whom he viewed as rivals. Perhaps Bragg himself provided a clue to this aspect of his being in a letter to one of his early army friends, Lt. James Duncan, which he penned to justify insubordinate writings that had led to his being court-martialed in 1844. "With an unconquerable thirst for action," he explained, "I feel I can never rest without some excitement." These are words of a young man, but this restlessness within Bragg's soul seemed not to mellow with age. Bragg was never able, apparently, to conquer or quell his "thirst for action." He was by nature a man looking for a fight.[4]

Delving more deeply into Bragg's personality, one can discern an essential complication that would inevitably cause misunderstandings and alienation: Bragg had a divided nature. He was a completely different man within his inner circle than what was conveyed by the persona that he projected publicly and in less intimate relationships. Of course, everyone to a degree maintains a certain amount of privacy to protect their vulnerabilities. But some build an impenetrable barrier to such an extent that no one suspects the existence of the hidden element. A modern term for this syndrome is compartmentalization. One component of Bragg's private side was his incongruous idealism, previously discussed, and another was his soft spot for the suffering. Bragg revealed his hidden side only to those he let into his close circle: his wife Elise, staff members whom he treated as family, and medical officers who noted his tender care for the wounded and sick. He reserved his humanity for these few, leaving others to perceive only the harsh, stern, belligerent commander who could not get along with anyone.

This was the Bragg known to his soldiers, and it won him few friends among the ranks. As a Texas soldier wrote to a friend, "Bragg is very unpopular with his troops, and justly so. He seems to vent his evil spleen at the causes of his unpopularity by arresting his generals." As historian William C. Davis wrote, "Braxton Bragg had fostered a toxic command culture in the Army of Tennessee that was felt all the way down through the ranks."[5]

Civilians in the Confederacy also primarily knew only this side of Bragg. As Mary Chesnut wrote of him while her husband traveled to mediate the dispute following Chickamauga: "I think a general worthless whose subalterns quarrel with him. Something wrong about the man. Good generals are adored by their soldiers." Even Jefferson Davis's wife Varina noted Bragg's predilection for conflict, of which she warned her husband during the last days of the Confederacy. After the fall of Richmond when Davis fled southward with government officials, Varina "begged him not to give Bragg a role in this crisis: '… let me entreat you not to send B.B. to command here … the country will be ruined by its intestine feuds if you do so.'"[6]

Wife Elise was one of the few who progressed through both phases of relating to Braxton Bragg: experiencing first the outer, then his inner nature. After they fell in love she was delighted by the revelation that there was a kinder, gentler Braxton Bragg. While a newlywed she explained Bragg's duality in a letter to a cousin:

> I once censured Colonel Bragg for being too cold and reserved. I little knew the depth of affection concealed *under such an exterior*. He is an ardent and devoted husband fonder of displaying his affection in a thousand little tendernesses than even myself.[7]

Yet for casual acquaintances, dealing with a man so tightly guarded can undermine trust. A person on the outside might instinctively suspect that Bragg was hiding something, or at least being less than forthright.

This two-sided nature of Bragg contrasted sharply with Polk's frank singleness of mind and heart. Polk behaved in the same manner toward all, high and low, and his disposition did not change over time or when under adversity. Throughout his life, acquaintances' and intimates' descriptions of him remain remarkably consistent. A clear demarcation between the two men is this: Polk got along with virtually everyone except Bragg, whereas Bragg got along with very few—and clashed with many.

These are the contrasts between Bragg and Polk. Yet, despite their discord, Bragg and Polk shared some surprising, fundamental similarities. Both were intelligent, energetic advocates of what they believed to be right. Both were born and raised in North Carolina, educated at West Point, became sugar planters in Lafourche Parish, Louisiana, and, oddly, neither man had a middle name. Both were by nature forthright and passionate and had an optimistic streak. (Bragg's remained largely hidden, but found public expression in his habit, criticized by his brother John, of prematurely declaring victory.) Each tended to rush headlong into new phases of life, leaving the past behind and throwing himself fully and enthusiastically into the next endeavor. A family member referred to this predilection when he wrote to Polk about his "tear-away tendencies," describing the trait as the "Polkism of your nature." Perhaps it was this that moved Elise Bragg to label Polk "a wild enthusiast," but her husband shared the same characteristic, as evidenced by his brother's assessment of Bragg's excitable, brash nature. Both generals cared for the welfare of their men, Bragg specifically as to medical care. On several occasions he even conducted hospital inspections himself, to the astonishment of surgeons in charge. Polk also dedicated much thought and direction regarding the efficiency of hospitals in his command. In 1863 he addressed a lengthy letter to Richmond outlining detailed recommendations for better administration of the army's medical facilities. To help improve hospital care he worked closely with his medical director, Dr. Preston B. Scott, "known far and wide as a man of warm heart and charitable impulses, beloved by patients." After Polk's death Dr. Scott was placed in charge of all military hospitals in Mississippi and Alabama.[8]

Most importantly, both generals ardently believed that the cause for which they fought was pure and just, and sacrificed everything they had to it. The war wiped out Polk's fortune in a single stroke, when a massive cotton fire raged through New Orleans warehouses on the eve of the city's fall in April 1862. Bragg's plantation, Bivouac, produced and thrived for a time after he went to war, but before long it was taken by Federal authorities, never to be recovered. Even Polk's son acknowledged Bragg's dedication to the Confederacy, in words that could just as well have applied to his father: "[I]n all matters touching [Bragg's] private duty to the cause of the South he was unselfishness itself. No man loved it better, no man gave it more devoted service, none laid his all upon the altar more ungrudgingly, and no one would have laid down his life for it more cheerfully."[9]

Historians have largely ignored the striking similarities between the high-ranking antagonists of the Army of Tennessee. Instead, they focus on the Bragg vs. Polk controversy, portraying it primarily in one of two ways. The story currently in vogue is that Bragg was a general in a difficult position, which a balky Polk made worse by victimizing and plotting against him at every turn. An alternative view found in earlier writings is that incompetent Bragg was the malevolent plotter who clashed with everyone, his personality problems attributable to poor health and an inferiority complex from childhood. Each version paints either Bragg or Polk as the evildoer solely at fault. The question is, should we not dispense with this good guy/bad guy scenario that belongs only in cartoons and is not at all helpful in understanding real life. One can examine the story without exaggerating to the point of caricature, and by refraining from taking sides. Rather than holding either one or the other to blame, it seems more reasonable to attribute their clash to an unfortunate combination of personalities. Given each man's nature, considering similarities as well as differences, it was perhaps inevitable that they would butt heads.

In the beginning this book postulated that in order to understand Leonidas Polk and those aspects of his army service that have so troubled historians, it is necessary also to understand Braxton Bragg. Hopefully the analysis offered herein has shed some light on each man. In addition, the goal has been to re-examine the dynamic between them and propose a more accurate theory in lieu of the prevailing doctrine that Leonidas Polk generated the friction between these two generals, and by extension, was responsible for undermining the army's mission. If the inherent nature of both men brought them inexorably to loggerheads, perhaps neither is at fault. But as to the broader question of why the Army of Tennessee went so wrong during the American Civil War, responsibility rests with its longtime commander for the many reasons demonstrated here, in particular his penchant for warring against those on his own side. His clearly stated declaration shifting blame from himself to subordinates, and the many instances in which he aggressively put it into action, serve as ample evidence for this objective conclusion.

By way of a final thought regarding this broad question, imagine that in December 1861 Braxton Bragg accepted President Davis's offer of command over the Trans-Mississippi, and he continued in that theater for the duration of the war. It almost takes one's breath away to retrace mentally the narrative of an Army of Tennessee under another commander—say, the tactful, "Old Reliable" military master William Hardee with his comrade-friend of unlimited talent, Patrick Cleburne, second in command. How differently would the history of the Army of Tennessee now read? One can never know, but there is a sure sense that personality conflict would not have dominated the storyline.

Dr. Preston B. Scott, after first serving as an assistant to Dr. David Yandell under General Sidney Johnston, became medical director for Polk's Corps. His father was an influential agricultural innovator in Kentucky, and his younger brother served as a physician for a Kentucky regiment. After the war he was president of the United Confederate Veterans' Association of Confederate Army and Navy Surgeons (*Texas Medical Journal*, August 1900).

Such an exercise counters a doctrine currently making the rounds in academic history departments: that generals do not matter, nor did they have the profound influence or deserve the attention that earlier hero-worshipping historians gave them. Now, the theory goes, the only worthwhile story of the military centers on the common soldier or sailor, while the *real, true* history of the war belongs exclusively to certain categories of civilians, namely women and enslaved people. Of course their perspectives are important and interesting, but they also leave out a great deal. Hypothetically picturing the Army of Tennessee without Braxton Bragg dramatically demonstrates that *who the leader is*—his character, personality, strengths and weaknesses—*does matter.*

Last Words

While Leonidas Polk's life was cut short by the war, Bragg survived the bloody years, and after surrender went on to engage in various careers. Initially he and Elise lived on his brother's plantation in Alabama where Bragg oversaw cotton cultivation. In 1867 he landed a job as superintendent at the New Orleans Water Works, and in 1870 worked for a time as an agent with Jefferson Davis's life insurance company. The following year he was hired as chairman of the Board of River, Harbor and Bay Improvements in Mobile, but became embroiled in disputes with city officials and was dismissed.

In 1874 Bragg took a job as railroad inspector for the State of Texas after moving to Galveston. There, on September 27, 1876, he died suddenly after collapsing in the street. Such a no-nonsense death, eschewing prolonged illness or death-bed sentiments or even memorable last words, seems somehow fitting for Bragg. Amidst much honor he was eulogized and buried at Magnolia Cemetery in Mobile beneath an elaborate gravestone which Elise (who could ill afford it) decorated with fresh flowers every month for the rest of her life. She was buried beside him

Braxton Bragg's grave, Magnolia Cemetery, Mobile, Alabama (photograph by Justin Dubois, used with permission).

after her death exactly 32 years later on the same date as her beloved husband's demise.

During his last years Bragg never wrote about the war other than in private correspondence and contributions to others' efforts. He refrained from writing to defend or explain his military career for public consumption, saying only, "I dare not tell the truth, and dare not tell lies."[1]

Polk remained buried at St. Paul's Church in Augusta, Georgia, where his wife Frances joined him upon her death in 1875. Not until 1945 did his diocese of Louisiana finally call him home, and he and Frances were reburied that year in the chancel of Christ Church, New Orleans.

Polk and Bragg shared one final similarity: each man's time on earth ended abruptly and dramatically, without lingering farewells; however, it was Polk who

Memorial plaque over Leonidas and Frances Polk's crypt in the chancel of Christ Church Cathedral, New Orleans, Louisiana (photograph by the author).

laid down his life on the field of battle. Yet to the end Bragg never saw Polk as a true soldier. Perhaps the dying words uttered by Confederate general John Adams, who had previously served under Polk, should put that issue to rest. Leading his brigade into the deadly storm at the Battle of Franklin on November 30, 1864, Adams was shot when his horse leapt onto the Federal parapet. As the body of his faithful mount lay sprawled across the enemy works, Federals brought the mortally wounded rider behind their lines where an officer gave Adams a drink of water. The merciful Yankee gazed sadly upon the Southern general lying upon the soil of his home state and expressed sympathy over his foe's imminent death. In response John Adams reportedly proclaimed: "It is the fate of a soldier to die for his country."[2] Whether or not Adams actually mouthed those lofty words, their self-evident verity affirms, contrary to Braxton Bragg's belief, that Leonidas Polk was, most assuredly and unquestionably, a soldier.

Chapter Notes

Introduction

1. Quoted in Samuel J. Martin, *General Braxton Bragg, C.S.A.* (Jefferson, N.C.: McFarland, 2011), 117.
2. Martin, *General Braxton Bragg*, 119.

Chapter 1

1. Joseph H. Parks, *General Leonidas Polk, C.S.A.: The Fighting Bishop* (Baton Rouge: Louisiana State University Press, 1962), 150–51.
2. Parks, *General Leonidas Polk*, 28.
3. Steven E. Woodworth, *Jefferson Davis and His Generals: The Failure of Confederate Command in the West* (Lawrence: University Press of Kansas, 1990), 28.
4. Huston Horn, *Leonidas Polk: Warrior Bishop of the Confederacy* (Lawrence: University of Kansas Press, 2019), 20–21.
5. Parks, *General Leonidas Polk*, 45.
6. Parks, *General Leonidas Polk*, 91–92; Horn, *Leonidas Polk*, 94–95.
7. Craig L. Symonds, *Stonewall of the West: Patrick Cleburne & The Civil War* (Lawrence: University Press of Kansas, 1994), 249.
8. Horn, *Leonidas Polk*, 104.
9. Parks, *General Leonidas Polk*, 109–14; Horn, *Leonidas Polk*, 141.
10. Parks, *General Leonidas Polk*, 157, 159.
11. Parks, *General Leonidas Polk*, 168; Horn, *Leonidas Polk*, 159.
12. Woodworth, *Jefferson Davis and His Generals*, 29.
13. Parks, *General Leonidas Polk*, 166.
14. Horn, *Leonidas Polk*, 474n43.
15. Letter to Frances Polk, June 19, 1861, Leonidas Polk Papers (University of the South Archives, Sewanee, Tennessee).
16. Albert Castel, *Decision in the West: The Atlanta Campaign of 1864* (Lawrence: University Press of Kansas, 1992), 46.
17. Parks, *General Leonidas Polk*, 166–67; William J. Cooper, Jr., *Jefferson Davis, American* (New York: Vintage, 2000), 382.
18. Charles P. Roland, *Albert Sidney Johnston: Soldier of Three Republics* (Lexington: University Press of Kentucky, 2001), 260; Horn, *Leonidas Polk*, 156–57.
19. Parks, *General Leonidas Polk*, 167, 170.

Chapter 2

1. Parks, *General Leonidas Polk*, 180, 185.
2. *The War of the Rebellion: A Compilation of the Official Records of the Union and Confederate Armies* (hereafter OR), Vol. III, 141–12.
3. Thomas L. Connelly, *Army of the Heartland: The Army of Tennessee, 1861–1862* (Baton Rouge: Louisiana State University Press, 1967), 52.
4. Connelly, *Army of the Heartland*, 44, emphasis added.
5. Stanley F. Horn, *The Army of Tennessee* (Norman: University of Oklahoma Press, 1941), 44.
6. Connelly, *Army of the Heartland*, 40, 52, 52n11, emphasis added.
7. Earl J. Hess, *The Civil War in the West: Victory and Defeat from the Appalachians to the Mississippi* (Chapel Hill: University of North Carolina Press, 2012), 14; Joseph L. Harsh, *Confederate Tide Rising: Robert E. Lee and the Making of Southern Strategy* (Kent: Kent State University Press, 1998), 24; Jefferson Davis, *The Rise of the Confederate Government* (New York: Barnes and Noble, 2010), 372.
8. Davis, *The Rise*, 372.
9. Woodworth, *Jefferson Davis and His Generals*, 39; Hess, *The Civil War in the West*, 9.
10. Hess, *The Civil War in the West*, 12.
11. Davis, *The Rise of the Confederate Government*, 372; Letter from Thomas Yeatman, August 21, 1861, Leonidas Polk Papers.
12. Horn, *Leonidas Polk*, 177; Glenn Tucker, *Chickamauga: Bloody Battle in the West* (Dayton: Morningside Bookshop, 1984), 103.
13. Nathaniel Cheairs Hughes, Jr., and Roy P. Stonesifer, Jr., *The Life and Wars of Gideon J. Pillow* (Chapel Hill: University of North Carolina Press, 1993), 168, 193–94.
14. Quoted in Eric Wittenberg, *We Ride a Whirlwind: Sherman and Johnston at Bennett Place* (Burlington, N.C.: Fox Run, 2017), 113.
15. Glenn Robins, *The Bishop of the Old South: The Ministry and Civil War Legacy of Leonidas Polk* (Macon: Mercer University Press, 2006), 163.
16. Parks, *General Leonidas Polk*, 186.
17. Parks, *General Leonidas Polk*, 187, 202; Horn, *Leonidas Polk*, 166–67, 186; Timothy B. Smith, *Shiloh: Conquer or Perish* (Lawrence: University Press of Kansas, 2014), 5; Horn, *Leonidas Polk*, 218.

18. Alfred Roman, *The Military Operations of General Beauregard, Volume I* (New York: Da Capo, 1994), 234, Horn, *Leonidas Polk*, 217–18.

Chapter 3

1. Martin, *General Braxton Bragg*, 111–13, 116; Timothy B. Smith, *Shiloh: Conquer or Perish* (Lawrence: University Press of Kansas), 35.
2. Horn, *Leonidas Polk*, 457n39, 459n57, 465n53, 147.
3. Grady McWhiney, *Braxton Bragg and Confederate Defeat* (Tuscaloosa: University of Alabama Press, 1969), 97, 273.
4. McWhiney, *Braxton Bragg*, 148, 150, 172; Martin, *General Braxton Bragg*, 86.
5. McWhiney, *Braxton Bragg*, 197, 199, 205.
6. McWhiney, *Braxton Bragg*, 211; Larry J. Daniel, *Shiloh: The Battle That Changed the Civil War* (New York: Simon & Schuster, 1997), 97.
7. Martin, *General Braxton Bragg*, 114, 119; Connelly, *Autumn of Glory*, 20.
8. Thomas L. Connelly, *Autumn of Glory: The Army of Tennessee, 1862–1865* (Baton Rouge: Louisiana State University Press, 1971), 11; Smith, *Shiloh: Conquer or Perish*, 19.
9. Smith, *Shiloh: Conquer or Perish*, 18.
10. Daniel, *Shiloh*, 117.
11. Smith, *Shiloh: Conquer or Perish*, 73.
12. Daniel, *Shiloh*, 121.
13. Connelly, *Army of the Heartland*, 155; Smith, *Shiloh: Conquer or Perish*, 63; Parks, *General Leonidas Polk*, 228.
14. Daniel, *Shiloh*, 122; Connelly, *Army of the Heartland*, 155, emphasis added.
15. Connelly, *Army of the Heartland*, 155; Parks, *General Leonidas Polk*, 228, emphasis added.
16. Smith, *Shiloh: Conquer or Perish*, 63.
17. Smith, *Shiloh: Conquer or Perish*, 64; James Lee McDonough, *Shiloh—In Hell Before Night* (Knoxville: University of Tennessee Press, 1977), 77; Connelly, *Army of the Heartland*, 155.
18. O. Edward Cunningham, *Shiloh and the Western Campaign of 1862* (El Dorado Hills, CA: Savas Beatie, 2007), 128.
19. Smith, *Shiloh: Conquer or Perish*, 69–70.
20. Daniel, *Shiloh*, 128, emphasis added; Smith, *Shiloh: Conquer or Perish*, 67, 69.
21. Daniel, *Shiloh*, 125; Smith, *Shiloh: Conquer or Perish*, 73.
22. Smith, *Shiloh: Conquer or Perish*, 72, 74; Daniel, *Shiloh*, 128; McDonough, *Shiloh—In Hell Before Night*, 80.
23. Daniel, *Shiloh*, 128, 129, emphasis added; McDonough, *Shiloh—In Hell Before Night*, 81; Smith, *Shiloh: Conquer or Perish*, 75; Connelly, *Army of the Heartland*, 157.
24. Smith, *Shiloh: Conquer or Perish*, 73; Daniel, *Shiloh*, 128.
25. Smith, *Shiloh: Conquer or Perish*, 48, 108.
26. Smith, *Shiloh: Conquer or Perish*, 108–10.
27. Smith, *Shiloh: Conquer or Perish*, 110–11.
28. Smith *Shiloh: Conquer or Perish*, 129.
29. Daniel, *Shiloh*, 168, emphasis added.
30. Smith, *Shiloh: Conquer or Perish*, 212–13.
31. Smith, *Shiloh: Conquer or Perish*, 220–21; Parks, *General Leonidas Polk*, 234; Cunningham, *Shiloh and the Western Campaign*, 300.
32. Smith, *Shiloh: Conquer or Perish*, 215–16, 231–32.
33. Russell S. Bonds, *Stealing the General: The Great Locomotive Chase and the First Medal of Honor* (Yardley, PA: Westholme, 2007).
34. Smith, *Shiloh: Conquer or Perish*, 232.
35. Woodworth, *Jefferson Davis and His Generals*, 102.
36. Connelly, *Army of the Heartland*, 169–70; Woodworth, *Jefferson Davis and His Generals*, 102; McWhiney, *Braxton Bragg and Confederate Defeat*, 243.
37. Woodworth, *Jefferson Davis and His Generals*, 102; Connelly, *Army of the Heartland*, 170; Letter to Daughter, April 6, 1863, Leonidas Polk Papers; Parks, *General Leonidas Polk*, 236.
38. Cunningham, *Shiloh and the Western Campaign of 1862*, 333; McDonough, *Shiloh—In Hell Before Night*, 82; Smith, *Shiloh: Conquer or Perish*, 250.
39. Smith, *Shiloh: Conquer or Perish*, 268–69.
40. Smith, *Shiloh: Conquer or Perish*, 352–54; Roman, *Military Operations of General Beauregard*, 313.
41. Smith, *Shiloh: Conquer or Perish*, 352–53, 359, 364.
42. Horn, *Leonidas Polk*, 233; Smith, *Shiloh: Conquer or Perish*, 404.
43. Parks, *General Leonidas Polk*, 240.
44. Mary Gorton McBride and Ann Mathison McLaurin, *Randall Lee Gibson of Louisiana: Confederate General and New South Reformer* (Baton Rouge: Louisiana State University Press, 2007), 59; Earl J. Hess, *Braxton Bragg: The Most Hated Man of the Confederacy* (Chapel Hill: University of North Carolina Press, 2016), 35; Don Carlos Seitz, *Braxton Bragg, General of the Confederacy* (reprint by Literary Licensing of 1923 original), 112, 116–17; McWhiney, *Braxton Bragg and Confederate Defeat*, 239.
45. Hess, *Braxton Bragg*, 102.
46. Parks, *General Leonidas Polk*, 240.

Chapter 4

1. McWhiney, *Braxton Bragg and Confederate Defeat*, 255.
2. Emory M. Thomas, *Robert E. Lee: A Biography* (New York: W.W. Norton, 1995), 247; Clifford Dowdey and Louis H. Manarin, eds., *The Wartime Papers of Robert E. Lee* (New York: Da Capo, 1961), 238.
3. Larry J. Daniel, *Conquered: Why the Army of Tennessee Failed* (Chapel Hill: University of North Carolina Press, 2019), 38.
4. Brian Steel Wills, *A Battle from the Start: The*

Life of Nathan Bedford Forrest (New York: HarperCollins, 1992), 82–83.

5. Earl J. Hess, *Banners to the Breeze: The Kentucky Campaign, Corinth, and Stones River* (Lincoln: University of Nebraska Press, 2000), 21. "Banners to the breeze" was a slogan Bragg employed in his address to the troops as they embarked on their massive movement two months earlier.

6. Christopher L. Kolakowski, *The Civil War at Perryville: Battling for the Bluegrass* (Charleston, S.C.: The History Press, 2009), 49.

7. Kenneth W. Noe, *Perryville: This Grand Havoc of Battle* (Lexington: University Press of Kentucky, 2001), 73–74.

8. Letter to General Braxton Bragg, September 30, 1862, Leonidas Polk Papers.

9. Letter from John Wharton, October 5, 1862, Leonidas Polk Papers; Kolakowski, *The Civil War at Perryville*, 78; *OR*, Vol. XVI, Part 2, 897.

10. Kolakowski, *The Civil War at Perryville*, 78–79.

11. *OR*, XVI, Part 2, 903.

12. Noe, *Perryville*, 130, 132–33.

13. Noe, *Perryville*, 132.

14. Connelly, *Army of the Heartland*, 256; Noe, *Perryville*, 132, emphasis added.

15. Letter from Braxton Bragg, October 7, 1862, Leonidas Polk Papers; Christopher Losson, *Tennessee's Forgotten Warriors: Frank Cheatham and His Confederate Division* (Knoxville: University of Tennessee Press, 1989), 65.

16. Connelly, *Army of the Heartland*, 262; Kolakowski, *The Civil War at Perryville*, 97–98.

17. Losson, *Tennessee's Forgotten Warriors*, 66; Noe, *Perryville*, 175.

18. Losson, *Tennessee's Forgotten Warriors*, 66; Connelly, *Army of the Heartland*, 263; Noe, *Perryville*, 186, 204; Kolakowski, *The Civil War at Perryville*, 108.

19. Losson, *Tennessee's Forgotten Warriors*, 69–70.

20. Losson, *Tennessee's Forgotten Warriors*, 71, 73; Connelly, *Army of the Heartland*, 264.

21. James Lee McDonough, *War in Kentucky: From Shiloh to Perryville* (Knoxville: University of Tennessee Press, 1994), 284.

22. Kolakowski, *The Civil War at Perryville*, 133; St. John Richardson Liddell, *Liddell's Record*, ed. Nathaniel Cheairs, Jr. (Baton Rouge: Louisiana State University Press, 1985), 93–94, 96.

23. Kolakowski, *The Civil War at Perryville*, 136; Noe, *Perryville*, 285.

24. Noe, *Perryville*, 308, 310.

25. Noe, *Perryville*, 310; Stuart W. Sanders, *Maney's Confederate Brigade at the Battle of Perryville* (Charleston, S.C.: The History Press, 2014), 9–10.

26. Connelly, *Army of the Heartland*, 266–27; Noe, *Perryville*, 328–29.

27. Letter from Braxton Bragg to Samuel Cooper, Adjutant General, October 12, 1862, Leonidas Polk Papers.

28. Letter from Braxton Bragg, October 1, 1862, Leonidas Polk Papers.

29. Liddell, *Liddell's Record*, 97–98; Letter from Braxton Bragg, October 16, 1862, Leonidas Polk Papers; Noe, *Perryville*, 337.

Chapter 5

1. Christopher L. Kolakowski, *The Stones River and Tullahoma Campaigns: This Army Does Not Retreat* (Charleston, S.C.: The History Press, 2011), 38–41.

2. Quoted in Horn, *Leonidas Polk*, 281.

3. Kolakowski, *The Stones River and Tullahoma Campaigns*, 90.

4. Kolakowski, *The Stones River and Tullahoma Campaigns*, 37, 41, 175.

5. Kolakowski, *The Stones River and Tullahoma Campaigns*, 43; Larry J. Daniel, *Battle of Stones River: The Forgotten Conflict between the Confederate Army of Tennessee and the Union Army of the Cumberland* (Baton Rouge: Louisiana State University Press, 2012), 226; Larry J. Daniel, *Conquered: Why the Army of Tennessee Failed* (Chapel Hill: University of North Carolina Press, 2019), 78.

6. Kolakowski, *The Stones River and Tullahoma Campaigns*, 46; Daniel, *Battle of Stones River*, 51.

7. Peter Cozzens, *This Terrible Sound: The Battle of Chickamauga* (Urbana: University of Illinois Press, 1994), 295.

8. Kolakowski, *The Stones River and Tullahoma Campaigns*, 50; Daniel, *Battle of Stones River*, 88.

9. Kolakowski, *The Stones River and Tullahoma Campaigns*, 52; Daniel *The Battle of Stones River*, 93.

10. Daniel, *The Battle of Stones River*, 104.

11. Daniel, *The Battle of Stones River*, 105, 107–09.

12. Kolakowski, *The Stones River and Tullahoma Campaigns*, 59; Daniel, *The Battle of Stones River*, 110, 112–13.

13. Daniel, *The Battle of Stones River*, 113–14; Losson, *Tennessee's Forgotten Warriors*, 85.

14. Losson, *Tennessee's Forgotten Warriors*, 84.

15. Daniel, *The Battle of Stones River*, 126; Losson, *Tennessee's Forgotten Warriors*, 85.

16. Losson, *Tennessee's Forgotten Warriors*, 85; Daniel, *The Battle of Stones River*, 117.

17. Daniel, *The Battle of Stones River*, 162; Daniel, *Conquered*, 80, 82, and see Hess, *Banners to the Breeze*, 214 and *Braxton Bragg*, 98, 105; Connelly, *Autumn of Glory*, 58; Field Marshal Viscount Wolseley, *The American Civil War: An English View*, ed. James A. Rawley (Mechanicsburg, PA: Stackpole Books, 2002), 180.

18. Kolakowski, *The Stones River and Tullahoma Campaigns*, 71-2, emphasis added.

19. Losson, *Tennessee's Forgotten Warriors*, 87–88.

20. Losson, *Tennessee's Forgotten Warriors*, 87; Daniel, *Battle of Stones RiverI* 161; Kolakowski, *The Stones River and Tullahoma Campaigns*, 77, 79;

Peter Cozzens, *No Better Place to Die: The Battle of Stones River* (Urbana: University of Illinois Press, 1990), 164.

21. Daniel, *Battle of Stones River*, 163–64, emphasis added; Cozzens, *No Better Place to DieI* 162.

22. Cozzens, *No Better Place to Die*, 164.

23. Daniel, *Battle of Stones River*, 165–66, 168; Hess, *Banners to the Breeze*, 214; Kolakowski, *The Stones River and Tullahoma Campaigns*, 80; Cozzens, *No Place to Die*, 165.

24. Kolakowski, *The Stones River and Tullahoma Campaigns*, 77.

25. Parks, *General Leonidas Polk*, 289.

26. Cozzens, *No Better Place to Die*, 166; Kolakowski, *The Stones River and Tullahoma Campaigns*, 81.

27. Kolakowski, *The Stones River and Tullahoma Campaigns*, 81, emphasis added; Daniel, *Battle of Stones River*, 174.

28. Daniel, *Battle of Stones River*, 173; Connelly, *Autumn of Glory*, 49–50.

29. Connelly, *Autumn of Glory*, 62; Daniel, *Battle of Stones River*, 181.

30. Cozzens, *No Better Place to Die*, 180–81.

31. Daniel, *Battle of Stones River*, 181, 184; Cozzens, *No Better Place to Die*, 183.

32. Daniel, *Battle of Stones River*, 185, 189; Kolakowski, *The Stones River and Tullahoma Campaigns*, 85.

33. Daniel, *Battle of Stones River*, 196, 198; Parks, *General Leonidas Polk*, 291.

34. Daniel, *Battle of Stones River*, 198.

35. Kolakowski, *The Stones River and Tullahoma Campaigns*, 89.

36. Kolakowski, *The Stones River and Tullahoma Campaigns*, 104.

37. David A. Powell and Eric J. Wittenberg, *Tullahoma: The Forgotten Campaign That Changed the Course of the Civil War* (El Dorado Hills, CA: Savas Beatie, 2020), 211.

38. Powell and Wittenberg, *Tullahoma*, 220; Kolakowski, *The Stones River and Tullahoma Campaigns*, 123.

39. Kolakowski, *The Stones River and Tullahoma Campaigns*, 127.

40. Parks, *General Leonidas Polk*, 315, 318–19; Horn, *The Army of Tennessee*, 236–37; Connelly, *Autumn of Glory*, 133; Powell and Wittenberg, *Tullahoma*, 317–18, 335, 352; Charles Todd Quintard, *Doctor Quintard Chaplain C.S.A. and Second Bishop of Tennessee: Being His Story of the War (1861–1865)*, ed. Rev. Arthur Howard Noll (Sewanee: The University Press of Sewanee Tennessee, 1905), 79.

41. Quoted in Powell and Wittenberg, *Tullahoma*, 327.

42. Parks, *General Leonidas Polk*, 316.

Chapter 6

1. Connelly, *Autumn of Glory*, 430.

2. Liddell, *Liddell's Record*, 106; Connelly, *Autumn of Glory*, 413.

3. Quoted in McWhiney, *Braxton Bragg and Confederate Defeat*, 259; Hess, *Braxton Bragg*, 219.

4. Connelly, *Autumn of Glory*, 70–71, 228; Wolseley, *The American Civil War*, 178, 181.

5. Quoted in Earl J. Hess, *Braxton Bragg: The Most Hated Man of the Confederacy* (Chapel Hill: University of North Carolina Press, 2016), 196.

6. Noe, *Perryville*, 18.

7. Cozzens, *This Terrible Sound*, 3–4.

8. Connelly, *Autumn of Glory*, 70.

9. Daniel, *Conquered*, 64.

10. McWhiney, *Braxton Bragg and Confederate Defeat*, 182; Martin, *General Braxton Bragg*, 163.

11. Liddell, *Liddell's Record*, 117.

12. McWhiney, *Braxton Bragg and Confederate Defeat*, 275; Nancy Disher Baird, *David Wendel Yandell: Physician of Old Louisville* (Lexington: University Press of Kentucky, 1978), 50, emphasis added.

13. McWhiney, *Braxton Bragg and Confederate Defeat*, 275, emphasis in original.

14. Noe, *Perryville*, 57; Martin, *General Braxton Bragg*, 115.

15. Daniel, *Shiloh: The Battle That Changed the Civil War*, 97.

16. Martin, *General Braxton Bragg*, 89; Letter from Braxton Bragg, October 16, 1862, Leonidas Polk Papers.

17. Connelly, *Autumn of Glory*, 22; McWhiney, *Braxton Bragg and Confederate Defeat*, 325.

18. McWhiney, *Braxton Bragg and Confederate Defeat*, 326–27; Hess, *Banners to the Breeze*, 115.

19. McWhiney, *Braxton Bragg and Confederate Defeat*, 327.

20. Hess, *Braxton Bragg*, 126.

21. Connelly, *Autumn of Glory*, 74–75.

22. Seitz, *Braxton Bragg*, 276; Daniel, *Conquered*, 92.

23. Connelly, *Autumn of Glory*, 75; Letter from Braxton Bragg, January 30, 1863, Leonidas Polk Papers.

24. Seitz, *Braxton Bragg*, 276; Connelly, *Autumn of Glory*, 80.

25. Letter to President Jefferson Davis, March 30, 1863, Leonidas Polk Papers.

26. Hess, *Braxton Bragg*, 122–23.

27. Hess, *Braxton Bragg*, 137.

28. Nathaniel Cheairs Hughes, Jr., and Thomas Clayton Ware, *Theodore O'Hara: Poet-Soldier of the Old South* (Knoxville: University of Tennessee Press, 1998); William C. Davis, *Breckinridge: Statesman, Soldier, Symbol* (Lexington: University Press of Kentucky, 2010), 350.

29. Davis, *Breckinridge*, 352.

30. Peter Cozzens, *No Better Place to Die: The Battle of Stones River* (Urbana: University of Illinois Press, 1990), 177; Daniel, *Battle of Stones River*, 182.

31. Robert Garlick Hill Kean, *Inside the Confederate Government: The Diary of Robert Garlick Hill Kean*, ed. Edward Younger (Baton Rouge: Louisiana State University Press, 1957), 42.

32. William C. Davis, *Diary of a Confederate*

Soldier: John S. Jackman of the Orphan Brigade (Columbia: University of South Carolina Press, 1990), 75.

33. William C. Davis, *Jefferson Davis: The Man and His Hour* (New York: HarperCollins, 1991), 585.

34. Parks, *General Leonidas Polk*, 212, 381.

35. Charles C. Jones, Jr., Late Lieut. Col. of Artillery, CSA, ed., *President Davis' Military Family,* www.perseus.tufts.edu/hopper/text?doc=Perseus%3Atest%3A2001.05.0144%3Achapter%3D3, last accessed July 2018; McWhiney, *Braxton Bragg and Confederate Defeat*, 382.

36. Letter from John M. Huger, February 15, 1863, Digital Library of Tennessee, Tennessee State Library and Archives, http://cdm15138.contentdm.oclc.org/cdm/ref/collection/p15138coll6/id/5862.

37. Letter from W.D. Gale, March 27, 1863, emphasis in original, Digital Library of Tennessee, Tennessee State Library and Archives, http://cdm15138.contentdm.oclc.org/cdm/ref/collection/p15138coll6/id/5795.

38. Seitz, *Braxton Bragg*, 257, emphasis added.

39. Seitz, *Braxton Bragg*, 290.

40. https://historical.ha.com/itm/autographs/military-figures/leonidas-polk-autograph-letter-signed/a/6093-34186.s, last accessed May 2023. The full text of the note reads as follows:

    Hd qtr Polks Corps
    Shelbyville, Apr 2/63
General
I send you a paper received to-day through the Adj Genl office of the Army at Tullahoma.

It is not the paper I asked Capt Robertson to send me. And I thought myself very explicit in asking him for the Report you wanted—his report to General Bragg. I have promptly asked him for a copy of that report. It shall be sent you as soon as received.

As you may not have seen that since notwithstanding it is addressed to your a.a.g. I enclose it.
    Respectfully
    Yr. Ot. St:
    L. Polk
    Mj Genl Breckenridge

41. Seitz, *Braxton Bragg*, 291.

42. Letter from Braxton Bragg to Samuel Cooper, Adjutant General, October 12, 1862, Leonidas Polk Papers.

43. Martin, *General Braxton Bragg*, 259.

44. Kolakowski, *The Stones River and Tullahoma Campaigns*, 102; Lt. Col. James Arthur Lyon Fremantle, *The Fremantle Diary: Being the Journal of Lieutenant Colonel James Arthur Lyon Fremantle, Coldstream Guards, and his Three Months in the Southern States*, ed. Walter Lord (Boston: Little, Brown, 1954), 129.

Chapter 7

1. McWhiney, *Braxton Bragg and Confederate Defeat*, 306; quoted in McDonough, *War in Kentucky*, 230.

2. *OR*, XVI, Part 2, 898; Connelly, *Army of the Heartland*, 245; Letter from Braxton Bragg to Samuel Cooper, Adjutant General, October 12, 1862, Leonidas Polk Papers, emphasis added.

3. *OR*, Vol. XVI, Part 2, 901.

4. McDonough, *War in Kentucky*, 230; Woodworth, *Jefferson Davis and His Generals*, 156–57.

5. Herman Hattaway and Archer Jones, *How the North Won: A Military History of the Civil War* (Urbana: University of Illinois Press, 1983), 257.

6. Connelly, *Army of the Heartland*, 233.

7. Connelly, *Army of the Heartland*, 245, 248.

8. Horn, *The Army of Tennessee*, 179, emphasis added; Connelly, *Army of the Heartland*, 247–48, emphasis added.

9. Quoted in Horn, *Leonidas Polk*, 263; Woodworth, *Jefferson Davis and His Generals*, 176.

10. Noe, *Perryville*, 133.

11. Horn, *The Army of Tennessee*, 180, 182.

12. Connelly, *Army of the Heartland*, 157.

13. Noe, *Perryville*, 156–57.

14. Sanders, *Maney's Confederate Brigade at the Battle of Perryville*, 10.

15. Woodworth, *Jefferson Davis and His Generals*, 158.

16. McDonough, *War in Kentucky*, 230; McWhiney, *Braxton Bragg and Confederate Defeat*, 306.

17. Connelly, *Army of the Heartland*, 260–61.

18. Noe, *Perryville*, 158, emphasis added.

19. David A. Powell, *The Chickamauga Campaign: A Mad Irregular Battle* (El Dorado Hills, CA: Savas Beatie, 2014), 47.

20. Daniel, *Conquered*, 53.

Chapter 8

1. Letter from William Hardee, July 27, 1863, Leonidas Polk Papers.

2. Letter to Kenneth Rayner, August 14, 1863, Leonidas Polk Papers, emphasis in original.

3. Letter to Stephen Elliott, August 15, 1863, Leonidas Polk Papers.

4. Letter to Susan Rayner, August 15, 1863, Leonidas Polk Papers; David A. Powell, *A Mad Irregular Battle: From the Crossing of the Tennessee River Through the Second Day, August 22—September 19, 1863* (El Dorado Hills, CA: Savas Beatie, 2014), 70.

5. Quoted in Hess, *Braxton Bragg*, 150.

6. Horn, *The Army of Tennessee*, 253.

7. Cozzens, *This Terrible Sound*, 83; Horn, *The Army of Tennessee*, 253, emphasis added.

8. Connelly, *Autumn of Glory*, 188–89.

9. Woodworth, *Jefferson Davis and His Generals*, 231, 233.

10. Horn, *The Army of Tennessee*, 253.

11. Cozzens, *This Terrible Sound*, 83.

12. Powell, *A Mad Irregular Battle*, 180–81, 184.

13. Cozzens, *This Terrible Sound*, 83; Powell, *A Mad Irregular Battle*, 184.

14. W.M. Polk Letter to Archibald Gracie, Jr., December 18, 1911, Leonidas Polk Papers

15. Connelly, *Autumn of Glory*, 216–17.
16. Connelly, *Autumn of Glory*, 217.
17. Seitz, *Braxton Bragg*, 359.
18. Seitz, *Braxton Bragg*, 344.
19. Woodworth, *Jefferson Davis and His Generals*, 235–36, xiii.
20. Judith Lee Hallock, *Braxton Bragg and Confederate Defeat*, Vol. II (Tuscaloosa: University of Alabama Press, 1969), 72.
21. Cozzens, *This Terrible Sound*, 306–07.
22. Cozzens, *This Terrible Sound*, 310.
23. Martin, *General Braxton Bragg*, 310.
24. Hess, *Braxton Bragg*, 164.
25. William Lee White, *Bushwacking on a Grand Scale: The Battle of Chickamauga, September 18–20, 1863* (El Dorado Hills, CA: Savas Beatie, 2013), 72; Daniel, *Conquered*, 187.
26. Connelly, *Autumn of Glory*, 217, emphasis added.
27. William Glenn Robertson, "A Tale of Two Orders: Chickamauga, September 20, 1863," in Jones and Sword, eds., *Gateway to the Confederacy*, 139, emphasis added.
28. Letter to W. M. Polk from James H. Polk, August 5, 1913, Leonidas Polk Papers.
29. Connelly, *Autumn of Glory*, 220.
30. Connelly, *Autumn of Glory*, 199, emphasis added, 209, 221; Daniel, *Conquered*, 187–8.
31. Hallock, *Braxton Bragg and Confederate Defeat II*, 74–5.
32. Losson, *Tennessee's Forgotten Warriors*, 110.
33. Connelly, *Autumn of Glory*, 223–4.
34. David A. Powell, *Glory or the Grave: The Breakthrough, the Union Collapse, and the Defense of Horseshoe Ridge, September 20, 1863* (California: Savas Beatie, 2015), 550.
35. Powell, *Glory or the Grave*, 617, 619.
36. Powell, *Glory or the Grave*, 624, 629–30, 637.
37. Quoted in David A. Powell, *Barren Victory: The Retreat into Chattanooga, the Confederate Pursuit, and the Aftermath of the Battle, September 21 to October 20, 1863* (El Dorado Hills, CA: Savas Beatie, 2016), 5.
38. Powell, *Barren Victory*, 6–7.
39. Powell, *Barren Victory*, 23–24.
40. Scott Bowden and Bill Ward, *Last Chance for Victory: Robert E. Lee and the Gettysburg Campaign* (Cambridge: Da Capo, 2001), 206.
41. Horn, *Leonidas Polk*, 343; Daniel, *Conquered*, 193.
42. Liddell, *Liddell's Record*, 152.
43. Hallock, *Braxton Bragg and Confederate Defeat II*, 103, emphasis added.
44. Stephen M. Hood, *The Lost Papers of Confederate General John Bell Hood* (El Dorado Hills, CA: Savas Beatie, 2015), 190–91.
45. Connelly, *Autumn of Glory*, 236; Leroy Riley Gresham, *The War Outside My Window: The Civil War Diary of LeRoy Wiley Gresham, 1860–1865*, ed. Janet Elizabeth Croon (El Dorado Hills, CA: Savas Beatie, 2018), 257–58.
46. Horn, *Leonidas Polk*, 348, 395.
47. Daniel, *Conquered*, 194; Chesnut, *Diary*, 482.
48. Lanny Kelton Smith, *The Stone's River Campaign: 26 December 1862–5 January 1863*, Army of Tennessee (Lanny Smith, 2010).
49. Gresham, *The War Outside My Window*, 266.
50. Martin, *General Braxton Bragg*, 278, 108–09.
51. Connelly, *Autumn of Glory*, 253–54.
52. Richard M. McMurry, *The Civil Wars of General Joseph E. Johnston, Confederate States Army, Volume I* (El Dorado Hills, CA: Savas Beatie, 2023), 25.
53. Hess, *Braxton Bragg*, 194, 198.
54. Jeffrey Wm. Hunt, *Meade and Lee at Bristoe Station* (El Dorado Hills, CA: Savas Beatie, 2019), 44; Wiley Sword, *Mountains Touched with Fire: Chattanooga Besieged, 1863* (New York: St. Martin's Press, 1995), 296.
55. Sword, *Mountains Touched With Fire*, 236.
56. Martin, *General Braxton Bragg*, 379, 387.
57. quoted in Hess, *Braxton Bragg*, 222.
58. Rod Gragg, *Confederate Goliath: The Battle of Fort Fisher* (Baton Rouge: Louisiana State University Press, 1991, updated ed., 2006), 99.
59. Daniel W. Barefoot, *General Robert F. Hoke: Lee's Modest Warrior* (Winston-Salem, NC: John F. Blair, 1996), 257, 269.
60. Barefoot, *General Robert F. Hoke*, 298.
61. Martin, *General Braxton Bragg*, 387.

Chapter 9

1. Parks, *General Leonidas Polk*, 353.
2. Parks, *General Leonidas Polk*, 356–57; General Samuel G. French, *Two Wars: The Autobiography & Diary of Gen. Samuel G. French, C.S.A.* (Huntington, W.V.: Blue Acorn Press, 1999), 185.
3. Parks, *General Leonidas Polk*, 357.
4. Buck T. Foster, *Sherman's Mississippi Campaign* (Tuscaloosa: University of Alabama Press, 2006), 15.
5. Foster, *Sherman's Mississippi Campaign*, 15–16.
6. Charles Bracelen Flood, *Grant and Sherman: The Friendship that Won the Civil War* (New York: Harper Perennial, 2005), 228; Foster, *Sherman's Mississippi Campaign*, 21.
7. Parks, *General Leonidas Polk*, 358.
8. Foster, *Sherman's Mississippi Campaign*, 18, 22; Parks, *General Leonidas Polk*, 358.
9. Foster, *Sherman's Mississippi Campaign*, 25–26; Ben Wynne, *Mississippi's Civil War: A Narrative History* (Macon: Mercer University Press, 2006), 149.
10. Parks, *General Leonidas Polk*, 358; Connelly, *Autumn of Glory*, 294.
11. Parks, *General Leonidas Polk*, 359; Foster, *Sherman's Mississippi Campaign*, 57.
12. Wynne, *Mississippi's Civil War*, 149; French, *Two Wars*, 188; Foster, *Sherman's Mississippi Campaign*, 57; Connelly, *Autumn of Glory*, 294.
13. Connelly, *Autumn of Glory*, 294; William M. Polk, M.D., *Leonidas Polk; Bishop and General*,

Vol. II (Old South Books reprint of New York: Longmans, Green, & Co., 1915), 326; Foster, *Sherman's Mississippi Campaign*, 19, 37, 38, 57, 73; French, *Two Wars*, 188.

14. Foster, *Sherman's Mississippi Campaign*, 48–49.
15. Foster, *Sherman's Mississippi Campaign*, 57–58.
16. Foster, *Sherman's Mississippi Campaign*, 60, 64–65.
17. Foster, *Sherman's Mississippi Campaign*, 65.
18. Foster, *Sherman's Mississippi Campaign*, 68.
19. Foster, *Sherman's Mississippi Campaign*, 72; French, *Two Wars*, 188–89.
20. Wynne, *Mississippi's Civil War*, 153; Foster, *Sherman's Mississippi Campaign*, 71, 73–74.
21. Parks, *General Leonidas Polk*, 359–60.
22. Foster, *Sherman's Mississippi Campaign*, 22, 73, 83–84.
23. Foster, *Sherman's Mississippi Campaign*, 75–77.
24. Foster, *Sherman's Mississippi Campaign*, 79, 81, 86, 88–89.
25. Foster, *Sherman's Mississippi Campaign*, 25, 89.
26. Parks, *General Leonidas Polk*, 360; Shelby Foote, *The Civil War: A Narrative, Vol. II. Fredericksburg to Meridian* (New York: Vintage, 1963), 925.
27. Foote, *The Civil War Vol. II*, 925–26.
28. *The War of the Rebellion: A Compilation of the Official Records of the Union and Confederate Armies* 128 vols. (Washington, D.C., 1880–1901) Series I, Vol. 32, pt. 2, 752–3; Parks, *General Leonidas Polk*, 360–61.
29. Wynne, *Mississippi's Civil War*, 154; Foote, *The Civil War*, 932–33.
30. Foote, *The Civil War*, 934; Foster, *Sherman's Mississippi Campaign*, 89, emphasis added.
31. Foote, *The Civil War*, 934; Flood, *Grant and Sherman*, 229.
32. Special thanks are due to John Evans of Atlanta, Georgia, for his understanding and admonition that "Okolona is the key." *OR*, Series I, Vol. 32, Part 2, 684–85, 720; Wills, *A Battle from the Start*, 158.
33. Wynne, *Mississippi's Civil War*, 154–55, emphasis added.
34. Gresham, *The War Outside My Window*, 291.
35. Wynne, *Mississippi's Civil War*, 155; Parks, *General Leonidas Polk*, 357.
36. Flood, *Grant and Sherman*, 229; Robert C. Black, III, *The Railroads of the Confederacy* (Chapel Hill: University of North Carolina Press, 1998), 241; Letter from L.J. Fleming, May 2, 1864, Leonidas Polk Papers; Foote, *The Civil War*, 937; Horn, *Leonidas Polk*, 534n16.
37. Parks, *General Leonidas Polk*, 363; *Demopolis Times*, February 24, 1864, Leonidas Polk Papers.
38. Connelly, *Army of the Heartland*, 5.
39. Flood, *Grant and Sherman*, 229; Ben Wynne, *A Hard Trip: A History of the 15th Mississippi Infantry, CSA* (Macon: Mercer University Press, 2010), 117–18.

40. Wynne, *Mississippi's Civil War*, 157; Gresham, *The War Outside My Window*, 290.
41. Wynne, *Mississippi's Civil War*, 152.
42. John R. Scales, *The Battles and Campaigns of Confederate General Nathan Bedford Forrest* (El Dorado Hills, CA: Savas Beatie, 2017), 242; Robert Selph Henry: *First with the Most: Nathan Bedford Forrest* (New York: Konecky and Konecky, 1992), 220–21.
43. Rudy H. Leverett, *Legend of the Free State of Jones* (Jackson: University Press of Mississippi, 1984), 105.
44. Leverett, *Legend*, 3.
45. Horn, *Leonidas Polk*, 359; Leverett, *Legend*, 37, 45.
46. Leverett, *Legend*, 88–89, 95–96, 99, 103.
47. Leverett, *Legend*, 95.
48. Leverett, *Legend*, 105.
49. Horn, *Leonidas Polk*, 380.
50. Ludwell H. Johnson, *North Against South: The American Iliad 1848-1877* (Columbia, S.C.: Foundation for American Education, 1993), 116–17.
51. Quoted in Johnson, *North Against South*, 117.

Chapter 10

1. Parks, *General Leonidas Polk*, 371, 373.
2. *OR*, Series I, Vol. 38, Part 2, 661, 676.
3. Letter to Samuel Cooper, May 6, 1864, Leonidas Polk Papers.
4. Horn, *Leonidas Polk*, 387; Letter from Braxton Bragg, May 23, 1864, Leonidas Polk Papers.
5. Daniel, *Conquered*, 285.
6. French, *Two Wars*, 194.
7. Daniel, *Conquered*, 286.
8. Connelly, *Autumn of Glory*, 336; *OR*, Vol. XXXVIII, Part 4, 663; Connelly, *Autumn of Glory*, 339; Philip L. Secrist, *The Battle of Resaca: Atlanta Campaign, 1864* (Macon: Mercer University Press, 2010), 14–16.
9. Connelly, *Autumn of Glory*, 341; Steven E. Woodworth, *Nothing But Victory: The Army of the Tennessee 1861-1865* (New York: Alfred A. Knopf, 2005), 497.
10. Horn, *Leonidas Polk*, 395.
11. Secrist, *The Battle of Resaca*, 42, 80.
12. Secrist, *The Battle of Resaca*, 43.
13. Parks, *General Leonidas Polk*, 377.
14. Connelly, *Autumn of Glory*, 334n28, 344.
15. Horn, *Leonidas Polk*, 400.
16. Connelly, *Autumn of Glory*, 346.
17. Connelly, *Autumn of Glory*, 347.
18. Connelly, *Autumn of Glory*, 348.
19. Connelly, *Autumn of Glory*, 351–52; French, *Two Wars*, 198.
20. French, *Two Wars*, 198.
21. Robert D. Jenkins, Sr., *The Cassville Affairs and the Failed Confederate Strategy in the Atlanta Campaign* (Macon: Mercer University Press, expected publication date 2024)

22. Horn, *Leonidas Polk*, 405; Brad Butkovich, *The Battle of Pickett's Mill: Along the Dead-Line* (Charleston, S.C.: The History Press, 2013), 40.

23. Russell W. Blount, Jr., *The Battles of New Hope Church* (Gretna, LA: Pelican, 2010), 53, 59–60.

24. Connelly, *Autumn of Glory*, 355.

25. Quoted in Butkovich, *The Battle of Pickett's Mill*, 152; Blount, *The Battles of New Hope Church*, 126.

26. Blount, *The Battles of New Hope Church*, 123; Connelly, *Autumn of Glory*, 356.

27. Connelly, *Autumn of Glory*, 357.

28. Horn, *Leonidas PolkI* 412; Quintard, *Doctor Quintard Chaplain*, 97; Charles Todd Quintard, *The Confederate Soldier's Pocket Manual of Devotions including Balm for the Weary and the Wounded*, Sam Davis Elliott, introd. (Macon: Mercer University Press, 2009), xvii.

29. Sam Watkins, *Co. Aytch or a Side Show of the Big Show*, ed. Philip Leigh (Yardley, PA: Westholme, 2013), 167.

30. Castel, *Decision in the West*, 275–76.

31. Castel, *Decision in the West*, 276.

32. Parks, *General Leonidas Polk*, 382; Nathaniel Cheairs Hughes, Jr., *The Pride of the Confederate Artillery: The Washington Artillery in the Army of Tennessee* (Baton Rouge: Louisiana State University Press, 1997), 189.

33. Quintard, *Doctor Quintard Chaplain*, 98–99.

34. Robins, *The Bishop of the Old South*, 195.

35. Quintard, *Doctor Quintard Chaplain*, 99; *Funeral Services at the Burial of the Right Reverend Leonidas Polk, D.D.*, anglicanhistory.org/usa/lpolk/funeral1864.html.

36. Horn, *The Army of Tennessee*, 332.

37. Quintard, *Doctor Quintard Chaplain*, 173–74.

Chapter 11

1. Watkins, *Co. Aytch*, 164; Ridley Wills, II, *Old Enough to Die* (Franklin, TN: Hillsboro Press, 1996), 124.

2. Horn, *Leonidas Polk*, 184, 201–02.

3. Robins, *The Bishop of the Old South*, 214.

4. Powell, *The Chickamauga Campaign*, 47; Noe, *Perryville*, 57; Castel, *Decision in the West*, 45–46.

5. Richard M. McMurry, *Atlanta 1864: Last Chance for the Confederacy* (Lincoln: University of Nebraska Press, 2000), 7, 67.

6. Connelly, *Army of the Heartland*, 47.

7. Fremantle, *The Fremantle Diary*, 111; Gen. G. Moxley Sorrel, *Recollections of a Confederate Staff Officer* (Dayton: Morningside Bookshop, 1978 reprint of 1905 original), 197–98; Watkins, *Co. Aytch*, 164. This is not the page cited in Connelly's footnote, but the events on the cited page occur far before Watkins came under Polk's command. This is the only instance where Watkins describes Polk.

8. Connelly, *Army of the Heartland*, 217, 248, 259; *Autumn of Glory*, 220.

9. McDonough, *Shiloh—In Hell Before Night*, 35, 59, 191.

10. McDonough, *War in Kentucky*, 27, 63, 65, 230.

11. Daniel, *Conquered*, 38; Eric A. Jacobson, *For Cause and for Country: A Study of the Affair at Spring Hill and the Battle of Franklin* (Franklin, TN: O'More, 2013), 13.

12. Letter to Daughter, April 6, 1863; Letter to Frances Polk, April 16, 1863; Letter to Kenneth Rayner, August 14, 1863, all in Leonidas Polk Papers.

13. William Glenn Robertson, *River of Death: The Chickamauga Campaign, Volume One: The Fall of Chattanooga* (Chapel Hill: University of North Carolina Press, 2018), 55, 73.

14. Letter from William Hardee, July 27, 1863, Leonidas Polk Papers.

15. Robertson, *River of Death*, 66; Parks, *General Leonidas Polk*, 41–54.

16. Robertson, *River of Death*, 67–68.

17. Robertson, *River of Death*, 5, 54, 68–69, 73, 265, 365.

18. Robertson, *River of Death*, 47, 50, 93.

19. Robertson, *River of Death*, 47, 59, emphasis added; McWhiney, *Braxton Bragg and Confederate Defeat*, 117, 122; Martin, *General Braxton Bragg*, 86, 382, 466.

20. Robertson, *River of Death*, 51, 55.

21. Robertson, *River of Death*, 66, 258–59.

22. Robertson, *River of Death*, 54–55, 59.

23. Hess, *Braxton Bragg*, 123; McWhiney, *Braxton Bragg and Confederate Defeat*, 35–51; Martin, *General Braxton Bragg*, 22.

24. Robertson, *River of Death*, 58, 68.

25. Robertson, *River of Death*, 69.

26. Robertson, *River of Death*, 51.

27. Robertson, *River of Death*, 56, emphasis added.

28. Robertson, *River of Death*, 55, 68.

29. Robertson, *River of Death*, 68, 164.

30. Robertson, *A Tale of Two Orders*, 129, 153.

31. Daniel, *Battle of Stones River*, 127.

32. Powell, *A Mad Irregular Battle*, 47; Cooper, *Jefferson Davis, American*, 42.

33. Cooper, *Jefferson Davis, American*, 382; Hess, *The Civil War in the West*, 15, emphasis added; Hess, *Banners to the Breeze*, 115, emphasis added; Woodworth, *Jefferson Davis and His Generals*, 31; Robertson, *River of Death*, 67–68; McMurry, *Atlanta 1864*, 7, emphasis added.

34. Parks, *General Leonidas Polk*, 168.

35. Woodworth, *Jefferson Davis and His Generals*, 185; Powell, *Glory or the Grave*, 28.

36. T. Michael Parrish, *Richard Taylor: Soldier Prince of Dixie* (Chapel Hill: University of North Carolina Press, 1992), 153.

37. Daniel, *Conquered*, 256–57, 380n28, 92, 93.

38. Taylor, *Destruction*, 94; Parks, *General Leonidas Polk*, 250; Parrish, *Richard Taylor*, 125–27; Ezra J. Warner, *Generals in Gray: Lives of the Confederate Commanders* (Baton Rouge: Louisiana State University Press, 1959), 166; Samuel W. Mitcham, Jr., *The Encyclopedia of Confederate Generals* (Washington, D.C.: Regnery, 2022), 352.

39. Hess, *Braxton Bragg*, 148, emphasis added.
40. Powell, *Glory or the Grave*, 28.
41. Letter to Frances Polk, May 27, 1864, Leonidas Polk Papers; Letter from W.D. Gale to William Huger, October 31, 1863, Leonidas Polk Papers.
42. Martin, *General Braxton Bragg*, 117; Powell, *Glory or the Grave*, 159; Robertson, *River of Death*, 224; French, *Two Wars*, 189–90.
43. Parks, *General Leonidas Polk*, 146.
44. Horn, *Leonidas Polk*, 166–67; quoted in Parks, *General Leonidas Polk*, 375.
45. Noe, *Perryville*, 57; Woodworth, *Jefferson Davis and His Generals*, 26; Robertson, *River of Death*, 224.
46. Daniel, *Conquered*, 149, 153.
47. Powell, *A Mad Irregular Battle*, 180.
48. Parks, *General Leonidas Polk*, 169; Martin, *General Braxton Bragg*, 118; Woodworth, *Jefferson Davis and His Generals*, 239.
49. Foote, *The Civil War*, 934; Powell, *A Mad Irregular Battle*, 70.
50. Letter from Jefferson Davis to William M. Polk, December 15, 1879, Leonidas Polk Papers; Watkins, *Co. Aytch*, 164.
51. Parks, *General Leonidas Polk*, 115, 170.
52. Fremantle, *The Fremantle Diary*, 111, 114.
53. Liddell, *Liddell's Record*, 67, 101; French, *Two Wars*, 202.
54. Dennis L. Peterson, *Confederate Cabinet Departments and Secretaries* (Jefferson, N.C.: McFarland, 2016), 184; Connelly, *Autumn of Glory*, 147; Hess, *The Civil War in the West*, 190.
55. Parks, *General Leonidas Polk*, 310; letter from General Joseph Johnston, March 3, 1863, Leonidas Polk Papers.
56. Letter to William Hardee, July 30, 1863, Leonidas Polk Papers.
57. Hess, *Braxton Bragg*, 159; Robertson, *River of Death*, 365.
58. *OR*, Series I, Vol. 32, Part 2, pp. 725, 779–81; Letter to W.M. Polk from General Stephen D. Lee, November 19, 1875, Leonidas Polk Papers.
59. Horn, *Leonidas Polk*, 383; Connelly, *Autumn of Glory*, 373–74.
60. Connelly, *Autumn of Glory*, 324; Parks, *General Leonidas Polk*, 368–69.
61. Connelly, *Autumn of Glory*, 344.

Chapter 12

1. Parks, *General Leonidas Polk*, 89, 115; Losson, *Tennessee's Forgotten Warriors*, 116, 151; Connelly, *Autumn of Glory*, 215.
2. Losson, *Tennessee's Forgotten Warriors*, 115.
3. Parks, *General Leonidas Polk*, 112; letter to dear Daughter, March 2, 1862, Leonidas Polk papers.
4. Sarah A. Dorsey, *Recollections of Henry Watkins Allen* (New Orleans: James A. Gresham, 1866), 70; https://www.monticello.org/research-education/thomas-jefferson-encyclopedia/seal-united-states.
5. Quoted in Parks, *General Leonidas Polk*, 375.

6. Jack Hurst, *Men of Fire: Grant, Forrest, and the Campaign that Decided the Civil War* (New York: Basic Books, 2007), 160–61.
7. Connelly, *Army of the Heartland*, 245.
8. Connelly, *Autumn of Glory*, 169.
9. Connelly, *Autumn of Glory*, 220–22.
10. Robertson, "A Tale of Two Orders" in *Gateway to the Confederacy*, 129.
11. Stephen Cushman, "Ambrose Bierce, Chickamauga, and Ways to Write History" in *Gateway to the Confederacy: New Perspectives on the Chickamauga and Chattanooga Campaigns, 1862–1863* (Baton Rouge: Louisiana State Press, 2014), 258.
12. Quoted in Robert D. Jenkins, Sr., *To the Gates of Atlanta: From Kennesaw Mountain to Peachtree Creek, 1–19 July 1864* (Macon: Mercer University Press, 2015), 136, emphasis added.
13. Parks, *Leonidas Polk*, 102–04, 163.
14. Horn, *Leonidas Polk*, 104, 124.

Chapter 13

1. Bishop Stephen Elliott, *Funeral Services at the Burial of the Right Rev. Leonidas Polk, D.D. together with the Sermon delivered in St. Paul's Church, Augusta, Ga., on June 29, 1864!* http://anglicanhistory.org/usa/lpolk/funeral1864.html, 12.
2. Russell S. Bonds, *War Like the Thunderbolt: The Battle and Burning of Atlanta* (Yardley, PA: Westholme2009), 63.
3. Robert D. Jenkins, Sr., *To the Gates of Atlanta*, 154, 158.
4. Martin, *General Braxton Bragg*, 22.
5. Hess, *Braxton Bragg*, 141; Alexander Mendoza, *Confederate Struggle for Command* (College Station: Texas A&M University Press, 2008), 69; William C. Davis and Sue Heth Bell, eds., *The Whartons' War: The Civil War Correspondence of General Gabriel C. Wharton & Anne Radford Wharton, 1863–1865* (Chapel Hill: University of North Carolina Press, 2022), 199.
6. Chesnut, *Mary Chesnut's Civil War Diary*, ed. C. Vann Woodward (New Haven: Yale University Press, 1981), 482; Burke Davis, *The Long Surrender* (New York: Random House, 1985), 109–10.
7. Martin, *General Braxton Bragg*, 71, emphasis added.
8. Horn, *Leonidas Polk*, 162; McWhiney, *Braxton Bragg and Confederate Defeat*, 183–84; *OR*, Series I, Vol. 23, Part 2, 747–49; Glenna R. Schroeder-Lean, *Confederate Hospitals on the Move: Samuel H. Stout and the Army of Tennessee* (Columbia: University of South Carolina Press, 1994), 144.
9. Quoted in Cozzens, *This Terrible Sound*, 4–5.

Last Words

1. Martin, *General Braxton Bragg*, 467.
2. Bryan W. Lane, *Tennessee Hero: Confederate Brigadier General John Adams* (Charleston, S.C.: The History Press, 2017), 152; Jacobson, *For Cause and For Countryl* 427–31.

Bibliography

Barefoot, Daniel W. *General Robert F. Hoke: Lee's Modest Warrior*. Winston-Salem, N.C.: John F. Blair, 1996.

Black, Robert C. *The Railroads of the Confederacy*. Chapel Hill: University of North Carolina Press, 1998.

Blount, Russell W., Jr. *The Battles of New Hope Church*. Gretna, LA: Pelican, 2010.

Bonds, Russell S. *Stealing the General: The Great Locomotive Chase and the First Medal of Honor*. Yardley, PA: Westholme, 2007.

_____. *War Like the Thunderbolt: The Battle and Burning of Atlanta*. Yardley, PA: Westholme, 2009.

Butkovich, Brad. *The Battle of Allatoona Pass: Civil War Skirmish in Bartow County, Georgia* Charleston, S.C.: The History Press, 2014.

_____. *The Battle of Pickett's Mill: Along the Dead-Line*. Charleston, S.C.: The History Press, 2013.

Castel, Albert. *Decision in the West: The Atlanta Campaign of 1864*. Lawrence: University Press of Kansas, 1992.

Chesnut, Mary. *Mary Chestnut's Civil War Diary*. C. Vann Woodward, ed. New Haven: Yale University Press, 1981.

Connelly, Thomas L. *Army of the Heartland: The Army of Tennessee, 1861–1862*. Baton Rouge: Louisiana State University Press, 1967.

_____. *Autumn of Glory: The Army of Tennessee, 1862–1865*. Baton Rouge: Louisiana State University Press, 1971.

Cooper, William J., Jr. *Jefferson Davis, American*. New York: Vintage, 2000.

Cozzens, Peter. *No Better Place to Die: The Battle of Stones River*. Urbana: University of Illinois Press, 1990.

_____. *This Terrible Sound: The Battle of Chickamauga*. Urbana: University of Illinois Press, 1994.

Cunningham, O. Edward. *Shiloh and the Western Campaign of 1862*. El Dorado Hills, CA: Savas Beatie, 2007.

Cushman, Stephen. "Ambrose Bierce, Chickamauga, and Ways to Write History" in *Gateway to the Confederacy: New Perspectives on the Chickamauga and Chattanooga Campaigns, 1862–1863*. Baton Rouge: Louisiana State University Press, 2014.

Daniel, Larry J. *Battle of Stones River: The Forgotten Conflict between the Confederate Army of Tennessee and the Union Army of the Cumberland*. Baton Rouge: Louisiana State University Press, 2012.

_____. *Conquered: Why the Army of Tennessee Failed*. Chapel Hill: University of North Carolina Press, 2019.

_____. *Shiloh: The Battle That Changed the Civil War*. New York: Simon & Schuster, 1997.

Davis, Burke. *The Long Surrender*. New York: Random House, 1985.

Davis, Jefferson. *The Rise of the Confederate Government*. Ben Wynne, ed. New York: Barnes and Noble, 2010.

Davis, William C. *Breckinridge: Statesman, Soldier, Symbol*. Lexington: University Press of Kentucky, 2010.

_____. *Diary of a Confederate Soldier: John S. Jackman of the Orphan Brigade*. Columbia: University of South Carolina Press, 1990.

Davis, William C., and Sue Heth Bell, eds. *The Whartons' War: The Civil War Correspondence of General Gabriel C. Wharton & Anne Radford Wharton, 1863–1865*. Chapel Hill: University of North Carolina Press, 2022.

Dorsey, Sarah A. *Recollections Of Henry Watkins Allen*. New Orleans: James A. Gresham, 1866.

Dowdey, Clifford, and Louis H. Manarin, eds. *The Wartime Papers of Robert E. Lee*. New York: Da Capo, 1961.

Flood, Charles Bracelen. *Grant and Sherman: The Friendship That Won the Civil War*. New York: Harper Perennial, 2005.

Foote, Shelby. *The Civil War: A Narrative, Vol. II. Fredericksburg to Meridian*. New York: Vintage, 1963.

Foster, Buck T. *Sherman's Mississippi Campaign*. Tuscaloosa: University of Alabama Press, 2006).

Fremantle, Lt. Col. James Arthur Lyon. *The Fremantle Diary: Being the Journal of Lieutenant Colonel James Arthur Lyon Fremantle, Coldstream Guards, and His Three Months in the Southern States*. Walter Lord, ed. Boston: Little, Brown, 1954.

French, General Samuel G. *Two Wars: The Autobiography & Diary of Gen. Samuel G. French, C.S.A.* Huntington, W.V.: Blue Acorn Press, 1999.

Gragg, Rod. *Confederate Goliath: The Battle of Fort Fisher*. Baton Rouge: Louisiana State University Press, 1991, updated ed., 2006.

Gresham, LeRoy. *The War Outside My Window: The Civil War Diary of LeRoy Wiley Gresham, 1860–1865*. Janet Elizabeth Croon, ed. El Dorado Hills, CA: Savas Beatie, 2018.

Hallock, Judith Lee. *Braxton Bragg and Confederate Defeat, Vol. II*. Tuscaloosa: University of Alabama Press, 1969.

Harsh, Joseph L. *Confederate Tide Rising: Robert E. Lee and the Making of Southern Strategy, 1861–1862*. Kent: Kent State University Press, 1998.

Hattaway, Herman, and Archer Jones. *How the North Won: A Military History of the Civil War*. Urbana: University of Illinois Press, 1983.

Henry, Robert Selph. *First with the Most: Nathan Bedford Forrest*. New York: Konecky and Konecky, 1992.

Hess, Earl J. *Banners to the Breeze: The Kentucky Campaign, Corinth, and Stones River*. Lincoln: University of Nebraska Press, 2000.

_____. *Braxton Bragg: The Most Hated Man in the Confederacy*. Chapel Hill: University of North Carolina Press, 2016.

_____. *The Civil War in the West: Victory and Defeat from the Appalachians to the Mississippi*. Chapel Hill: University of North Carolina Press, 2012.

Hood, Stephen M. *The Lost Papers of Confederate General John Bell Hood*. El Dorado Hills, CA: Savas Beatie, 2015.

Horn, Huston. *Leonidas Polk: Warrior Bishop of the Confederacy*. Lawrence: University Press of Kansas, 2018.

Horn, Stanley F. *The Army of Tennessee*. Norman: University of Oklahoma Press, 1941.

Hughes, Nathaniel Cheairs, Jr. *The Pride of the Confederate Artillery: The Washington Artillery in the Army of Tennessee*. Baton Rouge: Louisiana State University Press, 1997.

_____, and Thomas Clayton Ware. *Theodore O'Hara: Poet-Soldier of the Old South*. Knoxville: University of Tennessee Press, 1998.

_____, and Roy P. Stonesifer. *The Life and Wars of Gideon J. Pillow*. Chapel Hill: University of North Carolina Press, 1993.

Hunt, Jeffrey Wm. *Meade and Lee at Bristoe Station: The Problems of Command and Strategy After Gettysburg, from Brandy Station to the Buckland Races, August 1 to October 31, 1863*. El Dorado Hills, CA: Savas Beatie, 2019.

Hurst, Jack. *Men of Fire: Grant, Forrest, and the Campaign that Decided the Civil War*. New York: Basic Books, 2007.

Jacobson, Eric A., and Richard A. Rupp: *For Cause & for Country: A Study of the Affair at Spring Hill and the Battle of Franklin*. Franklin, TN: O'More, 2013.

Jenkins, Robert D., Sr. *The Cassville Affairs, and the Failed Confederate Strategy in the Atlanta Campaign*. Macon: Mercer University Press, 2024.

_____. *To the Gates of Atlanta: From Kennesaw Mountain to Peachtree Creek, 1–19 July 1864*. Macon: Mercer University Press, 2015.

Johnson, Ludwell H. *North Against South: The American Iliad 1848–1877*. Columbia, S.C.: Foundation for American Education, 1993.

Jones, Evan C., and Wiley Sword, eds. *Gateway to the Confederacy: New Perspectives on the Chickamauga and Chattanooga Campaigns, 1862–1863*. Baton Rouge: Louisiana State Press, 2014.

Kean, Robert Garlick Hill. *Inside the Confederate Government: The Diary of Robert Garlick Hill Kean*. Edward Younger, ed. Baton Rouge: Louisiana State University Press, 1957.

Kolakowski, Christopher L. *The Civil War at Perryville: Battling for the Bluegrass*. Charleston, S.C.: The History Press, 2009.

_____. *The Stones River and Tullahoma Campaigns: This Army Does Not Retreat*. Charleston, S.C.: The History Press, 2011.

Lane, Bryan W. *Tennessee Hero: Confederate Brigadier General John Adams*. Charleston, S.C.: The History Press, 2017.

Leverett, Rudy H. *Legend of the Free State of Jones*. Jackson: University Press of Mississippi, 1984.

Liddell, St. John Richardson. *Liddell's Record*. Nathaniel Cheairs Hughes, Jr., ed. Baton Rouge: Louisiana State Press, 1985.

Losson, Christopher. *Tennessee's Forgotten Warriors: Frank Cheatham and His Confederate Division*. Knoxville: The University of Tennessee Press, 1989.

Martin, Samuel J. *General Braxton Bragg, C.S.A.* Jefferson, N.C.: McFarland, 2011.

McBride, Mary Gorton, and Ann Mathison McLaurin. *Randall Lee Gibson of Louisiana: Confederate General and New South Reformer*. Baton Rouge: Louisiana State University Press, 2007.

McDonough, James Lee. *Shiloh—In Hell Before Night*. Knoxville: University of Tennessee Press, 1977.

_____. *War in Kentucky: From Shiloh to Perryville*. Knoxville: University of Tennessee Press, 1994.

McMurry, Richard M. *Atlanta 1864: Last Chance for the Confederacy*. Lincoln: University of Nebraska Press, 2000.

_____. *The Civil Wars of General Joseph E. Johnston, Confederate States Army*. El Dorado Hills, CA: Savas Beatie, 2023.

McWhiney, Grady. *Braxton Bragg and Confederate Defeat, Vol. I*. Tuscaloosa: University of Alabama Press, 1969.

Mendoza, Alexander. *Confederate Struggle for Command*. College Station. Texas A&M University Press, 2008.

Mitcham, Samuel W., Jr. *Bust Hell Wide Open: The Life of Nathan Bedford Forrest*. Washington, D.C.: Regency History, 2016.

_____. *The Encyclopedia of Confederate Generals: The Definitive Guide to the 426 Leaders of the South's War Effort*. Washington, D.C.: Regnery, 2022.

Noe, Kenneth W. *Perryville: This Grand Havoc of*

Battle. Lexington: University Press of Kentucky, 2001.

Parks, Joseph H. *General Leonidas Polk, C.S.A.: The Fighting Bishop*. Baton Rouge: Louisiana State University Press, 1962.

Parrish, T. Michael. *Richard Taylor: Soldier Prince of Dixie*. Chapel Hill: University of North Carolina Press, 1992.

Peterson, Dennis L. *Confederate Cabinet Departments and Secretaries*. Jefferson, N.C.: McFarland, 2016.

Polk, Leonidas Papers. University of the South Library. Sewanee, Tennessee.

Polk, William M., M.D. *Leonidas Polk; Bishop and General, Vol. II*. Old South Books reprint of New York: Longmans, Green, and Co., 1915.

Powell, David A. *The Chickamauga Campaign. A Mad Irregular Battle: From the Crossing of the Tennessee River Through the Second Day, August 22–September 19, 1863*. El Dorado Hills, CA: Savas Beatie, 2014.

_____. *The Chickamauga Campaign. Barren Victory: The Retreat Into Chattanooga, the Confederate Pursuit, and the Aftermath of the Battle, September 21 to October 20, 1863*. El Dorado Hills, CA: Savas Beatie, 2016.

_____. *The Chickamauga Campaign. Glory or the Grave: The Breakthrough, the Union Collapse, and the Defense of Horseshoe Ridge, September 20, 1863*. El Dorado Hills, CA: Savas Beatie, 2015.

_____. "A Legend in the Making: Nathan Bedford Forrest at Chickamauga" in *Gateway to the Confederacy: New Perspectives on the Chickamauga and Chattanooga Campaigns, 1862–1863*. Baton Rouge: Louisiana State Press, 2014.

_____, and Eric J. Wittenberg. *Tullahoma: The Forgotten Campaign that Changed the Course of the Civil War, June–July 4, 1863*. El Dorado Hills, CA: Savas Beatie, 2020.

Quintard, Charles Todd. *The Confederate Soldier's Pocket Manual of Devotions Including Balm for the Weary and the Wounded*. Sam Davis Elliott, introd. Macon: Mercer University Press, 2009.

_____. *Doctor Quintard Chaplain C.S.A. and Second Bishop of Tennessee: Being His Story of the War (1861–1865)*. Rev. Arthur Howard Noll, ed. Sewanee: The University Press of Sewanee Tennessee, 1905.

Robertson, William Glenn. *River of Death: The Chickamauga Campaign. Volume One: The Fall of Chattanooga*. Chapel Hill: University of North Carolina Press, 2018.

_____. "A Tale of Two Orders: Chickamauga, September 20, 1863" in *Gateway to the Confederacy: New Perspectives on the Chickamauga and Chattanooga Campaigns, 1862–1863*. Baton Rouge: Louisiana State University Press, 2014.

Robins, Glenn. *The Bishop of the Old South: The Ministry and Civil War Legacy of Leonidas Polk*. Macon: Mercer University Press, 2006.

Roland, Charles P. *Albert Sidney Johnston: Soldier of Three Republics*. Lexington: University of Kentucky Press, 2001.

Roman, Alfred. *The Military Operations of General Beauregard, Volumes I and II*. New York: Da Capo, 1994.

Sanders, Stuart W. *Maney's Confederate Brigade at the Battle of Perryville*. Charleston, S.C.: The History Press, 2014.

Scales, John R. *The Battles and Campaigns of Confederate General Nathan Bedford Forrest*. El Dorado Hills, CA: Savas Beatie, 2017.

Schroeder-Leon, Glenna R. *Confederate Hospitals on the Move: Samuel H. Stout and the Army of Tennessee*. Columbia: University of South Carolina Press, 1994.

Secrist, Philip L. *The Battle of Resaca: Atlanta Campaign, 1864*. Macon, GA: Mercer University Press, 2010.

Seitz, Don Carlos. *Braxton Bragg: General of the Confederacy*. Reprinted by Literary Licensing, original 1923.

Smith, Lanny Kelton. *The Stones River Campaign: 26 December 1862–5 January, 1863, Army of Tennessee*. Lanny Smith, 2010.

Smith, Timothy B. *Shiloh: Conquer or Perish*. Lawrence: University Press of Kansas, 2014.

Sorrel, Gen. G. Moxley. *Recollections of a Confederate Staff Officer*. Dayton: Morningside Bookshop, 1978 reprint of 1905 original.

Symonds, Craig L. *Stonewall of the West: Patrick Cleburne & The Civil War*. Lawrence: University Press of Kansas, 1994.

Taylor, Richard. *Destruction and Reconstruction*. Charles P. Roland, ed. Waltham, MA: Blaisdell, 1968.

Thomas, Emory M. *Robert E. Lee: A Biography*. New York: W.W. Norton, 1995.

Tucker, Glenn. *Chickamauga: Bloody Battle in the West*. Dayton: Morningside Bookshop, 1984.

The War of the Rebellion: A Compilation of the Official Records of the Union and Confederate Armies. 128 volumes. Washington, D.C.: Government Printing Office, 1880–1901.

Warner, Ezra J. *Generals in Blue: Lives of the Union Commanders*. Baton Rouge: Louisiana State University Press, 1964.

_____. *Generals in Gray: Lives of the Confederate Commanders*. Baton Rouge: Louisiana State University Press, 1959.

Watkins, Sam. *Co. Aytch or a Side Show of the Big Show*. Philip Leigh, ed. Yardley, PA: Westholme, 2013.

White, William Lee. *Bushwacking on a Grand Scale: The Battle of Chickamauga, September 18–20, 1863*. El Dorado Hills, CA: Savas Beatie, 2013.

Wills, Brian Steel. *A Battle from the Start: The Life of Nathan Bedford Forrest*. New York: HarperCollins, 1992.

Wills, Ridley, II. *Old Enough to Die*. Franklin, TN: Hillsboro Press, 1996.

Wittenberg, Eric J. *We Ride a Whirlwind: Sherman and Johnston at Bennett Place*. Burlington, N.C.: Fox Run, 2017.

Wolseley, Field Marshal Viscount. *The American*

Civil War: An English View. James A. Rawley, ed. Mechanicsburg, PA: Stackpole Books, 2002.

Woodworth, Steven E. *Jefferson Davis and His Generals: The Failure of Confederate Command in the West.* Lawrence: University Press of Kansas, 1990.

_____. *Nothing But Victory: The Army of the Tennessee 1861–1865.* New York: Alfred A. Knopf, 2005.

_____. *While God Is Marching On: The Religious World of Civil War Soldiers.* Lawrence: University Press of Kansas, 2001.

Wynne, Ben. *A Hard Trip: A History of the 15th Mississippi Infantry, CSA.* Macon: Mercer University Press, 2010.

_____. *Mississippi's Civil War: A Narrative History.* Macon: Mercer University Press, 2006.

Index

Numbers in ***bold italics*** indicate pages with illustrations.

Adams, Daniel W. 68, 69, 70, 123, 124
Adams, John 211
Adams, W. Wirt 144
Allatoona railroad cut 167
Allen, W. Henry 44, 200
Altimore (Polk slave) 76
Anderson, J. Patton 35, 58, 65, 66, 67, 89, 105, 114, 115, 185
Anderson, Richard H. 134, 135
Anderson, Robert 16, 17
Andrews's Raid 39
Army of Tennessee (Confederate) 7, 45, 48, 60, 61, 74, 77, 78, 80, 83, 85, 90, 91, 107, 109, 110, 111, 117, 118, 119, 126, 129, 131, 132, 133, 134, 135, 136, 139, 140, 143, 144, 160, 164, 166, 172, 174, 175, 178, 179, 186, 190, 196, 197, 201, 206, 208, 209
Army of the Cumberland 62, 63, 70, 109, 160, 161
Army of the Mississippi 24, 31, 47, 49
Army of the Ohio 28, 43, 47, 49, 50, 61, 160, 165
Army of the Tennessee (Union) 141, 160, 161, 162
Atlanta, Georgia 93, 119, 130, 131, 133, 154, 160, 170, 171, 172, 198, 202, 203, 205
Atlanta Campaign 128, 158, 160, 163, 164, 174, 187, 191, 197, 198
Augusta, Georgia 126, 147, 172, 211

Banks, Nathaniel P. 81, 142
Bardstown, Kentucky 47, 49, 50, 58, 101, 103, 104, 116, 176, 202
Bate, William B. 168, 169, 170
Baton Rouge, Louisiana 9, 203
Battle of Antietam 49, 108
Battle of Baton Rouge 37, 90
Battle of Bentonville 139

Battle of Big Bethel 12, 125
Battle of Belmont 173
Battle of Chickamauga 31, 36, 63, 84, 101, 109, 111, 113, 114, 119, 128, 131, 133, 134, 135, 136, 155, 163, 176, 178, 179, 180, 185, 193, 196, 199, 201, 202, 206; battle plan 116, 120, 196–197; Confederate victory 128, 129, 130, 131, 141, 189; Longstreet left wing commander 116, 118, 124, 125, 126, 127; Snodgrass Hill/Horseshoe Ridge 126, 127
Battle of Corinth 62, 63
Battle of Dallas 167–168
Battle of Franklin (Tenn.) 7–8, 211
Battle of Gettysburg 26, 76, 77, 109, 136
Battle of Malvern Hill 26, 100
Battle of Missionary Ridge 135, 136–137, 140, 191, 202
Battle of Murfreesboro 45, 59, 62–72, ***73***, 77, 83, 84, 85, 90, 91, 92, 93, 96, 111, 113, 128, 129, 130, 132, 134; Nashville Pike 63, 67; retreat from Murfreesboro 72, 85, 86, 89, 91; Round Forest 67, 68, 69, 70, 71, 89, 201; Slaughter Pen 66, 67; Stone's River 62, 63, 72
Battle of New Hope Church 167
Battle of Okolona 149, 154
Battle of Perryville 48, 52–57, 58, 59, 60, 61, 63, 64, 66, 68, 72, 75, 77, 81, 83, 84, 90, 102, 104, 105, 106, 107, 108, 109, 111, 116, 128, 139, 177, 189; acoustic shadow 107; Bragg's attack orders to Polk 47–48, 50, 51, 52–53, 58, 95, 98, 100, 101, 102, 103, 104, 105, 106, 107, 108, 176, 177, 178, 201; Doctor's Creek 51, 52, 54, 104; first street combat of Civil War 57; Peters Hill 52, 57, 105, 106;

Polk's near capture 56–57; retreat from Kentucky 58–59, 60, 83, 84, 108
Battle of Pickett's Mill 167, 168
Battle of Resaca 161, 164
Battle of Shiloh 28, 30, 34–43, 46, 55, 58, 64, 68, 81, 82, 84, 91, 111, 118, 123, 128, 154, 158, 177, 181; Allen, Henry (4th Louisiana) 44; Beauregard, P.G.T. (army commander) 39, 41, 42, 43; Bragg's criticism of 11th Louisiana 37–38; Bragg's objection to April 6 withdrawal order 39, 40, 41; Confederate march to battlefield 29–33, 43; Confederate retreat 43; council of war on eve of battle 33; death of A. S. Johnston 39, 46; Grant's formidable artillery line 38–39; Hornets' Nest 37; improvised Confederate field command 36, 42; Shiloh Church 35, 41
Battle of Stone's River *see* Battle of Murfreesboro
Battle of the Wilderness 136
Battle of Trafalgar 132
Battles of Seven Days 125, 134
Beatty, Samuel 71, 72
Beauregard, Pierre Gustave T. 24, ***25***, 27, 28, 29, 30, 31, 32, 34, 36, 39, 40, 46, 91, 92, 181, 188, 195
Belmont, Missouri 17
Benjamin, Judah 187
Bostick, J. Litton 173
Bowden, Scott (historian) 129
Bowling Green, Kentucky 21, 22
Bragg, Braxton 1, 2, 24, ***26***, 27, 33, 34, 45, 61, 78, 82, 84, 86, 91, 92, 93, 98, 121, 139, 169, 177, 178, 181, 182, 183, 204, 205, 206, 208, 210, 211; Army of

227

Index

Tennessee commander 46, 47, 48, 49, 50, 60, 61, 62, 73, 74, 75, 77, 78, 79, 80, 83, 84, 86, 87, 88, 90, 91, 94, 95, 96, 97, 100, 101, 102, 103, 106, 108, 109, 111, 112, 113, 114, 116, 123, 124, 125, 127, 128, 129, 130, 134, 135, 136, 137, 144, 148, 173, 174, 176, 182, 183, 184, 185, 186, 188, 189, 190, 196, 197, 199, 200, 202, 205, 206, 208, 209; background 25, 26; baptism and confirmation 99, 169; Battle of Murfreesboro 62, 67, 68, 69, 70, 71, 72, 79; Battle of Perryville 51, 53, 54, 56, 58, 59, 79, 84; Battle of Shiloh 31, 44, 178; Bivouac (plantation) 25, 26, 27, 43, 83, 208; burial place 210, *210*; chief-of-staff to A.S. Johnston 24, 28, 31, 36, 37, 184; circular letter (January 11, 1863) 85–88, 93, 94, 97, 98, 135, 183, 189; circular letter (April 13, 1863) 95–98, 178, 179, 180, 183, 184, 189; Corinth concentration 24, 27; corps commander 29, 31, 32, 33, 34, 35, 41, 42, 43, 44, 79; correspondence with wife 1, 27, 38, 43, 44, 45, 46, 82, 84, 117, 118, 122, 177, 178, 184; death 210, 211; devotion to Confederate cause 26, 79, 83, 137, 208; disciplinarian 25, 26, 27, 84; dismissal of Polk from army 109, 133, 140, 178, 190, 199; Fort Fisher, North Carolina 79, 137, 138; health problems 75, 83, 182, 196, 204, 205, 208; hostility toward Polk 1, 27, 32, 37, 46, 46–47, 48, 51, 52, 77, 78, 79, 80, 81, 83, 84, 88, 95, 97, 98, 99, 109, 115, 116, 130, 161, 178, 179, 186, 188, 189, 193, 199, 205, 207, 208; idealism/optimism 83, 137, 206, 207; intelligence lapses 73, 100, 101, 102, 103, 105, 106, 108, 111, 112, 113, 116, 123; leadership style 36–37, 78, 79, 80, 88, 126, 130, 132, 134, 179, 206; letter to Davis, Feb. 1863 absolving self of blame 94, 97, 98, 138, 178, 204, 209; marriage to Elise 25, 26, 207; medical care for troops 72, 78, 130, 139, 206, 207; military adviser to Davis 88, 92, 135, 137, 139, 161, 162, 182, 185, 205; Murfreesboro, battle report 88–91, 93–95, 97, 132, 183; Pensacola command 26, 27, 81, 88, 89, 134, 188; Perryville battle reports 8–59, 84, 97, 98, 102, 178; petition for removal 126, 131, 133, 179, 190; post-war career 210; promotion to full general 46, 177; railroad movement of troops 46, 79, 80; religion 1, 98–99; resignation from Army of Tennessee 26, 94, 136, 137, 140, 190; staff officers 78, 80, 81, 88, 130, 137, 183, 206; Trans-Mississippi offer of command 27, 209

Bragg, Elise (wife) 1, 2, 25, 27, 28, 45, 82, 91, 98, 135, 137, 138, 177, 179, 182, 184, 193, 206, 207, 210–211

Bragg, John (brother) 78, 81, 138, 207

Brandon, Mississippi 145

Breckinridge, John C. 24, 34, 37, 41, 61, *61*, 67, 68, 69, 70, 71, 85, 88, 89, 90, *90*, 91, 93, 93–94, 98, 117, 123, 124, 127, 132, 137, 179, 183, 186, 199, 201, 204; note from Polk re Murfreesboro battle report 95–96, *96*, 97

Brent, George 85

Bryantsville, Kentucky supply depot 49, 58, 101, 103

Buchanan, Pres. James 10, 90

Buckner, Simon Bolivar 47, 49, 58, 60, 72, 74, 98, 105, 111, 112, 114, 116, 130, 134, 186, 189, 196

Buell, Don Carlos 28, 39, 43, 46, 47, 48, 49, 50, 51, 52, 54, 58, 61, 62, 63, 93, 101, 102, 103, 104, 105, 106, 107, 108, 116, 202

Burns, Ken 156

Butler, Benjamin 137

Butler, Edward G.W., Jr. 173

Cairo, Illinois 15, 16, 18
Calhoun, Georgia 164, 165, 198
Camp Breckinridge, Kentucky 102, 103
Camp Dick Robinson, Kentucky 15, 16, 17, 101–102
Cantey, James 160, 161, 162, *162*, 163, 164, 202
Captured and Abandoned Property Act 159
Carnes, William 54, 115
Cassville, Georgia 165, 166
Castel, Albert 12, 174
Chalmers, James R. 48, 65, 66, 68, 70, 155
Champion Hill battlefield 144
Chattahoochee River (Georgia) 119
Chattanooga, Tennessee 26, 46, 60, 75, 77, 80, 93, 109, 110, 131, 141, 160, 182, 188, 190, 192, 193, 195, 196, 197, 201

Cheatham, Benjamin Franklin 29, 30, 33, 35, 41, 42, 47, 52, 53, 54, 55, *55*, 56, 58, 60, 61, *61*, 62, 64, 65, 66, 67, 72, 76, 90, 91, 93–94, 105, 112, 114, 116, 117, 121, 127, 134, 135, 150, 177, 190, 199

Cherokee Springs, Georgia 196
Chesnut, James 92, 131, 132
Chesnut, Mary 131, 173, 206
Cincinnati, Ohio 16, 47
Clark, Charles 30, 31, 35, 36, *37*
Clayton, Sallie 171–172
Cleburne, Patrick 7–8, 34, 35, 47, 48, 50, 56, 60, 63, 64, 72, 85, 117, 123, 126, 127, 134, *135*, 150, 167, 173, 193, 209
Clinton, Mississippi 143, 144
Coltart, John G. 64, 65, 69, 96
Columbia, Tennessee 6, 7, 83
Columbus, Kentucky 15, 16, 17, 18, 19, 20, 21, 22, 23, 72, 173, 177, 192, 200
Connelly, Thomas 15, 16, 28, 31, 34, 40, 41, 55, 67, 77, 78, 85, 104, 107, 112, 114, 117, 118, 119, 120, 121, 122, 123, 124, 131, 135, 143, 164, 174, 175, 176, 177, 192, 196, 198, 200, 201
Cooper, Samuel 58, 59, 87, 89, 102, 160, 161, 179
Corinth, Mississippi 1, 24, 27, 28, 29, 30, 31, 32, 46
Cozzens, Peter 68, 69–70, 71, 79, 89, 112, 113, 114, 116, 119, 121, 122, 186, 191, 202
Cracker Line 136
Crittenden, George B. (Confederate) 22, 24
Crittenden, Thomas L. (Union) 63, 72, 100, 101, 112, 113, 114, 115, 116, 126
Cumberland Gap 21
Cumberland River 28, 92
Cunningham, Edward 38, 41

Dallas, Georgia 167
Dalton, Georgia 140, 143, 160, 161, 163
Daniel, Larry 30, 32, 34, 37, 67, 68, 69, 108, 121, 124, 131, 161, 162, 178, 187, 188, 189, 192–193
Danville, Kentucky 103
Davis, Jefferson (Confederate president) 10, *10*, 12, 13, 15, 17, 24, 27, 46, 82, 84, 85, 86, 88, 91, 92, 111, 130, 133, 134, 137, 140, 174, 176, 181, 186, 187, 193, 194, 195, 197, 204, 206, 209, 210; friendship with

Polk from West Point 4, 6, 10, 185, 186, 187; Polk's concern over leadership of 109, 110; reticence to remove Bragg 84, 91, 132, 135, 136, 139, 189; visits to Army of Tennessee 60, 131, 132, 189
Davis, Jefferson C. (Union general) 64, 65
Davis, Stephen 187, 196
Davis, Varina 207
Davis, William C. 206
Deas, Zachariah C. 115
Decatur, Mississippi 147
Demopolis, Alabama 141, 142, 147, 148, 150, 152
Dilworth, William 170
Donelson, Daniel S. 53, 54, 55, 57, 65, 68, 70
Dorsey, Sarah 200
Duck River (Tennessee) 74
Duke, Basil W. 61, *61*, 175
Duncan, James 182, 183, 206

Eastport, Mississippi 28
Elliott, Bishop Stephen 1, 99, 110, 182, 193, 204
Ellis, Towson 43
Emancipation Proclamation 49
Enterprise, Mississippi 133, 140, 148, 151
Episcopal Church 6, 10, 48
Etowah River (Georgia) 166, 167
Ewell, Richard S. 134, 187

Fleming, L.J. 151, 152
Flood, Charles Bracelen 153
Foote, Andrew H. 22
Foote, Shelby 119, 121, 122, 193
Forrest, Nathan Bedford 47, 73, 113, 114, 116, 129, 140, 143, 148, 149, 150, 151, 153, 154, 155, *155*, 160, 197; conflict with Bragg 129, 131, 134, 155; cooperation, harmony with Polk 129, 154, 155
Fort Craig, Kentucky 49
Fort Donelson, Tennessee 22, 28, 58, 72, 154, 200
Fort Fisher, North Carolina 79, 137, 138, 185
Fort Henry, Tennessee 22, 28, 58, 200
Fort Pickens, Florida 26
Fort Pillow, Tennessee 22
Fort Sumter, South Carolina 16, 27
Foster, Buck T. 141, 142, 143, 144, 145, 146, 147, 150
Frankfort, Kentucky 47, 49, 50, 101, 103, 104, 105, 202

Fremantle, Arthur 99, 175, 194, 195
Frémont, John 15, 16, 20
French, Samuel G. 140, 143, 144, 145, 153, 160, 161, 162, 164, 165, 166, 191, 192, 194, 195

Gale, William D. 93, 94, 95, 164, 165, 190, 198
Galveston, Texas 210
Garfield, James A. 73
Gibson, Randall L. 33, 38, 43, 44, *44*, 68, 91
Gilbert, Charles C. 52, 53, 57, 101, 104, 107
Gladden, Adley H. 33, 89
Gooding, Michael 56, 64
Gorgas, Josiah 137, *138*, 182, 205
Gracie, Archibald, Jr. 115, 202
Granger, Gordon 126
Grant, Ulysses S. 15, 16, 17, 18, 19, 20, 28, *29*, 38, 39, 40, 42, 43, 63, 69, 72, 76, 141, 142, 146, 147, 148, 160, 196, 200
Gresham, LeRoy 131, 134, 151, 153
Grierson, Benjamin 148

Halleck, Henry W. 22, *22*, 28, 46, 141, 142, 152
Hallock, Judith 119, 122, 124
Hanson, Roger W. *61*, 71
Hardage house 168, 169
Hardee, William J. 24, 31, 36, 40, 41, 42, 47, 48, 51, 52, 54, 56, 58, 59, 60, 61, *61*, 63, 67, 71, 74, 75, 76, 85, 88, 98, 102, 103, 105, 108, 109, *111*, 128, 133, 135, 136, 140, 165, 166, 167, 168, 169, 170, 180, 184, 186, 190, 192, 196, 201, 204, 205, 209
Hardee's Corps 24, 29, 30, 31, 33, 34, 56, 60, 62, 74, 85, 89, 104, 109, 111, 116, 125, 164
Harris, Gov. Isham (Tennessee) 15, 16, 128
Harrodsburg, Kentucky 48, 51, 57, 58, 59, 102, 104, 106
Hartsville, Tennessee 60
Hattaway, Herman 103, 104
Hawes, Richard 49, 101, 102
Hazen, William B. 69, 72, 201
Hess, Earl 18, 43, 67, 69, 88, 121, 122, 185–186, 190, 196, 197
Heth, Henry 49
Hill, D.H. 111, 114, 116, 117, 120, 121, 122, 123, 124, *125*, 126, 127, 129, 134, 179, 182, 189, 196, 197
Hillsboro, Mississippi 147
Hindman, Thomas C. 66, 111, 112, 114, 125, 130, 131, 134, 189
Hoke, Robert F. 138, 139
Holmes, Theophilus H. 134

Hood, John Bell 7, 69, 94, 161, 163, 164, 165, 167, 168, 169, 170, 187; baptism 163–164, 165, 167; Cassville controversy 165, 166; Chickamauga wound 131; commander, Army of Tennessee 94; intrigue against Johnston 166, 187, 205
Hood, Stephen 187
Hooker, Joseph 167, 182, 187
Hopkins, Bishop John Henry 9
Horn, Huston 11–12, 19, 25, 157, 193
Horn, Stanley F. 16, 104, 113, 121
Howard, Oliver O. 170
Huger, Benjamin 134
Huger, John 91–93, 94, 96–97
Huger, William 92, 190
Hunt, Henry J. 26, 27, 182
Hurlbut, Stephen A. 28, 43, 144

inauguration Kentucky Confederate governor 49, 50, 51, 101, 102
Island No. 10 22

Jackson, John K. 68, 70, 115
Jackson, Stonewall 80, 81, 125, 131, 134, 176, 187, 201
Jackson, Tennessee 27
Jackson, William "Red" 168
Jackson, Mississippi 140, 143, 145, 151, 153
Jacobson, Eric 179
Jefferson, Thomas 200
Jenkins, Robert D., Sr. 166
Johnson, Bushrod R. 35, 56, 126, 127
Johnston, Albert Sidney 4, 13, 15, 21, 22, 24, 27, 28, 29, 32, 34, 36, 37, 39, 46, 69, 82, 91, 177, 181, 184, 185
Johnston, Joseph E. 24, 39, 48, 81, 82, 86, 87, 91, 93, 104, 111, 130, 133, 139, 140, 169, 170, 171, 179, 180, 196; baptism 165, 167; commander, Army of Tennessee 86, 91, 135, 140, 143, 148, 160, 161, 162, 163, 164, 165, 166, 167, 168, 174, 190, 197, 198, 202, 202, 205; Department of the West 60, 74, 84, 195, 196; relieved from army command 94, 204–205; tribute upon Polk's death 172
Johnston, Lydia 165
Johnston, William Preston 32, 91
Jones, Archer 103, 104
Jones, Samuel 188, *188*, 189
Jones County, Mississippi 156, 157, 158
Jordan, Thomas 29, 41

Index

Kean, Robert 89
Keith, Squire 56
Kennesaw Mountain, Georgia 168, 169
Kentucky Campaign 41, 46–59, 60, 66, 79, 80, 84, 85, 92, 98, 101–108, 155, 178, 184
Kentucky neutrality 15–20, 177
Kirby Smith, Edmund 26, 45, 46, 47, 49, 50, 51, 58, 59, 60, 82, 84, 101, 102, 103, 104, 105, 108, 187
Knight, Newton 157
Knoxville, Tennessee 126, 136, 189
Kolakowski, Christopher 50, 68, 70, 72
Kurtz, Wilbur 170

LaFayette, Georgia 112, 114
Lafourche Parish, Louisiana 44, 207
Lee, Pollock 36, 117, 118, 119, 120, 121, 122, 123, 125
Lee, Robert Edward 11, 13, 46, 61, 63, 77, 90, 91, 94, 100, 108, 109, 125, 126, 131, 133, 134, 136, 187, 192
Lee, Stephen D. 140, 143, 146, 148, 160, 197
Lee and Gordon's Mill 112, 113, 114, 116, 196
Leverett, Rudy 156, 157
Lexington, Kentucky 15, 47, 51
Liddell, St. John R. 52, 56, 57, 59, 72, 77, 80, 106, 128, 129, 130, 195
Lincoln, Abraham 15, 18, 49, 62, 187
Lockett, Samuel H. 40, 44
Logan, John A. 164
Longstreet, James 116, 118, 124, 126, **126**, 127, 128, 133, 134, 136, 172, 176, 179, 187, 189, 201
Loomis, John Q. 54, 64, 65, 96
Loring, William W. 140, 143, 144, 145, 160, 161, 162, 164
Losson, Christopher 199
Louisville, Kentucky 16, 47, 49, 50, 101, 198
Lovell, Mansfield 24, 38,
Lowrey, Mark P. 167, 193
Lowry, Robert 157, 158, **158**

Mackall, William W. 88, 130, 137, 165
Macon, Georgia 131, 134, 151
Magoffin, Beriah (Kentucky governor) 15, 16
Magruder, John 100, 134
Maney, George E. 35, 53, 54, 55, 65, 66, 115, 127, 128, **128**

Manigault, Arthur M. 64, 65, 66, 67, 67, 115
March to the Sea 146–147, 150, 151
Marietta, Georgia 129, 167
Martin, Samuel J. 120, 121, 122, 191
Maury, Dabney H. 140
Maury, Henry 157
Maury, Matthew Fontaine 21, 192
Maury County, Tennessee 6, 7, 43
McClelland, George B. 45, 63, 187
McClernand, John A. 28, 35, 37
McCook, Alexander M. 43, 50, 51, 53, 55, 63–64, 101, 103, 114; bad whiskey 56; capture of papers and clothing 56, 72; singing voice 63
McCown, John P. 60, 62, 63, 64, 72, 93–94
McDonough, James 100, 102, 103, 106, 177
McIlvaine, Charles Pettit 5, 181
McLean, Eugene 173
McLean, Margaret 173
McLemore's Cove 111, 114, 116, 130
McMurry, Richard 174, 186, 187, 196
McPherson, James B. 144, 145, 161, 162, 163, **163**
McWhiney, Grady 40, 92, 100, 106, 119, 177
Meade, Bishop William 11, 12, 181
Memphis, Tennessee 15, 142, 149, 192, 197
Memphis & Charleston Railroad 28, 39
Mendenhall, John 72
Meridian, Mississippi 140, 141, 142, 143, 146, 147, 148, 150, 151, 153, 154, 163, 197
Meridian Campaign 141–154, 156, 193, 197; Battle of Okolona 149; burning of Jackson 145; destruction of Meridian 148, 151; evacuation of stores from Meridian 148, 153; Forrest's cavalry 143, 148, 149, 150, 153, 197 railroad repair 151–152; Selma, Alabama (Sherman's objective) 141, 142, 146, 150, 152; Sherman's near capture 147; Sooy Smith's cavalry 143, 147, 148, 149, 150, 151, 152, 153, 197
Mill Springs, Kentucky 22
Minty, Robert H.G. 74

Mississippi River 10–11, 13, 15, 18, 20, 21, 24, 77, 141, 158, 181, 186, 192, 195, 198
Mitchel, Ormsby M. 39
Mobile, Alabama 24, 66, 92, 140, 141, 143, 144, 146, 147, 150, 152, 157, 160, 161, 162, 163, 197, 202, 210
Mobile & Ohio Railroad 28, 29, 142, 143, 146, 149, 150, 151, 152
Morgan, John Hunt 60, **61**, 85
Morton, Mississippi 145, 146, 147, 153
Munfordville, Kentucky 49, 74, 103
Murfreesboro, Tennessee 60, 61, 62, 69, 72, 73, 74, 85

Nashville, Tennessee 15, 28, 46, 47, 60, 62, 93, 141
Natchez, Mississippi 151, 156
Negley, James S. 67, 68, 72
Nelson, Adm. Horatio 132
Nelson, William "Bull" 16, 17
New Orleans, Louisiana 9, 12, 24, 25, 26, 38, 58, 92, 142, 166, 198, 208, 211
Niles, Dexter 202–203
Noe, Kenneth 51, 52, 53, 79, 105, 107, 174, 192, 201
Nott, Dr. Josiah 40, 85

O'Hara, Theodore 88, 89
Okolona, Mississippi 143, 149, 150
Oostanaula River (Georgia) 161, 164
Orphan Brigade 90
Otey, Bishop James 3, **5**, **76**, 194
Otey, Mercer 76

Paducah, Kentucky 18, 20
Palmer, Joseph B. 68, 69, 70, 72
Parks, Joseph H. 30, 41, 70, 194
Parsons, Charles 54
Pea Vine Church/Road 112, 113, 116
Pensacola, Florida 24, 26, 88
Perryville, Kentucky 47, 51, 53, 54, 104, 105, 106
Pillow, Gideon J. 19–20, 71, 72, 88, 173, 199
Pine Mountain, Georgia 168, 169, 170, 171, 172, 192
Pittsburg Landing, Tennessee 28, 29, 30, 39, 43
Polk, Elizabeth (daughter) 92, 110
Polk, Frances Devereux (wife) 6, 110, 181, 184, 203, 211
Polk, James H. (nephew) 123
Polk, Katherine (daughter) 93, 110

Index

Polk, Leonidas 1, 2, 3, **4**, 6, 7, 8, 9, 10, 11, 12, 13, 14, 15, 16, 17, 18, 19, 20, 21, 22, 23, 24, 25, 27, 28, 41, 57, 60, 61, **61**, 72, 76, 81, 84, 86, 90, 92, **92**, 93, 95, 96, 97, 99, 103, 104, 109, 110, 112, 120, 122, 128, 130, 161, 162, 163, 165, 166, 167, 168, 170, 173, 174, 175, **175**, 177, 180, 182, 183, 184, 185, 186, 187, 190, 191, 195, 196, 197, 203, 204, 211; Battle of Chickamauga 110, 117; Battle of Murfreesboro 62, 67, 68, 69, 70, 71, 72, 195; Battle of Perryville 48, 52–57, 58, 59, 64, 102, 177, 202; Battle of Shiloh 29, 34, 35, 36, 37, 38, 40, 41, 200; battlefield leadership, courage 36, 38, 42, 56, 114, 176, 191, 192, 195; Bishop of Louisiana 1, 8–9, 14, 25, 85, 100, 106, 163, 165, 167, 168, 172, 173, 175, 176, 177, 181, 182, 189, 191, 192, 193, 194, 203; breakfast myth, Chickamauga 116–123, 176; burial place 172, 211, **211**; Cassville controversy 165–166; cholera 8; Columbus, Kentucky command 15, 16, 18, 19, 20–21, 22, 23, 24, 173; communication problems with Bragg 41, 50, 51, 101, 107, 117, 178, 200–201; comparison to Thomas Jefferson 200; conflict with Bragg 27, 37, 44, 78, 79, 102, 178, 179, 182, 207, 208; corps commander 29, 30, 31, 32, 33, 34, 36, 37, 38, 40, 42, 43, 55, 74, 75, 105, 106, 108, 113, 114, 124, 164, 165, 172, 175, 188; correspondence with Davis re Bragg 75, 87, 132, 133, 136, 139, 140, 179, 185, 186, 187, 191; correspondence with wife 11, 12, 13, 41, 43, 45, 51, 52, 179, 182; death 127, 171, 172, 178, 192, 208, 210, 211; Department of Alabama, Mississippi and E. Louisiana 81, 133, 140, 143, 144, 146, 147, 148, 150, 151, 152, 153, 155, 156, 157, 158, 159, 160, 191, 197; devotion to Confederate cause 1, 208; dismissal from Bragg's army 79, 125, 130, 131, 134, 178, 179, 180, 189; Episcopal cleric 6, 163, 181, 199; funeral 126, 172; general's commission, CSA 11, 12, 13, 174, 181, 186, 193; leadership style 155, 156, 173, 176; Leighton (plantation) 8–9, **9**, 25; magnanimity 25, 176, 199, 200, 204, 207; marriage to Frances Devereux 6, 181; medical care for troops 207–208; Missionary Bishop of the Southwest 7, 191–192, 199; near capture at Perryville 56–57; orders to reinforce Johnston, May 1864 160, 161, 162; Pea Vine Road/Rock Creek Church 111–116, 202; promotion to lieutenant general 84; railroads 140, 151–152, 156, 160, 162, 197; religious conversion 5–6, 181; resignations from army (attempted) 13, 176, 181; seminary 6, 181; slaves 8, 76, 203; West Point 3–6, 175, 176, 181, 185, 186, 194, 195, 207; wing commander, Chickamauga 116, 118, 123, 124, 125, 126, 127, 12, 176, 201; wing commander, Kentucky 47, 48, 49, 50, 54, 55, 56
Polk, Lucius (nephew) 127
Polk, Marshall T. (cousin) 35, **36**, 123
Polk, Susan (sister) 110
Polk, Dr. William M. (son) 30, 115, 123, 197, 208
Polk's Corps 60, 61, 62, 64, 66, 67, 72, 74, 77, 85, 89, 106, 111, 115, 128, 133, 167, 168; flag 47, **48**
Pontotoc, Mississippi 149
Port Hudson, Louisiana 109, 140
Powell, David A. 74, 108, 113, 114, 121, 129, 174, 185, 186, 190, 191, 192, 193
Prentiss, Benjamin M. 28, 38, 40
Prentiss, Mississippi 140
Preston, William 68, 69, 70, 71, 92, 189

Quintard, Charles Todd 3, **5**, 57, 75, 98–99, **99**, 168, 170, 171, 172

Raleigh *Standard* 110
Rayner, Kenneth 110, 179, 182
Ready, Mattie 61, **61**, 85
Resaca, Georgia 161, 162, 163, 164, 174, 202
Richardson, Dr. T.G. 78, 136, 137
Richmond, William B. 129
Richmond, Kentucky 47
Richmond, Virginia 6, 11, 13, 18, 20, 60, 84, 85, 87, 89, 91, 92, 93, 94, 131, 134, 135, 136, 137, 138, 139, 152, 166, 169, 179, 181, 185, 186, 187, 189, 190, 198, 205, 206, 207
Ringgold, Georgia 113
Roberts, George W. 66, 67
Robertson, Felix 89, 96, 97, 132, 179
Robertson, William Glenn 121, 122, 180–185, 186, 191, 192, 197, 201–202
Robins, Glenn 20
Rock Spring Church, Georgia 112, 114, 202
Rocky Face Ridge 161
Rome, Georgia 73, 160, 161, 162, 164, 174
Rosecrans, William S. 62, 63, **63**, 67, 70, 72, 73, 74, 75, 77, 85, 101, 109, 110, 111, 113, 116, 123, 126, 129, 131, 185, 195, 196, 201
Rossville, Georgia 113, 126, 129
Rousseau, Lovell H. 51, 54
Ruggles, Daniel 24, 31, 32, 33, 38, 43
Russell, Robert 35, 36, 38, 41, 42, 82

St. John's Chapel (Columbia, Tennessee) 7, **8**, 43
St. John's Church (Thibodaux, Louisiana) 25
St. Luke's Church (Atlanta) 171
St. Paul's Church (Augusta) 172, 211
Savannah, Georgia 146, 147
Savannah, Tennessee 28
Schaefer, Frederick 67
Schofield, John M. 165
Scott, Dr. Preston B. 208
Secession 10, 26, 156, 158
Secrist, Philip 164
Seddon, James 131
Seitz, Don Carlos 118
Selma, Alabama 141, 142, 143, 146, 147, 150, 152, 153, 197
Shelbyville, Kentucky 50
Shelbyville, Tennessee 72, 73, 74
Sheridan, Philip H. 52, 57, 65, 66, 67, 70, 107
Sherman, William Tecumseh 20, 26, 28, 35, 37, 41, 69, 83, 119, 141, 142, **142**, 143, 144, 145, 146, 147, 148, 149, 150, 151, 152, 153, 154, 155, 156, 157, 160, 163, 164, 165, 167, 168, 170, 182, 193, 197, 198, 201
Siege of Chattanooga 113, 129, 131, 136, 137, 144
Sill, Joshua W. 50, 51, 58, 64, 67, 101, 103
Simonson, Peter 127, 170
slavery 202–203, 209

Smith, Charles F. 28
Smith, Edmund Kirby *see* Kirby Smith, Edmund
Smith, Lanny 132
Smith, Preston 35, 53, 64, 65, 115
Smith, Thomas B. 69
Smith, Timothy 30, 32, 38, 40, 41, 42, 43, 180
Smith, William "Baldy" 136
Smith, William Sooy 143, 147, 148, *149*, 150, 153, 197
Smith County, Mississippi 157
Snake Creek Gap 161, 162
Sorrel, Moxley 175, 176
Southern Railroad 143, 146, 152, 157
Sparta, Tennessee 47
Spence, Philip B. 128
Stanford's Mississippi Battery 54, 115
Stanton, Edwin M. 62
Steedman, James 126, 127
Stephens, William 35, 36
Stevenson, Carter L. 49, 60
Stewart, Alexander Peter 35, 36, 42, 53, 65, 66, 67, 69, 74, 125, 167
Stout, Dr. Samuel 78
Stovall, Marcellus 123, 124
Strahl, Otho F. 115
Streight, Abel D. 73
Stuart, J.E.B. 4, 54
Sumner, Edwin V. "Bull" 173

Taylor, Richard 80, *81*, 187, 188, 189
Tennessee River 28, 29, 76, 109, 160, 201
Terrill, William 54
Thibodaux, Louisiana 25

Thomas, George H. 16, 22, 26, 63, 71, 123, 124, 126, 127, 129, 182
Thrasher, John Sidney 131
Trans-Mississippi 60, 82, 84, 158, 196
Tucker, Glenn 19
Tullahoma, Tennessee 60, 72, 74, 75, 86, 91
Tullahoma Campaign 63, 73–75, 77, 109, 111, 185, 195
Tupelo, Mississippi 46

United States Military Academy (West Point) 3–6, 26, 123, 175, 176, 181, 185, 186, 194, 195, 207; disciplinary action in drawing class 4–5, 181; Polk's academic standing 6; religion 5–6, 181
The University of the South 3, *4*, 9, 75, 168, 172, 175, 192, 200, 203; cornerstone 3, *5*, 9, 75, 76, 171, 172; opening in 1868 172

Van Cleve, Horatio P. 71
Van Dorn, Earl 24
Vaughan, Alfred J. 64, 65, 66, 67
Versailles, Kentucky 51, 52, 53, 105
Vicksburg, Mississippi *7*, 60, 76, 82, 84, 109, 140, 141, 142, 143, 148, 150, 151, 152, 156, 196
Virginia Theological Seminary 6, 11

Waagner, Gustave 17
Walker, W.H.T. 112, 114, 116, 121, 124, 127

Wallace, Lew 28, 29, 42
Wallace, W.H.L. 28, 38
Warm Springs, Georgia 137
Washington Artillery 70
Waterhouse, Allen 35, 37
Watkins, Sam 127, 128, 170, 173, 175, 176, 194
West Point *see* United States Military Academy
West Point, Mississippi 149
Western & Atlantic Railroad 39, 160, 161, 163
Wharton, John A. 50, 53
Wheeler, Joseph 60, 62, 74, 76, 105, 155
White, Lee 121
Whitfield, George 151, 152
Whiting, William H. Chase 134, 138
Wilder, John T. 49, 74, 192
Wills, Brian Steel 150
Wilmington, North Carolina 137, 138, 185
Withers, Jones M. 32, 47, 53, 60, 62, 64, 65, *66*, 67, 68, 72, 89, 96, 105
Wittenberg, Eric 74
Wolseley, Field Marshal Garnet J., Viscount 67, 78
Wood, S.A.M. 47, 54, 56
Wood, Thomas J. 100
Woodruff, William 64
Woodworth, Steven 11–12, 17, 39, 40, 42, 74, 100, 102, 103, 104, 106, 112, 113, 118, 119, 121, 122, 133, 161, 176, 177, 178, 186, 191, 192, 193, 202
Wynne, Ben 143, 146, 150, 153

Yandell, Dr. David 81, *82*